S0-DVE-876

Dedication

This book is dedicated to members of the Catholic community who in faith participated in the research and development of this sizable undertaking. Many people contributed helpful suggestions to portions of this text. Our gratitude is expressed to all of them collectively.

Thanks go to the children, Fr. Bill Kernan and the supportive community of St. Francis of Assisi Parish.

PRAYER BEFORE
A CRUCIFIX

Look down on me, good and gentle Jesus. Make my soul strong in faith, hope and love. Make me really sorry for my sins so I will never sin again.

I am sad when I see the wounds on your hands and feet, and think of the words of your prophet, David: "They have pierced my hands and feet, they have hurt all my bones."

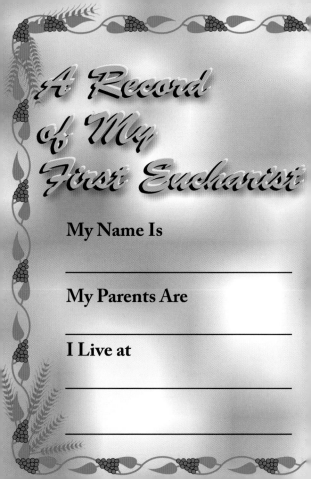

A Record of My First Eucharist

My Name Is

_____

My Parents Are

_____

I Live at

_____

_____

I received **My First Holy Communion**

in the Parish of

St Therese of the Child Jesus

in the City of

Portland, Oregon

on the _Fifth_ Day

of _May_

in _2013_

I was baptized on _____
in the Church of

_____

"Let the children come to me, and do not prevent them; for the kingdom of heaven belongs to such as these." After he placed his hands on them, he went away. re: Matt 19:14-15

My Mass and Holy Communion Book

A *New* Mass and Prayer Book for Today's Catholic Community

*Illustrations were created specifically for
My Mass and Holy Communion Book
by pastelist Teresa Biernacki, USA.*

**Published by
Devon Trading Corporation
New Jersey**

Nihil Obstat

*I have concluded that the materials
presented in this work are free of
doctrinal or moral errors.*

Bernadeane M. Carr, STL
Censor Librorum
4 October 2011

Imprimatur

*In accord with 1983 CIC 827 § 3, permission
to publish this work is hereby granted.*

✠ Robert H. Brom
Bishop of San Diego
4 October 2011

My Mass and Holy Communion Book

Sacred Mass Vessels 12

The Mass 14

How We Live 62

Prayer 63

Prayers 65

The Rosary 74

The Sacraments 110

Sacrament of
Reconciliation 112

10 Commandments............ 114

2 Great Commandments 117

The Beatitudes 118

Stations of The Cross 120

Prayers ... Sayings 126

Prayer to My
Guardian Angel............... 127

Boys and Girls:

This is your very own Mass and Communion book. You can use it in Church and at home for a long time.

This book can help you to understand the Mass. The beautiful pictures show what the priest is doing at the altar. What to do and what to say during Mass is explained.

Your book is full of special sections. In the prayer section, you can read your prayers until you learn them. There is a place for you to add your favorite sayings or other prayers.

The Rosary tells about the life of Jesus and his family. The words about Jesus are from the Bible.

The Stations of the Cross show how much Jesus loved us.

Being a Catholic means following Jesus and learning what Jesus teaches us. When we receive the Sacraments we follow Jesus. He wants all of us to obey the Commandments and to live the Beatitudes.

May you continue to grow in the Way of Jesus who is Truth and Life.
—*Peace be to you*

Vessels Used During the Mass

During the Mass special vessels are used to hold the water, wine and bread. Vessels are made from different materials.

The sacred vessels used during the Mass are the Chalice and Paten. Because they hold Jesus' Body and Blood, they are blessed. They are made of very precious materials to signify how special the celebration of the Mass is. Silver and gold as well as other precious materials may be used according to tradition.

CHALICE — *Or Cup, is used to hold the wine which becomes the Blood of Jesus. It is made of gold, silver or other precious materials.*

PATEN — *Or Plate, is used to hold the bread which becomes the Body of Jesus. A Bowl may also be used.*

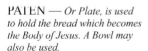

INTRODUCTION TO THE HOLY MASS

The Mass is the center of our worship of God. Together with the priest, our family, friends and neighbors, we celebrate the sacrifice of Jesus Christ. During the Mass, God speaks to us in the Bible readings and the priest's teachings. We pray, sing and praise the Father, Son and Holy Spirit.

Jesus is with us in many ways. In the Mass, he is especially with us in the

Eucharistic food. Jesus offers himself to our heavenly Father for everyone. We offer ourselves with Jesus to our heavenly Father.

Under the appearances of bread and wine, Jesus becomes food for our souls as the priest says the words, *"This is my Body. This is my Blood."* At Mass, everyone joins in the celebration of thanksgiving and love *through Jesus, with Jesus and in Jesus.*

ORDER OF THE HOLY MASS

INTRODUCTORY RITES

We Stand

As a Catholic community, we celebrate the Holy Sacrifice of the Mass.

ENTRANCE

If not sung, it is recited by all or some of the people.

←*THE ENTRANCE PROCESSION is led by altar servers. Next, the reader carries the Lectionary from which the Word of God is read to the people, followed by the priest. When the ministers and priest reach the altar, they bow. The priest kisses the altar in reverence because the altar is the symbol of Christ. Then he says the greeting.*

GREETING

PRIEST: In the name of the Father, and of the Son, and of the Holy Spirit.

PEOPLE: Amen.

PRIEST: The grace of our Lord Jesus Christ, and the love of God, and the communion of the Holy Spirit be with you all.

Or the priest says other prayers like,

PRIEST: Grace to you and peace from God our Father and the Lord Jesus Christ.

PEOPLE: And with your spirit.

*When the Rite of Blessing and Sprinkling
of Holy Water is celebrated, it takes
the place of the Penitential Rite — the
Confiteor and the Kyrie are not said.*

PENITENTIAL ACT

PRIEST: Brethren (brothers and sisters),
    let us acknowledge our sins,
and so prepare ourselves to celebrate
the sacred mysteries.
    (or similar words)

PRIEST AND PEOPLE:
I confess to almighty God,
and to you, my brothers and sisters,
that I have greatly sinned,
in my thoughts and in my words,
in what I have done and in what I have
    failed to do,
(They strike their breast)
through my fault, through my fault,
through my most grievous fault;

**therefore I ask blessed Mary
     ever-Virgin,
all the Angels and Saints,
and you, my brothers and sisters,
to pray for me to the Lord our God.**

The priest says the following absolution.

PRIEST:

May almighty God have mercy on us,

forgive us our sins,

and bring us to everlasting life.

PEOPLE: Amen.

KYRIE

PRIEST: Lord, have mercy.

PEOPLE: Lord, have mercy.

PRIEST: Christ, have mercy.

PEOPLE: Christ, have mercy.

PRIEST: Lord, have mercy.

PEOPLE: Lord, have mercy.

GLORIA

The Gloria is not said during Lent.

PRIEST AND PEOPLE:
Glory to God in the highest,
  and on earth peace to people
  of good will.

We praise you,
  we bless you,
  we adore you,
  we glorify you,
  we give you thanks for your
  great glory,
Lord God, heavenly King,
O God, almighty Father.

Lord Jesus Christ, Only Begotten Son,
Lord God, Lamb of God, Son of the
  Father,
    you take away the sins of the world,
      have mercy on us;
    you take away the sins of the world,
      receive our prayer;
    you are seated at the right hand of
    the Father,

have mercy on us.
For you alone are the Holy One,
you alone are the Lord,
you alone are the Most High,
  Jesus Christ, with the Holy Spirit,
  in the glory of God the Father. Amen.

COLLECT

PRIEST: Let us pray.

*The priest and people pray silently. Then
the priest says the opening prayer and
concludes:*

PRIEST: …for ever and ever.

PEOPLE: Amen.

LITURGY
OF THE WORD

*God speaks to us through readings from
the Bible in the Old Testament and the
New Testament.*

THE FIRST READING

Ending the reading:

READER: The word of the Lord.
PEOPLE: Thanks be to God.

RESPONSORIAL PSALM

We repeat the response sung or said by the reader. After each verse, we repeat the response.

SECOND READING

At the end:

READER: The word of the Lord.

PEOPLE: Thanks be to God.

GOSPEL ACCLAMATION

*After the reader's or choir's alleluia,
we say or sing alleluia.*

PEOPLE: ALLELUIA!

*The alleluia or other chant may be
omitted if not sung.
The alleluia is not sung during Lent.*

GOSPEL

DEACON OR PRIEST: The Lord
be with you.

PEOPLE: And with your spirit.

DEACON OR PRIEST: A reading
from the holy Gospel according to N—.
*The priest or deacon makes the Sign of the
Cross on the book, on his forehead, lips and
breast. We may do so, too.*

and Holy Communion Book

PEOPLE: Glory to you, O Lord.

At the end:

DEACON OR PRIEST: The Gospel of the Lord.

**PEOPLE: Praise to you,
        Lord Jesus Christ.**

We Sit

THE HOMILY

Listening to the priest explaining the readings from the Bible helps us put God's message into practice. We learn about Jesus' life and his teaching from the Gospels. The Gospels are taken from the writings of the 4 evangelists: Matthew, Mark, Luke and John. You will find their writings in the New Testament of the Bible.

PROFESSION OF FAITH

*When we say the Creed, we believe
everything God teaches us.*

PRIEST AND PEOPLE:
I believe in one God,
the Father almighty,
maker of heaven and earth,
of all things visible and invisible.

I believe in one Lord Jesus Christ,
the Only Begotten Son of God,
born of the Father before all ages,
God from God, Light from Light,
true God from true God,
begotten, not made,
    consubstantial with the Father;

through him all things were made.

For us men and for our salvation
he came down from heaven,

All bow during these three lines
and by the Holy Spirit was incarnate
of the Virgin Mary,
and became man.

For our sake he was crucified under
Pontius Pilate,
he suffered death, and was buried,
and rose again on the third day
in accordance with the Scriptures.
He ascended into heaven
and is seated at the right hand of
the Father.

He will come again in glory
to judge the living and the dead

and his kingdom will have no end.

I believe in the Holy Spirit,
the Lord, the giver of life,
who proceeds from the Father and
the Son,
who with the Father and the Son
is adored and glorified,
who has spoken through the prophets.
I believe in one, holy, catholic and
apostolic Church.
I confess one Baptism for
the forgiveness of sins
and I look forward to the
resurrection of thc dcad
and the life of the world to come.
Amen.

The Apostles' Creed may be said instead, see page 67.

UNIVERSAL PRAYER OR PRAYER OF THE FAITHFUL

We unite with our community, the entire Church and all people, to pray for their needs. After each intention is said, we say:

PEOPLE: Lord hear our prayer.
(or similar words)

The priest ends with a concluding prayer. We say:

PEOPLE: Amen.

We Sit

LITURGY OF THE EUCHARIST

As in the early days of the Church, we bring our gifts to the altar. Our offerings of bread and wine are presented. The priest places the bread and wine on the altar as the preparation song is sung. →

Preparation of the Bread

Holding the paten with the bread slightly above the altar, the priest says:

PRIEST: Blessed are you, Lord

God of all creation,

for through your goodness we have

received the bread we offer you:

fruit of the earth and work

of human hands,

it will become for us the bread of life.

The priest places the paten with the bread on the altar.

PEOPLE: Blessed be God for ever.

Preparation of the Wine

Holding the chalice of wine slightly above the altar, the priest says:

PRIEST: Blessed are you, Lord

God of all creation,

for through your goodness we have

received the wine we offer you:

fruit of the vine and work

of human hands

it will become our spiritual drink.

The priest sets the chalice on the altar.

PEOPLE: Blessed be God for ever.

PRAYER OVER THE OFFERINGS

PRIEST: Pray, brethren (brothers and sisters),
that my sacrifice and yours
may be acceptable to God,
the almighty Father.

We Stand

PEOPLE: May the Lord accept the
sacrifice at your hands
for the praise and glory of his name,
for our good and the good of all his
holy Church.

The priest asks God to accept our gifts.
At the end, we say:

PEOPLE: Amen.

EUCHARISTIC PRAYER

The priest begins the most important part of the Mass, the Eucharistic Prayer.

We join in with prayers of praise and thanksgiving.

PRIEST: The Lord be with you.

PEOPLE: And with your spirit.

PRIEST: Lift up your hearts.

PEOPLE: We lift them up to the Lord.

PRIEST: Let us give thanks to the Lord our God.

PEOPLE: It is right and just.

PREFACE

The priest continues giving God thanks and praise for saving us.

We join in with the song of the saints and angels.

PREFACE ACCLAMATION

PRIEST AND PEOPLE:

Holy, Holy, Holy Lord
> **God of hosts.**
Heaven and earth are full of
> **your glory.**
Hosanna in the highest.
Blessed is he who comes in the
> **name of the Lord.**
Hosanna in the highest.

We Kneel

In this part of the Eucharistic Prayer, the priest recalls the words of Jesus and prays for the Church,

MY MASS

*peace and salvation. He asks the Father
to accept these offerings.*

*He calls upon the Holy Spirit so that
the gifts of bread and wine will
become the Body and Blood of
Jesus. The priest says the same
words Jesus spoke during the
Last Supper.*

Taking the bread, the priest proclaims:

PRIEST:
> TAKE THIS, ALL OF YOU, AND EAT OF IT,
> FOR THIS IS MY BODY,
> WHICH WILL BE GIVEN UP FOR YOU.

**THE BREAD BECOMES THE BODY OF
CHRIST. Jesus is present to us in the Eucharist.
Jesus gives us his own Body and Blood that we
might have life everlasting.** →

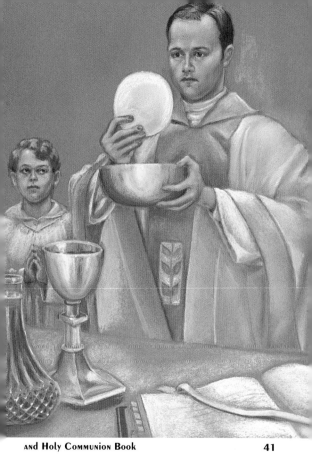

The priest, taking the chalice, bends slightly and says:

PRIEST: TAKE THIS, ALL OF YOU,
    AND DRINK FROM IT,
   FOR THIS IS THE CHALICE OF MY BLOOD,
   THE BLOOD OF THE NEW AND ETERNAL
     COVENANT,
   WHICH WILL BE POURED OUT FOR YOU
    AND FOR MANY
   FOR THE FORGIVENESS OF SINS.
DO THIS IN MEMORY OF ME.

THE WINE BECOMES THE BLOOD OF CHRIST. We celebrate and adore Jesus, present in the bread and wine. →

PRIEST: The mystery of faith.

PEOPLE: We proclaim your Death, O Lord, and profess your Resurrection until you come again.

or

When we eat this Bread and drink this Cup, we proclaim your Death, O Lord, until you come again.

or

Save us, Savior of the world, for by your Cross and Resurrection you have set us free.

Next we remember the life, death and resurrection of Jesus. We pray in our hearts as the priest prays for members of our Church, especially for those who have died.

At the end of the priest's prayer, we say "The Great Amen" →

PRIEST:
Through him,
and with him,
and in him,
O God, almighty Father,
in the unity of the Holy Spirit,
all glory and honor is yours,
for ever and ever.

PEOPLE: Amen.

COMMUNION RITE

THE LORD'S PRAYER

PRIEST: At the Savior's command
and formed by divine teaching,
we dare to say:

We Stand

PRIEST AND PEOPLE:

Our Father,
who art in
heaven,
hallowed be thy name;
thy kingdom come,

thy will be done
   on earth as it is in heaven.

Give us this day our
   daily bread,
and forgive us our
   trespasses
as we forgive those who
   trespass against us;
and lead us not into
   temptation,
but deliver us from evil.

PRIEST:

Deliver us, Lord, we pray, from every evil,

graciously grant us peace in our days,

that, by the help of your mercy,

we may be always free from sin

and safe from all distress,

as we await the blessed hope

and the coming of our Savior, Jesus Christ.

DOXOLOGY

PEOPLE: For the kingdom,

the power, and the glory are yours,

now and for ever.

The Church is a community. Before
receiving Jesus, we wish each other
the peace of Jesus Christ. This is a sign
of forgiveness and being in unity
as our community.

SIGN OF PEACE

PRIEST:
Lord Jesus Christ,
who said to your Apostles:
Peace I leave you, my peace I give you,
look not on our sins,
but on the faith of your Church,
and graciously grant her peace and unity
in accordance with your will.

He joins hands.

Who live and reign for ever and ever.

PEOPLE: Amen.

PRIEST: The peace of the Lord be with
you always.

PEOPLE: And with your spirit.

DEACON OR PRIEST: Let us offer
each other the sign of peace.

SIGN OF PEACE

FRACTION OF THE BREAD

*The priest breaks the host
over the paten. He places a small piece
in the chalice, saying quietly:* →

PRIEST: May this mingling of the Body
and Blood of our Lord Jesus Christ
bring eternal life to us who receive it.

We sing or say:

**PEOPLE: Lamb of God, you take
away the sins of the world,
have mercy on us.
Lamb of God, you take away the sins
of the world,
have mercy on us.
Lamb of God, you take away the sins
of the world,
grant us peace.**

We get ready to receive Jesus. We ask Jesus to keep us faithful and to never be parted from him.

COMMUNION

The priest genuflects and takes the host in his hand. Holding the host up, he says:

PRIEST:

Behold the Lamb of God,

behold him who takes away

 the sins of the world.

Blessed are those called to

the supper of the Lamb.

PRIEST AND PEOPLE:

Lord, I am not worthy

that you should enter under my roof,

but only say the word

and my soul shall be healed.

The priest, facing the altar, says quietly:

PRIEST: May the Body of Christ
keep me safe for eternal life.

Taking the chalice, the priest says quietly:

May the Blood of Christ
keep me safe for eternal life.

We walk up to receive Jesus in Communion.

(See the picture on the next page.)

*Before the priest gives each of us Jesus, he
raises a host and shows it to us saying:*

MINISTER, DEACON OR PRIEST:
The Body of Christ.

WE SAY: Amen.

MINISTER, DEACON OR PRIEST:
The Blood of Christ.

WE SAY: Amen.

PRAYER AFTER COMMUNION

After Communion, we talk to Jesus in our
hearts. →

PRIEST: Let us pray.
Then the priest says the Prayer
after Communion.
At the end, of which we say:

PEOPLE: Amen.

CONCLUDING RITES

We heard the Word, received Jesus,
prayed in unity with the Spirit. Now,
we leave the Church. It is time to go
out and do good works. By loving others,
we show how much we love Jesus.

PRIEST: The Lord be with you.

PEOPLE: And with your spirit.

The priest blesses the people. →

FINAL BLESSING

PRIEST: May almighty God bless you,
the Father, and the Son,
✠ and the Holy Spirit.

PEOPLE: Amen.

DISMISSAL

PRIEST OR DEACON:
Go forth, the Mass is ended.
*(Other words may be used. On Easter
Sunday, alleluias are added.)*

PEOPLE: Thanks be to God.

(We add alleluias on Easter.)

How We Live

As Catholics, we live our lives keeping in touch with God through prayer. We follow the will of God by keeping his commandments. We worship God together in community and individually.

Worship is giving honor and praise to God. Our Baptism calls us to honor God and follow Jesus. We worship God in the Mass, through the reading of the Scriptures and receiving Holy Communion. When we receive Jesus in the Eucharist, we are given the grace to live our Catholic faith and follow Jesus more completely.

PRAYER

Prayer is an important part of being a Catholic. To follow Jesus and to be closer to our heavenly Father, we pray. Through prayer, we come to know God as our very own Father.

WHAT IS PRAYER?

Praying is talking and listening to God. Praying is a two-way conversation. Listening and talking to God are very important. That is why we need to set aside a special time to listen to God. A good time to pray is at the start of the day — before all the other things we like to do — and at the end of the day, after a full day of activities.

How do we pray?

There are many different ways to pray. We can pray by speaking from our hearts to God. We can also say prayers that come from the Bible. There are memorized prayers and group prayers, too. Prayers have many different messages. There are prayers that ask God for what we need and prayers for giving thanks. There are prayers that ask for others' needs, and prayers for forgiveness. There are prayers of sorrow, and prayers of joy. There are prayers to adore God and praise Him for everything that is holy. The greatest prayer of all is the Holy Mass.

PRAYERS

Say during the day, or when the need arises.

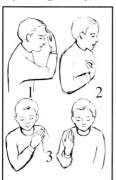

SIGN OF THE CROSS

(1) In the name of the Father,
(2) and of the Son, and of the
(3) Holy Spirit, Amen.

MORNING OFFERING

Heavenly Father, I believe in you and hope in you. I love you above all things. Thank you for bringing me safely through the night. Today, I give myself and everything I do to you. Keep me from evil. Bless my family, friends and all those I love. In Jesus' name I pray. Amen.

EVENING PRAYER

Heavenly Father, thank you for this day. Thank you for our many blessings. Please forgive anything that I did knowingly or unknowingly that displeased you. Please forgive anything I did that hurt others. Father, help me to do better in following Jesus tomorrow. Bless my family and friends all through the night. In Jesus' name I pray. Amen.

Apostles' Creed

I believe in God,
  the Father almighty,
Creator of heaven and earth,
and in Jesus Christ, his only Son,
  our Lord,

All bow up to and including the words "Virgin Mary"

who was conceived by the Holy Spirit,
born of the Virgin Mary,
suffered under Pontius Pilate,
was crucified, died and was buried;
he descended into hell;
on the third day he arose again from
    the dead;
he ascended into heaven,
and is seated at the right hand of God the
  Father almighty;
from there he will come to judge the
  living and the dead.

I believe in the Holy Spirit,
  the holy catholic Church,
  the communion of saints,
  the forgiveness of sins,
  the resurrection of the body,
  and life everlasting. Amen.

Our Father

See pages 46 & 47.

Hail Mary

Hail Mary, full of grace, the Lord is with you. Blessed are you among women, and blessed is the fruit of your womb, Jesus. Holy Mary, Mother of God, pray for us sinners, now, and at the hour of our death. Amen.

Glory to the Father

Glory to the Father, and to the Son, and to the Holy Spirit: as it was in the beginning, is now, and will be for ever. Amen.

Hail, Holy Queen

Hail, holy Queen, Mother of mercy; hail our life, our sweetness and our hope. To you do we cry, poor banished children of Eve. To you do we send up our sighs, mourning and weeping in this valley of tears. Turn then, most gracious Advocate, your eyes of mercy toward us. And after this our exile show unto us the blessed fruit of your womb, Jesus. O clement, O loving, O sweet Virgin Mary.

The Memorare

Remember, O most gracious Virgin Mary, that never was it known that anyone who fled to your protection, implored your help or sought your intercession, was left unaided. Inspired

with this confidence, I fly to you O Virgin of virgins, my Mother; to you do I come, before you I stand, sinful and sorrowful. O Mother of the Word Incarnate, despise not my petitions, but in your mercy hear and answer me. Amen.

Act of Contrition

My God,
I am sorry for my sins with all my heart.
In choosing to do wrong
and failing to do good,
I have sinned against you
whom I should love above all things.

I firmly intend, with your help,
to do penance,
to sin no more,
and to avoid whatever leads me to sin.

Our Savior Jesus Christ
suffered and died for us.
In his name, my God, have mercy.

Grace Before Meals

Bless us, O Lord, and these your gifts,
which we are about to receive
from your goodness, through Christ our
Lord. Amen.

St. Francis of Assisi, grew up as Francesco Bernadone from 1181–1226 A.D. Francis saw the face of God in everything. He began the Franciscan religious order which spread all over the world.

Prayer of
St. Francis of Assisi

Lord, make me an instrument of your
  peace.

Where there is hatred, let me sow
  love;

 Where there is injury, pardon;

 Where there is doubt, faith;

 Where there is despair, hope;

 Where there is darkness, light;

 And where there is sadness, joy.

O divine Master, grant that I may not
  so much seek to be consoled as to
  console;
  to be understood as to understand;
  to be loved as to love.

For it is in giving that we receive, it
  is in pardoning that we are
  pardoned,
  and it is in dying that we are born
  to eternal life.

The Rosary

The Rosary is a prayer. It was developed a long time ago. At first, the Rosary was much different. Today, we say the Rosary developed by St. Louis de Montfort in the 1700's with the newest addition by Pope John Paul II, the Luminous Mysteries. The Luminous Mysteries remind us how Jesus is the "light of the world" *(John 8:12)*. The Rosary is made of 20 Mysteries (200 Hail Mary beads) divided into 4 groups — The Joyful, Sorrowful, Glorious and the Luminous Mysteries.

Praying the Rosary helps us think about Jesus, what he did for us and how Mary and Jesus love us very much.

WHEN TO PRAY
THE ROSARY

The Mysteries focus on the life of Jesus and are said in the same order each week. Starting on Monday pray the Joyful followed by the Sorrowful, Glorious and Luminous Mysteries. Friday repeats the Sorrowful Mysteries, Saturday the Joyful and Sunday the Glorious Mysteries.

- *Pray the 5 Joyful Mysteries every Monday and Saturday.*

- *Pray the 5 Sorrowful Mysteries every Tuesday and Friday.*

- *Pray the 5 Glorious Mysteries every Wednesday and Sunday.*

- *Pray the 5 Luminous Mysteries every Thursday.*

How to pray the Rosary

The illustration to the right shows with which beads the Apostles' Creed, the Our Father, Hail Mary and Glory to the Father are prayed.

1. Apostles' Creed
2. Say 1 Our Father
3. Say 3 Hail Marys
4. Say 1 Glory to the Father

For each Mystery

5. Announce the Mystery and decade
6. Followed with 1 Our Father
7. Say 10 Hail Marys
8. Say 1 Glory to the Father

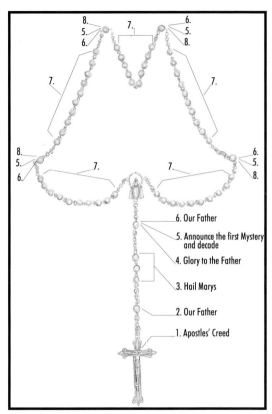

8.
5.
6.
7.
6.
5.
8.
7.
7.
8.
5.
6.
6.
5.
8.
7.
7.
6. Our Father
5. Announce the first Mystery and decade
4. Glory to the Father
3. Hail Marys
2. Our Father
1. Apostles' Creed

The 5 Joyful Mysteries

1. The Annunciation

The angel Gabriel was sent from God to ... Mary. The angel said, "Hail, favored one! The Lord is with you. You have found favor with God. Behold, you will conceive in your womb and bear a son, and you shall name him Jesus." Mary said, "Behold, I am the handmaid of the Lord. May it be done to me according to your word." *(re: Luke 1:26-28, 30-31, 38)*

Like Mary, help me to humbly say "yes"
to God.
(Say 1 Our Father,
10 Hail Marys, 1 Glory to the Father)

2. The Visitation

Mary set out and traveled to the hill country ... she entered the house of Zechariah and greeted Elizabeth. When Elizabeth heard Mary's greeting, the infant leaped in her womb, and Elizabeth, filled with the holy Spirit, cried out... and said, "Most blessed are you among women, and blessed is the fruit of your womb." *(re: Luke 1: 39-42)*

When the Holy Spirit fills my soul, it is God's grace and love that abound.
(Say 1 Our Father,
10 Hail Marys, 1 Glory to the Father)

3. The Birth of Jesus

While they (Mary and Joseph) were in Bethlehem, the time came for her to have her child, and she gave birth to her firstborn son. She wrapped him in swaddling clothes and laid him in a manger, because there was no room for them in the inn. *(re: Luke 2: 6-7)*

May I receive the grace to be poor
in spirit.
(Say 1 Our Father,
10 Hail Marys, 1 Glory to the Father)

4. The Presentation of Jesus

According to the law of Moses, they took
Jesus up to Jerusalem to present him to
the Lord. Now there was a man in
Jerusalem whose name was Simeon. This
man was righteous and devout... And
when the parents brought in the child
Jesus... he took him into his arms and
blessed God... *(re: Luke 2:22-25, 27-28)*

Help me to be obedient like Jesus, Mary
and Joseph were to the laws of God.
(Say 1 Our Father,
10 Hail Marys, 1 Glory to the Father)

5. Finding Jesus in the Temple

When Jesus was twelve years old, they went up to Jerusalem according to festival custom. After they had completed its days, as they were returning, the boy Jesus remained behind in Jerusalem, but his parents did not know it. Not finding him, they returned to Jerusalem to look for him. After three days they found him in the temple, sitting in the midst of the teachers, listening to them and asking them questions, and all who heard him were astounded at his understanding and his answers... He went ... to Nazareth, and was obedient to them... And Jesus advanced (in) wisdom and age and favor before God and man. *(re: Luke 2: 42-47, 51-52)*

Lord, help me to grow in knowledge
and piety.
(Say 1 Our Father,
10 Hail Marys, 1 Glory to the Father)

The 5 Sorrowful Mysteries

1. Agony in the Garden

Jesus came with the disciples to a place called Gethsemane... and he began to feel sorrow and distress. He advanced a little and fell prostrate in prayer, saying, "My Father, if it is possible, let this cup pass from me; yet, not as I will, but as you will." *(re: Matt 26: 36, 37, 39 & Luke 22:42)*

Heavenly Father, when it is difficult
to do the right thing, help me to do
what is right.
(Say 1 Our Father,
10 Hail Marys, 1 Glory to the Father)

2. Scourging at the Pillar

They bound Jesus, led him away, and handed him over to Pilate. Pilate questioned him, "Are you the king of the Jews?" Jesus answered, "My kingdom does not belong to this world. You say I am a king. For this I was born and for this I came into the world, to testify to the truth." Then Pilate said, "I find this man not guilty. Therefore I shall have him flogged and then release him." Then Pilate took Jesus and had him scourged.

(re: Mark 15: 1, 2; John 18: 36, 37; Luke 23: 4, 16; John 19: 1)

Jesus you love us so much that you
suffered for our sins so we would
be purified.
(Say 1 Our Father,
10 Hail Marys, 1 Glory to the Father)

3. Crowning of Thorns

The soldiers led Jesus away inside the palace. They stripped off his clothes and threw a scarlet cloak about him. Weaving a crown out of thorns, they placed it on his head... and kneeling before him, they mocked him, saying, "Hail! King of the Jews!" *(re: Mark 15:16; Matt 27: 28, 29)*

Give me strength and courage to follow
you even when others hurt me and
put me down.
(Say 1 Our Father,
10 Hail Marys, 1 Glory to the Father)

4. Carrying of the Cross

Carrying the cross himself he went out to what is called the Place of the Skull.

(re: John 19:17)

Following Jesus is sometimes difficult. Jesus tells us that following him may not always feel good.

"If anyone wishes to come after me, he must deny himself and take up his cross daily and follow me."

(re: Luke 9:23)

When my cross is heavy, Lord, help me
to have patience and follow your will in
my life.
(Say 1 Our Father,
10 Hail Marys, 1 Glory to the Father)

5. The Crucifixion

When they came to the place called the Skull, they crucified him... Then Jesus said, "Father, forgive them, they know not what they do." Now one of the criminals hanging there... said, "Jesus, remember me when you come into your kingdom." ...Darkness came over the whole land until three in the afternoon because of an eclipse of the sun. Then the veil of the temple was torn down the middle. Jesus cried out in a loud voice, "Father, into your hands I commend my spirit"; and when he had said this he breathed his last.

(re: Luke 23:33-34, 39, 42, 44-46)

Jesus you sacrificed yourself for my sins
that I, and all the world, might be saved.
Help me to have true sorrow for my sins.
(Say 1 Our Father,
10 Hail Marys, 1 Glory to the Father)

The 5 Glorious Mysteries

1. The Resurrection of Jesus

At daybreak on the first day of the week they took the spices they had prepared and went to the tomb. And behold, there was a great earthquake; for an angel of the Lord descended from heaven, approached, rolled back the stone... the angel said... "Do not be afraid! I know that you are seeking Jesus the crucified. He is not here, for he has been raised just as he said. Come and see the place where he lay." *(re: Luke 24:1; Matt 28:2, 5, 6)*

Jesus help me to know the joy of your resurrection and always believe in you.
(Say 1 Our Father,
10 Hail Marys, 1 Glory to the Father)

2. The Ascension of Jesus

Then Jesus led them (out) as far as Bethany, raised his hands, and blessed them. Then Jesus... said to them, "All power in heaven and on earth has been given to me. Go therefore, and make disciples of all nations, baptizing them in the name of the Father, and of the Son, and of the holy Spirit... behold, I am with you always, until the end of the age." As he blessed them he parted from them and was taken up to heaven.

(re: Luke 24:50-51; Matt 28:18-19, 20)

Help me to share my faith and hope in
you with others. Let me never be distant
from you.
(Say 1 Our Father,
10 Hail Marys, 1 Glory to the Father)

3. The Descent of the Holy Spirit upon the Apostles

When the time for Pentecost was fulfilled, they were in one place together. And suddenly there came from the sky a noise like a strong driving wind.... Then there appeared to them tongues as of fire, which parted and came to rest on each one of them. And they were all filled with the holy Spirit and began to speak in different tongues, as the Spirit enabled them to proclaim ... the mighty acts of God. *(re: Acts 2:1-4, 11)*

Through the gifts of the Holy Spirit,
help me to love God and others more.
(Say 1 Our Father,
10 Hail Marys, 1 Glory to the Father)

4. The Assumption of Mary

Blessed are you, daughter, by the Most
High God, above all the women on earth.

(re: Judith 13:18)

Mary, you were assumed into Heaven as
a sign of our hope to also live in heaven.
Because of Jesus, may I too be given
eternal happiness.
**(Say 1 Our Father,
10 Hail Marys, 1 Glory to the Father)**

5. The Crowning of Mary as Queen of Heaven and Earth

A great sign appeared in the sky, a woman clothed with the sun, with the moon under her feet, and on her head a crown of twelve stars. Who is this that comes forth like the dawn, as beautiful as the moon, as resplendent as the sun?

(re: Rev. 12:1; Song of Songs, 6:10)

Mary, my queen and my mother, help me to remain faithful to you and the will of God.
(*Say 1 Our Father,
10 Hail Marys, 1 Glory to the Father*)

1. The Baptism of Jesus in the Jordan

Jesus is made known as the Son of God by a sign from heaven. Jesus obediently accepted the mission God the Father gave him. When we are baptized, we join the family of God and are called to be obedient like Jesus. **Re: Matthew 3:13-17 or John 1:28-34**

MYSTERIES

In 2002, Pope John Paul II declared a year of the Rosary and added Mysteries to the Rosary. The new Luminous Mysteries remind us how Jesus is the

2. The Wedding Feast at Cana

Jesus does his first miracle, encouraged by his mother, to help people believe in him. When our mothers ask us to do something, may we be ready as Jesus was and believe that Jesus helps us. **Re: John 2:1-12**

3. The Proclamation of the Kingdom of God and Call to Conversion

Jesus heals the sick and forgives their sins because of their faith. May we grow in faith, asking Jesus' forgiveness, and follow what he says. **Re: Mark 2:1-12**

of Light

"light of the world" (John 8:12). The five mysteries include the important parts of Christ's public life. They show us how Jesus is the light of the world.

4. The Transfiguration

Jesus' divinity shines forth as Moses and Elijah talk with Jesus. God the Father asks us to listen to his son, Jesus, with whom He is pleased. When we follow Jesus in what we say and do, we also please the Father.
Re: Matthew 17:1-8

5. The Institution of the Eucharist

During the Last Supper, Jesus gave us his Body and Blood for the first time. When we receive Jesus in the Eucharist, we remember the ways Jesus shows his love for us, especially by dying for us on the cross.
Re: Luke 22:14-20

The Sacraments

Sacraments are visible signs established by Christ in which God's life is given to us. The sacraments are entrusted to the Church. They touch every important part of our Christian life of faith. At the Last Supper, Jesus gave us the Eucharist. The Eucharist is the sacrament of Christ's Body and Blood. The Eucharist is at the center of our sacramental life.

The 7 sacraments are divided into three groups.

1. Sacraments of Initiation
- Baptism
- Confirmation
- Eucharist

2. Sacraments of Healing
- Penance / Reconciliation
- Anointing of the Sick

3. Sacraments at the Service of Communion
- Holy Orders
- Matrimony

While they were eating, Jesus took bread, said the blessing, broke it, and giving it to his disciples said, "Take and eat; this is my body." Then he took a cup, gave thanks, and gave it to them, saying, "Drink from it, all of you, for this is my blood of the covenant, which will be shed on behalf of many for the forgiveness of sins." (re: Matt 26:26-28)

THE SACRAMENT of RECONCILIATION

hen we sin, it is important to reconcile ourselves with God. Through the Sacrament of Reconciliation we are forgiven for offending God, our family and our friends. To make a good confession, start by saying a prayer.

PRAYER BEFORE RECONCILIATION

God the Father, help me to remember those times in my thoughts and in my deeds when I may have offended you, or hurt others by not keeping your commandments. With the help of the Holy Spirit, I confess my sins. *(Pages 114-116 will help)*

Confessing our Sins

1. Begin by making the Sign of the Cross and greeting the priest: *"Bless me Father, for I have sinned."*

2. Continue saying: *"This is my first confession ..."* or *"My last confession was... (weeks, months, years)".*

3. While confessing your sins to the priest, he helps you make a good confession. Answer his questions without hiding anything out of fear or shame. Place your trust in God, a merciful Father who wants to forgive you.

4. Following your confession, say: *"I am sorry for these and all of my sins."*

5. The priest assigns you a penance and offers advice. The penance helps you become a better Catholic. It may be a prayer, an offering, works of mercy, service, or sacrifice.

6. Say an Act of Contrition (see page 70-71), expressing sorrow for your sins.

7. The priest, acting in the person of Christ, absolves you from your sins saying the Prayer of Absolution, while you are making the Sign of the Cross and say, *"Amen."*

8. The priest offers some proclamation of praise, such as *"Give thanks to the Lord, for He is good,"* to which you respond, *"His mercy endures forever."*

9. The priest dismisses you. Because sin causes harm, you must seek to repair the damage by completing your penance.

Prayer After Reconciliation

God the Father, Son and Holy Spirit, thank you for forgiving me. I promise to be better, love more and grow strong in your grace. Amen.

The 10 Commandments

Loving God above all things

1. I am the Lord your God: you shall not have strange gods before me.

We believe in God and love God — no person or thing is more important.

2. You shall not take the name of the Lord your God in vain.

We use God's name with love because it is holy.

3. Remember to keep holy the Lord's Day.

We pray, go to Church and attend Mass on Sunday and holy days.

Loving our neighbor

4. Honor your father and your mother.

We listen to and obey our parents and those who care for us.

5. You shall not kill.
  We should respect each person's life
    and dignity.

6. You shall not commit adultery.
  We are faithful to our loved ones.

7. You shall not steal.
  We must never take anything which
    does not belong to us.

*8. You shall not bear false witness against your
  neighbor.*
  We always tell the truth, and are
    careful not to gossip.

9. You shall not covet your neighbor's wife.
  We are thankful for those God has
    given us to love.

10. You shall not covet your neighbor's goods.
  We appreciate all the things God has
    given us.

(re: Exodus 20:2-17; Deuteronomy 5:6-21)

The 2 Great Commandments

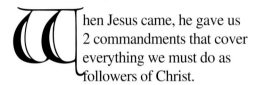When Jesus came, he gave us 2 commandments that cover everything we must do as followers of Christ.

"You shall love the Lord, your God, with all your heart, with all your soul, and with all your mind. This is the greatest and the first commandment.

The second is like it: You shall love your neighbor as yourself. "

(re: Matt 22: 37-39)

The Beatitudes

True happiness is following the teachings of Jesus.

Blessed are the poor in spirit,
for theirs is the kingdom of heaven.

Blessed are they who mourn,
for they will be comforted.

Blessed are the meek,
for they will inherit the land.

Blessed are they who hunger and thirst
for righteousness,
for they will be satisfied.

Blessed are the merciful,
for they will be shown mercy.

Blessed are the clean of heart,
for they will see God.

Blessed are the peacemakers,
for they will be called children of God.

Blessed are they who are persecuted for the sake of righteousness,
  for theirs is the kingdom of heaven.

Blessed are you when they insult you and persecute you and utter every kind of evil against you (falsely) because of me. Rejoice and be glad, for your reward will be great in heaven. (re: Matt 5: 3-12)

THE STATIONS OF THE CROSS

Kneel in front of the altar and say:

Jesus, you loved me so much that you died for my sins and rose again so I might share in eternal life with you, the Father and the Holy Spirit. May these Stations of the Cross help me to realize that love.

At each station, think about what happened to Jesus. Think about how he suffered for us and how much he loves us.

At each station say:
1 Our Father,
1 Hail Mary and
1 Glory to the Father

1st Station
Jesus is Condemned to Death

2nd Station
Jesus Takes up His Cross

3rd Station
Jesus Falls the First Time

4th Station
Jesus Meets His Mother

5th Station
Simon of Cyrene Helps Jesus

6th Station
Veronica Wipes Jesus' Face

7th Station
Jesus Falls a Second Time

8th Station
Jesus Meets the Sorrowing Women

9th Station
Jesus Falls the Third Time

10th Station
Jesus' Clothes are Torn From Him

11th Station
Jesus is Nailed to the Cross

12th Station
Jesus Dies on the Cross

13th Station
Jesus is Taken From the Cross

14th Station
Jesus is Laid in the Tomb

15th Station
Jesus Rises From the Dead

prayers... thoughts... sayings...

_____

_____

_____

_____

_____

_____

_____

_____

_____

_____

_____

_____

_____

_____

Prayer to My Guardian Angel

Angel of God, my guardian dear, to whom God's love commits me here. Ever this day be at my side, to light and guard, to rule and guide. Amen

Printed in Korea

RETURN TO READING

RETURN

TO Reading

RANDALL E. DECKER

Hartnell College, Salinas, California

Boston *Little, Brown and Company* Toronto

Published simultaneously in Canada
by Little, Brown & Company (Canada) Limited

PRINTED IN THE UNITED STATES OF AMERICA

✳
✳
PREFACE
✳
✳

Necessity is perhaps as often the mother of a book as of an invention. This book was produced in an effort to satisfy one vital need, if not a necessity — the need for a worthwhile anthology-text for that widening range of "in-between" English classes. These are the classes which (for whatever controversial reason) are not yet ready for the rigors of, say, Aristotle and Bacon, yet are much too mature for a bland diet of essay-advice on dating behavior and the decline of school spirit.

A book to bridge this gap, it was believed, should introduce the student to the widest possible variety in good reading — a variety of form and style, of subject matter and authors and publications, variety in breadth and depth and viewpoint. It should provide real intellectual challenge for the most experienced reader of the class and still be within reasonable reach of the inexperienced. Such a book should develop some literary discrimination and critical ability in every kind of student reader. And it should, above all, give the student a taste of the real satisfactions to be derived from the printed word and stimulate him to further explorations in the various sources of good reading all about him.

RETURN TO READING is a careful attempt to do all these things — and many more.

Essays, stories, and poems were selected to provide mature reading, always with some degree of literary merit and sophistication. Although it is not intended primarily as a writing improvement text, a student's serious attention to the reading involved will reflect in his own increasing maturity of ideas and self-expression.

Flexibility in potential uses has been another quality anxiously sought. "Questions for reflection, discussion, or writing," for instance, are grouped for full flexibility; instructors, as we know, have widely differing approaches to anthology selections — that, of course, is the way it should be. The questions can be used entirely as casual aids for studying, for formal assignments, or for informal class discussions, impromptu talks, or panel discussions. Writing assignments, when desired, can easily be selected or developed from the list — for short essay-type answers or fully developed compositions — without restrictions imposed by rigid categories such as Questions-on-Content, Topics-for-Themes, and the like. The differing lengths of essays and question-groups will also provide flexibility; some will adapt as one-day supplementary assignments, and others will require two or more days if treated thoroughly.

Apparatus in the book itself has been kept light, however, again to give the instructor complete control. Although it has been the editor's theory, for example, that vocabulary is better studied in context than in lists, the instructor will find it a simple matter, if he prefers, to provide advance lists of words. (Objective questions on content also have been omitted from the book itself, in an effort to avoid the usual mechanical filling in of squares or blanks, and instead to give the student full responsibility for the careful reading of the whole assignment.)

The instructor should not feel bound by the order of selections in RETURN TO READING. Although some are loosely grouped according to subject, these are easy to locate and keep together in any general rearrangement; although there are occasional headnote explanations of literary terms useful to full appreciation of the reading, these explanations are referred to by page number when the terms are used later; and, although in the questions there are frequent references to previously read essays, these questions can be omitted if necessary to accommodate some more useful arrangement.

The final section (which, of course, can provide only a nodding acquaintance with prose fiction and verse) can certainly be broken up and interspersed among the earlier units. Apparatus in this section has been omitted entirely, giving the instructor complete freedom to use the selections purely as "enjoyment" reading or to approach fiction and poetry in his own favorite ways.

Most of the contents of RETURN TO READING have been used in the editor's classes — successfully, or they would have been eliminated, as many others were. This is, we believe, a completely practical book.

The editor would like to express appreciation for the helpful criticism and suggestions provided by his friends and colleagues — especially Elizabeth H. Kaupp of the College of San Mateo and Raymond E. Early of the City College of San Francisco.

R. E. D.

CONTENTS

WHY "RETURN" — AND HOW

This Book's Purpose 3

A Suggested Way to Use this Book 4

VIEWS OF PRACTICAL MATTERS

The Institute for Propaganda Analysis, HOW TO DETECT PROPAGANDA   7

Keith Monroe, THEY MADE THE CIGAR RESPECTABLE   15

Cornelia Otis Skinner, WOMEN ARE MISGUIDED   25

Samuel S. Leibowitz, NINE WORDS THAT CAN STOP JUVENILE

    DELINQUENCY   30

Hubert H. Humphrey, A PLAN TO SAVE TREES, LAND, AND BOYS . . .   37

Shirley L. Povich, BASKETBALL IS FOR THE BIRDS   47

Ken D. Loeffler with Harry T. Paxton, I SAY BASKETBALL'S OUR BEST

    GAME   54

Gertrude Samuels, from A FORCE OF YOUTH AS A FORCE FOR PEACE   .   66

Paul Conklin, "WE DON'T WANT TO BE WON"   72

Marquis Childs, PEACE CORPS   76

Peter F. Drucker, HOW TO BE AN EMPLOYEE   79

Aldous Huxley, THE SHAPE OF THINGS IN 1986   94

EXPLORING THE PAST

Rachel Carson, MOTHER SEA: THE GRAY BEGINNINGS 103

Nathaniel Benchley, THE $24 SWINDLE 114

Jack London, THE EARTHQUAKE 120

Bruce Catton, from A STILLNESS AT APPOMATTOX 128

John K. Townsend, from A HUNTING PARTY ON THE SNAKE RIVER . . 134

Peter Lyon, WYATT EARP AND BAT MASTERSON 137

Joseph Stocker, THE IMMORTAL MODEL T 148

A CASUAL LOOK AROUND

George Nelson, OUT OF THE TRACKLESS BUSH, A NATIONAL CAPITAL . 155

Time Magazine, BRAZIL'S WILD WEST 162

Patrick O'Donovan, ANCHORAGE 165

The New Yorker, CANDY 171

Eugene Burdick, from THE UNITED STATES NAVY 175

Alan Devoe, EVERYONE A NATURALIST 186

Charles G. Finney, WESTERN GLADIATOR 192

David Cort, SURVIVAL IN THE ZOO 200

Jack Kerouac, ALONE ON A MOUNTAINTOP 206

Time Magazine, THE ROOTS OF HOME 218

VIEWS OF MAN AS HE SEES HIMSELF

Philip Wylie, SCIENCE HAS SPOILED MY SUPPER 231

Henry David Thoreau, from ECONOMY 239

Lin Yutang, MAN, THE ONLY WORKING ANIMAL 242

Sloan Wilson, HAPPY IDLE HOURS BECOME A RAT RACE 246

Joseph Wood Krutch, SPORTSMAN OR PREDATOR? 256

H. L. Mencken, from ON THE MEANING OF LIFE 264

A. Cressy Morrison, SEVEN REASONS WHY A SCIENTIST BELIEVES IN GOD 268

Arthur H. Tasker, OCTOBER BLIZZARD 273

William D. Blair, Jr., JOURNEY INTO FEAR 279

James P. Cornette, LET THEM BUILD TENTS 287

Robert Paul Smith, HOW NOT TO LISTEN 291

Stephen Vincent Benét, FREEDOM'S A HARD-BOUGHT THING 297

Patrick Henry, LIBERTY OR DEATH 312

David Lawrence, THE BIG PRISON 315

Norman Cousins, TRIUMPH OVER THE BULLY 319

John F. Kennedy, INAUGURAL ADDRESS, 1961 322

SIMPLE ENJOYMENT

Some Last Advice 329

John Mason Brown, BETWEEN THE DARK AND THE DAYLIGHT 330

James Thurber, COURTSHIP THROUGH THE AGES 336

E. B. White, DOG TRAINING 341

Bill Helmer, MEXICAN HEY RIDE 344

Edna St. Vincent Millay, FIRST FIG 350

William Saroyan, THE SUMMER OF THE BEAUTIFUL WHITE HORSE . . 350

Phyllis McGinley, SEASON AT THE SHORE 357

Ambrose Bierce, THE BOARDED WINDOW 358

Carl Sandburg, CHICAGO 362

Julian Mitchell, LAMENT FOR THE COWBOY LIFE 364

William E. Barrett, SEÑOR PAYROLL 365

Stephen Crane, "I EXPLAIN THE SILVERED PASSING . . ." 368

Oscar Hammerstein, II, HELLO, YOUNG LOVERS 369

Robert Fontaine, MY MOTHER'S HANDS 370

Frederick Eckman, LOVE LIES A-BLEEDING 375

Guy de Maupassant, THE JEWELS OF M. LANTIN 375

William Shakespeare, O MISTRESS MINE 382

Emily Dickinson, "HOPE" IS THE THING WITH FEATHERS 382

Walt Whitman, BEAT! BEAT! DRUMS! 383

William Ernest Henley, INVICTUS 384

Edwin Arlington Robinson, RICHARD CORY 384

A. E. Housman, "IS MY TEAM PLOWING . . . ?" 385

Shirley Jackson, CHARLES 386

Ogden Nash, TO A SMALL BOY 390

Edgar Allan Poe, THE CASK OF AMONTILLADO 391

Karl Shapiro, AUTO WRECK 398

Frank O'Connor, MY OEDIPUS COMPLEX 399

Edna St. Vincent Millay, GOD'S WORLD 410

INDEX, 411

RETURN TO READING

WHY "RETURN" —AND HOW

THERE WAS A TIME when everyone who seriously expected to become educated, in school or out, was a diligent reader. Today, it seems, a great many young people go to college and wait there for learning to take place, to enter painlessly by osmosis while sitting passively in a classroom. But it seldom does.

Presumably every student using this book has at least some interest in becoming an educated person, either for "practical" purposes (a more profitable career, a more impressive social life) or for the less easily defined satisfaction that comes simply from *knowing* and *understanding*. Some people, unfortunately, must rely entirely on first-hand experience for their mental and cultural development. There is nothing wrong, of course, with first-hand experience — as far as it goes. But what a confining life it is for the person who knows *only* what he can learn in his own narrow canyon. It is a great deal like going through life half-blind and half-deaf, unable to really see and hear what the rest of the world is like.

A sensible RETURN TO READING can prevent such a fate.

Probably some students, although they want, vaguely, to see outside their own narrow canyons, never quite get around to reading anything not absolutely required by teachers — or by the social necessity of keeping up with the Dodgers or the local weddings. Sometimes the cause for this negligence is pure mental laziness (and people with this chronic affliction will never be really educated, whatever else they may be), but often the cause is simply poor reading ability. And this, itself, has been caused by *not* reading. Faulty reading habits, inadequate vocabulary, and a limited stock of ideas with which to cope with the ideas of others combine to make the whole business such a disagreeable task that the student seldom does any reading, the only possible *cure* for his trouble. A vicious circle? Yes — but it can be broken, although not easily once adult habits are formed. And so the years go by, and after a while the non-reader becomes more or less reconciled to not really understanding or enjoying many of the conversations around him; to not really understanding or enjoying the exciting, important things happening in his community, in the world; to not really understanding or enjoying people themselves very well — because he is too limited in his sources of ideas and information. He becomes reconciled to just wondering what there is about reading that causes some people to do it deliberately. He becomes reconciled, yes — and he may live a satisfactory life, as a good husband and father, as a successful businessman perhaps, or as a member of the City Council. But he will always wish — at least secretly, and maybe frankly, if you ask him — that he had learned to read and enjoy it.

Understanding and enjoyment — these are the benefits of reading. Reading *can* be enjoyable for anyone with ordinary intelligence — at least, after those first difficult stages of learning to do it with real and mature understanding. There can be real and lasting enjoyment (of the deeper sort than mere hilarity, understand) in good reading about all sorts of things — about the sale of Manhattan, for instance, by Indians with no right to sell it, or about the life cycle of a rattlesnake or some fellow's wacky impressions of auto-driving in Mexico, about the population explosion or Brazil's new capital, or about another man's ideas of God or freedom or basketball — all to be found in this book, by the way.

This Book's Purpose

RETURN TO READING, we hope, will prove enjoyable and informative if you are one of those who are already "readers," and, if you are not, will help to break through your "vicious circle" of non-reading. One course or two, however — and one small book — are not enough to completely over-come any serious reading deficiencies you may have. Your vocabulary, for example, will not be good in a few months if it is not good now. There are more than 500,000 words in the English language, and here we can cap-ture only a comparative few of them; and some of these will soon be lost again. But by the end of the course you will have made at least a start; and, more important, you will have developed a word *consciousness*, an in-terest in words, because they are no longer mere classroom gimmicks but tools people actually do use in trying to communicate — with *you*.

You will develop a new consciousness of *ideas*, too — the ideas and ex-periences people try to share with you in their writings; you will find your-self interested in far more things than you now believe possible. One in-terest will lead to another, and another, and still another.

You will notice that the variety in RETURN TO READING is not limited to that of subject matter. The book includes long and short essays, some old and some new, some "deep" and some merely amusing; stories; a few poems. A part of the reading you will find easy; some of it will be a rung or two above your most comfortable level in ideas, vocabulary, and struc-ture. (For how else can we climb a ladder except by reaching higher than we already are?) The selections, too, were written by a wide variety of people: Some are world-famous authors, statesmen, philosophers, journal-ists, or poets. Others are almost unknown except for this one contribution.

The selections are arranged in five categories, depending on our inter-pretation of the average reader's probable purpose in reading them. But many could have been classified in other ways; the categories themselves are arbitrary. If, in reading an article on Wyatt Earp, you discover some-thing of modern-day, practical concern as well as of historical interest, if you learn something of a different philosophy of life, and at the same time have fun in the reading — good! Then at least four of the five categories have converged in one piece of writing, and you certainly will have found it rewarding to read.

A Suggested Way to Use This Book

As time goes on, you will develop your own best system for reading or study. Certainly if reading is to be any kind of pleasure we cannot be worrying about every sentence we read, feverishly consulting our dictionary, trying to memorize facts, and fretting over hidden meanings. *Much* reading, in fact, should be done without any "study" at all. But a portion of your reading each day should be done *with* careful study and with a dictionary handy. Here is a suggested plan, step by step:

(1) Read the headnotes preceding the selection itself. In them will be suggestions for better understanding and appreciation of the reading to follow.

(2) Then read the selection itself, this first time almost entirely for whatever enjoyment or new ideas you can get from a quick, casual reading. Do *not* stop to look up new words unless the sentence in which they are used is meaningless until you do. But have a red pencil in hand and draw a quick line under all words you are doubtful about, then go on.

(3) When finished with the first reading put the book down and think over, for a few minutes, what you have read.

(4) Then use the dictionary to help you understand the words you have underlined. Do not make the mistake of finding the first or the shortest definition and trying to memorize it. Instead, look at the various meanings, and for the word's use as a noun, verb, modifier. *Think* about them. Pronounce the word to yourself. Use it in a few sentences. Identify it with similar words you already know. Then see how the author has used it.

(5) After you understand all the words, read and ponder briefly the questions and remarks which follow the selection.

(6) Then re-read the essay, pausing sometimes to think and to *question*, underlining important ideas, marking sentences or phrases that seem to you especially interesting, wrong, amusing, or well-expressed.

(7) Then return to the questions at the end. You probably will find that you have already provided the answers. If not, give them further thought, referring again to the essay or to earlier explanations

(page references are usually given in parentheses) wherever necessary for thorough understanding.

(8) Next, try to evaluate the selection. Sometimes you will think it successful, sometimes not. But *why?* Here are three questions we can ask ourselves in trying to make an intelligent criticism of any creative endeavor, whether it be an essay or story or poem — or, for that matter, a building, a song, a braided rug, or a flower garden:

(a) *What was the creator's purpose?* If we take a building that was designed to be a library and use it instead as a church, we would be most unfair to criticize the architect because he designed a poor church. Likewise, if an author is trying to explain a plan for lessening juvenile delinquency, we should not criticize him because he does not make us laugh in every paragraph. Or, if his purpose is merely to make us laugh, we should not condemn him because he teaches us nothing. So first decide what you think he was trying to do.

(b) *How well does he succeed?* If we think the architect was designing a church, we *are* justified in criticizing, favorably or unfavorably, depending on whether the building is successful and attractive as a *church*. If an author is trying to convince us that we should favor a modern-day version of the old Civilian Conservation Corps, we do have a right to expect sound reasoning and clear explanations. If he is telling us about the hazards of driving in Mexico, exaggerating with the obvious intention of making us laugh, we have a right to expect at least a few chuckles.

(c) *Was it worth doing?* Many things are written and published that succeed in the author's intent all right — but simply were not worth bothering about. Some of the selections in this book may appear that way to you. If so, part of the reason *might* lie in your own personal tastes or lack of experience, or in your mood at the moment, and you should allow for this when criticizing the worth of the author's endeavor. But most of these selections were written for ordinary people like us — adults, with no great knowledge of or passionate interest in the subjects written about. If we try, we can picture the *average* reader of the publication in which the selection originally appeared, and judge its worth accordingly.

(9) Your last step should be whatever writing your instructor has assigned, or to plan anything he might ask you to write about in class. Just as your reading skill progresses, you will find that you are also becoming a more competent *writer*. Your increasing experience in *reading* good writing; your study of the various techniques good writers use; your growing ability to cope with and express intangible ideas — all these will reflect, even though imperceptibly at first, in your own ability to communicate with others.

All of this takes a great deal of time and trouble, you say? Especially for one little essay about rattlesnakes, for example, or one man's account of his summer on a Washington mountaintop? Perhaps — but a great deal of time and trouble *only* if your ability to read with understanding is deficient in the beginning. In that case, of course, you must realize that it is high time you *are* investing some extra time and energy to correct the deficiency. And, at this stage, every time you grapple with a new idea or a new piece of information, or admire the way an author has expressed it, and every time you try to make his words a part of your own vocabulary, you are just that much nearer being able to understand and appreciate all sorts of other things besides — within books and without — things which *are* of concern to you.

And, after all, that is how most really mature and educated people got that way.

✳ ✳
VIEWS
✳ ✳ OF
✳ PRACTICAL MATTERS

✳
✳
✳
✳
✳
✳
✳
✳
✳
✳
✳
✳
✳
✳
✳
✳

The Institute for Propaganda Analysis

HOW TO DETECT PROPAGANDA

THE INSTITUTE FOR PROPAGANDA ANALYSIS *was founded in 1937 and remained under the supervision of Clyde R. Miller, faculty member, administrative officer, and public relations director of Teachers College at Columbia University. It was financed in part by Edward A. Filene, the Boston merchant, who had heard about the approach Mr. Miller was developing in his classroom for the understanding of propaganda. Until the Institute became one of the first "casualties" of World War II, thousands of American schools and other organizations used its special pamphlets and monthly bulletins which identified and analyzed current propaganda.*

HOW TO DETECT PROPAGANDA, *a chapter from the pamphlet* Propaganda Analysis, *is primarily an explanation, which is one of the four basic kinds of prose* writing. Known as **exposition,** or **expository** writing, its purpose is to "expose" or lay bare the author's ideas or information for someone else's understanding. (The three other basic kinds of writing are argument, narration, and description, all of which will be discussed later.)

The authors have used various common techniques in developing "How to Detect Propaganda" into an easy-to-understand exposition: **dividing** and **classifying** their materials; constantly **defining** their terms, beginning with "propaganda" itself (the whole essay, in a way, is a definition of "propaganda"); and using numerous **examples** to demonstrate what they mean. The result is an article that almost anyone can read.

An understanding of these expository methods, of course, is extremely useful in our own writing of compositions, essay examinations, term papers, and business letters, reports, and office memorandums — nearly all the writing most of us ever have to do is expository. But the understanding is perhaps even more valuable for efficient reading, especially of explanations more difficult than this one, enabling us to take full advantage of any aids the author provides.

1   IF AMERICAN citizens are to have clear understanding of present-day conditions and what to do about them, they must be able to recognize propaganda, to analyze it, and to appraise it.

2   But what is propaganda?

3   As generally understood, *propaganda is expression of opinion or action by individuals or groups deliberately designed to influence opinions or actions of other individuals or groups with reference to predetermined ends.* Thus propaganda differs from scientific analysis. The propagandist is trying to "put something across," good or bad, whereas the scientist is trying to discover truth and fact. Often the propagandist does not want careful scrutiny and criticism; he wants to bring about a specific action. Because the action may be socially beneficial or socially harmful to millions of people, it is necessary to focus upon the propagandist and his activities the searchlight of scientific scrutiny. Socially desirable propaganda will not suffer from such examination, but the opposite type will be detected and revealed for what it is.

4   We are fooled by propaganda chiefly because we don't recognize it when we see it. It may be fun to be fooled but, as the cigarette ads used to say, it is more fun to know. We can more easily recognize

propaganda when we see it if we are familiar with the seven common propaganda devices. These are:

1. The Name Calling Device
2. The Glittering Generalities Device
3. The Transfer Device
4. The Testimonial Device
5. The Plain Folks Device
6. The Card Stacking Device
7. The Band Wagon Device

5   Why are we fooled by these devices? Because they appeal to our emotions rather than to our reason. They make us believe and do something we would not believe or do if we thought about it calmly, dispassionately. In examining these devices, note that they work most effectively at those times when we are too lazy to think for ourselves; also, they tie into emotions which sway us to be "for" or "against" nations, races, religions, ideals, economic and political policies and practices, and so on through automobiles, cigarettes, radios, toothpastes, presidents, and wars. With our emotions stirred, it may be fun to be fooled by these propaganda devices, but it is more fun and infinitely more to our own interests to know how they work.

6   Lincoln must have had in mind citizens who could balance their emotions with intelligence when he made his remark: ". . . but you can't fool all of the people all of the time."

Name Calling

7   "Name Calling" is a device to make us form a judgment without examining the evidence on which it should be based. Here the propagandist appeals to our hate and fear. He does this by giving "bad names" to those individuals, groups, nations, races, policies, practices, beliefs, and ideals which he would have us condemn and reject. For centuries the name "heretic" was bad. Thousands were oppressed, tortured, or put to death as heretics. Anybody who dissented from popular or group belief or practice was in danger of being called a heretic. In the light of today's knowledge, some heresies were bad and some were good. Many of the pioneers of modern science were called heretics; witness the cases of Copernicus, Galileo, Bruno. Today's bad names include: Fascist, demagogue, dictator,

Red, financial oligarchy, Communist, muckraker, alien, outside agi-
tator, economic royalist, Utopian, rabble-rouser, trouble-maker,
Tory, Constitution-wrecker.

8   "Al" Smith called Roosevelt a Communist by implication when
he said in his Liberty League speech, "There can be only one capital, Washington or Moscow." When "Al" Smith was running for
the presidency many called him a tool of the Pope, saying in effect,
"We must choose between Washington and Rome." That implied
that Mr. Smith, if elected President, would take his orders from the
Pope. Likewise Mr. Justice Hugo Black has been associated with a
bad name, Ku Klux Klan. In these cases some propagandists have
tried to make us form judgments without examining essential evidence and implications. "Al Smith is a Catholic. He must never be
President." "Roosevelt is a Red. Defeat his program." "Hugo Black
is or was a Klansman. Take him out of the Supreme Court."

9   Use of "bad names" without presentation of their essential meaning, without all their pertinent implications, comprises perhaps the
most common of all propaganda devices. Those who want to *maintain* the *status quo* apply bad names to those who would change
it. . . . Those who want to *change* the *status quo* apply bad names
to those who would maintain it. For example, the *Daily Worker*
and the *American Guardian* apply bad names to conservative Re-
publicans and Democrats.

Glittering Generalities

10   "Glittering Generalities" is a device by which the propagandist
identifies his program with virtue by use of "virtue words." Here he
appeals to our emotions of love, generosity, and brotherhood. He
uses words like truth, freedom, honor, liberty, social justice, public
service, the right to work, loyalty, progress, democracy, the American
way, Constitution-defender. These words suggest shining ideals. All
persons of good will believe in these ideals. Hence the propagandist,
by identifying his individual group, nation, race, policy, practice, or
belief with such ideals, seeks to win us to his cause. As Name Calling
is a device to make us form a judgment to *reject and condemn*,
without examining the evidence, Glittering Generalities is a device
to make us *accept and approve*, without examining the evidence.

11   For example, use of the phrases, "the right to work" and "social

justice," may be a device to make us accept programs for meeting labor-capital problems, which, if we examined them critically, we would not accept at all.

12   In the Name Calling and Glittering Generalities devices, words are used to stir up our emotions and to befog our thinking. In one device "bad words" are used to make us mad; in the other "good words" are used to make us glad.

13   The propagandist is most effective in the use of these devices when his words make us create devils to fight or gods to adore. By his use of the "bad words," we personify as a "devil" some nation, race, group, individual, policy, practice, or ideal; we are made fighting mad to destroy it. By use of "good words," we personify as a godlike idol some nation, race, group, etc. Words which are "bad" to some are "good" to others, or may be made so. Thus, to some the New Deal is "a prophecy of social salvation" while to others it is "an omen of social disaster."

14   From consideration of names, "bad" and "good," we pass to institutions and symbols, also "bad" and "good." We see these in the next device.

Transfer

15   "Transfer" is a device by which the propagandist carries over the authority, sanction, and prestige of something we respect and revere to something he would have us accept. For example, most of us respect and revere our church and our nation. If the propagandist succeeds in getting church or nation to approve a campaign in behalf of some program, he thereby transfers its authority, sanction, and prestige to that program. Thus we may accept something which otherwise we might reject.

16   In the Transfer device, symbols are constantly used. The cross represents the Christian Church. The flag represents the nation. Cartoons like Uncle Sam represent a consensus of public opinion. Those symbols stir emotions. At their very sight, with the speed of light, is aroused the whole complex of feelings we have with respect to church or nation. A cartoonist by having Uncle Sam disapprove a budget for unemployment relief would have us feel that the whole United States disapproves relief costs. By drawing an Uncle Sam who approves the same budget, the cartoonist would have us feel

that the American people approve it. Thus the Transfer device is used both for and against causes and ideas.

Testimonial

17 The "Testimonial" is a device to make us accept anything from a patent medicine or a cigarette to a program of national policy. In this device the propagandist makes use of testimonials. "When I feel tired, I smoke a Camel and get the grandest 'lift.' " "We believe the John L. Lewis plan of labor organization is splendid; C.I.O. should be supported." This device works in reverse also; counter-testimonials may be employed. Seldom are these used against commercial products like patent medicines and cigarettes, but they are constantly employed in social, economic, and political issues. "We believe that the John L. Lewis plan of labor organization is bad; C.I.O. should not be supported."

Plain Folks

18 "Plain Folks" is a device used by politicians, labor leaders, businessmen, and even by ministers and educators to win our confidence by appearing to be people like ourselves — "just plain folks among the neighbors." In election years especially do candidates show their devotion to little children and the common, homey things of life. They have front porch campaigns. For the newspaper men they raid the kitchen cupboard, finding there some of the good wife's apple pie. They go to country picnics; they attend service at the old frame church; they pitch hay and go fishing; they show their belief in home and mother. In short, they would win our votes by showing that they're just as common as the rest of us — "just plain folks" — and, therefore, wise and good. Business men often are "plain folks" with the factory hands. Even distillers use the device. "It's our family's whiskey, neighbor; and neighbor, it's your price."

Card Stacking

19 "Card Stacking" is a device in which the propagandist employs all the arts of deception to win our support for himself, his group, nation, race, policy, practice, belief, or ideal. He stacks the cards against the truth. He uses under-emphasis and over-emphasis to dodge issues and evade facts. He resorts to lies, censorship, and distortion.

He omits facts. He offers false testimony. He creates a smoke screen of clamor by raising a new issue when he wants an embarrassing matter forgotten. He draws a red herring across the trail to confuse and divert those in quest of facts he does not want revealed. He makes the unreal appear real and the real appear unreal. He lets half-truth masquerade as truth. By the Card Stacking device, a mediocre candidate, through the "build-up," is made to appear an intellectual titan; an ordinary prize fighter, a probable world champion; a worthless patent medicine, a beneficent cure. By means of this device propagandists would convince us that a ruthless war of aggression is a crusade for righteousness. Some member nations of the Non-Intervention Committee send their troops to intervene in Spain. Card Stacking employs sham, hypocrisy, effrontery.

The Band Wagon

20 The "Band Wagon" is a device to make us follow the crowd, to accept the propagandist's program en masse. Here his theme is: "Everybody's doing it." His techniques range from those of medicine show to dramatic spectacle. He hires a hall, fills a great stadium, marches a million men in parade. He employs symbols, colors, music, movement, all the dramatic arts. He appeals to the desire, common to most of us, to "follow the crowd." Because he wants us to "follow the crowd" in masses, he directs his appeal to groups held together by common ties of nationality, religion, race, environment, sex, vocation. Thus propagandists campaigning for or against a program will appeal to us as Catholics, Protestants, or Jews; as members of the Nordic race or as Negroes; as farmers or as school teachers; as housewives or as miners. All the artifices of flattery are used to harness the fears and hatreds, prejudices, and biases, convictions and ideals common to the group; thus emotion is made to push and pull the group on to the Band Wagon. In newspaper article and in the spoken word this device is also found. "Don't throw your vote away. Vote for our candidate. He's sure to win." Nearly every candidate wins in every election — before the votes are in.

Propaganda and Emotion

21 Observe that in all these devices our emotion is the stuff with which propagandists work. Without it they are helpless; with it, harnessing

it to their purposes, they can make us glow with pride or burn with hatred, they can make us zealots in behalf of the program they espouse. As we said at the beginning, propaganda as generally understood is expression of opinion or action by individuals or groups with reference to predetermined ends. Without the appeal to our emotion — to our fears and to our courage, to our selfishness and unselfishness, to our loves and to our hates — propagandists would influence few opinions and few actions.

22   To say this is not to condemn emotion, an essential part of life, or to assert that all predetermined ends of propagandists are "bad." What we mean is that the intelligent citizen does not want propagandists to utilize his emotions, even to the attainment of "good" ends, without knowing what is going on. He does not want to be "used" in the attainment of ends he may later consider "bad." He does not want to be gullible. He does not want to be fooled. He does not want to be duped, even in a "good" cause. He wants to know the facts and among these is included the fact of the utilization of his emotions.

23   Keeping in mind the seven common propaganda devices, turn to today's newspapers and almost immediately you can spot examples of them all. At election time or during any campaign, Plain Folks and Band Wagon are common. Card Stacking is hardest to detect because it is adroitly executed or because we lack the information necessary to nail the lie. A little practice with the daily newspapers in detecting these propaganda devices soon enables us to detect them elsewhere — in radio, news-reel, books, magazines, and in expression of labor unions, business groups, churches, schools, political parties.

QUESTIONS FOR REFLECTION, DISCUSSION, OR WRITING

(1) Why do you suppose the authors considered it especially important to make this essay as simple and clear as possible? For what kind of reading audience was it written?

(2) Examine the essay and show where and how the authors have used *division* and *classification* to make their writing easy to read and understand. Where have they used *definition? Examples?*

(3) Where else, in your day-by-day reading or study, is *exposition* the primary type of writing?

(4) How many of the "seven devices of propaganda" can you find examples of in today's newspapers, magazines, brochures (for schools, occupations, Armed Forces, etc.), or television programs? Propaganda in advertising is, of course, the most easily detected; but try to find examples also in news stories (the men in the Kremlin, for instance, are experts at propaganda — as are many people who write our own news stories), editorials, syndicated columns, cartoons, panel programs — places where the unsuspecting reader or listener is most apt to be "fooled." Remember that erroneous information, unless given for "predetermined ends," is not considered propaganda, however dangerous it might be.

(5) Have you ever been the innocent victim of propaganda? An account of this experience and its results might provide suitable material for composition.

(6) Can you think of any occasion when it might be *best,* either personally or for the common good, for people to be "fooled"? Might there be times when it is best to let our feelings be appealed to, rather than our reason? Defend your stand, if this is assigned, in good composition form.

Keith Monroe

THEY MADE THE CIGAR RESPECTABLE

KEITH MONROE, *who lives in Santa Monica, California, has been a newspaper editor, advertising agency copy chief, and aircraft public relations man. His free-lance articles have appeared in* Saturday Evening Post, Cosmopolitan, Esquire, Reader's Digest, True, *and many other periodicals.*

HARPER'S MAGAZINE, *in which this essay was published in January 1959, is a well respected "quality" magazine, published in New York. Founded in 1850, it has always been devoted to public affairs and literature in various forms: the essay, prose fiction, and poetry.*

THEY MADE THE CIGAR RESPECTABLE *is another expository essay (see p. 8), an explanation of how a successful propaganda campaign has restored the cigar's lost popularity. Unlike the preceding exposition, however, large portions of this essay are* narration, *or* narrative *writing (the telling of events in time sequence, as in a story), used here to assist in the explanation.*

The author has made frequent (though seldom very original) use of two kinds of figures of speech *— our two most common kinds, the* simile *and the* metaphor. *Awareness of figures of speech and their capabilities can heighten our appreciation of much worthwhile reading, from science textbooks to modern poetry.*

Both *metaphors and* similes *are short,* vivid *comparisons, either stated or* implied; *but they are not literal comparisons, as when we say, "Your car is like my car," which is presumably a plain statement of fact. Metaphors and similes are more imaginative, used less to inform than to make vivid or forceful impressions. Both are comparisons of* unlikes, *but unlikes that do have some interesting point of* likeness *which the author has noticed. The simile (which is often classified as a metaphor itself, a special kind) expresses such a similarity directly, usually with the word "as" or "like" ("as old-fashioned as chin whiskers," par. 26 below). But the metaphor merely suggests the comparison and is worded as if the two unlikes were the same thing ("rolled back the tide of public distaste," par. 3, or "the thunder of the big games," par. 33). It would occur to few readers to take such expressions literally, but figuratively they make their points well.*

Many *expressions which started as bright metaphors, however, have been absorbed into our everyday working language and have lost, or nearly lost, their value as figures of speech — e.g., the* leg *of a chair, the* head *of a nail, or someone's iron* will *or steel* nerve. *In this essay we have, for example,* "undercover *work" (par. 3), "low pressure* propaganda" *(5), "pin* money" *(14), and "people* softened up" *(43).*

1   SUPPOSE YOU WERE a manufacturer whose product was steadily falling into disfavor. Previously bought by millions, like the button shoe or the high collar, it was now scorned except by oldsters too stubborn to change, and by bums too ignorant to care. Your sales were sinking toward the bankruptcy point. What would you do?

2   The problem is an old one. Few businessmen who have faced it have ever solved it, except by flight into some other line of work. It wiped out the fletchers and the blacksmiths. It defeated the makers of corsets and gas lights and stereoscopes. But it has not defeated one present-day group of manufacturers.

3   They have met this problem in our generation and have conquered it, after a fight for survival which only recently has seemed securely won. In ten years of studied undercover work they have rolled back the tide of public distaste, thereby almost literally rescuing their product from the gutter and themselves from limbo.

4   The men by whom — or for whom — this miracle was performed are the cigar makers. There are around forty fairly big ones today, and around 4,000 small ones. They are the smart survivors of the

27,000 who flourished before World War I, and they survived because they gambled part of their fast-shrinking bankrolls on a public
relations campaign.

5   What saved them was pervasive low pressure propaganda, which
was brought to bear long before the cigarette was publicly associated
with lung cancer; the pressure was so invisible and imperceptible
that most people never noticed it even though it reversed their attitude toward cigars. Among public relations wizards, the "cigar campaign" is recognized as one of the great classics of their art.

6   Perhaps the reader does not smoke cigars and therefore thinks
that this campaign did not sway him. But if he is under fifty, let him
ask himself if he feels any prejudice against cigars today — and then
let him think back twenty years. Around 1935 how did cigar-smokers
look to him? Didn't they seem rather lowbrow and crude? Or else
pitiably old-fashioned? Wouldn't he have been taken aback to see
a young man of good family puffing a stogie?

7   If the reader is a lady, let her recall how she reacted to cigar smoke
in the thirties. Does her nose wrinkle today as it did then? Let her
remember the many parlors in which cigar fumes, if anyone had
dared to generate them, would have seemed shamefully offensive.
Is she shocked today if a gentleman lights a cigar in her home?

8   The answers seem beyond dispute, at least statistically. Public
opinion pollsters recently found that 90 per cent of American women
no longer object to cigar smoking by men. Of all American men, 40
per cent now smoke cigars at least occasionally, and they start young,
at the average age of twenty-three. Cigar sales, which were down to
$225 million a year when the manufacturers kittied up for their
campaign, have soared to $550 million.

9   This is still a cut below the majestic old days of $650 million
annual sales in the first decades of the century. But the sales curve,
which dropped steeply from 1920 to 1936, has climbed ever since,
and in recent years has gone up at the rate of 2 per cent a year. In
the last three years an estimated 1,500,000 new men have become
cigar-smokers.

10 Perhaps the curve would eventually have gone up anyway, without pushing by propagandists. Public taste runs in mysterious waves.
There is no sure way of telling when, or why, people will change
their minds en masse. (One of many examples is the strange lettuce

market of 1930. For unknown reasons, housewives simply weren't in
the mood to buy lettuce that year. The price plummeted, but lettuce
didn't sell at any price. Lettuce growers and speculators went broke,
lettuce fields were abandoned and left to rot. Then, over one week-
end, an army of women from Maine to Mexico began asking their
grocers for lettuce. Prices climbed to ten-year highs and shattered
fortunes were rebuilt in a few weeks, as women kept on buying
lettuce.)

A *Prop for Villains*

11   The cigar has survived several such violent ups and downs. Columbus brought it back from the New World and showed Spanish
nobility how the Indians smoked it. It became so much the rage
that professors of smoking set up salons to teach both sexes how to
light up, how to blow smoke rings, and a few other tricks still used
by cigar-smokers today.

12   Cigars grew so popular that Pope Urban VIII had to issue a bull
against priests who smoked while saying mass. The interior of St.
Peter's itself was sometimes so gray with cigar haze that Innocent X
finally threatened smokers with excommunication. This almost
killed the cigar in Europe.

13   But the Vatican's attitude changed later, and cigar-manufacturing
became a papal prerogative. In 1851 the Secretary to the Papal
States warned that anyone who disseminated anti-cigar propaganda
would be jailed. Cigars were hotly controversial by then. Not only
were prohibitionists preaching against them, but in 1848 cigar-
smokers were pursued by mobs and lynched in the streets of Milan.
It wasn't that the Milanese found cigar odor as obnoxious as all that;
they hated it for ideological reasons. The cigar was a symbol of their
Austrian rulers. All cigars in Milan were imported by the Austrian
government, but boycotted by nationalists, so a cheroot in the
mouth was emblematic of an 1848-style collaborationist.

14   There were cigar stores in America before the Revolution. One in
Lancaster, Pennsylvania, was opened in 1770 and is still owned by
the same family. The earliest cigar-makers in this country were colonial dames, who rolled them by hand and sold them to itinerant
peddlers for pin money. These good wives sampled their own wares

as a matter of course. In colonial days cigar smoking was no less ladylike than cigarette smoking is today.

15   The first world war came closer to killing the cigar than any other event had. During that war, men switched to cigarettes. Until then the cigarette had seemed vaguely degenerate. Almost nobody smoked it except mysterious Orientals, absinthe drinkers, Tenderloin girls, and other slinky characters. But the doughboys, burdened with bulkier equipment than any warriors since the Crusaders, discovered the advantages of the handy little pack in an outside pocket. They learned to enjoy a quick puff at odd moments in the trenches. Suddenly a cigarette was a he-man's pleasure.

16   This trend started by default, because cigars weren't in the field. Service men had yearned for cigars in the early months of the war, so Washington had ordered millions for distribution to the armed forces. Unfortunately its policy was to buy from the lowest bidders.

17   "Many bidders for cigar contracts," the Cigar Institute of America records bitterly, "were neither experienced nor reputable. It was their practice to produce something that had the appearance of a cigar, deliver it to government depots, then disappear with their profit. Much of this product was in no condition for anything but the incinerator. It was moldy or dried or wormy, or the most sordid combination of assorted vegetables and wrapping paper."

18   So the AEF tried cigarettes. Soon all the armies of the Allied and the Central Powers were smoking them too. Cigarette manufacturers shrewdly reinvested their profits in massive advertising and distribution drives which led to complete saturation of their markets.

19   By 1920 they were strong enough to suggest that women might smoke too. They began cautiously, with advertisements which showed winsome and fashionable girls imploring men to "Blow Some My Way." Finally they risked a picture of a girl actually smoking. Another barrier between the sexes fell, and millions of women bought cigarettes.

20   Meanwhile, trainloads of war-surplus cigars were being dumped on civilians. Retailers put baskets of cigars in their stores with signs like "Take a handful for 5 cents" and "Free cigars with every purchase." Only the most hardened roughnecks could smoke them at any price. A cigar in the mouth became the mark of a tough mug.

21   The infant movie industry noticed this. Thrifty casting directors realized they didn't need a good actor to play a house detective, gangster, or ward heeler. All they needed was a $5-a-day extra with plug hat and cigar.

22   Movie audiences learned to identify the cigar-smoker as the villain. The impact of Hollywood on our folkways has been felt many times. This time it knocked cigars out of the mouths of almost everyone except Grandpa. Without malice aforethought, the movie-makers nearly finished off the cigar-makers.

23   Dealers buried cigars on bottom counters, and stopped bothering to humidify them. Four of every five cigar factories closed. In 1933 most of the remaining manufacturers sat down in one room to form the Cigar Manufacturers Association.

The Indirect Approach

24   They were a jealous and suspicious crowd: Cubans, Puerto Ricans, New Yorkers and Southerners and New Englanders. Each considered his product a work of art, and was as egoistic as a chef or a novelist. No one would agree to anything smacking of standardization. No system of classifying cigar shapes or sizes would suit them — nor has, to this day. "Perfecto" or "Panatela" can mean almost anything in length and thickness, depending on which company is doing the labeling.

25   However, the manufacturers did agree to hire a market-research man. But when he recommended spending $150,000 on publicity to make cigar-smoking fashionable, the CMA shuddered and voted him down.

26   Another two years passed. Cigars were becoming as old-fashioned as chin whiskers. Then the sales curve took a feeble turn upward. Why? Some tobacco men said cigar sales had followed the prosperity graph downward, and now would follow it up again. Others noted that Cremo, Dutch Masters, and Bayuk Phillies had lashed out on their own with vigorous advertising; perhaps they were pulling the whole industry upward.

27   Not until 1940, when the "national defense" boom had failed to bring prosperity to them, did the cigar-makers pull out their check-books and agree on joint, bold action. They would finance a subtle

but widespread promotion to stop Americans' drift away from cigars.

28   The manufacturers rented offices in Rockefeller Center, established the Cigar Institute of America, and hired a manager: Berthold Nussbaum, an adman who had wrestled for years with cigar-company accounts.

29   Mr. Nussbaum remembered the blunder of the movie men, who wasted vast sums bellowing "Movies Are Your Best Entertainment." (Their billboards, banners, radio commercials, and newspaper pages were hastily canceled when someone pointed out that the initials of the slogan spelled MAYBE. But even when reborn as "Motion Pictures Are Your Best Entertainment" the campaign flopped.) He knew that a blatant smoke-more-cigars theme would merely remind people that few cigars were being smoked.

30   When the meat packers had wanted to sell more bacon, he remembered, they had sought the advice of the legendary Ivy Lee, a public relations counsel who believed in persuasion by indirection. Mr. Lee had sprinkled the newspapers with statements from doctors urging people to eat bigger breakfasts. The doctors never mentioned bacon. But millions of people bought bacon, because a big breakfast usually includes bacon and eggs.

31   Mr. Nussbaum devised an even more oblique approach. His campaign did not urge anybody to do anything. Instead he sent emissaries to newspaper offices, empty-handed. They bore no mimeographed press releases, no invitations to press conferences. They had nothing in writing — but they discreetly passed the word to news photographers that there would be cash prizes each month for the best published photos of people smoking cigars.

32   Cameramen, who had previously suggested to a cigar-smoking subject that he hide his cigar before posing, now decided that he looked better with cigar. They sometimes went so far as to offer him one if he didn't have it. News pictures began to show cigars in the mouths of the Duke of Windsor, Lauritz Melchior, Darryl Zanuck, Benny Goodman. When American wire-service men photographed Winston Churchill, they waited patiently for chances to catch him with cigar in teeth.

33   By text as well as by photo, cigars eased into newspapers and magazines. Cigar Institute agents had begun feeding copy to editors.

The nation heard cigars mentioned casually amid the thunder of the big games. There were reminders of Churchill's fifteen cigars a day; of the five-dollar Havanas Coolidge had cherished, and the humidor Roosevelt kept for distinguished visitors; of Babe Ruth's passion for expensive Perfectos, and Douglas MacArthur's habit of sitting down with a cigar to mull a military problem.

34   Cigar sales showed a walloping increase of one billion in 1941. Mr. Nussbaum died of a heart attack the week before Pearl Harbor, but the manufacturers kept their campaign rolling. As their new manager they picked Harry W. McHose, fresh from Lexington, Kentucky, where he had been a publicity man for American Tobacco Company during the government's monopoly suit against cigarette manufacturers.

Cigars Are For Heroes

35   Mr. McHose saw that the new war threatened final ruin of the cigar business if the government repeated its 1917 policy. He persuaded Washington to buy only from established cigar-makers. Cigars for the armed forces were as good as those for civilians, and service men asked for more and more. The first Allied soldier to land in France was reported to be a young American paratrooper who arrived bolt upright with a lighted cigar in his mouth. The Cigar Institute, naturally, prevented this incident from being overlooked.

36   By 1944 there was a world-wide cigar shortage. Manufacturers could not keep up with the demand. They had only 36,000 factory workers, with no hope of hiring more while the war lasted. But they knew that even if they made enough cigars for everyone who wanted them, sales would be far below the eight-billion peak of 1910. Mr. McHose kept hatching ideas.

37   He had plenty of problems. Younger men by no means overwhelmed cigar counters. Women still complained about the "vile smell." Hollywood still used cigars incessantly as a prop for heavies.

38   Mr. McHose begged Hollywood to stop putting stogies in the mouths of Edward G. Robinson and his ilk. Hollywood paid no attention. Finally he loaded a briefcase and stormed the studios in person.

39   He showed movie magnates a tabulation which revealed that

27,500,000 people a week passed cigar counters near theaters. "Whenever you make a movie with a good cigar scene," he offered, "I'll put posters advertising it on 25,000 cigar counters across the nation. Free of charges."

40   Free advertising is meat and drink to showmen. Hollywood heavies stopped smoking, and heroes started. Tyrone Power puffed cigar smoke all over the screen in "Blood and Sand." So did Gary Cooper as Sergeant York. When the Cigar Institute heard that Hollywood was filming George Gershwin's life story, it hastened to concoct twenty-five pages of alleged historical data about Gershwin's cigar-smoking. The subsequent movie showed Gershwin wreathed in smoke at each high point of triumph or delight. In "Saratoga Trunk," Gary Cooper flourished Havanas intermittently, and Ingrid Bergman cooed, "A house isn't really a house unless it has about it the scent of a good cigar after breakfast."

41   If they thought about it at all, men may have been puzzled that cigar counters were all flaunting movie posters. But movie patronage picked up. By the end of 1947 the Cigar Institute was able to boast that forty major movies of that year contained "good cigar scenes" and that "Seldom, if ever, is a cigar misused today in action or dialogue."

42   Mr. McHose combed literature for endorsements of cigars. Robert Louis Stevenson, he found, had advised women never to marry a non-smoker. Bert Leston Taylor had suggested that when things go wrong it is a good idea to "meditate on interstellar spaces, / And smoke a mild seegar." Bulwer-Lytton called the cigar "as great a comfort to a man as a good cry to a woman." Thackeray called it "a kind companion, a gentle stimulant, an amiable anodyne, a cementer of friendship." Kipling wrote "A woman is only a woman, but a good cigar is a smoke!"

43   People softened up toward cigars. Without analyzing why, men began smoking them and women did not protest. Cigar missionaries kept the vogue growing. Boxes of cigars became prizes on radio shows. Store-window displays urged cigars for Father's Day and Christmas. Service clubs and the American Legion posts presented cigars to boys entering the armed forces. Elks gave them away to new fathers.

44   A painting of a young father surrounded by stacks of cigar boxes

turned up on the cover of *Coronet*. Cigars got into male fashion pictures. The Cigar Institute persuaded the Veterans of Foreign Wars to send a humidor of costly cigars to Lord Mountbatten as a gift for the royal wedding, and wangled newsreel coverage. It organized the Cigar Bowl football game in Tampa, and lined up a radio network to broadcast it, although fifteen other "bowl" games were already booked for the same day.

45 These feats led to Mr. McHose's election as president of the American Public Relations Association. In 1947 he departed to conquer new fields, but the Cigar Institute still campaigns more or less invisibly. It has recently persuaded some airlines to relax their long-standing taboo against cigar-smoking on planes; several luxury flights now offer cigars to passengers. Amy Vanderbilt has issued a guide to "The Good Manners of Cigar Smoking." Newsreels show today's jet aces chewing cigars, not gum.

46 The Cigar Institute now uses paid advertising as well as the other kind. It began spending the major portion of its budget on advertisements in 1949, and bought $350,000 worth last year. Its present director, Eugene L. Raymond, says "The CIA is subtly wooing younger men in its ads, by soliciting testimonials from baseball and other sports figures whom the younger element lionizes." Individual manufacturers have even begun to slant advertising to women: General Cigar used the headline, "America's first cigar ad for women only," and Bayuk gave this advice to women, "Be glad your husband smokes cigars."

47 There are still a few cigar counters which let cigars get so dry that only a subhuman could enjoy them, but such counters are far rarer than they were a few years ago. The public relations counsel of the Cigar Institute, Lynn Farnol, says, "Humidification and the care of cigars are now the beginning of the industry bible. Mr. Raymond has spoken at the Cigar Clinics in every major city in America on this subject."

48 Cigar men decline to harp on the fact that cigar-smokers apparently are not nearly as susceptible to lung cancer as cigarette-smokers. There is no pseudo-medical lore in their campaigns. Nor are there any veiled cracks at competition. Cigar men are doing all right as it is. Maybe their propaganda hasn't changed your mind about cigars, but it has certainly changed a lot of other minds.

QUESTIONS FOR REFLECTION, DISCUSSION, OR WRITING

(1) In addition to the *metaphors* and *similes* mentioned in the headnotes, there are at least 15 others which are, or have been, such *figures of speech*. List as many as you can find, identify each as to whether metaphor or simile, and comment on its freshness and present effectiveness as either a workaday or a figurative expression.

(2) How many of the "seven devices of propaganda" did the cigar industry use in the campaign? Were any propaganda techniques used which do not fit into one of the seven categories?

(3) Explain, using fresh examples as necessary, the difference between low pressure and high pressure propaganda. Between low pressure and high pressure in personal salesmanship.

(4) Why do you suppose cigar men "decline to harp on the fact that cigar-smokers apparently are not nearly as susceptible to lung cancer as cigarette-smokers" (par. 48)? The author says they are "doing all right as it is." Do you think any businessman is ever doing so "all right" that he would not like to do better? If you were a cigar manufacturer, would you pass up this opportunity to convert smokers to your product? Why, or why not?

(5) What other styles or national habits have become popular again after a period of disuse? Do you suppose any of these comebacks were the result of similar low pressure propaganda campaigns? High pressure campaigns? Explain.

(6) Aside from the fashions or habits in smoking, what others can you think of that were once considered unfeminine but are now acceptable for women — or, once considered effeminate, now acceptable for men? To what extent do you think propaganda may have influenced these changes?

(7) Your account of some drastic change of style or popular habit could be written in good composition form. Keep your purpose *expository*, with no attempt to influence your readers' opinions.

Cornelia Otis Skinner
WOMEN ARE MISGUIDED

CORNELIA OTIS SKINNER, *a native of Chicago and resident of New York, has achieved fame in various fields: as a Broadway actress and producer, as a play-wright, poet, and author. She has written such books as* Nuts in May, The Ape in Me, *and* Bottoms Up! *and co-authored (with Emily Kimbrough) the best-seller* Our Hearts Were Young and Gay.

LIFE *Magazine, where "Women Are Misguided" first appeared Dec. 24, 1956, was started in 1936. It is owned by Time, Inc. (also publishers of* Time, Fortune, *and* Sports Illustrated), *which had previously purchased the 53-year-old humorous weekly* Life, *retired it, and gave its name to the new publication. The "new"* Life *is the oldest of the "picture magazines" and the largest, with a weekly circulation of well over 6 million. The editors now attempt to give much more than mere picture coverage of world events and include a wide variety of both photographs and essays, chosen to appeal to all kinds and ages of people.*

WOMEN ARE MISGUIDED *is an example of one kind of* **informal essay**, *a classification which is pretty well described by its name. Usually shorter than the* **formal essay**, *it is also less elaborately organized and more "chatty" in style. In informal essays we usually find a free use of first person pronouns* (I, me); *contractions ("don't," par. 1 below); coined words and expressions ("a sort of we-are-the-leaders girls' college attitude," par. 11); and colloquialisms ("had crashed the gates," par. 3, and "okay," par. 11). Informal essays are less serious in apparent purpose than formal essays; although many do contain a worthwhile "message" or observation of some kind, their primary purpose is most often to entertain, to please in some other way, or occasionally the opposite, to "get a rise" out of readers, much like the fellow who manipulates the bull-session into an argument, then sits back and enjoys the fun.*

The following selection, however, is a particular type of informal essay, known as the **familiar essay**, *a term applied to the more personal, intimate kind. The author of a familiar essay writes about his own experiences, ideas, or prejudices, always in a light style and usually with humor.*

1   I HAPPEN not to be what is known as a "woman's woman." The female who is proud of the fact that she is a "woman's woman" is as ludicrous to me as the manhood-triumphant male who boasts of being a "man's man." I am quite content to be a woman but I don't regard my state as a remarkable accomplishment. I am not inordinately proud of my sex any more than I am inordinately proud of mankind as a whole. And I am anything but proud of the unwomanly way in which women's women are behaving these days.

2   Being completely nonpartisan when it comes to the comparative merits and superiorities of the two sexes, I am always astonished when I run across the earnestly vigorous partisans, those "what-women-are-doing" enthusiasts who still go under the outdated term

of feminists. There are still an astonishing number of American women who get all worked up over American women, hailing each new distinction of any member of the sisterhood as one more goal for their team. And often as not, the more unfeminine the achievement, the more rapturous the cheers.

3   I have been exposed to this attitude all my life, for my mother was awfully impressed by the emancipated female "who did things." To be sure, when I was a child women had not been doing things for too many years as far as the professions or civic affairs were concerned, and my mother thought those who did were wonderful. There was a female general practitioner that mother thought was especially wonderful—only, I'm sure, because she had crashed the gates of the medical profession, for as a person she was a fright, resembling a tweed-clad horse with a definite mustache and smelling of leather and disinfectant. I called her "Dr. Spook." She was one of the Emancipated Women all right, and the first shackle from which she had emancipated herself was charm.

4   I had to put up with Dr. Spook because she was the first woman doctor in our neighborhood. To be the *first* woman to accomplish any unusual feat has always been heralded, especially by other women, as being something remarkably splendid. Woman will go to all lengths in her incomprehensible scuffle to prove herself the equal of man. In 1901 Mrs. Anna Edson Taylor had herself nailed into a steel-bound barrel, shoved out into the rapids of the Niagara River and swept down over the falls. She goes down in the pages of history as the first person to survive this idiotic act. Whether or not it proved women to be the equal of men in courage and shock absorption, it certainly proved that they can be equally asinine.

5   A surprising number of women in this country still maintain that they can do anything better than a man can. This is a pity, for if a woman *can* do a man's job better than he, and if she lets him know it, she is no true woman. It is certainly not to be questioned that in many fields women are on a par of excellence with men. In others, their excellence might be summed up by the words of Dr. Samuel Johnson: "Sir, a woman preaching is like a dog's walking on his hind legs. It is not done well; but you are surprised to find it done at all."

6   Whether they do them well or not, there are certain trades I

wish the girls had not taken up. For instance, that of the hospital technician. I have never had a blood count taken or other medical tests performed upon me by anyone but a very brisk, very terrifying, young Miss Efficiency, smugly competent, aloofly impersonal and about as compassionate as an armadillo.

7   Then there are those lady headwaiters who go by the euphemistic title of "hostesses." For me they strike a chilling note. A headwaiter leads one directly to a table with an anticipatory flourish that whets the appetite. A head waitress, after considerable hesitancy, takes a mysteriously circuitous route to what proves to be the most distant table, as though she thought it best not to let one be seen. It is rather like being shown to a pew at a funeral.

8   I also feel curiously uncomfortable about all-girl orchestras. I am ready to grant that the female musician can be every inch the equal of the male artist, if not occasionally the superior. But the sight of a woman playing a peculiarly unwomanly instrument is so distracting that one spends the time watching her instead of listening to the sounds she produces. There is no logical reason why female musicians should be confined to the piano, the harp, the violin, the viola and an occasional flute. And there are no logical grounds, artistic or physical, for objection to a woman's playing on a bassoon or pounding a kettledrum or venting interesting sounds by means of a tuba. But she looks ridiculous. The English conductor Sir Thomas Beecham apparently shares my dim view of lady musicians. When, on a guest tour of this country, he discovered women in the symphony orchestras, he fulminated: "Women are like the vultures on the battlefield: they appear after everyone else is dead. . . . The sooner they're allowed to run their course, the sooner the present era will blow up in ineptitude, inefficiency and incompetence. There will be five years of no music, and at the end people will say, 'Now we'll start over.' "

9   Actually there was recently a talented young female bassoonist who gave up a promising career on that sturdy instrument, not to do something more feminine but to take up bullfighting. This is Patricia Hayes of San Angelo, Texas, who has had spectacular success in the arenas of Mexico and Portugal. Unfortunately she is not America's only matadoress. Pat McCormick (also from Texas) has slaughtered more than 125 bulls since 1952, and Bette Ford, a

former model from McKeesport, Pa., has accounted for more than 53 bulls since 1954.

10 It is obvious that in time there will hardly be a job that women will not try to tackle. I don't know if as yet the carpenter's union has admitted any women to their ranks, and so far we do not employ many lady paper hangers, plumbers or garage mechanics. As far as I know, the Brotherhood of Locomotive Engineers is still a brotherhood. Trains are my favorite means of transportation, but the day I look through the cab window of the Century and see, seated behind the throttle, a woman wearing goggles and one of those caps made of bed-ticking, I will take a plane. And the day a woman wins a heavyweight or even a bantamweight championship over a male pugilist (and there have been lady boxers), I will take up lavender and lace.

11 Women have plenty of champions among the sociologists and anthropologists who have proved her equality to man. If she is equal, the fact is not too disturbing. What is disturbing is the inordinate pride we flaunt in our accomplishments, a sort of we-are-the-leaders girls' college attitude — which is okay as long as one is a girl in college. If a woman can do a job as well as a man, so what? As for all those women's groups and committees, I think they are fine if they are accomplishing fine things. They are to be commended for proving themselves constructive, valuable *citizens,* but not for proving themselves constructive, valuable *women.* Any step toward the betterment of this sorry world is a splendid thing. But the fact that the public benefactor is a woman doesn't make it any more splendid.

12 Ladies, we have won our case, but for heaven's sake let's stop trying to prove it over and over again. By setting ourselves up as a race apart and special we lose many of the delights and fulfillments of being women. In the long run, we cannot do without men and men cannot do without us — not unless we drive them to it with our shrill cheering for our own accomplishments. If ever the day approaches when men *can* do without us, I will take out citizenship papers in another and more agreeable planet.

QUESTIONS FOR REFLECTION, DISCUSSION, OR WRITING

(1) What characteristics of this essay permit it to be classified as an *informal essay?* As a *familiar essay?* Be specific.

(2) Miss Skinner has used several figures of speech (see p. 15), including both similes ("like being shown to a pew at a funeral," par. 7) and metaphors ("the first shackle," par. 3), some old and some new. Find as many of each as you can and comment on their originality and effectiveness.

(3) If you see the reason for including this familiar essay in the "Practical Matters" division of the book, explain. If not, where might it have been more appropriately located? Why?

(4) Explain in your own words what is meant by the term "feminist." Do you think Miss Skinner is completely fair in her denunciation of feminism? Why, or why not?

(5) Do you agree that if "a woman *can* do a man's job better than he, and if she lets him know it, she is no true woman" (par. 5)? Explain.

(6) An interesting composition might be based on your own views — either pro or con — of women in certain occupations not mentioned by Miss Skinner in her essay.

Samuel S. Leibowitz

NINE WORDS THAT CAN STOP
JUVENILE DELINQUENCY

SAMUEL S. LEIBOWITZ, *who wrote this selection, was admitted to the New York bar in 1917 and practiced as a criminal lawyer until 1941. Since that time he has served as judge in the Kings County Court, Brooklyn.*

THIS WEEK, *in which "Nine Words . . ." appeared Dec. 15, 1957, has been published since 1935 by United Newspapers Magazine Corporation of New York. Used as a Sunday "magazine supplement" by more than 40 metropolitan newspapers throughout the country, the weekly distribution of* This Week *is approximately 13 million.*

NINE WORDS THAT CAN STOP JUVENILE DELINQUENCY *was obviously written for one specific purpose: to convince readers that the author's recommendation is sound. And this is what we should have in mind when we attempt to judge the worth of the article.*

If we are to become critical and discriminating readers (important, certainly, if we are to make the most of our capabilities as either students or citizens) we must learn to evaluate fairly the worth of what we read. And, always, the writer's **purpose** *is the yardstick by which we should measure his writing, just as purpose is the success-measure of any other endeavor. (However little we may like riding in helicopters ourselves, we'd hardly criticize them because they will not operate under water or bore holes for fenceposts!) But once having found the author's purpose in writing (or purposes, perhaps, but usually with only one of them primary), we are in a position to judge his success intelligently, and then the worthwhileness of his endeavor. At first this is done consciously, even laboriously; but later it becomes nearly automatic to evaluate as we read. And that is the way it should be.*

1   I HAVE SPENT my life "inside" crime — 21 years as a criminal lawyer, 16 years as a judge in the criminal courts. I have studied the criminal from his first young scrape with the law to his last walk to the electric chair; I have dissected his background, the forces that produced him, the unresolved conflicts inside him that warp him to crime.

2   Ask me for examples of juvenile crime and I need only invite you into my courtroom, any day, any week. I had just recently before me a youth of 17 who hurled liquid lye in another student's face. One of our Children's Court judges was attacked by a boy in court who hit him on the head with a chair. Another youth hurled an inkwell into the face of a teacher. Every criminal courts judge in this country is witness to the terrible fact that teen-agers are replacing adults on the dockets of the criminal courts.

3   We judges are all sickeningly aware of this development, but our awareness is tinged with hopelessness. The Senate Sub-Committee on Juvenile Delinquency has announced that "we are losing our battle against juvenile delinquency." J. Edgar Hoover has seconded this pronouncement. We flail at the problem with a jumble of unco-ordinated "solutions": teen-age curfews, more playgrounds, punishing parents for their teen-ager's crimes, getting more social workers, setting up a Federal delinquency bureau, establishing psychiatric committees to research the adolescent psyche.

4   There is a feeling of despair, almost panic, about these "solu-

tions." To me, sitting on the bench in the capacity of society's conscience, in day-to-day contact with the problem, these "solutions" are treatments of the effect rather than the cause. I have felt for some time that our approach is like putting bandages on a sore that can be healed only by changing the blood stream.

5   It has seemed to me that something down deep, simple but basic, must have disappeared from our way of life to have caused this revolt toward crime among our young people. But what was it? For several years I searched through the debris of the young, ruined lives brought before me, trying to find a lead, but without results.

6   Then, last summer, with court out of session, I had an idea that I felt might be worth pursuing: I would go to the country that had the *lowest* rate of juvenile delinquency and see if I could find there some clue to how and why our nation had jumped the track.

7   What Western country has the lowest juvenile delinquency rate? Italy, by far, as the box on these pages shows. Even allowing for differences in each country in the tabulation of their statistics, the picture is a shocking one for Americans.

Found: A Vital Element

8   But why is it that Italy's delinquency rate is so low? For weeks, last summer, I toured Italian cities, trying to get the answers. Eventually I was rewarded with the revelation I was seeking: I found an element there, a basic, vital element of living that is disappearing in this country and which, to my mind, is the most effective solution to the malady of young delinquency.

9   In Italy, I was given remarkable co-operation. Police commissioners, school superintendents, officials of cities, told me what I wanted to know, took me where I wanted to go.

10   An important police official asked me if it were really true that teen-agers attacked police in this country. I had to tell him it was.

11   "Ah, this is very hard for us to believe," he said. "No Italian youth would ever lay hands on a police officer."

12   A Naples school superintendent asked me if thrill murders are figments of journalists' imaginations.

13   "No," I informed him, "they are all too true. Three high-school boys, good boys with no marks against them, take a walk along the river, see a bum sleeping, suddenly get a grotesque urge to torture

him. They burn his feet, torture him in other ways, end up by throwing him in the river. Could that happen here in Italy?"

14   "We have no such crimes," the superintendent said. "We have the delinquency of stealing, of misbehaving, but boys in this country commit boy wrongs, within the bounds of the boy's world."

15   "But how do you keep him there, how do you keep the boy from bursting out?" I asked.

16   From all parts of Italy, from every official, I received the same answer: *The young people in Italy respect authority.* They have a respect that starts in the home and carries over into the school, the city streets, the courts. I went into many Italian homes to see for myself what the experts were talking about. I found that even in the house of the poorest laborer, the father was respected by the wife and the children as the head of the family. He was the leader of that family, and ruled his brood with varying degrees of love and tenderness and firmness. His household had rules to live by, and the child who disobeyed them was punished.

17   "*The child who respects his father and mother, too, will respect his teacher, the laws of his country, the policeman, the elders around him,*" a high-school principal in Milan told me. Thus, from the ancient wisdom of the Italians, who have the best-behaved teen-agers in the Western world, I found the nine-word principle that I think can do more for us than all the committees, ordinances and multi-million-dollar programs combined:

PUT FATHER BACK AT THE HEAD OF THE FAMILY.

18   These nine words spell out the tragedy of the American teen-ager. He has been raised in a household where "obey" is a dirty word, and where the mother has put herself at the head of the family. Well, in my opinion no woman looks good wearing a man's pants. We are becoming a nation of matriarchs. How many times have you heard a father say, "John, it's time to go to bed," or words to that effect, only to be topped by mother saying, "Oh, Harry, leave the boy alone. Stop picking on him."

19   The result has been that father has slowly, albeit grudgingly, abrogated his leadership. In upper and middle-class homes we have the additional specter of "permissive" psychology at work. There the combination of mother wielding absolute power in a permissive

household where Johnny is rarely if ever disciplined has produced the confused, rebellious unhappy teen-ager who floods our traffic courts, our criminal courts and later our divorce dockets. Twenty-five per cent of all U.S. marriages now end in divorce or legal separation — isn't that a shocking and incredible statistic? One out of four marriages a failure!

Discipline Is the Key

20   And why not? Isn't divorce the result of delinquency grown up, a natural outgrowth of the teen-ager's inability to cope with a world he was never prepared for?

21   How many parents have stood before me, after I have sentenced their children to prison, and asked, "Judge, what did I do that was wrong? I sacrificed for him, gave him a good life, put him through school . . ."

22   It's not what they *did*, it's what they did *not* do. They did not put father in charge of the family, but let him surrender his rightful and needful leadership to mother. They did not teach their child discipline.

23   No child can be reared doing only what he likes. He must be disciplined to also do things he does not want to do, if it's in the best interests of the family. For that is how, realistically, the world will treat him when he gets older. The child does not want an undisciplined, do-as-you-please, "permissive" world. It makes him unhappy, confuses him. He wants the solid walls of rules and of discipline around him, defining his world, giving him a large free area but telling him exactly how far he can go.

24   In my boyhood I had that discipline, and I'm very glad I did. I was raised on Essex Street, a dismal slum on New York's lower East Side. My father ran a little dry goods store and barely made enough for us to live on. But he was the head of our house, and I respected him. When I was 16, and he told me to be home at 12, I broke my neck to get there on time.

25   Many a teen-ager today roams around until two or three in the morning, and considers his parent impertinent if he so much as asks if he had a good time.

26   A home where the father is not the recognized chief of the family is not much better off, to my way of thinking, than a home broken

BELOW: *statistics based on official reports show percentage of crimes in each country committed by offenders 18 or under.*

	Sex Crimes	Homi-cides		Sex Crimes	Homi-cides
Italy	2%	½ of 1%	Germany	15%	2%
France	7%	8%	Britain	15%	1%
Belgium	12%	1%	United States	35%	12%

by divorce. Of course, there are some homes afflicted with "problem fathers" — alcoholics, etc. — but I am speaking about the average family. *Every time that mother overrules father, undermines his authority and his standing in the eyes of the child, she knocks a piece off the foundation on which the child stands.*

27 Old-fashioned idea? Yes sir, I know the sorrowful plight of your children as you yourself do not know it, and I can tell you that if you want a sound family, growing sound children in its soil, then you will ask yourself: is father the real head of our family? If not, there is no reason why you cannot rebuild your relations, especially if you are young.

A Mother's Responsibility

28 How the twig is bent is how the tree grows, and if your child learns to respect the single authority of his father in the important personality-forming period before the age of six, then chances are he will know how to handle authority without disastrous rebellion in later life.

29 Recently Pope Pius XII spoke words of wisdom on this subject: "God created man and woman," His Holiness said, "as persons equal in rank and dignity and no one can say that woman is in any way inferior to man. But wives must submit themselves to their husbands as the church does to God. Women have a three-fold mission of truth, love and feminine action."

30 Does that mean the women must forsake their role as child-rearers? Not at all. Let me make it clear that what I suggest is only a matter of emphasis and does not drastically change a mother's position in the family. She has the same day-to-day, hour-to-hour responsibility she has always had, but she focuses authority and finality and discipline on her husband. When there are disagree-

ments and problems, they are discussed and argued, but not in front of the children. Beware of sowing a storm, for you will reap a hurricane.

31   We have single leadership in every walk of our lives — the school principal, the city's mayor, the commanding officer, the president of your club. Why shouldn't the family have the same advantage?

32   If mothers would understand that much of their importance lies in building up the father image for the child, they would achieve the deep satisfaction of children who turn out well.

33   And no mother would ever have to stand before me with tears in her eyes, and ask: "What did I do that was wrong, Judge — what did I do that was wrong?"

QUESTIONS FOR REFLECTION, DISCUSSION, OR WRITING

(1) Carefully give this article the evaluation test: (a) *purpose?* (b) *success* in achieving it? and (c) *worthwhileness?*

(2) Compare the apparent purpose of this article and that (or those) of "Women Are Misguided." Do you think Miss Skinner was really trying to *convince* us of anything? If not, what was her primary purpose?

(3) In "Nine Words . . ." Judge Leibowitz is very emphatic in his statements, allowing very few qualifications (if's, possibly's, etc.). Do you see any weaknesses in such a presentation?

(4) Do you think he is allowing *enough* for "differences in each country in the tabulation of their statistics" (par. 7)? If Judge Leibowitz and his figures are correct, does it then follow that adult Italians have more respect for authority than do adults of other countries? If not, how can this be explained?

(5) What about the "jumble of uncoordinated solutions" (pars. 3-4)? Do you share in his "feeling of despair, almost panic," about these solutions? Or do you think that some of them may be basic enough to treat the "cause" itself, rather than the "effect"?

(6) Do you agree that "divorce is the result of delinquency grown up"? Defend your answer.

(7) It has sometimes been said that "because men *aren't* men, women *have* to be." Do you agree with this theory? Explain it and defend your answer.

(8) Among your acquaintances, what results — of any kind — have you seen in families where the father has "abrogated his leadership" (par. 18)?

Does it seem to you that any of the juvenile delinquents or near-delinquents you may have known are the results of such abrogation of the father's leadership? What do you think are the causes of the others? (Within your own field of acquaintances there is undoubtedly the topic for a good analytical type of composition.)

Hubert H. Humphrey

A PLAN TO SAVE TREES, LAND, AND BOYS

HUBERT H. HUMPHREY, *the author of this essay, is a former pharmacist, professor of political science, and Minneapolis mayor, who has been active in Minnesota and national politics since the New Deal days. As a U.S. Senator from Minnesota since 1948, he has long been known as one of the leading "liberals" of the Democratic party.*

(A liberal, briefly, is one who feels, in contrast to the "conservative," less bound by established practices, more inclined to experiment with change. To the political liberal, eager to adapt governmental forms and practices to changing times, the political conservative often seems a "reactionary"; this conservative, on the other hand, is apt to consider the Humphrey type of liberal as a "radical.")

A PLAN TO SAVE TREES, LAND, AND BOYS, *first published in* Harper's Magazine *(see p. 15) in January 1959, is another* **argument,** *or* **argumentative** *essay, and as such should be read skeptically but with an open mind. (An author's primary purpose in argument, of course, is to convince us of something or perhaps to influence our actions.) When reading or hearing any sincere argument, we should be willing to "listen to reason" but should remember that the debater's job is to win us to his side, and that he is obligated to present only his side of the matter; it is up to us to find out if there is another valid side and examine it, too, before committing ourselves one way or the other.*

1   EVERY DAY the news bears evidence of an appalling waste of young lives. Shocking juvenile crimes are commonplace on page one. But no less distressing are the countless minor transgressions more briefly reported from the crowded dockets of magistrates, desk sergeants, and juvenile court judges.

2   The cost to the United States is beyond all calculation.

3   This waste of human resources is matched in another field by an

outrageous dissipation of our resources of soil and water. From the tidewater East to the mountains of the Far West, wind and water and fire gnaw at the hill slopes and fill our lakes and streams with topsoil. Despite encouraging progress made by conservation programs, sluicing rains tear new gorges in the earth. Millions of acres of cut-over forest lands lie abandoned to brush, wind, fire, and insects — ugly and unproductive, at a time when the U.S. Forest Service predicts that our need for lumber and other wood products is rising beyond our expected forest yields.

4   Muddied and polluted lakes and streams mock the tourist brochures of dozens of States. Park and forest campsites and trails are deteriorating. Even these neglected facilities are crowded today — would-be campers often find only dim echoes of the refreshing outdoor experiences that our parents took for granted fifty years ago.

5   Such a waste of both human and natural resources need not be tolerated. This was proved a generation ago in a nine-year national experiment that gave us a blueprint for conservation that can teach us a lot today.

6   The idea for the Civilian Conservation Corps sprang into action almost overnight in March 1933, during the magnificent ferment of the first hundred days of Roosevelt's New Deal. It became one of the most successful projects of the 'thirties, acclaimed by both parties.

7   The theory was simple: we had a lot of young men out of work; outdoor work was good for young men: therefore, let's get the boys out into the woods! Within weeks, the first experimental CCC camp was in operation at Camp Roosevelt, two hours west of Washington, D.C., in the green woods of the George Washington National Forest. Reserve Army officers were called back on active duty to supervise the boys, and out into the woods they went with shovel and axe. Within a few months, camps began to mushroom throughout the country, with about 200 boys in each. Within a year, the CCC enrollment had hit its average of 300,000 and until the early 'forties the CCC boys were working in nearly 2,600 camps in the state and national parks and forests.

8   What started as a "make-work" project rapidly developed into the most comprehensive program for the management and conser-

vation of natural resources that any nation had ever undertaken. Frankly improvising, the professional conservationists of the U.S. Forest Service, the National Park Service, the Bureau of Reclamation, the Bureau of Indian Affairs, and the Soil Conservation Service shifted into high-gear projects that had only been dreams of forestry and conservation technicians.

9   Conservationists who had despaired of moving beyond the first giant step taken by the pioneers of the Teddy Roosevelt-Gifford Pinchot era — when the major national park and forest areas were set aside for public use — suddenly awoke to find a new force at work. Raw brain and muscle, willing and enthusiastic, became available almost overnight for the long-dreamed work of forest-fire prevention, erosion control, timber-stand improvement, new outdoor recreational facilities, and earth-dam reservoirs.

10   As the waste motion came under control — as the boys from New York and Chicago, Chattanooga and Los Angeles and a thousand cities and villages across the nation were trained into effective, skillful teams — millions of acres of land were transformed by reforestation, strip-cropping, gully-stabilization, and forest fire control.

11   What happened to the CCC boys themselves — eventually almost three million of them — was also fascinating.

12   The boys put on solid weight. They grew taller. Many had their teeth attended to for the first time. They developed manual skills they had never suspected and later got specialized vocational training — truck-driving, machine maintenance, building-trades skills. Eventually, training became as important as the actual pick-and-shovel work of conservation. Skilled leaders emerged among the teams of boys and young men working against fire, erosion, and waste in ever more carefully planned projects.

How They Did It

13   Nine years of the CCC built into the national economy and, it may be, into the national character, some extraordinary values. A major start was made in using nearly untried techniques of forestry and soil conservation in the nation's timber and grazing lands, and our infinitely valuable watersheds. But in terms of the salvage and the strengthening of young lives, many hundreds of

thousands of them, the CCC may have made its most important contribution. Former CCC boys are today scattered throughout the leadership of American industry, government, and education — testimony to the social values of this great experiment. I have asked some of them what the CCC meant to them.

14   A typical comment comes from a Marine Fishery Research biologist:

15   It is my honest opinion that my experiences in the CCC during the critical years of my life better prepared me for my years of service overseas with the U.S. Army during World War II. . . . An enrollee enjoys a sense of accomplishment, a sense of having contributed something worthy to the nation.

16   My good friend, Congressman John Blatnik of Minnesota's forested 8th District, who had just finished teacher's college at the time, became a CCC camp educational adviser. This is what he says about his experience:

17   The CCC looked good, and believe me, it was good to me. . . . We worked in warm weather and in cold. There was plenty to do, but we were young. We liked the work; we liked the life; and especially, we liked the opportunity to be a recognized part of American life. . . . [The CCC] was a great movement to renew a spirit of adventure in youth, and to dramatize the protection and restoration of our natural resources.

18   World War II killed off the CCC, but in its nine years some great steps had been taken. The teams of boys planted nearly three billion trees, built over 150,000 miles of trails and fire lanes. They strung 85,000 miles of new telephone lines and put up 4,000 fire towers, 45,000 bridges, and thousands of buildings.

19   They built several million check dams against soil erosion, and did improvement cuttings and thinnings on about four million acres of forests. They saved millions of acres by prompt fighting of small fires before they got out of control and protected the trees from attacks by insects and diseases. They also helped replace sagebrush with forage grasses on nearly forty million acres of brushy range lands. Altogether, the value of their work has been estimated at one and a half billion dollars — in 1940 dollars, too!

20   What did it cost? An even $1,000 each year per boy — for everything — overhead, salaries, everything.

How Much Should We Invest?

21   The demand of World War II mobilization drained away the CCC's manpower, but the conservation needs remained. The job the CCC did until 1942 in putting our forests and farm lands into shape was by no means finished, though the work was put aside "temporarily." Conservation programs went on a strictly maintenance basis during the war and have never been resumed on the scale needed.

22   Today, the children born during World War II are our teenagers — and they are finding a crowded world — not only in the cities, but in the outdoor recreational areas. More than fifty million visitors are now using the National Forests alone each year.

23   A critical shortage of forest products will come by the year 2,000 if we do not expand our forestry programs *now*. Trees take time to grow. And, although our agricultural abundance is a concern today, demographers are predicting scarcity to come, if we continue to allow wind and water to wear away our topsoil at the present rate.

24   Last summer, the Natural Resources Council, made up of the heads of nationally important conservation groups, completed a searching estimate of the total job needed to bring the corrosive actions of man against nature under control, and to rebuild the productive capacity of our lands and waters enough to sustain the predicted population of fifty years from now.

25   They came up with some hard figures. Over a ten-year intensive program, they said, we need to invest $3 billion to put our forests into adequate productive shape; $4.5 billion to halt the loss of topsoil and protect vital watersheds; $1 billion to stabilize the soils and increase the forage yields on our Western range lands; $2 billion for the upgrading and expanding of the areas of outdoor recreational facilities; and another $1 billion to improve refuges for wildlife. Many of these represent planned programs in the files of both federal and state conservation agencies. They do not include the huge conservation needs of our new state of Alaska.

26   Take just one major resource — forest lands. Professional forest-ters estimate we have 275 million understocked forest acres in need of timberstand improvement, thinning, eliminating diseased

trees, and reducing fire hazard. Another 52 million acres of open, unproductive land should be replanted in trees.

27   Water and topsoil are not inexhaustible. Yet hundreds of thousands of streams dump silt into our reservoirs and harbors. Stream banks can be stabilized — but only by human hands planting protective vegetation. Federal and state conservation agencies have simply not been able to tackle these and other conservation jobs on anywhere near the scale demanded. Manpower shortages and lack of funds, not ignorance, are holding them back. There is work enough to employ several hundred thousand men for a decade or more — at useful, not make-work, jobs.

An Up-to-Date Corps

28   A giant step toward the *prevention* of delinquency and the improvement of physical fitness could be accomplished if the CCC were in existence today to provide not only healthful, useful outdoor work, but educational opportunities for boys and young men with too much time on their hands.

29   Drop-outs from high school, and even a considerable proportion of high-school graduates, find it increasingly difficult to secure jobs with any future. Despite the sharp increases in college enrollment, millions of young men will not go on to higher education. Instead, they will flow directly into a labor market which is at best inhospitable for teen-agers, and during recessions is forbidding.

30   I am convinced that we must again provide the kind of opportunity for creative work on the land that was given to American boys in the 'thirties. I introduced legislation to accomplish this during the last session of Congress, and Congressman Blatnik introduced a companion bill in the House. We expect to bring the measure up again in the new Congress, shortly after this article appears.

31   Briefly, the bill would establish a somewhat smaller, more flexible, and more education-oriented organization than the old CCC — a Youth Conservation Corps of 150,000 young men. It would be decentralized among the federal and state conservation agencies in relatively small groups as compared with the old 200-man CCC camps.

32   The boys would improve young timber stands by thinning, help

carve new access roads and trails into the forest areas, plant seed-lings on bare lands, stabilize eroding stream banks by hand-planting. They would construct picnic area facilities, retaining walls, erect earth dams to create upstream reservoirs, improve lakes, streams, and marshes for fish and wildlife, rebuild game cover, team up for fighting forest fires and reseeding deteriorated range lands.

33 It would be hard, dusty, and rugged work, but if I know Amer-ican boys they would fight to participate.

34 Recruitment and overall budgetary control, the responsibility for the maintenance of minimum standards for working hours, and for health and educational programs, would be in the hands of a Director under the Department of Health, Education, and Welfare. An advisory board from the Departments of Agriculture; Interior; and Health, Education, and Welfare would consult on policy with the Director.

35 But once the boys are processed through the YCC recruiting and orientation period, they should be assigned directly to small units of perhaps fifty or less under the immediate supervision and direc-tion of professional foresters and conservationists of the U.S. Forest Service, the National Park Service, the Fish and Wildlife Service, the Soil Conservation Service, and the state conservation depart-ments.

36 The boys would be put into on-the-job training situations throughout the conservation field — good, vigorous outdoor work under careful supervision. But, in addition, I propose the develop-ment of well-articulated health and educational programs for the enrollees quite apart from their conservation work. In fact, twenty per cent of their time is explicitly to be set aside for educational purposes, making use of the facilities of schools and junior colleges in the vicinity of the projects.

37 Enrollees would be paid at the current rate of a private in the Army — about $78 per month — plus subsistence, medical care, and other fringe benefits. They would sign up for one year, or for special "vacation period" enrollments for students. Enrollment would be open to any American boy, of course, regardless of race or creed or color, who is at least sixteen years old, and physically qualified.

38 Like the old CCC, the YCC would also provide for the enroll-

ing of a small percentage of more mature skilled woodsmen and other conservation workers to provide a leavening of older heads and skills for the groups of inexperienced young men. In areas close to or actually inside Indian reservations, special provision would be made to give work opportunities to tribesmen on their own lands. This would relieve an acute and chronic unemployment problem in the reservations, and also serve to lace the pool of manpower with another good measure of woods skills.

People Are Asking for —

39   There has been a heartening response to my proposal from around the nation. Juvenile court authorities, social welfare people, state and private conservation officials — and many young men themselves interested in enrolling in the corps — have written me all through 1958 suggesting minor changes, advocating different emphases but, without a single exception, strongly favoring the proposal.

40   A juvenile court judge in Ohio, for example, asked me if I would consider reducing the minimum age to sixteen. "In Ohio," he pointed out, "a boy may be released from school if he has passed the seventh grade and is sixteen years of age. Lowering the age to sixteen would therefore enable the boy who is maladjusted in school to get a working certificate and enroll in the Youth Conservation Corps. . . ."

41   A superintendent of a work camp for delinquent boys in Minnesota wrote that his seven years with the old CCC and his five years with the Minnesota Youth Conservation Commission were "the most satisfying of my life" and outlined detailed conservation projects which could be undertaken in his area.

42   Stressing that the group between fourteen and eighteen is his particular interest, a Missouri superintendent of schools said:

43   "We have no institution between the public school and reform school to take care of the boy who is (1) a poor student and not interested in school; (2) one who has family problems and is emotionally maladjusted; or (3) one who has no opportunity to earn the money he feels he needs and that to him is more important than an education."

44   Many correspondents raise tough questions. For example: what about something for the girls? That gets us into a whole series of

new considerations, and will be the subject, I am sure, of separate legislation and a separate program. The answer, of course, is that there *should* be something for the girls — something beyond the Scouting years, and of a serious, constructive nature — that would involve practical conservation work without the heavy, load-lifting duties of the young men.

45   Another interesting question is whether service in the YCC should be counted as part of the fulfillment of obligatory military service. Undeniably, the body-building of outdoor work would greatly increase the general state of physical fitness of our young men. Yet I strongly feel that young men would enroll in the conservation corps without the added incentive of being able to "write off" a year's reserve service requirement, and I am inclined to feel that at this time we should leave the military training to the numerous and competent Reserve and National Guard programs.

46   The CCC left no bad taste. Even the bitterest opponents of the New Deal had to admit that the CCC was a sound investment in both people and the land. And millions of American families taking to the fields and woods today constantly run across reminders of the constructive CCC work of a generation ago. Among them are thousands of loyal CCC "alumni" who take pride in revisiting the woods trails, recreational areas, and upstream reservoirs, the burgeoning stands of young timber, the renewed game cover and green stream banks on which they worked as very young men.

47   Americans, until our very recent urbanization, have always been outdoorsmen. Only recently has the privilege of living and working in the open been denied to so many of our younger generation. For hundreds of thousands of city boys, the opportunity to work on the land could enrich and strengthen their lives. Too, it might provide a new sense of meaning and purpose for young men growing up in a society in which the opportunity for creative accomplishment is becoming rarer each year. Eleanor Roosevelt once said that conservation programs in which young men worked to save our natural resources might serve as a "moral equivalent of war" needed to inspire young men's loyalties and their dreams.

48   I am convinced that young men in substantial numbers would seize the opportunity to roll up their sleeves and join a great national effort on the land. The challenge of a task that transcends

the mere earning of a living, the chance to participate in a purposeful effort, would be far more important to such young men than
the nominal wages and subsistence. I know a dozen young men
from stable, middle-income families who would give their eyeteeth
for such an opportunity.

49   And could anything more effectively and constructively channel
those restless energies that today are leading tens of thousands of
underprivileged boys in the direction of delinquency, violence, and
self-destruction?

QUESTIONS FOR REFLECTION, WRITING, OR DISCUSSION

(1) If you did not already know, would you guess this article to have been
written by a *liberal* or a *conservative?* Why?

(2) How successful do you consider the author's *argument* for his plan? Can
you find any weaknesses in it? If not, why do you suppose the plan has not
been enacted into law? (Several years have gone by since its proposal.)

(3) Sometimes strings of statistics can kill the readability of an article for
the average reader. Do you think Humphrey's frequent use of statistics in
paragraphs 18, 19, 25, and 26 have this effect? Or do they contribute more
than they detract from the job he was trying to do? If so, how?

(4) Humphrey's arguments could be grouped under two major headings.
What are they? To which has he given more space? To which has he given
greater emphasis? On what do you base your answer? Do you think he was
wise in his choice for emphasis?

(5) Explain clearly what you think Mrs. Roosevelt meant (par. 47) when
she said that conservation programs in which young men work to save our
natural resources might serve as a "moral equivalent of war." Do you think
young people need such a moral equivalent?

(6) Whatever you think of the plan in principle, would you be willing to
enroll in the YCC if it were in operation? If you had a 17-year-old son or
brother, would you want him to join, or do you think there might be some
bad effects which would make it inadvisable?

(7) Will the existence of a Peace Corps have any effect on the need for a
YCC? Any effect on the YCC's eventual chance for enactment? Explain.

(8) Considering juvenile delinquents, or borderline delinquents, that you
may have known, do you think such boys would voluntarily join the YCC?
If so, do you think they would benefit from it as much as Humphrey would
have us believe? Why, or why not? Would you be willing to spend *your*

hard-earned money, in the form of taxes, to provide such boys with "the opportunity for creative work on the land"? Defend your stand.

(9) What kinds of "practical conservation work" might serve as the basis for a girls' version of the YCC? Can you think of other serious difficulties that would require different handling from those of the boys? Do you think such problems could somehow be solved successfully?

Shirley L. Povich

BASKETBALL IS FOR THE BIRDS

SHIRLEY L. POVICH *has been sports editor and columnist for the* Washington (D.C.) Post *and* Times Herald *since 1946. He has received several citations and awards for outstanding sports writing and for his work as war correspondent in the Pacific area during World War II. A long-time member of the Baseball Writers Association of America, he served as its president in 1955.*

SPORTS ILLUSTRATED, *the original publisher of "Basketball Is for the Birds" on Dec. 8, 1958, is one of the publications of Time, Inc., in New York. Founded in 1954, it has reached a weekly circulation of approximately 900,000.*

BASKETBALL IS FOR THE BIRDS *illustrates some of the techniques of* **persuasion,** *which is usually classified as a special kind of argument; it, too, seeks to influence someone's opinion or attitude and, much more than* **logical argument,** *to get him to act in a certain way. But unlike logical argument, which appeals to* reason, *persuasion appeals to* emotion — *argument to the mind, you might say, and persuasion to the heart.*

In actual practice, however, persuasion and logical argument are often interwoven, and there is nothing unethical in such a combination — we may need to persuade someone even to listen to the logic of our argument! But the very fact that seeming logic may contain the less logical elements of persuasion is apt to catch the unwary reader (or listener) offguard and bring about an unwise conversion, based more on feeling than thinking.

In persuasive writing, as in everyday conversation, various methods and degrees of emotionalism may be employed: the author may merely use "tact" to create a favorable impression, or he may try to arouse the reader's sympathy, or his loyalty, or his indignation; he may even resort to one or more of the "seven devices of propaganda" (see p. 7); he may try to out-shout his victim or wear down his resistance by repetition ("Please, please, Daddy, just one more candy, please, Daddy, please!); or he may try to wither any opposition by the use of **sarcasm** *and* **exaggeration** *("and put the accent on carnival freaks who achieved upper space by growing into it," par. 2 below).*

Sarcasm and exaggeration, though sometimes highly successful, are tricky techniques for an author to use. There are two chief dangers: (1) The "thinking" audience is apt to consider him merely emotional — and dismiss everything he says as immature, irrational. (2) Some people who might have been persuaded may become annoyed instead, especially if the sarcasm seems excessive, too deliberately unkind.

Read this essay casually the first time, reacting naturally, as if reading it "on your own" in Sports Illustrated. *Afterward, try to analyze your reactions.*

1   THE LATE H. L. Mencken some years ago warned that the language was changing and wrote a book about it. A newly recognized entry in the American lexicon at that time was the word goon. Mencken's goons were simple, workaday strikebreakers who might have to bash in a few skulls to get the job done. America's latter-day goons are the biological blowups with runaway pituitary glands who play at basketball.

2   Basketball is for the birds — the gooney birds. The game lost this particular patron years back when it went vertical and put the accent on carnival freaks who achieved upper space by growing into it. They don't shoot baskets any more, they stuff them, like taxidermists.

3   In a single generation, there has been a revved-up degeneration of basketball from a game to a mess. It now offers a mad confection of absurdities, with ladder-size groundlings stretching their gristle in aerial dogfights amid the whistle screeches of apoplectic referees trying to enforce ridiculous rules that empty the game of interest.

4   Dr. James Naismith, an earnest man, could be justifiably spinning in his mausoleum in a schizophrenia of rage and despair at what they've done to the game he invented in 1891. When he inspired basketball by placing two peach baskets at opposite ends of a YMCA hall in Springfield, Mass., the sincere doctor could hardly foretell the degree to which his creation would become all fuzzed up by the senseless tinkerers who have grabbed hold of it. And if the native pride of peach trees is remembered, it is obvious that the tint of their fruit now is less the glow of ripeness than the blush of shame for their part in helping to bring basketball into the world.

5   The towering six-footers who were the giants of the basketball

court only a couple of decades ago and were eagerly sought for the important center jump need not apply any more unless they are content to be the game's runts. If the mere six-footer is permitted to suit up at all by coaches whose ruling passion is collecting two-legged giraffes with an eye-level approach to the basket, he is reduced to rooting around in the undergrowth of the forests of bone and marrow that rear above him. It is time for him to curse the utter normality of his glands which stunted his growth.

6   This basketball apostate makes confession that he is a one-time aficionado who couldn't wait to get up in the morning to play the game or watch it. That was in the era when it was a game, not a bewildering whistle-fest with the referees eager to bring to book the naughty-naughties who are so bold or so careless as to commit something of a firm nature, like laying a hand on the hem of an opponent's garment.

7   It used to be a game that could be comfortably won by a team total of 26 points, in the not-so-distant days when a slightly malevolent glance at an opponent with the ball was simply a frame of mind, not a personal foul. I read incredulously that the New York Knickerbockers averaged 112 points a game last season and finished last in their division of the pro league.

8   They've weighted the rules so heavily in favor of the team with the ball that the missed basket is now more incredible than the shot that is made. Referees not content with enforcing the letter of the rules impose no-no, musn't-touch injunctions that leave the defense in a constant state of fright lest their tactics be adjudged too manly.

9   The way they have it rigged and the way the coaches have wheeled in all available altitude, basketball and basket shooting now offer a close substitute interest for those doughty sportsmen who dream of shooting fish in a barrel. They've made the basketball court a virtual shooting gallery with the bull's-eye affixed to the rifle barrel, just to encourage success.

10   It has all served to simplify coaching skills. An eye for the basket isn't necessary as long as the coach can corral enough tall hands to plumb it. Then it becomes a game of can-you-top-this against rival coaches who counter with their own altitudinous tribes of basket shrinkers.

11   From time to time apologists for the game have made attempts to define the motivations that impel the buffs to attend these encounters, but their conclusions are almost invariably desultory and pathetic. The best that this observer, who has also delved into the matter, can say is that there is no accounting for people's tastes, because it is well known that some even like fried baby bees, kidney stew, Garroway, and yodeling, and some root for the Washington Senators.

12   This discouraged spectator, who has tried intermittently to warm toward the game in efforts to relive it up, finds nothing left to cheer for at a basketball contest. Who can applaud "Wilt the Stilt," or his ilk when they outflank the basket from above and pelt it like an open city? These fellows are biological accidents who ought to be more usefully employed, like hiring out as rainmakers and going to sow a few clouds.

13   Even that last precious motivation of healthy partisanship, the pleasure of rooting for somebody, evaporates at a basketball game in common outrage against the referee who is usually wronging both teams, as well as the spectators.

14   Basketball is always attended by a shrieking dissent from this character, who is trying to enforce fine-line rules that defy sensible interpretation. It is thus inevitable that the referee must wind up as the enemy of all cheering sections. King Solomon would have wisely disqualified himself as incompetent had he been asked to deliver a fair ruling on blocking vs. charging on the basketball court of today.

15   Nothing in the prospectus ever suggested that anybody should pay admission to watch a basketball referee perform, but their actions would seem to imply that they believe this to be the case. Most of them consider the basketball court as their public stage, having taken the cue from the late great Pat Kennedy, an extraordinary dramatist who invented the role of the domineering, infallible, showboat referee. The first indication of a rules infraction would set "Actor" Kennedy aquiver and his whistle to shrieking. His eyes bulged from their sockets, the veins showed purple in his neck as he tracked down the miscreant who had violated something about Kennedy's game. He would put the positive finger on the

culprit with an outward show of anger that others usually reserve for a rapist.

16   Kennedy's antics were at least diverting, but peopling the referee ranks now are only the lesser hams who have no reason to fancy themselves in his image. The result is pure cornball as, playing screech-owl tunes on their tin whistles, these Keystone cops blow the action to a stop apparently on whim.

17   The game, in fact, is crawling with would-be scene stealers. In that department the referees are hard pressed by the coaches on the players' benches. Modern coaches are a breed better born for the revival tents. They play to the crowd by kicking up a public fuss at every grievance real or fancied, and communicate by their gestures that the referees are utter no-goodniks.

18   The coaches warm up to their phony sympathy pitch with suitable and audible sighs and groans. Then come the head-in-hands gestures of utter despair, the falling to the knees in posture of prayer for greater justice, and then the arms flung wide in "Please, Almighty," supplication for deliverance from the fiends blowing whistles. For the most part it adds up to incitement to riot.

19   Among the pro teams, all this has filtered up from the colleges where the coaches first discovered that they, too, could be characters. As usual, the pros have improved on it, as they have done with most everything else from the colleges, so that in basketball you now have, in addition to the goons, the flip-top coach.

20   The basketball rules, in themselves, are enough to baffle anyone with an orderly mind. The game launched its popularity with simple restrictives like five players to a side and don't step outside the marked lines. Now it is a confounding jumble of personal fouls, traveling fouls, dribbling fouls, whistles, buzzers and bonuses for injured innocence.

21   It was not much overdrawn when somebody once said that the basketball people scribble new rules with a pen in each hand for fear of being caught up with. What was permitted last year is this year's foul. In the pro league, even last night's rule book is apt to be outmoded, with President Maurice Podoloff ordering revisions at any hour he can get his referees on the telephone.

22   The pros' mania for changing the rules cropped up again in

October when two new rules governing foul shots were adopted. There is actually the stipulation that one of the new rules would be considered official only during an allotted one-month tryout — a sort of rookie rule, as it were.

23   The other new rule of the pros deals with double fouls and now provides for a jump ball between the centers of the two teams. But wait. Identifying the centers apparently is not so simple in this modern age of basketball, because the rule takes care to spell out "If a dispute arises as to who is center of a team, it shall be resolved by the referees."

24   The once-respected place tags have gone from the game. Every position is now so freewheeling that the center, guards and forwards can be positively identified as such only by lip tattoo. It amounts to basketball's for-real version of the "Who's on First?" vaudeville routine of Abbott and Costello.

25   To add to the confusion, the colleges a few years back introduced a queer something called the "one-and-one" foul. The bright minds who thought that one up should be cited for deportation as saboteurs of the American way of life.

26   It is flabbergasting to know that the one-and-one foul, which is awarded victims of aggression, is sometimes two foul shots, sometimes one, depending on the inaccuracy of the man on the free-throw line. If he sinks his first free shot, he is deemed to have exacted the offender's debt to basketball society and the referee says that's all.

27   But if the fouled citizen misses his first free throw, he is now entitled to take another, honest. Failure is rewarded, success is penalized. It is George Orwell's 1984 in action. Black is white, Truth is false. Love is hate, and Big Brother Referee is always present.

28   The pros have gimmicked it up even more. Now there is a something extra called a bonus free throw. That goes to the aggrieved team if the fouls by the other side total as many as seven in any period. The spectator without a Comptometer is lost, and only certified public accountants can follow the scoring, except when the board lights up like a jackpot-hit machine.

29   In what exact year basketball began to go sour as a game cannot be precisely determined here, but there had to be alarm on a

certain night in 1949. That was when one man, Paul Arizin, of Villanova, scored 85 points in one game. To the basketball fundamentalists, that was as disgraceful as it was remarkable.

30   Later on a whirlybird named Bevo Francis of Rio Grande College made numerous descents on the basket and ladled in 113 points in one night against Ashland College. They've got some kind of a game all right, but it isn't basketball. What is happening reawakens for this disenchanted fellow a gratitude for one of America's most little-mentioned freedoms — the freedom to stay away from it.

QUESTIONS FOR REFLECTION, DISCUSSION, OR WRITING

(1) Which of the "seven devices of propaganda" does Povich use? Show where and justify your classification.

(2) In which paragraph did you first become aware that the author was using *sarcasm* in presenting his case against basketball? How many paragraphs can you find in which he uses neither sarcasm nor *exaggeration*?

(3) Does Povich use so much sarcasm that he actually weakens his case? Or do you consider his technique successful? Explain. What effect do you think it would have on most other readers?

(4) He has also made liberal use of metaphors (see p. 15), often *as* sarcasm. Examine several of these. Are they clever? Effective?

(5) To what extent do you find this essay a mixture of both *logical argument* and *persuasion* — appeals to both our reason and our emotion?

(6) Can you think of any practical *result* the author may have hoped to achieve by this essay, any *action* he hoped to influence? Explain.

(7) How do you suppose a sports magazine, undoubtedly read by thousands of basketball fans, could dare to print such an article as this? What could the magazine gain by it?

(8) A good topic for composition might be the defense of basketball against Povich's attack — or against any one of his charges. Another: an explanation of, defense of, or attack against one of the recent new rules of basketball.

(9) In paragraph 11, Povich says there is no accounting for people's tastes — a fact you have no doubt been aware of for some time. What other "tastes" do you find it hard to account for? Explain in composition form — using sarcasm, if you like.

(10) What event awakens *your* gratitude for "the freedom to stay away
from it" (par. 30)? An explanation of your reasons could also make a worthwhile composition.

Ken D. Loeffler with Harry T. Paxton

I SAY BASKETBALL'S OUR BEST GAME

KEN D. LOEFFLER *was a college basketball coach (Geneva, Yale, LaSalle,
Texas A. & M.) for 27 years, during which his teams won 310 games and lost
206. He also was a pro coach for three years (St. Louis and Denver). In 1957
he gave up college coaching and went to Monmouth College in West Long
Branch, N. J., where he is now a professor of business law. His collaborator
in the writing of "I Say Basketball . . . ,"* HARRY T. PAXTON, *has been in
journalism since 1936, with* The Saturday Evening Post *since 1942. He has
served as its sports editor since 1949, considering himself about two-thirds
editor and one-third writer; his by-line has appeared on approximately 70
Post articles.*

THE SATURDAY EVENING POST, *where this article first appeared Dec. 19, 1953,
traces its origin to 1728, with Benjamin Franklin as its founder. With a family-
type weekly circulation of over six million, it is published in Philadelphia by
the Curtis Publishing Company, also the publisher of* Ladies' Home Journal,
Holiday, *and* Jack and Jill.

I SAY BASKETBALL'S OUR BEST GAME *seems almost to be a direct reply to the
Povich attack we have just read — except that this was published five years
before Povich's article. The basketball controversy, of course, has been going
on much longer than that, and we might ask, with some justification, whether
it can really be called an "argument" at all — or are we, in comparing sports,
discussing a matter of simple taste, or personal preference.*

*For, no matter how much we may quarrel and scream and stamp our feet
about a matter of mere taste, we can have no argument; to argue is to assume that a sensible decision could, somehow, be reached. (And how could
even the small group of people in this class, for example, ever hope to decide
which is "better," apple pie or cherry pie? Or which is "prettier," blue or red?)
However, if we can reason the matter out, setting up certain logical criteria for
judging the worth of a sport (or car, or house plan, or what have you), then
we have something to measure merits against, and argument can take place —
with some hope, at least, for eventual agreement.*

*As you read this article, see to what extent the authors have set up such
criteria and measured basketball and other sports against them, attempting to
remove the matter from the area of mere personal taste.*

1   I'VE BEEN in athletics for more years than I like to count. I've played and coached most of our well-known sports. I don't think there is any question as to which one is the best game. It's basketball. To me this is so obvious that I am always surprised that anyone could fail to recognize it. Yet there are those who don't. Some people, such as unreconstructed baseball nuts, go so far as to make fun of the game.

2   You know the sort of things the critics say: Basketball players aren't really athletes. They're just physical freaks who stand around in their underwear and throw a ball at a hoop. Whenever one of them as much as lays a finger on another, a man with a whistle rushes up and puts a stop to it.

3   That's basketball? How silly can a critic get?

4   I've handled baseball teams, and football teams too. I've boxed and wrestled. I've taught tennis and coached lacrosse. The other sports can be fun, but the truth is that most of them are elementary compared to basketball. None involves such speed and intricacy of tactics. None demands such fast moving, fast thinking and all-round athletic skill.

5   In St. Louis two winters ago, after a La Salle College basketball game with St. Louis University, I was sitting around a table with a group of sports people that included Bill Veeck, then the owner of the baseball Browns. At one point the conversation began to drag, and a sportswriter friend nudged me and whispered, "Why don't you see if you can needle Veeck and stir up a little excitement?"

6   So I said to Veeck, "There's something I'd like to tell you. You baseball people pay your managers entirely too much money. All big league managers are being overpaid for the work they do. Why, any of the top college basketball coaches could win as many ball games with the same material you fellows have for a whole lot less money, and with a whole lot less headaches than they have in their own sport. They work three times as hard on drilling and planning for games. And they know more about handling men who really have to be handled, and more about getting men into real condition, than any baseball job ever required."

7   That stirred up excitement, all right. Naturally, Veeck leaped to the defense of his game. I was just talking for the sake of getting a discussion going, but I meant every word I said. I'm convinced that baseball gives the biggest, easiest money in sports.

8   When I used to play baseball at Penn State, it was a lark, coming as it did after a hard-running, painstaking basketball season.

9   Baseball is so slow. It is a leisurely series of events. The pitcher throws the ball, and if the batter hits it, a fielder goes after it and then perhaps throws it to another man. Most of the time the fielders don't do anything. They stand around while three men work — the pitcher, the catcher and the batter. Even these three are by no means in constant action. There is a pause after every pitch, and a pause after every play.

10   The manager has all the time in the world to decide what moves to make. And what decisions does he have to make, anyway? The game hasn't changed in my time. The situations are very cut and dried. Suppose there are runners on first and second with none out, and the man coming up to bat is a good bunter. What should the manager have him do? Ask any banker in the stands.

11   Or they'll go out and have a conference on the mound. "Let's see now, we have time to scrabble our brains a bit. What shall we throw to this batter? Let's try a double-reverse twist. All right. There it goes! What? Nothing happened? Throw that ball up there again!"

12   Contrast this to basketball. On a well-coached basketball team, everybody is moving all the time. There are five individual contests going on, between each man and his opponent, and a team contest is going on too. Each man has to relate his personal contest to the collective contest. The man with the ball is trying to out-maneuver his opponent and get a step on him. The four other men are trying to out-maneuver their opponents too. The man with the ball has to keep tabs on these other contests, so that if he can't defeat his opponent, he can give off the ball to the teammate who is in the best position to start a break-through.

13   All this goes on without a letup. Every time the ball changes hands — and it may change hands every second or two — a whole new set of situations is created. But there is no break while the

players sit down and hash things over. The action is continuous.

14   Football comes much closer to this than baseball. Football procedures aren't so standardized — the top coaches today make it a point to keep varying their tactics on both offense and defense. Nor is football just a sequence of individual performances. There is man-against-man effort, related to a team effort. However, like baseball, football is divided into a sequence of separate plays. After each one there is an interval of about thirty seconds for the players to adjust to the new circumstances. And as for skill and finesse, football compares to basketball as the bass drum does to the violin.

15   Football is a body-contact sport. Basketball is a noncontact sport. Whenever there is contact, a foul is supposed to be called against the man who was responsible for it. That makes basketball an easier game? On the contrary, it makes basketball a more difficult game. And I'm not speaking as a man who shrinks from the very thought of physical collision — in my own days as a participant, what I relished most were the contact sports, especially boxing and wrestling.

16   Quite often a fellow can be a good football player simply because he's rough. That's what the coach tells a man in football line play — first localize the opponent by hitting him. Bang him and then maneuver. There's always a bang before the maneuver.

17   The basketball player is denied this weapon. He has to stop his man without physically hitting him. He has to localize his opponent without benefit of the bash. He has to do it with his eyes, with his foot movements, with his body movements.

18   Too many people at basketball games seem only to watch the shooting. They don't realize how much else is going on. Spectators who really know the game, seeing somebody like Jim Pollard, of the Minneapolis Lakers, will forget about the ball and just watch Pollard. In my opinion, the best man playing basketball today is Jim Pollard — doing things without the ball.

19   Pollard doesn't need the ball. He spends his time inside, moving around. He's having a contest with his man, trying to get him out of position. He keeps maneuvering to get an angle of advantage on his opponent. He may get behind him so that the man can't see him, or so that, in his effort to watch Pollard, the man can't see

the ball. When Pollard does get a superior position on his opponent, then he wants the ball, and his teammates, if they are properly alert, will throw it to him and the score goes in.

20   Because of the rules against physical contact, and because the players generally aren't the thickset, heavy-muscled type, some people have the idea that basketball is a sissy game. Don't kid yourself. The fact that there is a penalty for banging into an opponent doesn't mean that nobody ever gets hit. If one of your stars breaks under the basket, and the opposition has a choice of fouling him or conceding a field goal, he is going to get fouled. They'll say to themselves, "We can't stop this big monkey anyway, so let's really cut him down."

21   Away from the court, I have seen slender basketball players step and jab and punch the daylights out of big football players who were in the road of their own muscles. I know I wouldn't want to fight a fellow like Jim Pollard. With those long arms, and quick as he is, he'd knock my head off. I wouldn't recommend to many 250-pound football players that they try to fight him either.

22   As far as endurance and stamina are concerned, a basketball player is comparable to a prize fighter. He must be able to go at top speed all night long. Football, although the risk of injury is greater, is restful in contrast to basketball. Studies have shown that out of the sixty minutes of playing time in a football game, there is a total of only about thirteen minutes in which the ball is actually in play.

23   Baseball? With the possible exception of the pitcher and the catcher, a fellow could stay out all night and, as long as he could drag himself to the ball park, he could still manage to play.

24   There is very little body contact in baseball, and few opportunities for men to get hurt. But when they do get hurt — why, if a ballplayer gets a small cut, you'd think he'd broken an arm. Many trainers will tell you that. This isn't a slap at the personal courage of ballplayers. It's just the nature of their game.

25   Once I had occasion to take a German doctor out to a big-league game. He was an eminent stomach specialist on his first visit to this country. The Boston Red Sox were playing. The great Ted Williams was in left field. There wasn't a ball hit in his direction the entire game. All he did that afternoon was to kick an occasional blade of

grass in the outfield and make three or four uneventful trips to the plate.

26   I said to the German doctor, "Do you know how much money this fellow gets paid? Eighty thousand dollars a year."

27   The doctor said, "Ah, America!"

28   If a young athlete is thinking about sports solely from the selfish standpoint of what's in it for him, he won't play football. There's too much chance of getting hurt. He won't play basketball either. There's too much work for too little return. He'll be a baseball player. Oh, he'll learn a little boxing and wrestling, so he can defend himself if thugs try to roll him for his baseball dough or if some drunken fraternity brother gets on him for not going out for football. He'll also take up tennis socially, so he can meet the right people.

29   I always loved to play tennis. I spent a couple of summers as a tennis pro at Hyannis Port, Massachusetts. But tennis can hardly be mentioned in the same breath with basketball and other team games. The team games demand so much more than the individual sports like tennis, where a fellow can be the most snobbish and selfish person imaginable and still be a crack player.

30   That reminds me of a radio sports forum I was on in Philadelphia last spring with a group that included Helen Sigel Wilson, a fine lady and golfer. We were talking about the merits of different sports, and the question of golf came up. I said, "Golf is no sport. Golf is going for a walk and taking a little ball along with you as a companion. It's good exercise, but it isn't a sport. Maybe it is when you're competing with somebody, but playing golf isn't a sport. It's like fishing. Is fishing a sport? Are we talking about sports or individual entertainment?"

31   Of course, Mrs. Wilson didn't agree with me about golf, any more than Bill Veeck agreed with me about baseball during that discussion in St. Louis that I mentioned earlier. Veeck's chief counterattack was, "Why, all you do in basketball is get a big goon and stand him out there near the basket and throw him the ball."

32   I'll concede this much: Some teams do play a brand of basketball that can give this impression. They get a fellow of mountainous size and build their whole offense around feeding the ball to him. This slows down the game. When two of these teams with big

pivot men play each other, then the game gets almost as slow as baseball — it's a contest between two pivot men, the way baseball is a contest between the pitcher and the batter. Here basketball is open to criticism — except that the critics talk as if these isolated cases were the general rule.

33   It is undeniable that height is an advantage in basketball — the only way you could change that would be to take away the basket and put a hole in the floor, and have the players stick the ball down there to register points. It is also true that the occasional boy who scales six-ten or more generally isn't a real athlete. He is a hardworking fellow who has learned to capitalize on his size and make certain specialized moves, like a baseball pitcher. There are as many goons on the mound as there are on the basketball court, believe me. But most of the tall boys in basketball aren't goons. Take such six-foot-six men as Jim Pollard or my La Salle boy, Tom Gola, who made just about every All-American team as a sophomore last year. They're no freaks, specializing in a few set maneuvers. They're athletes who can move with alacrity in any direction.

34   People ask, "Where do all these tall boys come from?" Well, not so many years ago, before big George Mikan began making $25,000 a year out of basketball, when a kid began sprouting up like a beanstalk, his father would moan, "I've got a freak on my hands." He'd assume his son had no chance in sports. The boy would wind up carrying the front end of the drum in the high-school band.

35   Nowadays, with a youngster like that, the father shouts, "I've got another Mikan!" and rushes out to buy him a basketball. When the kid gets to high school, he's on the basketball team, and they have a short man carrying the drum. Practicing with that basketball in his back yard from the time he was seven, this tall boy has developed grace and balance. Among the kids I see coming up today, the six-fives move just as well as the five-tens used to.

36   Those quick, agile six-foot-five-inch fellows are the ones I like to have on my team. I don't want a seven-foot man mountain. I don't want an offense that revolves around one big pivot man. That kills the game for the four other players. It kills it for the spectators. Not only that, I don't think such a static offense is ever as effective as a fast-moving, five-man attack.

37　　When I came to La Salle College in 1949 — I'd previously coached basketball at Geneva, at Yale and in the professional big leagues — the fair-haired boy was Larry Foust, who has since done well with Fort Wayne in the pro league. He was six-eleven and 250 pounds. The season before, he had played the traditional big man's role in the pivot. Success always hinged on whether Larry was having an "on" night.

38　　I converted the La Salle team to a mobile, screening type of offense — some sportswriters call it "the weave" — in which the players keep the ball circling back and forth, constantly sparring for openings. I took Larry Foust out of his set pivot position and made him part of the weave, with special responsibility for getting rebounds off the backboard.

39　　Larry, a good team player, accepted his new role graciously. Not so, a lot of outsiders. When we played in New York, a number of basketball writers said I was crazy not to use a fellow like Foust as a pivot man.

40　　What they didn't see was that with Foust no longer in the middle, jamming the doorway to the basket, every man on the team now had a chance to break in there and score. Their incentive was greater. Where Foust had dominated the scoring the year before, now it was split between Foust, Frank Comerford, Jim Phelan, and Ace McCann. Foust made fewer points than the previous season, but the team average was seven points higher per game. Where La Salle had lost seven games the preceding year, this time we went through our schedule with only three defeats and qualified for the National Invitation Tournament. At this point we have made the National Invitation four straight times, incidentally, and in 1952 we won it.

41　　In recent years both the rule makers and the opposing coaches have developed ways of making things tougher for the big man who plays the pivot in basketball. The best defensive coaches now put the emphasis on intercepting the ball before it gets to the pivot man, by putting pressure on the feeders and playing somebody in front of the big boy. It's like rushing the passer in football.

42　　New tactics keep coming along all the time in basketball, and in football too. But baseball! Why, when anyone does something different there, it's so unusual that it creates a sensation. Take the time a few years back when Lou Boudreau got the idea of shifting all his fielders over to the right side against Ted Williams, who did his hitting in that direction. Boudreau was hailed as a genius. The only wonder to me was that somebody hadn't thought of it long ago. Football teams for years have been moving men over to the strong side. Basketball teams for years have been overswitching — playing to a man's right, for instance, if that's the way he likes to go.

43   Then there is that fad in baseball for using left-handed batters against right-handed pitchers, and right-handed batters against left-handed pitchers. In his eagerness to do something to earn his salary, one manager will put in a left-handed relief pitcher to face a left-handed hitter. Then the other manager will switch to a right-handed pinch hitter. Then they counter some more. The strategy is terrific, and while it's going on everybody has time for a bottle of pop and a hot dog.

44   At Yale I handled the jayvee baseball team for several years. We won three fourths of our games. "Smoky" Joe Wood, who used to be a big-league pitcher, was the head baseball coach. It was a privilege to be associated with him. Joe Wood was a great athlete and a great student of any sport. But there's so little to study, comparatively speaking, in baseball.

45   I go to a lot of sports banquets, and I hear a lot of speeches. The dullest by far are the baseball speakers. The average young ballplayer can't get out of his own way when he stands up to speak. Most of the older men, the managers and coaches, tell the same flat stories over and over. I go to a banquet one week, and a baseball veteran is describing how far Babe Ruth hit one. If I hear him at another banquet the next week, Babe Ruth is still hitting that same ball.

46   I'll wager that any good basketball coach can get up and talk about a different phase of his game's technique every night in the week. And I'll wager that the baseball managers cannot.

47   Some basketball old-timers can be as bad at banquets as the baseball old-timers. They'll get up and talk about "The good old game." That's the bunk. I played "the good old game" myself, back in the days of the original New York Celtics. After graduating from Penn State and going to work for a utility company in Pittsburgh,

I played professional basketball on the side with the Pittsburgh Morrys, champions of the old Central League.

48   The old game wasn't fast. It was slow. It was a game of rough play. We went up against the Celtics — against Nat Holman, Dutch Dehnert, Johnny Beckman and all the rest — and it was four wrestling matches plus the man with the ball. When Beckman would try to drive, I'd ram into him. They seldom called fouls for those things. You were permitted to have virtually all the contact you wanted. But there was none of the fine shading and screening and finesse that there is nowadays, when you are required to avoid contact.

49   The shooting wasn't so good as it is on the major college and pro teams today, either. In modern big-time basketball, the boys have to be good shots. Otherwise the opposing team can mass in a zone defense and keep you from getting any closer than fifteen to seventeen feet from the basket. You have to be able to sink four out of ten shots from twenty feet — if given time to get set — in order to beat this kind of defense.

50   You may say, "Then all you need to do is get five good shooters and send them out there." It isn't that simple. The difference between good coaches with five shooters and poor coaches with five shooters is that the good coaches create patterns that give better shooting opportunities. These patterns bring the ball closer, allow the boys more time to shoot, and result in higher percentages of successful shots.

51   In La Salle's kind of moving offense, the man with the ball is like a football quarterback. As he moves, he watches the defense, looking for one of the various holes our screening patterns are designed to open up. If he doesn't find one quickly, he gives the ball right over to another man, and that man becomes the quarterback. So we have a team of five quarterbacks.

52   This takes boys who can move fast and react fast. When I was with the Army Air Force during World War II, and stationed for a time at a training center in Roswell, New Mexico, it was an indisputable fact that fellows with basketball backgrounds made outstanding fliers. Their reactions were much quicker than, for instance, those of the average football player, who hadn't had all that ball handling and footwork.

53   Except for the T quarterback and a few other men on the squad,
not many football players have the nimbleness to do the things a
basketball player does. This also shows up in a sport like lacrosse —
I coached freshman lacrosse during a couple of my years at Yale.
Lacrosse is a good game. It's a rough sport, like football, but it also
requires deftness in handling a ball with a stick. Most of the football players who came out didn't have this — they were just big
men running up and down for exercise.

54   I started in college coaching in 1930. I'm also a law-school graduate and teach law courses at La Salle, but I never have broken
away from sports. In my time I have seen too many college athletes
who were not mentally qualified to be in a college. But very few of
these were basketball players. By and large, it takes an alert-minded
boy to play basketball. You'll find an occasional exception — a fellow the coach goes along with because he is tremendously gifted
from some physical standpoint. Basketball players don't always get
good grades, but if they concentrated on their studies the way they
do on the game, 90 per cent of them would be A students.

55   The coach had better have a quick mind too. A basketball coach
can do more to affect the outcome of a game, for better or worse,
than a coach in any other sport. And he has to do it more rapidly.
As a consequence, basketball coaches are subject to the occupational
disease of supersensitivity — they have quick boiling points. Ask
any official.

56   There are so many things to watch. Take substitutions. One of
your men is faked out of position by his opponent. Does that same
fake fool him a second time? If so, you should see it and get him
out of there without further delay and explain to him what he's
doing wrong. And you must be alert to signs that an individual is
getting weary, and rush in a fresh man to give him a rest.

57   You keep altering your offensive and defensive tactics to meet
the circumstances. When there is a time-out, we hold a meeting on
the bench. I ask each man, "Have you found out anything?" If one
fellow says, "Well, I can go past my man," or, "I can take my man
inside and beat him on the pivot," we start to look for him a little
more in that five-man pattern we have out there.

58   Another thing, a basketball coach has to be good at sizing up
people. He has to recognize when an official is of questionable

parentage. Seriously, I think that officiating is the biggest problem in basketball. Since all contact is a foul, depending on who caused the contact, a great deal rides on the official's judgment. You have varying interpretations. Some officials have better eyes than others. Some have more judicious minds.

59 Next to basketball, football is the toughest sport to coach. I handled the 150-pound team at Yale for a while — we were undefeated one year — and I was varsity line coach one season at the University of Denver. Football coaches spend long hours studying movies and mapping out different offenses and defenses. They have adjustments to make during a game too. But they have one decisive advantage over basketball coaches. They get those thirty seconds after each play in which to think.

60 The baseball coach or manager has the least to do during a game — and the most time to do it. The pitcher throws the ball, and if the batter hits it, you invariably can tell by where the ball goes what's going to happen. A smash down the third-base line will be good for two bases. A fly ball to center field will be an out. You could take away the fielders and mark out the field like a pinball board, and things would work out about the same. If the ball landed in a certain area between left and center, the two-base-hit light would flash on; if it went on the ground to the shortstop spot, that would register an out. Then you could dispense with all those high-salaried infielders and outfielders and just have the pitcher and the batter and the catcher.

61 Maybe this sounds ridiculous, but it isn't any more ridiculous than the comments some people make about basketball. There's room for a lot of different sports in this country. I enjoy many of them myself. But one game is clearly the best. It's the toughest all-round test of speed and stamina and skill and science. It's basketball.

QUESTIONS FOR REFLECTION, DISCUSSION, OR WRITING

(1) Make a list of the criteria these authors set up, either by direct statement or by implication, as a means of judging the value of a sport. How well do they succeed in showing that basketball comes nearer than other sports to meeting these requirements?

(2) Now return to the article by Povich and decide how well he manages this problem of argument. Which of the two selections seems more *reasonable* in approach? Which more *emotional?* Could one or the other, then, be considered more effective as argument-persuasion?

(3) Consider the many Loeffler-Paxton indictments of baseball. Do you agree with any or all of them? From the standpoint of player or spectator? Defend your opinion.

(4) Golf, according to this article, is "good exercise, but it isn't a sport" (par. 30). Do you share this opinion? Why, or why not?

(5) Considering the basketball players you have known personally, do you suppose if "they concentrated on their studies the way they do on the game, ninety per cent of them would be 'A' students" (par. 54)? Would this be more or less apt to be true of the football and baseball players you have known?

(6) How do you feel about the authors' advice to the young athlete (par. 28)? Do you believe many young athletes think about sports "solely from the selfish standpoint?" *Should* they? Organize your explanation or argument in good composition form.

(7) General Patton once remarked that he would always choose to have beside him on the battlefield a man who had played football. Compare this statement with Loeffler and Paxton's paragraph 52. Which of the *three* major sports do you think gives the best training for war combat in any or all of the armed services? Justify your opinions in a well-developed composition.

Gertrude Samuels

From A FORCE OF YOUTH
AS A FORCE FOR PEACE

GERTRUDE SAMUELS, *a member of the* New York Times *staff for several years, has written many articles on today's youth and also on the various newly emerging countries of the world. At the time this book was prepared she was in Israel, gathering material for news and feature stories. Her biography of Israel's Prime Minister Ben-Gurion,* B-G: Fighter of Goliaths, *has already been published.*

THE NEW YORK TIMES MAGAZINE, *published since 1896, is distributed with the more than 1¼ million copies of the* Times' *Sunday edition. Devoted to matters of general interest, the* Times Magazine *is written, however, for a somewhat more world-conscious audience than most other "Sunday supplements." The following article was published Feb. 5, 1961.*

A FORCE OF YOUTH AS A FORCE FOR PEACE *is reprinted here with minor omissions, parts which were significant only at the time of first publication. It is, in our book, the first of three short articles which pertain in some way to the Peace Corps. All were written before the beginning of actual Peace Corps operations, but the needs and the problems involved are just as pertinent now, perhaps just as controversial, as when these articles were written.*

1   THINK of the wonders skilled American personnel could work, building goodwill, building the peace. . . . I therefore propose that our inadequate efforts in this area be supplemented by a "peace corps" of talented young men willing and able to serve their country in this fashion for three years, as an alternative to peacetime Selective Service.

2   Of all the campaign statements by President Kennedy, this — his "peace corps" proposal, made last November at San Francisco — more than any other reached directly into the hearts and minds of thousands of young men and women throughout the country. Clearly, it articulated a longing and a question that have been spreading for some time among many groups, both young and old: How can the individual American do something positive and affirmative for peace? . . .

3   Why this concern? What are the needs abroad?

4   Nearly half the world lives in grinding poverty — on a per capita income of about $100 a year, compared with $2,166 a year in the United States. Two-thirds of the world is illiterate, compared with ninety-eight per cent of Americans who can read and write. Life expectancy, because of such diseases as malaria and tuberculosis, is thirty-six years in the poorer areas, compared with almost seventy years in America.

5   Vast amounts of money have been poured into these areas, unilaterally and through the United Nations, to help people, shattered by war or poverty, to leapfrog the centuries and develop a better life.

6   Yet all these efforts have proved unequal to the astronomical need. Reports from Congressional, United Nations and private

sources indicate that the demand is for many times the number of people and projects. One Congressman estimated after touring Asia that ten times the number of International Cooperation Administration specialists — or a total of 60,000 men — could well be used on farm development projects alone.

7   Just as crucial as the manpower problem is the psychological factor. Americans serving abroad are chiefly I. C. A. consultants to governments — well-paid specialists who work in the capitals and rarely meet the people. Native peoples in many areas have the idea that America is the inheritor of the colonial tradition, that Americans like to keep on a plane of superiority far from them. Thus foreign aid has fallen short, the experts say, because it has been insufficiently human and understandable; it has relied too much on military hardware and on steel and concrete projects that may be necessary for defense and development but, by themselves, cannot make friends for us.

8   Representative Henry S. Reuss of Wisconsin, on a Congressional mission to Cambodia not long ago, surveyed the "crowning jewel" of American aid in that country — a vast and beautiful superhighway from Pnompenh, the capital, to the sea. But it was a team of four American school teachers, working for UNESCO and going quietly from village to village in the Cambodian jungle to set up elementary schools for the first time in the country, who were idolized by the people. The only trouble was, he reported, that "we had four people working on it instead of forty or, better, 400."

9   The Soviet Union has seen the worth of the grassroots approach. Its foreign aid to under-developed countries today is close to that contributed by the United States — about $1 billion a year. Its technicians and projects reach deep into the villages of the receiving countries. More important than the projects themselves — many of which in Africa are literally "giveaway programs" to make friends with the so-called uncommitted countries — the Soviet technicians are there to entrench themselves with the people. They are, as one foreign diplomat put it, "always available."

10   The Soviet campaign to influence people is clearly on everyone's mind. C. P. Snow dramatically sums up this aspect of foreign aid in his book, *The Two Cultures and the Scientific Revolution.* He says:

11   "Since the gap between the rich countries and the poor can be removed, it will be. If we are short-sighted, inept, incapable either of goodwill or enlightened self-interest, then it may be removed to the accompaniment of war and starvation: but removed it will be. The questions are, how, and by whom."

12   The human picture of what is possible with a peace corps is glimpsed in the work of the major private agencies. Although they have only been able to scratch the surface of the problem, young Americans, volunteering for work with the agencies, have already been putting their idealism into practice in many countries.

13   The American Friends Service Committee (Quakers) sends some 500 young Americans abroad during the summer vacation to help rebuild villages and schools. The International Voluntary Service (I. V. S.), supported by the major world missionary groups, uses about 150 young Americans on a year-round basis.

14   Perhaps the best-known experiment, now in its third year, is Operation-Crossroads Africa, organized by Dr. James H. Robinson, Negro pastor, and director of the Morningside Community Center of New York.

15   In 1954, Dr. Robinson toured Africa and saw the urgent needs of the villages. Back home, he failed to interest anyone in his person-to-person approach ("Everyone thought the idea was crazy") until he got to Occidental College in Los Angeles; 900 students there pitched in to initiate plans to send ten students with him to spend the summer of 1958 helping Africans.

16   As the idea spread to other campuses, Dr. Robinson received 270 applications; he chose sixty out of the group, of whom seventeen were Negroes. They understood that this was neither a tourist joyride nor an African safari, but a tough work-camp mission in which they would live simply, travel hard, and be willing to accept the risks of malaria, dysentery and the primitive conditions of village life where few tourists or diplomats penetrate. Money for the project was raised by churches and civic groups, or contributed by the students themselves.

17   The first group, loaded with tropical medicine chests and zeal, went to impoverished villages in Liberia, Ghana, Nigeria, Sierra Leone and the French Cameroons (now the Republic of Cameroon), where they were joined by African students. Practically

every night there was an exchange of views about the United States and its role in Africa. "Always" there was the question of race relations.

18   The Americans were shocked at first to find that in many communities the educated élite scorned manual labor; African students would look on with amusement as Americans — boys and girls, Negro and white — went to work for their village. Finally, they were shamed into action and, as they began to work alongside the Americans, the illiterate villagers saw from the joint action that it was not undignified for the educated to work with their hands — "Work, it's okay," they said — and they, too, pitched in.

19   That summer, the Americans helped build a village water supply in the bush country of Gbendembu in Sierra Leone; a two-room, concrete block school and a stone chapel in the village of Buel in the French Cameroons; a seven-room school in a remote Ghanaian village. After working hours, they taught children elementary English, arithmetic, history and geography; the girls met with women's groups to teach homemaking and hygiene.

20   Since 1958, Operation-Crossroads Africa has grown to a project of 180 students, chosen from 700 applicants from Harvard, Yale, M. I. T., Howard University and seventy other colleges. The students divide into teams of fifteen to twenty, assigned to ten West African countries. Most students are white, some two dozen are from Southern states; almost half are women.

21   Last summer in the Sanniquelle District of Liberia, a team of Americans and one Canadian helped to build a library with materials from American firms in the country, working alongside African students from the University of Liberia. Sonja Bolling, 20-year-old junior of Howard University, taught school after the manual labor — mathematics and spelling to a class of thirty-five who ranged in age from nine to eighteen years.

22   At Prampram, a fishing village on the Ghana coast, fourteen American students joined thirty Ghanaian students in building a schoolhouse. They had no modern amenities; they brought water by bucket from the village well; they managed on gas lamps, cooked their own meals (mainly meat stews with tropical yams and rice), and experienced one case of malaria. The blue-jeaned girls soon learned it was easier to carry mortar pans and concrete blocks on

their heads; at lunch Americans and Africans shared coconuts and ideas for a better life.

23   The young Americans found they were not only creating a positive attitude for America, but also acquiring education themselves in foreign beliefs and social customs.

24   The "Farewell Address" to Operation-Crossroads Africa last year, printed by the Akugbene community of Nigeria and signed by the village elders, tells its own story:

25   We deeply appreciate your association with us in which our foreshore wall embarkment has been completed. . . . During your stay you so identified yourselves with us that we regarded you as members of our Akugbene community.

26   You have since your stay endured to put up with the uncomfortable lodgings we provided; you submitted yourselves to care for the health of our children. You took the trouble to conduct outdoor classes with our children. . . . How lonesome shall we feel your absence from our town, Akugbene, when we shall no more cast our eyes upon American dances and ways of life. . . .

QUESTIONS FOR REFLECTION, DISCUSSION, OR WRITING

(1) To what extent is the author's primary purpose one of argument? Has she used any persuasive tactics? How successful has she been in achieving her purpose? Was it worthwhile, in your estimation?

(2) Discuss "the idea [of many native peoples] that America is the inheritor of the colonial tradition, that Americans like to keep on a plane of superiority far from them" (par. 7). Do you think this idea is correct? If so, do you think individual Americans can be "blamed" for such an attitude? If it does our country harm, what should be done about it?

(3) Do you think it is necessary to live like a native in order to convince natives of our good will? Why, or why not?

(4) If a "vast and beautiful" superhighway through a country like Cambodia is not a wise use of foreign aid money, explain why not. Otherwise, defend the expense.

(5) Do you see any weakness in Miss Samuels' reliance on the Operations Crossroads example to show that a Peace Corps can work? Are there any ways in which the problems of Operations Crossroads were not typical of those the Peace Corps faces?

(6) Without necessarily reading his book, what do you suppose are the forces which make C. P. Snow so sure "the gap between the rich countries

and the poor countries" will be removed (par. 11)? Do you find alarming the implications of this statement? Can the gap be removed without, in the process, making ourselves "poor countries" too? Is it worth the risk?

(7) Did you ever, by choice or necessity, live for even a brief time (maybe only for a day) with people whose standard of living was much lower than your own? How did you react — inwardly, as well as outwardly? An account of the experience and its effects on you could make an excellent composition.

Paul Conklin
"WE DON'T WANT TO BE WON"

PAUL CONKLIN, *an Army veteran and graduate of Wayne State University (Detroit) and Columbia University, wrote from Lagos while this book was in preparation that he had been "having a go at free-lance writing and photography here in Nigeria for the past year — after three years on the staffs of the Worcester (Mass.) Gazette and the Minneapolis Star, and a growing weariness of 'beat' work." He continued, "Our present way of life will end when we are no longer solvent; within the next six months I will have to look for another job, I'm afraid."*

THE NEW REPUBLIC, *wherein "We Don't Want to Be Won" was first printed Feb. 20, 1961, has been published since 1914, in Washington, D.C. It has always fulfilled its avowed function as a liberal "journal of opinion," featuring current commentaries and book reviews.*

"WE DON'T WANT TO BE WON" *is an almost entirely objective report (i.e., the author keeps his own opinions and feelings out of it) of a personal interview, a common basis for news and feature stories. Interviewed are certain young Africans whose arguments in favor of "non-alignment" between the West and Communism may not sound very rational to us. But few of us now doubt that our eventual success in the struggle with Communism will partially depend on our attempt to understand such viewpoints, whether or not we approve of their logic.*

Ibadan, Nigeria

1   THE FIVE students came in bringing chairs and made themselves comfortable in the book-strewn dormitory room. They were polite but a bit wary. My wife and I had driven ninety miles from Lagos to University College on the outskirts of Ibadan in order to talk with them.

2   Outside the sun beat down with dazzling intensity on the school's handsome white buildings which were made to appear even whiter by the surrounding forest. Not far away this wall of green was pierced by the rooftops of a new housing development.

3   On the horizon was the skeletal transmitting tower of the Western Region's — and Africa's first — television network. Out of sight behind a ridge lay Ibadan, an immense, sprawling city of 600,000 people.

4   Four of the students were studying undergraduate physics. The fifth was doing graduate work in library science. One was president of the student council. Another edited the college weekly.

5   Two months earlier all five had abandoned their books for a day, and along with several hundred of their classmates had descended noisily on the federal house of parliament in Lagos to protest the signing of the Anglo-Nigerian Defense Pact. Before the ensuing fracas with the police had run its course, one of the physicists and the librarian had deliberately allowed themselves to be arrested and carried away in a paddy wagon for a date next morning with a Lagos magistrate.

6   The pact, then, was a natural starting place for a discussion. As their initial reserve melted the students spoke freely and with a vehemence tempered by frequent assurance that their American visitors should take nothing they said personally. Here is some of what they said, reported as accurately as memory allows.

7   "The mere idea of a pact is inconsistent with the neutral role every African nation should play. It makes us look hypocritical and ridiculous because our leaders have told the world we will follow a policy of non-alignment as far as the power blocs are concerned."

8   "Signing a pact with Britain means aligning ourselves with America and NATO, too. During the Suez crisis the British used our airbase at Kano. If de Gaulle and Abbas fail to reach an agreement, the West may use Kano to attack Algeria. The day will inevitably come when we find ourselves fighting at Britain's side against other Africans."

9   A gust of wind blew to the floor a leaflet announcing "regretfully," that the French acting troupe scheduled to appear on the

campus the following week was cancelling its engagement because the Nigerian-French diplomatic break had made transportation impossible.

10   "The British are deceitful," one of the group continued. "They tell us they want to help us but in reality take advantage of our inexperience as a new nation to increase their military capacity. They want to keep an eye on us because they fear us."

11   "Once we have given them a base we'll never get them off our soil. Cuba gave America the naval base at Guantanamo, but when relations deteriorated America refused to leave. The same thing will happen here because if there is any country with which we will quarrel in the future it will be Britain."

12   And then as a brutal afterthought one student added, "Why should we tie ourselves to a declining power that is no longer able to defend even itself?"

13   "Africans are weary of being pushed around like pawns on your Cold War chessboard. You take it for granted that we lack intelligence to make our own decisions and shape our own future. Russia and America haven't yet realized that Africa does not need to decide between capitalism and Communism. There are alternatives and we can find them."

14   "You Americans are the most obstinate people. You above all others should realize that Africa is not to be wooed like a child with no mind of its own. There is so much talk in the United States about winning Africa for the free world. Has it ever occurred to you that perhaps we don't want to be won, perhaps we don't regard your freedom as being particularly desirable?"

15   "Kennedy says he will send a peace corps to us, but to us this kind of peace means anti-Communism."

16   The five were in quick agreement that none wanted to have anything to do with President Kennedy's young emissaries from America.

17   "We are ready to receive your help, but help that comes from love, not pity. We don't want a patronizing pat on the back. We don't want your American superiority flaunted in our faces, because in fact we don't recognize this superiority."

18   "You must realize that when we talk like this it is not because we are pro-Communist. We want nothing to do with Communism. The

Hungaries repel us. We have never looked to Moscow for leadership. We have looked to the West but you have disappointed us."

19   "We may disagree with some of Nkrumah's internal policies, but as far as projecting Africa to the world goes, he is the leader we most admire. Nkrumah was right when he said that Ghana will not be free until all of Africa is free. We begrudge every inch of African soil that remains under the control of the white man. All Africans are brothers with a common history of oppression and a common destiny of freedom."

20   "Africa has reached a stage where it must stand on its own." His voice edged with scorn, the editor continued, "The English and Americans tell me that I am not a human being until I learn to speak English and wear a white shirt and tie. But I am an African. I cannot be a carbon copy of a white man. Likewise, Africa has to express itself as a continent with integrity."

21   "Put it another way. The West is a declining civilization. Where is the human race going to get the leaven it needs so badly if Africans — and Asians — are not allowed to express themselves as human beings?"

22   After this outburst the student took a long drink from a bottle of orange soda, looked at his watch and got up. It was time for lunch.

23   As they left, one turned in the doorway and said, "You know, Americans and Nigerians have one important trait in common. We both speak our minds."

QUESTIONS FOR REFLECTION, DISCUSSION, OR WRITING

(1) Americans have no monopoly of the use of metaphors and similes (see p. 15): these African students used them often for vivid expression. Find at least one in each of the following paragraphs: 7, 8, 10, 12-14, and 17-20. Identify each as to type (two are similes) and comment on their effectiveness.

(2) Does any part of this interview make Miss Samuels' enthusiasm ("A Force of Youth . . .") seem less well-founded? Explain.

(3) Do you think the small and weak countries of the world are justified in supporting neither the cause of "freedom" nor that of Communism (par. 7)? Does such non-alignment, at a time when the struggle between the two seems to be one of life-or-death, imply that one cause is as good — or as bad — as the other? Explain.

(4) Can you think of any logical "alternatives" to capitalism and Communism (par. 13)? If the Communists win the struggle for world domination, do you think Nigeria will have the opportunity to practice an alternative? What if capitalism wins the struggle?

(5) What would be a logical answer to the unfavorable remark about America and the naval base in Cuba (par. 11)? Or do you agree that we should leave Guantanamo to the Cubans? Defend your stand.

(6) How valid is the student's fear that the Peace Corps "kind of peace means anti-Communism" (par. 15)?

(7) Can you believe that any American would be so foolish or so tactless as to tell an African he must speak English and wear a white shirt and tie in order to be a human being? On what do you base your opinion?

(8) Examine the student's statement, "We don't want your American superiority flaunted in our faces, because in fact we don't recognize this superiority" (par. 17). Is this mere emotional talk? If Americans are not superior, then how can you (and the Nigerians) account for the centuries-long gap in our respective civilizations?

(9) Can you find any indications that the West is "a declining civilization" (par. 21)? Discuss.

Marquis Childs

PEACE CORPS

MARQUIS CHILDS, *a native of Iowa and resident of Washington, D.C., has been the recipient of many journalism awards. Author of various books, including* The Ragged Edge *and* Eisenhower, Captive Hero, *he is perhaps best known for his syndicated "Washington Column." It is distributed by United Features Syndicate and appears in daily newspapers, large and small, in all parts of the United States.*

PEACE CORPS *was one day's feature of Childs' column (in March of 1961). You will want to relate his opinions and warnings to what we have just read about the Peace Corps in the two preceding pieces.*

1   THE OVERWHELMING response to the Peace Corps shows once again the deep strain of idealism that is an important part of the American character. Americans, particularly young Americans, are earnestly searching for some "moral equivalent of war" that

will challenge their abilities and give them the sense of joining in an enterprise larger than personal gain.

2   The spirit is there and by the thousands young people are coming forward who want to put their talents to use in the difficult and demanding situations created by the tide of nationalism in Asia and Africa. But while this is a magnificent concept it is also full of the most perilous pitfalls. And unless it is administered with the utmost care and conscientiousness the net result can be almost more harm than good.

3   Those already familiar with volunteer efforts to send teachers and technicians to underdeveloped countries stress above everything else the problem of acceptance. They must be wanted and wanted not as saviors and innovators but as modest and devoted servants of the new national order.

4   The dependence of an ex-colonial nation on the talents of its ex-colonial masters and on others of the same race and culture acts as a constant irritant on the sensitivity and pride of even the most levelheaded persons in those nations where freedom is raw and new. Left wing and extremist parties are constantly seeking to exploit the presence of foreign advisors and technicians with the demand that Africans be left alone to work out their own destiny.

5   That this makes little sense in view of the fact that every kind of skill is needed is beside the point. Even after members of the Peace Corps have been invited in they will have to realize that a great many people in the country to which they are assigned will regard them with suspicion and hostility.

6   The campus wonder boy will not necessarily make the best Peace Corpsman, according to those who know the problem at firsthand. Those with experience, put the prerequisites in the following order: adaptability and flexibility, maturity, professional qualifications and motives.

7   Those who see themselves in the role of noble Messiahs had better stay home. They will only be frustrated, while they alienate those they are seeking to help. The ideal candidate for the Peace Corps must have the patience of Job, the forbearance of a saint and the digestive system of an ostrich.

8   The first question in putting the corps together is whether the

screening process will be sufficiently effective to weed out the misfits and detect the young who are intellectually and emotionally equipped for an exacting assignment. And a related question is whether the latter will come forward in sufficient numbers so that a small and a carefully worked out beginning can be made.

9   On this last score there seems little reason for doubt. Already under voluntary auspices a number of capable young people are doing tough jobs in difficult circumstances. Operation Crossroads Africa, in which young college students have worked long hours at hard labor side by side with Africans, was one of the projects that the Kennedy planners studied in developing the Peace Corps.

10   But Crossroads Africa was a summer assignment and the important thing for the Peace Corps is to find men and women who will stay the course. Experience with volunteers now in the field shows that when those who contract to stay for two years break their contracts and pull out after a few months the harm done is great.

11   If the concept of the Corps can be expanded, as President Kennedy has suggested, to cover services in this country it will help to win acceptance overseas. For, according to those working intensively at making the experiment a success, this will answer the sensitive and suspicious in the newly developing nations who say, "You have some bad spots right at home and wouldn't you do better to stay there and clean them up."

12   One idea put into the hopper is for the President to propose a United Nations Peace Corps, of which the American Corps would be a part. This would do away with any problem of acceptance. Individual countries could then decide what Peace Corpsmen they would invite in, and in that way there would be no question of the Corps becoming a mask for Communist agents using it as a means to get entry.

13   While this is still in the tentative idea stage there is something so yeasty and exciting about the whole concept that it cannot be ruled out. Once these things get started they tend to run away with even the boldest innovators.

QUESTIONS FOR REFLECTION, DISCUSSION, OR WRITING

(1) After reading "Peace Corps" could you classify Childs as either a liberal or a conservative? (See p. 37.) Explain why.

(2) How does this essay compare with Miss Samuels' treatment of the same subject? Does one seem more realistic than the other? In what respects? Has your "sandwiched" reading of "We Don't Want to Be Won" influenced your opinion? Which essay seems to you the more argumentative?

(3) Again we have the reference to a "moral equivalent of war" (par. 1). Is this term any more meaningful to you now than when you encountered it in Senator Humphrey's essay? Explain how the Peace Corps might serve as such a moral equivalent.

(4) What do you suppose would be the outcome if the rest of the world did leave Africans "alone to work out their own destiny" (par. 4)?

(5) Can you see any great need for a home Peace Corps (par. 11)? If so, do you think it should have been organized first? Explain your views on the subject.

(6) Childs seems to like the idea of a United Nations Peace Corps (pars. 12-13). Can you see any serious disadvantages to such a plan?

(7) Do you think participation in the present Peace Corps should exempt young men from the Army draft? Why, or why not?

(8) What is your opinion of permitting girls in the Peace Corps? How would you react if your young sister or daughter wanted to join and go into some African jungle to work? Explain.

(9) Have you ever considered applying for service in the Peace Corps? Why, or why not?

(10) In view of recent reports of actual Peace Corps operations, how valuable do you now consider this endeavor? How practical?

Peter F. Drucker
HOW TO BE AN EMPLOYEE

PETER F. DRUCKER, *who was born in Austria in 1909, has made an outstanding name for himself in the United States as economist and management consultant for numerous large corporations. He is also well known as an author in the fields of economics and business management. His writings include many magazine articles and books, among which are* Practice of Management, America's Next Twenty Years, *and* The Landmarks of Tomorrow.

FORTUNE, *which used "How to Be an Employee" in its May 1952 issue, was founded in 1930 and now has a circulation of more than 330,000. According to its original prospectus,* Fortune's *purpose "is to reflect Industrial Life in ink and paper and word and picture as the finest skyscraper reflects it in stone and steel and architecture." Much intensive research goes into the magazine's content, which, besides serving business executives (about eighty-five per cent of its readers), consistently relates American business to America itself and frequently includes articles and statistics on such subjects as community planning and education.*

HOW TO BE AN EMPLOYEE *is a good example of exposition (see p. 8), as indeed almost any "how-to" article should be, since its one function is to explain something — a process or operation — effectively.*

1   MOST OF YOU graduating today will be employees all your working life, working for somebody else and for a pay check. And so will most, if not all, of the thousands of other young Americans graduating this year in all the other schools and colleges across the country.

2   Ours has become a society of employees. A hundred years or so ago one out of every five Americans at work was employed, i.e., worked for somebody else. Today only one out of five is not employed but working for himself. And where fifty years ago "being employed" meant working as a factory laborer or as a farmhand, the employee of today is increasingly a middle-class person with a substantial formal education, holding a professional or management job requiring intellectual and technical skills. Indeed, two things have characterized American society during these last fifty years: the middle and upper classes have become employees; and middle-class and upper-class employees have been the fastest-growing groups in our working population — growing so fast that the industrial worker, that oldest child of the Industrial Revolution, has been losing in numerical importance despite the expansion of industrial production.

3   This is one of the most profound social changes any country has ever undergone. It is, however, a perhaps even greater change for the individual young man about to start. Whatever he does, in all likelihood he will do it as an employee; wherever he aims, he will have to reach it through being an employee.

4   Yet you will find little if anything written on what it is to be an employee. You can find a great deal of very dubious advice on how to get a job or how to get a promotion. You can also find a good deal on work in a chosen field, whether it be metallurgy or salesmanship, the machinist's trade or bookkeeping. Every one of these trades requires different skills, sets different standards, and requires a different preparation. Yet they all have employeeship in common. And increasingly, especially in the large business or in government, employeeship is more important to success than the special professional knowledge or skill. Certainly more people fail because they do not know the requirements of being an employee than because they do not adequately possess the skills of their trade; the higher you climb the ladder, the more you get into administrative or executive work, the greater the emphasis on ability to work within the organization rather than on technical competence or professional knowledge.

5   Being an employee is thus the one common characteristic of most careers today. The special profession or skill is visible and clearly defined; and a well-laid-out sequence of courses, degrees, and jobs leads into it. But being an employee is the foundation. And it is much more difficult to prepare for it. Yet there is no recorded information on the art of being an employee.

The Basic Skill

6   The first question we might ask is: what can you learn in college that will help you in being an employee? The schools teach a great many things of value to the future accountant, the future doctor, or the future electrician. Do they also teach anything of value to the future employee? The answer is: "Yes — they teach the one thing that it is perhaps most valuable for the future employee to know. But very few students bother to learn it."

7   This one basic skill is the ability to organize and express ideas in writing and in speaking.

8   As an employee you work with and through other people. This means that your success as an employee — and I am talking of much more here than getting promoted — will depend on your ability to communicate with people and to present your own thoughts and ideas to them so they will both understand what you are driving at and be persuaded. The letter, the report or memorandum, the ten-minute spoken "presentation" to a committee are basic tools of the employee.

9   If you work as a soda jerker you will, of course, not need much skill in expressing yourself to be effective. If you work on a machine your ability to express yourself will be of little importance. But as soon as you move one step up from the bottom, your effectiveness depends on your ability to reach others through the spoken or the written word. And the further away your job is from manual work, the larger the organization of which you are an employee, the more important it will be that you know how to convey your thoughts in writing or speaking. In the very large organization, whether it is the government, the large business corporation, or the Army, this ability to express oneself is perhaps the most important of all the skills a man can possess.

10   Of course, skill in expression is not enough by itself. You must have something to say in the first place. The popular picture of the engineer, for instance, is that of a man who works with a slide rule, T square, and compass. And engineering students reflect this picture in their attitude toward the written word as something quite irrelevant to their jobs. But the effectiveness of the engineer — and with it his usefulness — depends as much on his ability to make other people understand his work as it does on the quality of the work itself.

11   Expressing one's thoughts is one skill that the school can really teach, especially to people born without natural writing or speaking talent. Many other skills can be learned later — in this country there are literally thousands of places that offer training to adult people at work. But the foundations for skill in expression have to be laid early: an interest in and an ear for language; experience in organizing ideas and data, in brushing aside the irrelevant, in wedding outward form and inner content into one structure; and above all, the habit of verbal expression. If you do not lay these

foundations during your school years, you may never have an opportunity again.

12   If you were to ask me what strictly vocational courses there are in the typical college curriculum, my answer — now that the good old habit of the "theme a day" has virtually disappeared — would be: the writing of poetry and the writing of short stories. Not that I expect many of you to become poets or short-story writers — far from it. But these two courses offer the easiest way to obtain some skill in expression. They force one to be economical with language. They force one to organize thought. They demand of one that he give meaning to every word. They train the ear for language, its meaning, its precision, its overtones — and its pitfalls. Above all they force one to write.

13   I know very well that the typical employer does not understand this as yet, and that he may look with suspicion on a young college graduate who has majored, let us say, in short story writing. But the same employer will complain — and with good reason — that the young men whom he hires when they get out of college do not know how to write a simple report, do not know how to tell a simple story, and are in fact virtually illiterate. And he will conclude — rightly — that the young men are not really effective, and certainly not employees who are likely to go very far.

14   The next question to ask is: what kind of employee should you be? Pay no attention to what other people tell you. This is one question only you can answer. It involves a choice in four areas — a choice you alone can make, and one you cannot easily duck. But to make the choice you must first have tested yourself in the world of jobs for some time.

15   Here are the four decisions — first in brief outline, then in more detail:

16   1. Do you belong in a job calling primarily for faithfulness in the performance of routine work and promising security? Or do you belong in a job that offers a challenge to imagination and ingenuity — with the attendant penalty for failure?

17   2. Do you belong in a large organization or in a small organization? Do you work better through channels or through direct contacts? Do you enjoy more being a small cog in a big and powerful machine or a big wheel in a small machine?

¹⁸ 3. Should you start at the bottom and try to work your way up, or should you try to start near the top? On the lowest rung of the promotional ladder, with its solid and safe footing but also with a very long climb ahead? Or on the aerial trapeze of "a management trainee," or some other staff position close to management?

¹⁹ 4. Finally, are you going to be more effective and happy as a specialist or as a "generalist," that is, in an administrative job?

²⁰ Let me spell out what each of these four decisions involves:

²¹ The decision between secure routine work and insecure work challenging the imagination and ingenuity is the one decision most people find easiest to make. You know very soon what kind of person you are. Do you find real satisfaction in the precision, order, and system of a clearly laid-out job? Do you prefer the security not only of knowing what your work is today and what it is going to be tomorrow, but also security in your job, in your relationship to the people above, below, and next to you, and economic security? Or are you one of those people who tend to grow impatient with anything that looks like a "routine" job? These people are usually able to live in a confused situation in which their relations to the people around them are neither clear nor stable. And they tend to pay less attention to economic security, find it not too upsetting to change jobs, etc.

²² There is, of course, no such black-and-white distinction between people. The man who can do only painstaking detail work and has no imagination is not much good for anything. Neither is the self-styled "genius" who has nothing but grandiose ideas and no capacity for rigorous application to detail. But in practically everybody I have ever met there is a decided leaning one way or the other.

²³ The difference is one of basic personality. It is not too much affected by a man's experiences; for he is likely to be born with the one or the other. The need for economic security is often as not an outgrowth of a need for psychological security rather than a phenomenon of its own. But precisely because the difference is one of basic temperament, the analysis of what kind of temperament you possess is so vital. A man might be happy in work for which he has little *aptitude*; he might be quite successful in it. But he can be neither happy nor successful in a job for which he is *temperamentally* unfitted.

24   You hear a great many complaints today about the excessive security-consciousness of our young people. My complaint is the opposite: in the large organizations especially there are not enough job opportunities for those young people who need challenge and risk. Jobs in which there is greater emphasis on conscientious performance of well-organized duties rather than on imagination — especially for the beginner — are to be found, for instance, in the inside jobs in banking or insurance, which normally offer great job security but not rapid promotion or large pay. The same is true of most government work, of the railroad industry, particularly in the clerical and engineering branches, and of most public utilities. The bookkeeping and accounting areas, especially in the larger companies, are generally of this type too — though a successful comptroller is an accountant with great management and business imagination.

25   At the other extreme are such areas as buying, selling, and advertising, in which the emphasis is on adaptability, on imagination, and on a desire to do new and different things. In those areas, by and large, there is little security, either personal or economic. The rewards, however, are high and come more rapidly. Major premium on imagination — though of a different kind and coupled with dogged persistence on details — prevails in most research and engineering work. Jobs in production, as supervisor or executive, also demand much adaptability and imagination.

26   Contrary to popular belief, very small business requires, above all, close attention to daily routine. Running a neighborhood drugstore or a small grocery, or being a toy jobber, is largely attention to details. But in very small business there is also room for quite a few people of the other personality type — the innovator or imaginer. If successful, a man of this type soon ceases to be in a very small business. For the real innovator there is, still, no more promising opportunity in this country than that of building a large out of a very small business.

Big Company or Small?

27   Almost as important is the decision between working for a large and for a small organization. The difference is perhaps not so great as that between the secure, routine job and the insecure, imaginative job; but the wrong decision can be equally serious.

28   There are two basic differences between the large and the small enterprise. In the small enterprise you operate primarily through personal contacts. In the large enterprise you have established "policies," "channels" of organization, and fairly rigid procedures. In the small enterprise you have, moreover, immediate effectiveness in a very small area. You can see the effect of your work and of your decisions right away, once you are a little bit above the ground floor. In the large enterprise even the man at the top is only a cog in a big machine. To be sure, his actions affect a much greater area than the actions and decisions of the man in the small organization, but his effectiveness is remote, indirect, and elusive. In a small and even in a middle-sized business you are normally exposed to all kinds of experiences, and expected to do a great many things without too much help or guidance. In the large organization you are normally taught one thing thoroughly. In the small one the danger is of becoming a jack-of-all-trades and master of none. In the large one it is of becoming the man who knows more and more about less and less.

29   There is one other important thing to consider: do you derive a deep sense of satisfaction from being a member of a well-known organization — General Motors, the Bell Telephone System, the government? Or is it more important to you to be a well-known and important figure within your own small pond? There is a basic difference between the satisfaction that comes from being a member of a large, powerful, and generally known organization, and the one that comes from being a member of a family; between impersonal grandeur and personal — often much too personal — intimacy; between life in a small cubicle on the top floor of a skyscraper and life in a crossroads gas station.

Start at the Bottom, or . . . ?

30   You may well think it absurd to say that anyone has a choice between beginning at the bottom and beginning near the top. And indeed I do not mean that you have any choice between beginner's jobs and, let us say, a vice presidency at General Electric. But you do have a choice between a position at the bottom of the hierarchy and a staff position that is outside the hierarchy but in view of the top. It is an important choice.

31   In every organization, even the smallest, there are positions that, while subordinate, modestly paid, and usually filled with young and beginning employees, nonetheless are not at the bottom. There are positions as assistant to one of the bosses; there are positions as private secretary; there are liaison positions for various departments; and there are positions in staff capacities, in industrial engineering, in cost accounting, in personnel, etc. Every one of these gives a view of the whole rather than of only one small area. Every one of them normally brings the holder into the deliberations and discussions of the people at the top, if only as a silent audience or perhaps only as an errand boy. Every one of these positions is a position "near the top," however humble and badly paid it may be.

32   On the other hand the great majority of beginner's jobs are at the bottom, where you begin in a department or in a line of work in the lowest-paid and simplest function, and where you are expected to work your way up as you acquire more skill and more judgment.

33   Different people belong in these two kinds of jobs. In the first place, the job "near the top" is insecure. You are exposed to public view. Your position is ambiguous; by yourself you are a nobody — but you reflect the boss's status; in a relatively short time you may even speak for the boss. You may have real power and influence. In today's business and government organization the hand that writes the memo rules the committee; and the young staff man usually writes the memos, or at least the first draft. But for that very reason everybody is jealous of you. You are a youngster who has been admitted to the company of his betters, and is therefore expected to show unusual ability and above all unusual discretion and judgment. Good performance in such a position is often the key to rapid advancement. But to fall down may mean the end of all hopes of ever getting anywhere within the organization.

34   At the bottom, on the other hand, there are very few opportunities for making serious mistakes. You are amply protected by the whole apparatus of authority. The job itself is normally simple, requiring little judgment, discretion, or initiative. Even excellent performance in such a job is unlikely to speed promotion. But one also has to fall down in a rather spectacular fashion for it to be noticed by anyone but one's immediate superior.

Specialist or "Generalist"?

35   There are a great many careers in which the increasing emphasis is on specialization. You find these careers in engineering and in accounting, in production, in statistical work, and in teaching. But there is an increasing demand for people who are able to take in a great area at a glance, people who perhaps do not know too much about any one field — though one should always have one area of real competence. There is, in other words, a demand for people who are capable of seeing the forest rather than the trees, of making over-all judgments. And these "generalists" are particularly needed for administrative positions, where it is their job to see that other people do the work, where they have to plan for other people, to organize other people's work, to initiate it and appraise it.

36   The specialist understands one field; his concern is with technique, tools, media. He is a "trained" man; and his educational background is properly technical or professional. The generalist — and especially the administrator — deals with people; his concern is with leadership, with planning, with direction giving, and with coordination. He is an "educated" man; and the humanities are his strongest foundation. Very rarely is a specialist capable of being an administrator. And very rarely is a good generalist also a good specialist in a particular field. Any organization needs both kinds of people, though different organizations need them in different ratios. It is your job to find out, during your apprenticeship, into which of those two job categories you fit, and to plan your career accordingly.

37   Your first job may turn out to be the right job for you — but this is pure accident. Certainly you should not change jobs constantly or people will become suspicious — rightly — of your ability to hold any job. At the same time you must not look upon the first job as the final job; it is primarily a training job, an opportunity to analyze yourself and your fitness for being an employee.

The Importance of Being Fired

38   In fact there is a great deal to be said for being fired from the first job. One reason is that it is rarely an advantage to have started as an office boy in the organization; far too many people will still consider you a "green kid" after you have been there for twenty-five

years. But the major reason is that getting fired from the first job is the least painful and the least damaging way to learn how to take a setback. And whom the Lord loveth he teacheth early how to take a setback.

39   Nobody has ever lived, I daresay, who has not gone through a period when everything seemed to have collapsed and when years of work and life seemed to have gone up in smoke. No one can be spared this experience; but one can be prepared for it. The man who has been through earlier setbacks has learned that the world has not come to an end because he lost his job — not even in a depression. He has learned that he will somehow survive. He has learned, above all, that the way to behave in such a setback is not to collapse himself. But the man who comes up against it for the first time when he is forty-five is quite likely to collapse for good. For the things that people are apt to do when they receive the first nasty blow may destroy a mature man with a family, whereas a youth of twenty-five bounces right back.

40   Obviously you cannot contrive to get yourself fired. But you can always quit. And it is perhaps even more important to have quit once than to have been fired once. The man who walks out on his own volition acquires an inner independence that he will never quite lose.

When to Quit

41   To know when to quit is therefore one of the most important things — particularly for the beginner. For on the whole young people have a tendency to hang on to the first job long beyond the time when they should have quit for their own good.

42   One should quit when self-analysis shows that the job is the wrong job — that, say, it does not give the security and routine one requires, that it is a small-company rather than a big-organization job, that it is at the bottom rather than near the top, a specialist's rather than a generalist's job, etc. One should quit if the job demands behavior one considers morally indefensible, or if the whole atmosphere of the place is morally corrupting — if, for instance, only yes men and flatterers are tolerated.

43   One should also quit if the job does not offer the training one needs either in a specialty or in administration and the view of the

whole. The beginner not only has a right to expect training from his first five or ten years in a job; he has an obligation to get as much training as possible. A job in which young people are not given real training — though, of course, the training need not be a formal "training program" — does not measure up to what they have a right and a duty to expect.

44   But the most common reason why one should quit is the absence of promotional opportunities in the organization. That is a compelling reason.

45   I do not believe that chance of a promotion is the essence of a job. In fact there is no surer way to kill a job and one's own usefulness in it than to consider it as but one rung in the promotional ladder rather than as a job in itself that deserves serious effort and will return satisfaction, a sense of accomplishment, and pride. And one can be an important and respected member of an organization without ever having received a promotion; there are such people in practically every office. But the organization itself must offer fair promotional opportunities. Otherwise it stagnates, becomes corrupted, and in turn corrupts. The absence of promotional opportunities is demoralizing. And the sooner one gets out of a demoralizing situation, the better. There are three situations to watch out for:

46   The entire group may be so young that for years there will be no vacancies. That was a fairly common situation in business a few years back, as a result of the depression. Middle and lower management ranks in many companies were solidly filled with men in their forties and early fifties — men who were far too young to be retired but who had grown too old, during the bleak days of the 'Thirties, to be promotable themselves. As a result the people under them were bottled up; for it is a rare organization that will promote a young man around his older superior. If you find yourself caught in such a situation, get out fast. If you wait it will defeat you.

47   Another situation without promotional opportunities is one in which the group ahead of you is uniformly old — so old that it will have to be replaced long before you will be considered ready to move up. Stay away from organizations that have a uniform age structure throughout their executive group — old or young. The

only organization that offers fair promotional opportunities is one in which there is a balance of ages.

Who Gets Promoted?

48 And finally there is the situation in which all promotions go to members of a particular group — to which you do not belong. Some chemical companies, for instance, require a master's degree in chemistry for just about any job above sweeper. Some companies promote only engineering graduates, some government agencies only people who majored in economics, some railroads only male stenographers, some British insurance companies only members of the actuaries' association. Or all the good jobs may be reserved for members of the family. There may be adequate promotional opportunities in such an organization — but not for you.

49 On the whole there are proportionately more opportunities in the big organization than in the small one. But there is very real danger of getting lost in the big organization — whereas you are always visible in the small one. A young man should therefore stay in a large organization only if it has a definite promotional program which ensures that he will be considered and looked at. This may take several forms: it may be a formal appraisal and development program; it may be automatic promotion by seniority as in the pre-war Army; it may be an organization structure that actually makes out of the one big enterprise a number of small organizations in which everybody is again clearly visible (the technical term for this is "decentralization").

50 But techniques do not concern us here. What matters is that there should be both adequate opportunities and fair assurance that you will be eligible and considered for promotion. Let me repeat: to be promoted is not essential, either to happiness or to usefulness. To be considered for promotion is.

Your Life off the Job

51 I have only one more thing to say: to be an employee it is not enough that the job be right and that you be right for the job. It is also necessary that you have a meaningful life outside the job.

52 I am talking of having a genuine interest in something in which

you, on your own, can be, if not a master, at least an amateur expert. This something may be botany, or the history of your county, or chamber music, cabinetmaking, Christmas tree growing, or a thousand other things. But it is important in this "employee society" of ours to have a genuine interest outside of the job and to be serious about it.

53   I am not, as you might suspect, thinking of something that will keep you alive and interested during your retirement. I am speaking of keeping yourself alive, interested, and happy during your working life, and of a permanent source of self-respect and standing in the community outside and beyond your job. You will need such an interest when you hit the forties, that period in which most of us come to realize that we will never reach the goals we have set ourselves when younger — whether these are goals of achievement or of worldly success. You will need it because you should have one area in which you yourself impose standards of performance on your own work. Finally, you need it because you will find recognition and acceptance by other people working in the field, whether professional or amateur, as individuals rather than as members of an organization and as employees.

54   This is heretical philosophy these days when so many companies believe that the best employee is the man who lives, drinks, eats, and sleeps job and company. In actual experience those people who have no life outside their jobs are not the really successful people, not even from the viewpoint of the company. I have seen far too many of them shoot up like a rocket, because they had no interests except the job; but they also come down like the rocket's burned-out stick. The man who will make the greatest contribution to his company is the mature person — and you cannot have maturity if you have no life or interest outside the job. Our large companies are beginning to understand this. That so many of them encourage people to have "outside interests" or to develop "hobbies" as a preparation for retirement is the first sign of a change toward a more intelligent attitude. But quite apart from the self-interest of the employer, your own interest as an employee demands that you develop a major outside interest. It will make you happier, it will make you more effective, it will give you resistance against the setbacks and the blows that are the lot of everyone; and it will

make you a more effective, a more successful, and a more mature employee.

55 You have no doubt realized that I have not really talked about how to be an employee. I have talked about what to know before becoming an employee — which is something quite different. Perhaps "how to be an employee" can be learned only by being one. But one thing can be said. Being an employee means working with people; it means living and working in a society. Intelligence, in the last analysis, is therefore not the most important quality. What is decisive is character and integrity. If you work on your own, intelligence and ability may be sufficient. If you work with people you are going to fail unless you also have basic integrity. And integrity — character — is the one thing most, if not all, employers consider first.

56 There are many skills you might learn to be an employee, many abilities that are required. But fundamentally the one quality demanded of you will not be skill, knowledge, or talent, but character.

QUESTIONS FOR REFLECTION, DISCUSSION, OR WRITING

(1) Do you think this author himself has both "skill in expression" and "something to say in the first place" (par. 10)? Discuss, using specific illustrations from his writing to show what you mean.

(2) Where and how, if at all, does he use division and classification (see p. 8) in his exposition?

(3) How do you feel about Drucker's flat, unqualified statement that the "one basic skill [which students can learn in college] is the ability to organize and express ideas in writing and speaking" (par. 7)? How basic do you think this skill will be in your particular future work? Explain.

(4) In what ways can the even more "basic skill" of efficient and discriminating *reading* benefit a person's writing and speaking? Why do you suppose the author did not mention this?

(5) Discuss his rather surprising advice to take courses in writing poetry and short stories (par. 12). Can you see any benefit to the average future employee in such writing — or do you think it might even prove harmful? Explain.

(6) Do you agree that there is "a great deal to be said for being fired from the first job" (par. 38)? Perhaps in your own experience or circle of acquaintances there are examples which will help to form or demonstrate your opinion.

(7) Do you agree that to be a successful employee one must have a "meaningful life outside the job" (par. 51)? Or is it better to be so devoted to the job that one "lives and breathes" his work? Discuss Drucker's theory, again using real-life examples whenever possible.

(8) After studying again the "four decisions" a prospective employee should make (beginning with par. 15), carefully analyze yourself in relation to each piece of advice, then make your own tentative decision concerning each. A statement of your decisions and an explanation of your reasons (for all four or, perhaps, for only the most significant one) can provide a worthwhile topic for composition.

(9) Elaborate on Drucker's final statement that "fundamentally the one quality demanded of you will not be skill, knowledge, or talent, but character." Define "character" fully, as you think he is using it. Explain the *various* ways in which this quality might be particularly valuable to an employer.

Aldous Huxley
THE SHAPE OF THINGS IN 1986

ALDOUS HUXLEY, *member of an illustrious British family, is an author-philosopher now living in Los Angeles. He has written occasional magazine articles and engaged in various other forms of journalism. A few of his many well known books are* Brave New World, After Many a Summer Dies the Swan, Ape and Essence, The Genius and the Goddess, *and* Tomorrow and Tomorrow and Tomorrow. *Mr. Huxley has been the recipient of several awards, including that of the American Academy of Arts and Letters in 1959.*

TRUE *Magazine published "The Shape of Things in 1986" as a feature of its 25th anniversary issue in February 1961. This magazine for men, which now sells at the rate of about 2,300,000 copies a month, is published by the Fawcett Publishing Company (also owners of a spectacular array of other magazines:* True Police Cases, Startling Detective, Cavalier, Electronics Illustrated, Mechanix Illustrated, Motion Picture, True Confessions, *and* Woman's Day).

THE SHAPE OF THINGS IN 1986, *although an opinion piece, is expository in presentation. The author remains almost completely **objective** in his viewpoint, only occasionally permitting his own feelings to show through. As you read, notice the "structure" of the essay, the orderly classification and development of ideas. (Orderliness in any expository writing is desirable, of course; at the very least, it seems to reflect an author's respect and consideration for his readers.)*

1 MOST PROPHECY tends to oscillate between an extreme of gloom and the wildest optimism. The world, according to one set of seers, is headed for disaster; according to the others, the world is destined, within a generation or two, to become a kind of gigantic Disneyland, in which the human race will find perpetual happiness playing with an endless assortment of ever more ingenious mechanical toys.

2 When *True* asked me to take a look into the future for them, I decided to take a middle course. Like an accountant, I shall set forth the main items on the future's debit side and, over against them, its principal assets and credits. In the light of this record of coming profits and losses, it may be possible to guess where we shall stand twenty-five years from now.

3 The first and by far the most formidable item in the debit column is a huge biological fact — the current explosive increase in population. At the time of the birth of Christ the total number of people on our planet was probably about two hundred and fifty millions — the estimated population of the USA alone in 1986. When the Pilgrim Fathers landed, world population was about five hundred millions. Today there are almost three billions of us and there is every indication that, by the end of the present century, there will be six billions.

4 It is against the background of this unprecedented biological fact that the dramas of man's political, economic and social life are destined to be played. The most obvious danger confronting us is, of course, atomic war, and the most obvious causes of war are ideological fanaticism and the tradition of nationalism, with their corollaries of power politics, armament races and the balance of terror. But beneath these political and ideological causes of war lie deeper causes, and they spring from this exploding population and the ever-increasing pressure of numbers upon resources.

5 But before discussing these deep-seated causes of war, let me take a brief look at the United States in 1986. If good times and the current rate of increase are maintained, our population will be in the neighborhood of two hundred and fifty million. Nearly

one third of these people will live in the ten super-cities of Miami-Palm Beach, Washington-Baltimore, Philadelphia, New York, Boston, Cleveland, Detroit, Chicago, San Francisco and Los Angeles.

6 New York will have about twenty million inhabitants in 1986, Los Angeles more than fifteen million, Chicago about ten million, and so on down the line to the baby super-cities with no more than six or seven million. How will the traffic problems of these super-cities be handled? What will be the long-range effects of an environment that insulates a third of all children from any direct contact with nature and, when they grow up, makes them members of gigantic agglomerations of anonymous individuals with a helpless sense, in spite of the vote and democratic institutions, that they no longer control their own destinies?

7 America is a huge, rich and highly developed country, and while the fairly rapid population growth of the next twenty-five years will certainly cause a good deal of inconvenience, it will not be disastrous for us; nor will it increase the probability of war.

8 In the underdeveloped regions of the world, a very different state of affairs will prevail. Most countries in Asia, Africa and Latin America are increasing their populations at the rate of about two per cent a year. Some of them show an annual increase of three per cent — which means that their population will double in less than twenty-five years. The present very low standard of living in these countries can be maintained only if there is an annual increase of agricultural and industrial production of two or three per cent. If the standard is to be significantly raised, the increase of production must be at least four or five per cent per annum, and this increase will have to be kept up over a long period. All of the underdeveloped countries will find it difficult, and many may find it impossible, to achieve this.

9 Additionally, their mushrooming population will bring new problems in the educational field, health and social security programs, in housing and slum clearance. This means that, for the majority of the world's people, the next twenty-five years will be years of the bitterest disappointment. All of them will have won their political independence, but they will find that nationalism

and independence are no cure for poverty, illiteracy and bad government.

10 Frustration will breed social unrest at home and envious hatred of more prosperous nations abroad. Social unrest will culminate in chaos or revolution. Chaos and revolution will give place to dictatorships associated either with some kind of native fascism or, more probably, with international Communism.

11 So much for the major item on the debit side of the ledger. Let us now consider a few of the other unpleasant facts that will confront us. Perhaps the most unpleasant of these is the fact of Communist China. By 1986 China's population will be approaching the truly appalling figure of eleven hundred million. Most of these people will be no better off than the six hundred million living in Communist China today. But though consumer goods will be scarce, heavy industry will be highly developed. By means of forced labor and well directed planning an underdeveloped country is now able (with some help from highly industrialized countries abroad) to create an up-to-date armament industry and so to transform itself, within a couple of decades, into a first-class military power. A nation of more than a billion impoverished, passionately nationalistic and systematically indoctrinated people, with a government, in Mr. Nehru's words, less interested in peace than any other, and equipped with all the machinery of modern war, including in all probability the H-bomb, will represent for its near neighbors and the rest of the world the most menacing of dangers.

12 It may well be that, by 1986, the Soviet rulers will have officially admitted that danger. Within the next twenty-five years Russia may well have taken its place in the community of highly developed Western nations, leagued to defend themselves against the huge Have-Not Leviathan of the Orient. Meanwhile goodness only knows what Chinese imperialism in search of power, glory and *lebensraum* may choose to do.

13 Let us now turn to a less ominous and more exciting realm, and hazard a few guesses. By 1986 atomic power will be largely used wherever conventional fuels are scarce. In Britain, for example, domestic supplies of coal are almost exhausted. Twenty-five years from now atomic reactors will be supplying much of the power re-

quired to keep British industry running. In this country, with its huge resources in natural gas, petroleum and coal, the percentage of power produced by atomic reactors will be smaller than in parts of Europe and in such fuel-poor Asian countries as India.

14   Physicists in America, Britain and Russia are now working intensively on the problem of nuclear fusion. Can the H-bomb be tamed and set to work for the benefit of mankind? The difficulties are enormous, but they may be soluble. Whether they will have been solved by the year 1986 is anybody's guess.

15   And what about Space? By 1986 man will undoubtedly have landed on the moon and perhaps on Mars. But long before that space vehicles loaded with instruments will have brought back a great deal of information about our satellite and the nearer planets.

16   Of more practical importance will be the information supplied by space vehicles about our own planet. For example, we shall soon know far more about the world's weather than we know today. In the light of this new knowledge we may be able not merely to forecast, but even to control the weather.

17   The distinction between scientific and technological developments that profoundly affect ordinary life and those which do not, is useful and important. Some of the most science fiction-like discoveries and inventions of the next twenty-five years will leave most human lives almost unaffected. For example, commercial planes flying at three times the speed of sound will be spectacular; but they will not significantly change the general pattern of human life. Stepping up the speed of jet liners will produce no revolution comparable to that brought about by the original development of efficient flying machines.

18   Similarly the enormous changes in family life and social arrangements brought about by the mass production of automobiles, household appliances, radios and TV sets were initiated years ago. The development of gas turbines for cars, of ultrasonic washing machines and diathermic kitchen stoves, of TV in color and three dimensions, will represent a succession of spectacular advances. But these advances will not make a new revolution in human life comparable to that which was brought about by the relatively primitive cars, appliances and electronic devices of the past.

19   In the biological field we shall see advances that will affect human

life profoundly and in many ways. Using electron beams to produce controlled mutations, geneticists will create new varieties of plants for all kinds of special purposes. Many species of fungi, algae and bacteria will be domesticated, selectively bred and set to work producing starches, fats and proteins, or performing those fantastic feats of chemical transformation and synthesis, of which, up till now, natural organisms alone are capable.

20   In the medical field basic research in the life history of cells may help us to understand why some organisms develop malignant tumors and why all grow old and die. Twenty-five years from now there may be practical methods for preventing cancer and slowing down the aging process. (Let us hope, by that time, that an efficient and cheap birth-control pill will be on the market. If it isn't, these new techniques of death control will merely make it a little more difficult to solve the population problem.)

21   Meanwhile the pharmacologists will be hard at work. New "miracle drugs" will control the degenerative diseases which are the bane of aging populations. Even more revolutionary will be the coming discoveries of new mind-modifying and mood-changing drugs. Virtually non-toxic psychic energizers will make it possible for a man to become more alert, more capable of sustained attention and prolonged intellectual effort. Virtually non-toxic euphorics will transform depression and apathy into cheerfulness. Virtually non-toxic tranquillizers will turn hostility into kindliness. And along with these there will be virtually non-toxic evokers of visions, transfigurers of reality.

22   Men have always felt the need for chemical mind-modifiers and mood-changers, but up till now they have had to be content with such unreliable and dangerous drugs as opium and alcohol. Twenty-five years from now vodka and whisky may have been taken off the list of permitted drugs. Their places will have been taken, perhaps, by chemical substances which are more effective, less prejudicial to health and less liable to result in traffic accidents and crimes of violence.

23   From bio-chemistry we pass now to electronics and engineering. Among the developments in this field there are two which will undoubtedly exercise an enormous influence on human life during the next twenty-five years. Electronic computers are steadily grow-

ing bigger and better. (When new models are built that will work at the temperature of liquid helium, they will become smaller and better, far more complex and brain-like.) Among many other things, these improved thinking machines will permit us to forecast the consequences of any given course of action as it is likely to be affected by varying circumstances.

24   By 1986 it may have become possible to conduct the affairs of nations and indeed of the whole human race in a completely rational manner. Whether we shall take advantage of this possibility is another question. Being reasonable is dull, and most people find more enjoyment in prejudice, hatred and collective frenzy than in cool negotiation, democratic compromise and tolerance. The probability, I fear, is that our ends will be chosen for us by our passions and conditioned reflexes.

25   And here is another development which is destined to affect the pattern of living in many ways: automation. Automation will spread in factories and offices, not in the service industries. Barbers, manicurists, attorneys and undertakers will never be replaced by tape-controlled machines. But these devices and a host of electronic gadgets will undoubtedly replace many industrial workers, clerks and secretaries. To create jobs for these victims of technological unemployment, and at the same time to maintain purchasing power, it will be necessary to shorten work hours in every field, but without reducing salaries.

26   One of the major consequences of automation will be a considerable increase, for everybody except the mothers of young children, in leisure time. Leisure has its problems. Sex, drinking, looking at TV, watching other people play games and even playing games oneself are not enough. Something more purposeful and constructive is required to make leisure tolerable. The current do-it-yourself movement represents a first spontaneous and still rudimentary effort to find a solution for the problems of leisure. By 1986 this movement will probably have won social recognition, and appropriate education will have transformed our haphazard do-it-yourselfism into a movement of creative artisanship. Machines will produce the necessities of industrial civilization and do most of the routine work, leaving human beings free to use their minds and hands in craftsmanship, in mechanical tinkering and invention, in

the practice of an art either as a means of communication or, where there is no special talent, as a form of occupational therapy.

27   Ours may be an alarming world; but it is most certainly not a dull one. The next twenty-five years will confront mankind with difficult problems and enormous dangers, but they will also bring unprecedented opportunities. Will the books of our future destiny be balanced? Shall we emerge, after twenty-five years, in the black? Or will the debits of our biological and political situation out-weigh all our credits of wisdom and scientific knowledge, leaving us worse off in 1986 than we are in 1961?

28   All I will venture to answer is that we have enough intelligence and good will — if we will only use them — to overcome all our difficulties. Meanwhile let us never forget that time is against us. If 1986 is to be a good year, we must work fast and hard, beginning right now in 1961.

QUESTIONS FOR REFLECTION, DISCUSSION, OR WRITING

(1) Can you suggest anything the rest of the world can do as protection against the "Have-Not Leviathan of the Orient" (pars. 11-12)? Explain Huxley's metaphor. (It is also an *allusion,* to be discussed on page 207.)

(2) Explain what he means by "virtually non-toxic evokers of visions" (par. 21). Do you think such "evokers" represent progress?

(3) Would you like to see vodka and whisky taken off the market and replaced by safer and more effective "mind-modifiers and mood-changers" (par. 22) — perhaps in the form of pills or capsules? Why, or why not?

(4) If frustration and chaos in underdeveloped countries will be caused by population increases that are greater than agricultural and industrial increases (pars. 8-10; also refer to the still stronger threat expressed in par. 11 of "A Force of Youth as a Force for Peace"), then is there any solution other than birth control? What plans are underway now for prosperous countries to help these "have-nots" increase production and solve problems in "the educational field, health and social security programs, in housing and slum clearance"? How effective do you think this help can be?

(5) What are the greatest objections or drawbacks to the use of birth control to curb the world's "exploding population"? (As a good exercise in self-discipline, try to be completely *objective* in answering this question.)

(6) In paragraph 6, Huxley leaves some questions unanswered. Can you suggest ways in which the traffic problems of the "super-cities" may be handled?

(7) Another unanswered question concerns the long-range effects of super-city environment on children. First, study the question itself and be sure you understand its implications. Then try to answer it — and your answer can make an excellent small essay.

(8) Do you agree with Huxley's thesis (par. 24) that "being reasonable is dull, and most people find more enjoyment in prejudice, hatred and collective frenzy than in cool negotiation"? In providing a sensible and honest answer to this question, look first inward at yourself, then outward to your personal acquaintances, then at what you know of the conduct of national and world affairs. This answer, too, properly organized and well supported by examples, should be a good composition.

(9) Huxley concludes with the *subjective* admonition that "if 1986 is to be a good year, we must work fast and hard, beginning right now." What, if anything, can you do — right now — to help make 1986 a "good year"? Explain fully.

＊
＊

EXPLORING THE PAST

＊
＊
＊
＊
＊
＊
＊
＊
＊
＊
＊
＊
＊
＊
＊
＊
＊
＊
＊
＊
＊
＊
＊
＊
＊
＊
＊

Rachel Carson

MOTHER SEA: THE GRAY BEGINNINGS

RACHEL CARSON, *a native Pennsylvanian, is a member of the staff of the U.S. Fish and Wildlife Service and lives in Silver Spring, Md. She has received numerous science awards and is famous for a highly developed ability which many other scientists lack: the ability to explain technical information in language the average layman can understand. Three of her successful books are* Under the Sea Wind, The Sea Around Us, *and* The Edge of the Sea.

MOTHER SEA: THE GRAY BEGINNINGS *is the first chapter of the "best-seller"* The Sea Around Us. *The author, whose job here is essentially one of exposition, makes such skillful and constant use of two other basic types of writing (narration and description — no argumentation), interweaving them with her explanation, that they seem to be all one fabric.*

*She also uses various minor techniques in making her meanings vivid to the
non-scientist, and one of these is **personification**. This is a third kind of
figure of speech (see p. 15), really a special type of metaphor but usually classified as a "figure" in its own right. Personification, too, is used to convey
short, imaginative impressions — but by giving* inanimate *things the qualities
or powers of a person in order to describe their function or appearance.
("Mother Sea" itself is an example, as is "our planet's birth," par. 2.)*

> And the earth was without form, and void; and
> darkness was upon the face of the deep.
>
> — GENESIS

1   BEGINNINGS are apt to be shadowy, and so it is with the beginnings of the great mother of life, the sea. Many people have
debated how and when the earth got its ocean, and it is not surprising that their explanations do not always agree. For the plain
and inescapable truth is that no one was there to see, and in the
absence of eyewitness accounts there is bound to be a certain amount
of disagreement. So if I tell here the story of how the young planet
Earth acquired an ocean, it must be a story pieced together from
many sources and containing many whole chapters the details of
which we can only imagine. The story is founded on the testimony
of the earth's most ancient rocks, which were young when the
earth was young; on other evidence written on the face of the earth's
satellite, the moon; and on hints contained in the history of the sun
and the whole universe of star-filled space. For although no man
was there to witness this cosmic birth, the stars and the moon and
the rocks were there, and, indeed, had much to do with the fact
that there is an ocean.

2   The events of which I write must have occurred somewhat more
than 2 billion years ago. As nearly as science can tell that is the approximate age of the earth, and the ocean must be very nearly as old.
It is possible now to discover the age of the rocks that compose the
crust of the earth by measuring the rate of decay of the radioactive
materials they contain. The oldest rocks found anywhere on earth —
in Manitoba — are about 2.3 billion years old. Allowing 100 million
years or so for the cooling of the earth's materials to form a rocky
crust, we arrive at the supposition that the tempestuous and violent

events connected with our planet's birth occurred nearly 2½ billion years ago. But this is only a minimum estimate, for rocks indicating an even greater age may be found at any time.

3   The new earth, freshly torn from its parent sun, was a ball of whirling gases, intensely hot, rushing through the black spaces of the universe on a path and at a speed controlled by immense forces. Gradually the ball of flaming gases cooled. The gases began to liquefy, and Earth became a molten mass. The materials of this mass eventually became sorted out in a definite pattern: the heaviest in the center, the less heavy surrounding them, and the least heavy forming the outer rim. This is the pattern which persists today — a central sphere of molten iron, very nearly as hot as it was 2 billion years ago, an intermediate sphere of semi-plastic basalt, and a hard outer shell, relatively quite thin and composed of solid basalt and granite.

4   The outer shell of the young earth must have been a good many millions of years changing from the liquid to the solid state, and it is believed that, before this change was completed, an event of the greatest importance took place — the formation of the moon. The next time you stand on a beach at night, watching the moon's bright path across the water, and conscious of the moon-drawn tides, remember that the moon itself may have been born of a great tidal wave of earthly substance, torn off into space. And remember that if the moon was formed in this fashion, the event may have had much to do with shaping the ocean basins and the continents as we know them.

5   There were tides in the new earth, long before there was an ocean. In response to the pull of the sun the molten liquids of the earth's whole surface rose in tides that rolled unhindered around the globe and only gradually slackened and diminished as the earthly shell cooled, congealed and hardened. Those who believe that the moon is a child of earth say that during an early stage of the earth's development something happened that caused this rolling, viscid tide to gather speed and momentum and to rise to unimaginable heights. Apparently the force that created these greatest tides the earth has ever known was the force of resonance, for at this time the period of the solar tides had come to approach, then equal, the period of the free oscillation of the liquid earth. And so every sun tide was

given increased momentum by the push of the earth's oscillation, and each of the twice-daily tides was larger than the one before it. Physicists have calculated that, after 500 years of such monstrous, steadily increasing tides, those on the side toward the sun became too high for stability, and a great wave was torn away and hurled into space. But immediately, of course, the newly created satellite became subject to physical laws that sent it spinning in an orbit of its own about the earth. This is what we call the moon.

6   There are reasons for believing that this event took place after the earth's crust had become slightly hardened, instead of during its partly liquid state. There is to this day a great scar on the surface of the globe. This scar or depression holds the Pacific Ocean. According to some geophysicists, the floor of the Pacific is composed of basalt, the substance of the earth's middle layer, while all other oceans are floored with a thin layer of granite, which makes up most of the earth's outer layer. We immediately wonder what became of the Pacific's granite covering and the most convenient assumption is that it was torn away when the moon was formed. There is supporting evidence. The mean density of the moon is much less than that of the earth (3.3 compared with 5.5), suggesting that the moon took away none of the earth's heavy core, but that it is composed only of the granite and some of the basalt of the outer layers.

7   The birth of the moon probably helped shape other regions of the world's ocean besides the Pacific. When part of the crust was torn away, strains must have been set up in the remaining granite envelope. Perhaps the granite mass cracked open on the side opposite the moon scar. Perhaps, as the earth spun on its axis and rushed on its orbit through space, the cracks widened and the masses of granite began to drift apart, moving over a tarry, slowly hardening layer of basalt. Gradually the outer portions of the basalt layer became solid and the wandering continents came to rest, frozen into place with oceans between them. In spite of theories to the contrary, the weight of geologic evidence seems to be that the locations of the major ocean basins and the major continental land masses are today much the same as they have been since a very early period of the earth's history.

8   But this is to anticipate the story, for when the moon was born there was no ocean. The gradually cooling earth was enveloped in

heavy layers of cloud, which contained much of the water of the new planet. For a long time its surface was so hot that no moisture could fall without immediately being reconverted to steam. This dense, perpetually renewed cloud covering must have been thick enough that no rays of sunlight could penetrate it. And so the rough outlines of the continents and the empty ocean basins were sculptured out of the surface of the earth in darkness, in a Stygian world of heated rock and swirling clouds and gloom.

9   As soon as the earth's crust cooled enough, the rains began to fall. Never have there been such rains since that time. They fell continuously, day and night, days passing into months, into years, into centuries. They poured into the waiting ocean basins, or, falling upon the continental masses, drained away to become sea.

10   That primeval ocean, growing in bulk as the rains slowly filled its basins, must have been only faintly salt. But the falling rains were the symbol of the dissolution of the continents. From the moment the rains began to fall, the lands began to be worn away and carried to the sea. It is an endless, inexorable process that has never stopped — the dissolving of the rocks, the leaching out of their contained minerals, the carrying of the rock fragments and dissolved minerals to the ocean. And over the eons of time, the sea has grown ever more bitter with the salt of the continents.

11   In what manner the sea produced the mysterious and wonderful stuff called protoplasm we cannot say. In its warm, dimly lit waters the unknown conditions of temperature and pressure and saltiness must have been the critical ones for the creation of life from nonlife. At any rate they produced the result that neither the alchemists with their crucibles nor modern scientists in their laboratories have been able to achieve.

12   Before the first living cell was created, there may have been many trials and failures. It seems probable that, within the warm saltiness of the primeval sea, certain organic substances were fashioned from carbon dioxide, sulphur, nitrogen, phosphorus, potassium, and calcium. Perhaps these were transition steps from which the complex molecules of protoplasm arose — molecules that somehow acquired the ability to reproduce themselves and begin the endless stream of life. But at present no one is wise enough to be sure.

13   Those first living things may have been simple microorganisms

rather like some of the bacteria we know today — mysterious border-line forms that were not quite plants, not quite animals, barely over the intangible line that separates the non-living from the living. It is doubtful that this first life possessed the substance chlorophyll, with which plants in sunlight transform lifeless chemicals into the living stuff of their tissues. Little sunshine could enter their dim world, penetrating the cloud banks from which fell the endless rains. Probably the sea's first children lived on the organic substances then present in the ocean waters, or, like the iron and sulphur bacteria that exist today, lived directly on inorganic food.

14   All the while the cloud cover was thinning, the darkness of the nights alternated with palely illumined days, and finally the sun for the first time shone through upon the sea. By this time some of the living things that floated in the sea must have developed the magic of chlorophyll. Now they were able to take the carbon dioxide of the air and the water of the sea and of these elements, in sunlight, build the organic substances they needed. So the first true plants came into being.

15   Another group of organisms, lacking the chlorophyll but needing organic food, found they could make a way of life for themselves by devouring the plants. So the first animals arose, and from that day to this, every animal in the world has followed the habit it learned in the ancient seas and depends, directly or through complex food chains, on the plants for food and life.

16   As the years passed, and the centuries, and the millions of years, the stream of life grew more and more complex. From simple, one-celled creatures, others that were aggregations of specialized cells arose, and then creatures with organs for feeding, digesting, breath-ing, reproducing. Sponges grew on the rocky bottom of the sea's edge and coral animals built their habitations in warm, clear waters. Jellyfish swam and drifted in the sea. Worms evolved, and starfish, and hard-shelled creatures with many-jointed legs, the arthropods. The plants, too, progressed, from the microscopic algae to branched and curiously fruiting seaweeds that swayed with the tides and were plucked from the coastal rocks by the surf and cast adrift.

17   During all this time the continents had no life. There was little to induce living things to come ashore, forsaking their all-providing, all-embracing mother sea. The lands must have been bleak and

hostile beyond the power of words to describe. Imagine a whole continent of naked rock, across which no covering mantle of green had been drawn — a continent without soil, for there were no plants to aid in its formation and bind it to the rocks with their roots. Imagine a land of stone, a silent land, except for the sound of the rains and winds that swept across it. For there was no living voice, and no living thing moved over the surface of the rocks.

18   Meanwhile, the gradual cooling of the planet, which had first given the earth its hard granite crust, was progressing into its deeper layers; and as the interior slowly cooled and contracted, it drew away from the outer shell. This shell, accommodating itself to the shrinking sphere within it, fell into folds and wrinkles — the earth's first mountain ranges.

19   Geologists tell us that there must have been at least two periods of mountain building (often called "revolutions") in that dim period, so long ago that the rocks have no record of it, so long ago that the mountains themselves have long since been worn away. Then there came a third great period of upheaval and readjustment of the earth's crust, about a billion years ago, but of all its majestic mountains the only reminders today are the Laurentian hills of eastern Canada, and a great shield of granite over the flat country around Hudson Bay.

20   The epochs of mountain building only served to speed up the processes of erosion by which continents were worn down and their crumbling rock and contained minerals returned to the sea. The uplifted masses of the mountains were prey to the bitter cold of the upper atmosphere and under the attacks of frost and snow and ice the rocks cracked and crumbled away. The rains beat with greater violence upon the slopes of the hills and carried away the substance of the mountains in torrential streams. There was still no plant covering to modify and resist the power of the rains.

21   And in the sea, life continued to evolve. The earliest forms have left no fossils by which we can identify them. Probably they were soft-bodied, with no hard parts that could be preserved. Then, too, the rock layers formed in those early days have since been so altered by enormous heat and pressure, under the foldings of the earth's crust, that any fossils they might have contained would have been destroyed.

22   For the past 500 million years, however, the rocks have preserved
the fossil record. By the dawn of the Cambrian period, when the history of living things was first inscribed on rock pages, life in the sea
had progressed so far that all the main groups of backboneless or in-
vertebrate animals had been developed. But there were no animals
with backbones, no insects or spiders, and still no plant or animal
had been evolved that was capable of venturing onto the forbidding
land. So for more than three-fourths of geologic time the continents
were desolate and uninhabited, while the sea prepared the life that
was later to invade them and make them habitable. Meanwhile, with
violent tremblings of the earth and with the fire and smoke of roaring volcanoes, mountains rose and wore away, glaciers moved to and
fro over the earth, and the sea crept over the continents and again
receded.

23   It was not until Silurian time, some 350 million years ago, that the
first pioneer of land life crept out on the shore. It was an arthropod,
one of the great tribe that later produced crabs and lobsters and insects. It must have been something like a modern scorpion, but, unlike some of its descendants, it never wholly severed the ties that
united it to the sea. It lived a strange life, half-terrestrial, half-aquatic,
something like that of the ghost crabs that speed along the beaches
today, now and then dashing into the surf to moisten their gills.

24   Fish, tapered of body and stream-molded by the press of running
waters, were evolving in Silurian rivers. In times of drought, in the
drying pools and lagoons, the shortage of oxygen forced them to develop swim bladders for the storage of air. One form that possessed
an air-breathing lung was able to survive the dry periods by burying
itself in mud, leaving a passage to the surface through which it
breathed.

25   It is very doubtful that the animals alone would have succeeded
in colonizing the land, for only the plants had the power to bring
about the first amelioration of its harsh conditions. They helped
make soil of the crumbling rocks, they held back the soil from the
rains that would have swept it away, and little by little they softened
and subdued the bare rock, the lifeless desert. We know very little
about the first land plants, but they must have been closely related
to some of the larger seaweeds that had learned to live in the coastal
shallows, developing strengthened stems and grasping, rootlike hold-

fasts to resist the drag and pull of the waves. Perhaps it was in some coastal lowlands, periodically drained and flooded, that some such plants found it possible to survive, though separated from the sea. This also seems to have taken place in the Silurian period.

26   The mountains that had been thrown up by the Laurentian revolution gradually wore away, and as the sediments were washed from their summits and deposited on the lowlands, great areas of the continents sank under the load. The seas crept out of their basins and spread over the lands. Life fared well and was exceedingly abundant in those shallow, sunlit seas. But with the later retreat of the ocean water into the deeper basins, many creatures must have been left stranded in shallow, landlocked bays. Some of these animals found means to survive on land. The lakes, the shores of the rivers, and the coastal swamps of those days were the testing grounds in which plants and animals either became adapted to the new conditions or perished.

27   As the lands rose and the seas receded, a strange fishlike creature emerged on the land, and over the thousands of years its fins became legs, and instead of gills it developed lungs. In the Devonian sandstone this first amphibian left its footprint.

28   On land and sea the stream of life poured on. New forms evolved; some old ones declined and disappeared. On land the mosses and the ferns and the seed plants developed. The reptiles for a time dominated the earth, gigantic, grotesque, and terrifying. Birds learned to live and move in the ocean of air. The first small mammals lurked inconspicuously in hidden crannies of the earth as though in fear of the reptiles.

29   When they went ashore the animals that took up a land life carried with them a part of the sea in their bodies, a heritage which they passed on to their children and which even today links each land animal with its origin in the ancient sea. Fish, amphibian, and reptile, warm-blooded bird and mammal — each of us carries in our veins a salty stream in which the elements sodium, potassium, and calcium are combined in almost the same proportions as in sea water. This is our inheritance from the day, untold millions of years ago, when a remote ancestor, having progressed from the one-celled to the many-celled stage, first developed a circulatory system in which the fluid was merely the water of the sea. In the same way,

our lime-hardened skeletons are a heritage from the calcium-rich ocean of Cambrian time. Even the protoplasm that streams within each cell of our bodies has the chemical structure impressed upon all living matter when the first simple creatures were brought forth in the ancient sea. And as life itself began in the sea, so each of us begins his individual life in a miniature ocean within his mother's womb, and in the stages of his embryonic development repeats the steps by which his race evolved, from gill-breathing inhabitants of a water world to creatures able to live on land.

30   Some of the land animals later returned to the ocean. After perhaps 50 million years of land life, a number of reptiles entered the sea about 170 million years ago, in the Triassic period. They were huge and formidable creatures. Some had oarlike limbs by which they rowed through the water; some were web-footed, with long, serpentine necks. These grotesque monsters disappeared millions of year ago, but we remember them when we come upon a large sea turtle swimming many miles at sea, its barnacle-encrusted shell eloquent of its marine life. Much later, perhaps no more than 50 million years ago, some of the mammals, too, abandoned a land life for the ocean. Their descendants are the sea lions, seals, sea elephants, and whales of today.

31   Among the land mammals there was a race of creatures that took to an arboreal existence. Their hands underwent remarkable development, becoming skilled in manipulating and examining objects, and along with this skill came a superior brain power that compensated for what these comparatively small mammals lacked in strength. At last, perhaps somewhere in the vast interior of Asia, they descended from the trees and became again terrestrial. The past million years have seen their transformation into beings with the body and brain and spirit of man.

32   Eventually man, too, found his way back to the sea. Standing on its shores, he must have looked out upon it with wonder and curiosity, compounded with an unconscious recognition of his lineage. He could not physically re-enter the ocean as the seals and whales had done. But over the centuries, with all the skill and ingenuity and reasoning powers of his mind, he has sought to explore and investigate even its most remote parts, so that he might re-enter it mentally and imaginatively.

33 He built boats to venture out on its surface. Later he found ways to descend to the shallow parts of its floor, carrying with him the air that, as a land mammal long unaccustomed to aquatic life, he needed to breathe. Moving in fascination over the deep sea he could not enter, he found ways to probe its depths, he let down nets to capture its life, he invented mechanical eyes and ears that could re-create for his senses a world long lost, but a world that, in the deepest part of his subconscious mind, he had never wholly forgotten.

34 And yet he has returned to his mother sea only on her own terms. He cannot control or change the ocean as, in his brief tenancy of earth, he has subdued and plundered the continents. In the artificial world of his cities and towns, he often forgets the true nature of his planet and the long vistas of its history, in which the existence of the race of men has occupied a mere moment of time. The sense of all these things comes to him most clearly in the course of a long ocean voyage, when he watches day after day the receding rim of the horizon, ridged and furrowed by waves; when at night he becomes aware of the earth's rotation as the stars pass overhead; or when, alone in this world of water and sky, he feels the loneliness of his earth in space. And then, as never on land, he knows the truth that his world is a water world, a planet dominated by its covering mantle of ocean, in which the continents are but transient intrusions of land above the surface of the all-encircling sea.

QUESTIONS FOR REFLECTION, DISCUSSION, OR WRITING

(1) What do you think was Miss Carson's primary purpose in writing "Mother Sea . . ."? How well did she achieve this purpose? Was it worthwhile?

(2) The book from which this section was taken has been sold to many thousands (and perhaps read by millions) of ordinary people with no greater scientific background than yours. Apparently the average layman finds it quite readable. Do you? If so, try to analyze how Miss Carson has achieved readability with such a complicated scientific subject. If not, try to discover, in the essay or in yourself, just what caused the trouble.

(3) Locate as many examples of *personification* as you can find in "Mother Sea . . ." With what human function do most of them compare, figuratively,

the beginnings of the world? Does this seem to you an appropriate and useful choice of personification? Explain.

(4) Consider the quotation from the Biblical book of Genesis with which Miss Carson begins her essay. Do you consider this fitting, inasmuch as Genesis is devoted to the *creation* of the Earth and its creatures — by God — in "six days"?

(5) Can you reconcile the modern scientific explanation of the "gray beginnings" with the creation-beliefs of your own religion? If so, how? If not, then is atheism the only answer? (Don't be surprised if your instructor declines, in the classroom at least, to become involved in the matter!)

Nathaniel Benchley

THE $24 SWINDLE

NATHANIEL BENCHLEY, *former newspaper reporter and* Newsweek *drama critic, is a son of the famous humorist Robert Benchley and a successful novelist, playright, and essayist in his own right. His literary works include* Side Street *and* One to Grow On, *both novels;* The Frogs in Spring, *a play;* Robert Benchley, *a biography; and* The Great American Pastime, *a motion picture. He is a native of Manhattan, the island he writes about in this selection.*

AMERICAN HERITAGE, *the first publisher of "The $24 Swindle," in December 1959, is a bi-monthly book-magazine subtitled "The Magazine of History." Published in New York since 1954, beautifully illustrated and carefully authentic in subject matter, it is sponsored by two distinguished historical societies: the American Association for State and Local History, and the Society of American Historians.*

THE $24 SWINDLE *uses a tongue-in-cheek type of humor in giving the author's account of this historical event. Such a combination of history and humor could easily be crude, in poor taste. Your opinion of Benchley's success, then, should tell you a great deal about his ability as a writer. Forget about the more or less serious reading you have been doing so far and relax for this one.*

1   BY NOW it is probably too late to do anything about it, but the unsettling fact remains that the so-called sale of Manhattan Island to the Dutch in 1626 was a totally illegal deal; a group of Brooklyn Indians perpetrated the swindle, and they had no more right to sell Manhattan Island than the present mayor of White Plains would have to declare war on France. When the Manhattan Indians

found out about it they were understandably furious, but by that time the Dutch had too strong a foothold to be dislodged — by the Indians, at any rate — and the eventual arrival of one-way avenues and the Hamburg Heaven Crystal Room was only a matter of time.

2   To understand how this was brought about, it is important to know something about the local Indians of the period. They were all, or almost all, of Algonquian origin; those who later became known as the Manhattans were actually Weckquaesgeeks, who belonged to the Wappinger Confederation. Their main village was Nappeckamack, on the site of what is now Yonkers, and they had a fort called Nipinichsen, on the north bank of Spuyten Duyvil. They lived in little clusters of igloo-like bark huts, along the east bank of the Hudson River and the Westchester shore of Long Island Sound, and they used Manhattan ("the island of hills") for their hunting and fishing stations.

3   A path ran up the center of the wooded, craggy island, and its twenty-five miles or so of water front were dotted with small camps, from which the Indians conducted their food-gathering expeditions. The fishing was more rewarding than it is now; aside from the pediodic runs of shad, there were sturgeon and flatfish in considerable numbers, and there were massive oyster and clam beds all along the shore line. The squaws would shuck the oysters and dry them on sticks in the sun, and it must be assumed that ptomaine poisoning was either unknown to these Indians or else it was a way of life. At any rate, their discovered shell piles are many, and their burial mounds comparatively few. In addition to all these delicacies, every now and then a whale would get stranded on a sand bar down in the Narrows, and the braves would take out after it in their dugout canoes.

4   By general consent, the Weckquaesgeeks (and it is easy to see why the Dutch decided to call them Manhattans) occupied the northern three quarters of the island, and the Canarsees, who were members of the Montauk, or Long Island, branch of the Algonquians, had only the southern tip, plus all of what is now Brooklyn. But there was enough fish and game for all, and nobody bothered

By Nathaniel Benchley. © 1959 by American Heritage Publishing Co., Inc. Reprinted courtesy of *American Heritage* Magazine.

very much about boundaries. The game was fairly spectacular; there were deer, bears, wolves, porcupines, beaver, otter, moose, wildcats, grouse, and turkey, and there were even cases when an occasional bison would wander in from the west, just in time to find himself transformed into a buffalo robe.

5   In consequence of all this largess, the Indians were happy with their lot. They were well fixed for food and clothing (in addition to the fish and game, they grew corn, beans, pumpkins, and tobacco, which rounded out their diet with the proper epicurean touch), and their only real worries were the occasional and unexplained epidemics that decimated their numbers, and the periodic raids that the upstate Mohawks made to collect overdue tribute. It was the Mohawks, as a matter of fact, who later all but wiped out the Canarsees, in an act of unconscious retributive justice.

6   All the tribes of the area shared a common belief in a world after death, ruled over by a single Great Spirit, or Manitou, and their heaven was a precise place — it lay off to the southwest, possibly where Trenton, New Jersey, is now. It was a place where game was even more plentiful than in real life, and a great deal more plentiful than at the present moment, if the figures from Trenton authorities are at all accurate. About four times a year the Indians had dances, either for spring planting, or harvest, or thanksgiving, or the like, and they always made a big to-do when they set off on a hunting expedition. Their life was, in short, all that the out-of-door enthusiasts would have us believe is good and true in Nature.

7   The men wore their hair in a scalp lock that formed a brush from the forehead to the nape of the neck, the side hair usually being burnt off with hot rocks, and although they sometimes put feathers in their hair, they never used the Sioux-type war bonnet. They decorated their faces and upper bodies with stripes of red, yellow, and black, and, in order to ward off both mosquitoes and sunburn, they smeared themselves with either fish oil, eagle fat, or bear grease. To get to leeward of a Weckquaesgeek Indian on a hot day, even — or especially — if he was in a friendly mood, was an experience in itself.

8   Their relations with the white men were, initially, good. The Indians were agreeable, in their way, and their main reaction to

the coming of the white men was one of excited interest, like schoolchildren who have been joined by a newcomer with three ears. As far as anyone knows, the Florentine explorer Verrazano was the first to see Manhattan and its natives, in 1524, but no significant contact with the Indians is recorded until 1609, when Henry Hudson sailed up the river in search of a passage to the Orient. Unfortunately, a crewman of the *Half Moon* named John Coleman was fatally punctured by the Indians, more out of curiosity than anger on their part, and in the subsequent incidents between the natives and Hudson's men, a few Indians were killed.

9   There was, in fact, what amounted to a pitched battle off Fort Nipinichsen, when the *Half Moon's* cannon and the muskets of her crew did severe damage to the braves on the shore and in the canoes. But, everything considered, the relations were not too bad, and the Indians were quite impressed by the knives, kettles, awls, and blankets that Hudson's men traded for their furs. As far as they were concerned, a little bloodshed every now and then was inevitable, and the materials the fur traders brought made up for a great deal.

10   In the next fifteen years, more and more fur traders arrived on Manhattan, some of them even setting up storehouses on the southern tip of the island, and in all that time their dealings with the Indians were friendly. In 1625 the first livestock arrived — 103 sheep, cows, horses, and pigs — and they were the first such animals the Indians had ever seen. Almost every Indian family had its dogs, but beyond that the only animals they knew were wild, and the savages were overcome by not only the sight of the animals but also their by-products, such as milk, cheese, bacon, ham, and mutton.

11   From the Indians' point of view, something new and interesting was happening every day (their first view of the Dutch wooden shoes, for instance, was the cause for no end of giggling and general merriment), and since the Dutch were under strict orders to be as nice to the natives as possible, the untoward incidents were reduced to an absolute minimum. In passing, it is of interest to note that the rate of seduction of the Indian maidens was so small as to be practically negligible. Either they were afraid of their own menfolk, or the Dutch were unusually clumsy — or the eagle fat might pos-

sibly have had something to do with it. Whatever the reason, there was little or no sexual scuffling between the natives and the colonists.

12   Then, on May 4, 1626, Peter Minuit, sent by the Dutch West India Company to be the formal director-general of New Netherland, arrived on the *Sea-mew*. The Dutch knew that the French and the British, the latter with flanking colonies at Plymouth and Jamestown, would not be particularly pleased at the establishment of a Dutch colony in the area, and they also knew that they didn't have the strength to resist armed intervention by either nation. Consequently, they resolved to make their purchase of Manhattan as legal as possible, hoping that if the Indians appeared to back up their claims, the British or French might hesitate before starting any trouble. With this in mind, Minuit was instructed to make a legal purchase of the entire island, and he therefore did what seemed like the logical thing: he asked the first Indians he saw to ask their chief to come and hold council.

13   These Indians were, of course, a band of Canarsees who had set up a little village called Werpoes by a pond near what is now Worth Street, and their chief was a genial opportunist named Seyseys. When Seyseys learned that not only would Minuit give him valuable merchandise in exchange for the title of the island of Manhattan, but also that Minuit didn't know that the Weckquaesgeeks controlled its whole upper three quarters or more, he gladly volunteered to take his few people away, and let the Dutchmen hunt and fish and build things to their hearts' content. There is some reason to believe that Seyseys wasn't quite sure what it meant to sell land — the land was, after all, Mother Earth to the Indians, and they felt you could no more sell it outright than you could sell the sky — but he wasn't one to quibble over small points; he took the sixty guilders' worth* of knives, axes, clothing, and beads (and possibly rum), and went chortling back to Brooklyn. The Canarsees set up another village named Werpoes, to replace the one they had left behind, and everybody settled down and was happy.

14   Everybody was happy, that is, except the Weckquaesgeeks. At

* The sixty guilders has popularly been supposed to have been worth about $24, but some authorities claim that, considering the times and the flexible rates of exchange, it was probably nearer $2,000. At any rate, it was all found money as far as Seyseys was concerned.

first they had no idea that their land had been sold out from under them, but then more and more Dutch farmers began to arrive, and their unfenced cattle wandered off across the Indians' land, eating their corn and trampling their crops, and when the Indians complained, they were given a few trinkets in payment and told it was too bad, but the land was no longer theirs. It was then that the truth began to creep over them, and then there was absolutely nothing they could do. Even if they had wanted to make a fight about it, the Dutch had guns and they didn't, and the only thing the Indians could do was sullenly try to make the best of an impossible situation.

15 Matters might have continued at a slow boil for some time, if it hadn't been that a few of the Dutch violated all the standing orders and began to trade liquor and guns to the Indians in exchange for furs. They found that the Indians, being unaccustomed to liquor, were pushovers for a quick bargain after about one drink; the thing the Dutch didn't realize was the fact that an Indian with a hangover, a gun, and a burning sense of injustice was as dangerous as a platoon of dragoons. The mere sight of a red-eyed, dry-mouthed Indian, with a gun in his shaking hand and bits of dirt and grass clinging to his coating of days-old eagle fat, should have been enough to warn them to be careful — but it wasn't.

16 Inevitably, trouble developed; massacres were perpetrated by both sides, but as often as not it was the Dutch who were the aggressors. (In one spectacular display of perfidy they slaughtered a whole group of Weckquaesgeeks who had come to them for protection against the marauding Mohawks, and mangled them so badly that at first it looked like the work of other Indians.) As a result, by 1664, when the British fleet slipped in and quietly took New Amsterdam, there were very few Indians left on the island, and those who remained didn't really care about anything. They had succumbed not only to various kinds of diseases and to the white men but, more disastrously, they had been done in by the Mohawks from up one river, and by the Canarsees from across another.

17 It should be a lesson to us all.

QUESTIONS FOR REFLECTION, DISCUSSION, OR WRITING

(1) If any parts of this essay gave you a laugh (or even a faint internal grin), go back now and try to discover the *source* of the humor. What devices or techniques does the author use to produce it? Are there any similar attempts at humor that failed to amuse you? (Don't expect necessarily to get the same amusement the second time around — often humor stops being humorous when we start probing it.)

(2) Do you think humor was Benchley's *primary* purpose in writing "The $24 Swindle"? Or was it to give us information? How successful was he in each? Does the accomplishment of one purpose help or hinder the success of the other? Do you consider both worthwhile and in good taste, considering the rather tragic subject matter? Explain.

(3) Are you especially bothered in reading by his use of the complicated Indian names? Do you think the author expected all readers to master them? If not, why do you suppose he included them?

(4) Whose side, if any, do you think the author is on — that of the white man or of the Indian? Whose fault were the bloody massacres of the period described?

(5) What is the "lesson to us all" which the story can teach? Or does Benchley mean this to be taken seriously at all?

(6) If there were descendants of the Manhattan Indians still living on the island, do you think they could rightfully claim New York City as their own and demand that the white man move out? Explain your answer. In what ways, if any, would this situation differ from the actual situation in many African countries during recent years? Be logical in your reasoning.

Jack London

THE EARTHQUAKE

JACK LONDON (1876-1916) *was born in San Francisco but lived and worked in many parts of the world. His success, however, was achieved as a fiction writer: in 1905 he was the highest paid author in the United States; and when he died at the age of 40, he had written more than 40 books, several of which are still widely read in this country and abroad. Perhaps the two best known are* The Call of the Wild *and* The Sea Wolf.

THE EARTHQUAKE *was written by special assignment for* Collier's Magazine, *whose editors, hearing of the San Francisco catastrophe, had telegraphed Lon-*

don at his home 40 miles from the scene. This eye-witness report was printed in the May 5, 1906, issue. Although it shows some signs of hurried writing, it also contains much excellent dramatic description. (Collier's, "the national weekly," was discontinued in January 1957, after nearly 70 years of publication.)

1 THE EARTHQUAKE shook down in San Francisco hundreds of thousands of dollars' worth of walls and chimneys. But the conflagration that followed burned up hundreds of millions of dollars' worth of property. There is no estimating within hundreds of millions the actual damage wrought. Not in history has a modern imperial city been so completely destroyed. San Francisco is gone. Nothing remains of it but memories and a fringe of dwelling-houses on its outskirts. Its industrial section is wiped out. Its business section is wiped out. The factories and warehouses, the great stores and newspaper buildings, the hotels and the palaces of the nabobs, are all gone. Remains only the fringe of dwelling-houses on the outskirts of what was once San Francisco.

2 Within an hour after the earthquake shock the smoke of San Francisco's burning was a lurid tower visible a hundred miles away. And for three days and nights this lurid tower swayed in the sky, reddening the sun, darkening the day, and filling the land with smoke.

3 On Wednesday morning at a quarter past five came the earthquake. A minute later the flames were leaping upward. In a dozen different quarters south of Market Street, in the working-class ghetto, and in the factories, fires started. There was no opposing the flames. There was no organization, no communication. All the cunning adjustments of a twentieth century city had been smashed by the earthquake. The streets were humped into ridges and depressions, and piled with the debris of fallen walls. The steel rails were twisted into perpendicular and horizontal angles. The telephone and telegraph systems were disrupted. And the great water-mains had burst. All the shrewd contrivances and safe-guards of man had been thrown out of gear by thirty seconds' twitching of the earth-crust.

The Fire Made Its Own Draft

4 By Wednesday afternoon, inside of twelve hours, half the heart of the city was gone. At that time I watched the vast conflagration

from out on the bay. It was dead calm. Not a flicker of wind stirred.
Yet from every side wind was pouring in upon the city. East, west,
north, and south, strong winds were blowing upon the doomed
city. The heated air rising made an enormous suck. Thus did the
fire of itself build its own colossal chimney through the atmosphere.
Day and night this dead calm continued, and yet, near to the flames,
the wind was often half a gale, so mighty was the suck.

5   Wednesday night saw the destruction of the very heart of the
city. Dynamite was lavishly used, and many of San Francisco's
proudest structures were crumbled by man himself into ruins, but
there was no withstanding the onrush of the flames. Time and again
successful stands were made by the fire-fighters, and every time the
flames flanked around on either side, or came up from the rear, and
turned to defeat the hard-won victory.

6   An enumeration of the buildings destroyed would be a directory
of San Francisco. An enumeration of the buildings undestroyed
would be a line and several addresses. An enumeration of the deeds
of heroism would stock a library and bankrupt the Carnegie Medal
fund. An enumeration of the dead — will never be made. All vestiges
of them were destroyed by the flames. The number of the victims
of the earthquake will never be known. South of Market Street,
where the loss of life was particularly heavy, was the first to catch
fire.

7   Remarkable as it may seem, Wednesday night, while the whole
city crashed and roared into ruin, was a quiet night. There were no
crowds. There was no shouting and yelling. There was no hysteria,
no disorder. I passed Wednesday night in the path of the advancing
flames, and in all those terrible hours I saw not one woman who
wept, not one man who was excited, not one person who was in the
slightest degree panic-stricken.

8   Before the flames, throughout the night, fled tens of thousands
of homeless ones. Some were wrapped in blankets. Others carried
bundles of bedding and dear household treasures. Sometimes a
whole family was harnessed to a carriage or delivery wagon that was
weighted down with their possessions. Baby buggies, toy wagons,
and go-carts were used as trucks, while every other person was
dragging a trunk. Yet everybody was gracious. The most perfect

courtesy obtained. Never, in all San Francisco's history, were her people so kind and courteous as on this night of terror.

A *Caravan* of *Trunks*

9   All night these tens of thousands fled before the flames. Many of them, the poor people from the labor ghetto, had fled all day as well. They had left their homes burdened with possessions. Now and again they lightened up, flinging out upon the street clothing and treasures they had dragged for miles.

10   They held on longest to their trunks, and over these trunks many a strong man broke his heart that night. The hills of San Francisco are steep, and up these hills, mile after mile, were the trunks dragged. Everywhere were trunks, with across them lying their exhausted owners, men and women. Before the march of the flames were flung picket lines of soldiers. And a block at a time, as the flames advanced, these pickets retreated. One of their tasks was to keep the trunk-pullers moving. The exhausted creatures, stirred on by the menace of bayonets, would arise and struggle up the steep pavements, pausing from weakness every five or ten feet.

11   Often, after surmounting a heart-breaking hill, they would find another wall of flame advancing upon them at right angles and be compelled to change anew the line of their retreat. In the end, completely played out, after toiling for a dozen hours like giants, thousands of them were compelled to abandon their trunks. Here the shopkeepers and soft members of the middle class were at a disadvantage. But the working men dug holes in vacant lots and backyards and buried their trunks.

The Doomed City

12   At nine o'clock Wednesday evening I walked down through the very heart of the city. I walked through miles and miles of magnificent buildings and towering skyscrapers. Here was no fire. All was in perfect order. The police patrolled the streets. Every building had its watchman at the door. And yet it was doomed, all of it. There was no water. The dynamite was giving out. And at right angles two different conflagrations were sweeping down upon it.

13   At one o'clock in the morning I walked down through the same

section. Everything still stood intact. There was no fire. And yet there was a change. A rain of ashes was falling. The watchmen at the doors were gone. The police had been withdrawn. There were no firemen, no fire engines, no men fighting with dynamite. The district had been absolutely abandoned. I stood at the corner of Kearney and Market, in the very innermost heart of San Francisco. Kearney Street was deserted. Half a dozen blocks away it was burning on both sides. The street was a wall of flame, and against this wall of flame, silhouetted sharply, were two United States cavalrymen sitting their horses, calmly watching. That was all. Not another person was in sight. In the intact heart of the city two troopers sat their horses and watched.

Spread of the Conflagration

14   Surrender was complete. There was no water. The sewers had long since been pumped dry. There was no dynamite. Another fire had broken out further uptown, and now from three sides conflagrations were sweeping down. The fourth side had been burned earlier in the day. In that direction stood the tottering walls of the Examiner building, the burned-out Call building, the smoldering ruins of the Grand Hotel, and the gutted, devastated, dynamited Palace Hotel.

15   The following will illustrate the sweep of the flames and the inability of men to calculate their spread. At eight o'clock Wednesday evening I passed through Union Square. It was packed with refugees. Thousands of them had gone to bed on the grass. Government tents had been set up, supper was being cooked, and the refugees were lining up for free meals.

16   At half-past one in the morning three sides of Union Square were in flames. The fourth side, where stood the great St. Francis Hotel, was still holding out. An hour later, ignited from top and sides, the St. Francis was flaming heavenward. Union Square, heaped high with mountains of trunks, was deserted. Troops, refugees, and all had retreated.

A Fortune for a Horse!

17   It was at Union Square that I saw a man offering a thousand dollars for a team of horses. He was in charge of a truck piled high with

trunks for some hotel. It had been hauled here into what was considered safety, and the horses had been taken out. The flames were on three sides of the Square, and there were no horses.

18   Also, at this time, standing beside the truck, I urged a man to seek safety in flight. He was all but hemmed in by several conflagrations. He was an old man and he was on crutches. Said he, "Today is my birthday. Last night I was worth thirty thousand dollars. I bought five bottles of wine, some delicate fish, and other things for my birthday dinner. I have had no dinner, and all I own are these crutches."

19   I convinced him of his danger and started him limping on his way. An hour later, from a distance, I saw the truckload of trunks burning merrily in the middle of the street.

20   On Thursday morning, at a quarter past five, just twenty-four hours after the earthquake, I sat on the steps of a small residence on Nob Hill. With me sat Japanese, Italians, Chinese, and Negroes —a bit of the cosmopolitan flotsam of the wreck of the city. All about were the palaces of the nabob pioneers of Forty-nine. To the east and south, at right angles, were advancing two mighty walls of flame.

21   I went inside with the owner of the house on the steps of which I sat. He was cool and cheerful and hospitable. "Yesterday morning," he said, "I was worth six hundred thousand dollars. This morning this house is all I have left. It will go in fifteen minutes." He pointed to a large cabinet. "That is my wife's collection of china. This rug upon which we stand is a present. It cost fifteen hundred dollars. Try that piano. Listen to its tone. There are few like it. There are no horses. The flames will be here in fifteen minutes."

22   Outside, the old Mark Hopkins residence, a palace, was just catching fire. The troops were falling back and driving the refugees before them. From every side came the roaring of flames, the crashing of walls, and the detonations of dynamite.

The Dawn of the Second Day

23   I passed out of the house. Day was trying to dawn through the smoke-pall. A sickly light was creeping over the face of things. Once only the sun broke through the smoke-pall, blood-red, and

showing quarter its usual size. The smoke-pall itself, viewed from beneath, was a rose color that pulsed and fluttered with lavender shades. Then it turned to mauve and yellow and dun. There was no sun. And so dawned the second day on stricken San Francisco.

24   An hour later I was creeping past the shattered dome of the City Hall. Than it there was no better exhibit of the destructive forces of the earthquake. Most of the stone had been shaken from the great dome, leaving standing the naked framework of steel. Market Street was piled high with the wreckage, and across the wreckage lay the overthrown pillars of the City Hall shattered into short crosswise sections.

25   This section of the city, with the exception of the Mint and the Post-Office, was already a waste of smoking ruins. Here and there through the smoke, creeping warily under the shadows of tottering walls, emerged occasional men and women. It was like the meeting of the handful of survivors after the day of the end of the world.

Beeves Slaughtered and Roasted

26   On Mission Street lay a dozen steers, in a neat row stretching across the street, just as they had been struck down by the flying ruins of the earthquake. The fire had passed through afterward and roasted them. The human dead had been carried away before the fire came. At another place on Mission Street I saw a milk wagon. A steel telegraph pole had smashed down sheer through the driver's seat and crushed the front wheels. The milkcans lay scattered around.

27   All day Thursday and all Thursday night, all day Friday and Friday night, the flames still raged.

28   Friday night saw the flames finally conquered, though not until Russian Hill and Telegraph Hill had been swept and three-quarters of a mile of wharves and docks had been licked up.

The Last Stand

29   The great stand of the fire-fighters was made Thursday night on Van Ness Avenue. Had they failed here, the comparatively few remaining houses of the city would have been swept. Here were the magnificent residences of the second generation of San Francisco nabobs, and these, in a solid zone, were dynamited down across the

path of the fire. Here and there the flames leaped the zone, but these fires were beaten out, principally by the use of wet blankets and rugs.

30   San Francisco, at the present time, is like the crater of a volcano, around which are camped tens of thousands of refugees. At the Presidio alone are at least twenty thousand. All the surrounding cities and towns are jammed with the homeless ones, where they are being cared for by the relief committees. The refugees were carried free by the railroads to any point they wished to go, and it is estimated that over one hundred thousand people have left the peninsula on which San Francisco stood. The Government has the situation in hand, and, thanks to the immediate relief given by the whole United States, there is not the slightest possibility of a famine. The bankers and business men have already set about making preparations to rebuild San Francisco.

QUESTIONS FOR REFLECTION, DISCUSSION, OR WRITING

(1) A man reporting the destruction of his "home town" could easily become over-sentimental — and this would ruin his story for most readers. Do you see any evidence of this weakness in London's report, or does he remain objective (emotionally detached) in his viewpoint? Explain, using illustrations from the story.

(2) If you are not familiar with San Francisco's streets and buildings, does his frequent reference to them by name seriously hinder your understanding? Why, or why not?

(3) Does his occasional repetition (of facts and ways of stating them) annoy you? Find some examples of such repetition. Do you suppose they were due to carelessness, or do they serve some useful purpose?

(4) What were the "cunning adjustments," the "shrewd contrivances" (par. 3), which had been made inoperative by the earthquake? Would the still shrewder contrivances of a modern city be able to save it in case of a similar catastrophe?

(5) Comment on the effectiveness of the simple statement with which London concludes his report. We would expect him to end such a dramatic account with a sentence of great significance. What, if any, is this one's significance? Would it have been improved by greater eloquence? Explain.

(6) How can you explain the fact that all of the San Franciscans he saw (including, undoubtedly, many who were by nature highly excitable or un-

gracious) remained calm and gracious in the midst of such calamity (pars. 7-8)?

(7) Your own "eye-witness report" of some past catastrophe (although much less "catastrophic" than this one, we hope), and the behavior of the people involved, could make a good writing assignment.

Bruce Catton

From A STILLNESS AT APPOMATTOX

BRUCE CATTON, *who was the recipient of the Pulitzer Prize for historical work in 1954 and of the National Book Award the same year, started his career as reporter for various newspapers. Later he was director of information for the U.S. Department of Commerce. He has written many books, including* Mr. Lincoln's Army, Glory Road, A Stillness at Appomattox, The Hallowed Ground, *and* America Goes to War. *His special field of historical interest, of course, is the Civil War. Since 1954 he has been editor of* American Heritage *(see p. 114).*

A STILLNESS AT APPOMATTOX, *probably the best-known of Catton's books, concludes with the following narrative of that last morning of the Civil War. As you read, you will certainly notice that Catton's writing differs from the ordinary historical account; take time to pause and appreciate the ways in which he achieves this difference.*

1   FEDERAL infantry was on the road in the dark hours before dawn, with very little sleep and no breakfast at all. The men were told that if they hurried this was the day they could finish everything, and this inspired them. Yet they were no set of legendary heroes who never got tired or hungry or thought about personal discomfort. They were very human, given to griping when their stomachs were empty, and what really pulled them along this morning seems to have been the promise that at Appomattox Station rations would be issued. Most of the men who made the march that morning, one veteran admitted, did so because they figured it was the quickest way to get breakfast. Even so the straggling was abnormally heavy, and there were regiments in the column which had no more than seventy-five men with the colors.

2   It was Palm Sunday, with a blue cloudless sky, and the warm air had the smell of spring. The men came tramping up to the fields

by the railroad station with the early morning sun over their right shoulders, and they filed off to right and left, stacked arms, and began collecting wood for the fires with which they would cook the anticipated rations. The divisions from the Army of the James were in front, Ord and John Gibbon in the lead, and the V Corps was coming up close behind. Gibbon and Ord rode to a little house near the railroad where Sheridan had his headquarters, and Sheridan came out to greet them and explain the situation.

3   The Lynchburg Road lay about a mile north of cavalry head-quarters. It ran along a low ridge, partly concealed by timber, with a boggy little brook running along a shallow valley on the near side, and a couple of miles to the east it dipped down to a little hollow and ran through the village of Appomattox Court House. In and around and beyond this village, with its advance guard holding the breastworks half a mile west of it, was what remained of the Army of Northern Virginia. Off to the east, out of sight beyond hills and forests but not more than six or eight miles away, was Meade with the II Corps and the VI Corps, coming west on the Lynchburg Road to pound the Confederate rear. In effect, the Federals occupied three sides of a square — cavalry on the west, infantry on the south, Meade and the rest of the army on the east. The Rebel army was inside the square, and although the north side was open that did not matter because the Confederates could find neither food nor escape in that direction. Their only possible move was to fight their way west along the Lynchburg Road.

4   So Sheridan explained it, warning the generals that he expected the Rebels to attack at any moment and that they had better get ready to bring their troops up in support.

5   While he was talking the sound of musket fire came down from the ridge. It was sporadic, at first, as the skirmishers pecked away at each other, but it soon grew much heavier and there was the heavy booming of field artillery. The big push was on, and Sheridan sprang into the saddle, ordering the rest of his cavalry up into line and telling the officers to bring their infantry up as fast as they could. Then he was off, and the generals galloped back to put their men in motion.

6   The hopeful little breakfast fires died unnoticed, nothing ever
cooked on them, and the infantry took their muskets, got into
column, and went hurrying north to get astride of the Lynchburg
Road. The crossroad they were on led through heavy timber and
the men could see nothing, but the noise of the firing grew louder
and louder as they marched. Then, for the last time in their lives,
beyond the trees they heard the high, spine-tingling wail of the
Rebel yell, a last great shout of defiance flung against the morning
sky by a doomed army marching into the final sunset.

7   The Federals got across the Lynchburg Road, swung into line
of battle facing east, and marched toward the firing and the shouting. As they marched, dismounted cavalry came drifting back, and
the troopers waved their caps and cheered when they saw the
infantry, and called out: "Give it to 'em — we've got 'em in a tight
place!"

8   In a clearing there was Sheridan, talking with Griffin and other
officers of the V Corps; Sheridan, talking rapidly, pounding a palm
with his fist; and the battle line marched on and came under the
fire of Rebel artillery. One brigade went across somebody's farm,
just here, and as the firing grew heavier a shell blew the end out of
the farmer's chicken house, and the air was abruptly full of de-
moralized chickens, squawking indignantly, fluttering off in frantic
disorganized flight. And here was the last battle of the war, and the
men were marching up to the moment of apotheosis and glory —
but they were men who had not eaten for twenty-fours hours and
more, and they knew Virginia poultry from of old, and what had
begun as an attack on a Rebel battle line turned into a hilarious
chase after fugitive chickens. The battle smoke rolled down over
the crest, and shells were exploding and the farm buildings were
ablaze, and Federal officers were waving swords and barking orders
in scandalized indignation. But the soldiers whooped and laughed
and scrambled after their prey, and as the main battle line swept
on most of this brigade was either continuing to hunt chickens or
was building little fires and preparing to cook the ones that had
been caught.

9   The Confederates had scattered the cavalry, and most of the
troopers fled south, across the shallow valley that ran parallel with
the Lynchburg Road. As the last of them left the field the way

seemed to be open, and the Confederates who had driven them away raised a final shout of triumph — and then over the hill came the first lines of blue infantry, rifles tilted forward, and here was the end of everything: the Yankees had won the race and the way was closed forever and there was no going on any farther.

10 The blue lines grew longer and longer, and rank upon rank came into view, as if there was no end to them. A Federal officer remembered afterward that when he looked across at the Rebel lines it almost seemed as if there were more battle flags than soldiers. So small were the Southern regiments that the flags were all clustered together, and he got the strange feeling that the ground where the Army of Northern Virginia had been brought to bay had somehow blossomed out with a great row of poppies and roses.

11 So the two armies faced each other at long range, and the firing slackened and almost ceased.

12 Many times in the past these armies had paused to look at each other across empty fields, taking a final size-up before getting into the grapple. Now they were taking their last look, the Stars and Bars were about to go down forever and leave nothing behind but the stars and the memories, and it might have been a time for deep solemn thoughts. But the men who looked across the battlefield at each other were very tired and very hungry, and they did not have much room in their heads for anything except the thought of that weariness and that hunger, and the simple hope that they might live through the next half hour. One Union soldier wrote that he and his comrades reflected bitterly that they would not be here, waiting for the shooting to begin, if they had not innocently believed that tale about getting breakfast at Appomattox Station; and, he said, "we were angry with ourselves to think that for the hope of drawing rations we had been foolish enough to keep up and, by doing so, get in such a scrape." They did not mind the desultory artillery fire very much, he said, but "we dreaded the moment when the infantry should open on us."

13 Off toward the south Sheridan had all of his cavalry in line again, mounted now with pennons and guidons fluttering. The Federal infantry was advancing from the west and Sheridan was where he could hit the flank of the Rebels who were drawn up to oppose that infantry, and he spurred over to get some foot soldiers to stiffen

his own attack. General Griffin told Chamberlain to take his brigade and use it as Sheridan might direct. Men who saw Sheridan pointing out to Chamberlain the place where his brigade should attack remembered his final passionate injunction: "Now smash 'em, I tell you, smash 'em!"

14   Chamberlain got his men where Sheridan wanted them, and all of Ord's and Griffin's men were in line now, coming up on higher ground where they could see the whole field.

15   They could see the Confederate line drawing back from in front of them, crowned with its red battle flags, and all along the open country to the right they could see the whole cavalry corps of the Army of the Potomac trotting over to take position beyond Chamberlain's brigade. The sunlight gleamed brightly off the metal and the flags, and once again, for a last haunting moment, the way men make war looked grand and caught at the throat, as if some strange value beyond values were incomprehensively mixed up in it all.

16   Then Sheridan's bugles sounded, the clear notes slanting all across the field, and all of his brigades wheeled and swung into line, every saber raised high, every rider tense; and in another minute infantry and cavalry would drive in on the slim Confederate lines and crumple them and destroy them in a last savage burst of firing and cutting and clubbing.

17   Out from the Rebel lines came a lone rider, a young officer in a gray uniform, galloping madly, a staff in his hand with a white flag fluttering from the end of it. He rode up to Chamberlain's lines and someone there took him off to see Sheridan, and the firing stopped, and the watching Federals saw the Southerners wheeling their guns back and stacking their muskets as if they expected to fight no more.

18   All up and down the lines the men blinked at one another, unable to realize that the hour they had waited for so long was actually at hand. There was a truce, they could see that, and presently the word was passed that Grant and Lee were going to meet in the little village that lay now between the two lines, and no one could doubt that Lee was going to surrender. It was Palm Sunday, and they would all live to see Easter, and with the guns quieted it might be easier to comprehend the mystery and the promise of that day. Yet the fact of peace and no more killing and an open road

home seems to have been too big to grasp, right at the moment, and in the enormous silence that lay upon the field men remembered that they had marched far and were very tired, and they wondered when the wagon trains would come up with rations.

19   One of Ord's soldiers wrote that the army should have gone wild with joy, then and there; and yet, he said, somehow they did not. Later there would be frenzied cheering and crying and rejoicing, but now . . . now, for some reason, the men sat on the ground and looked across at the Confederate army and found themselves feeling as they had never dreamed that the moment of victory would make them feel.

20   ". . . I remember how we sat there and pitied and sympathized with these courageous Southern men who had fought for four long and dreary years all so stubbornly, so bravely and so well, and now, whipped, beaten, completely used up, were fully at our mercy — it was pitiful, sad, hard, and seemed to us altogether too bad." A Pennsylvanian in the V Corps dodged past the skirmish line and strolled into the lines of the nearest Confederate regiment, and half a century after the war he recalled it with a glow: ". . . as soon as I got among these boys I felt and was treated as well as if I had been among our own boys, and a person would of thought we were of the same Army and had been Fighting under the Same Flag."

21   Down by the roadside near Appomattox Court House, Sheridan and Ord and other officers sat and waited while a brown-bearded little man in a mud-spattered uniform rode up. They all saluted him, and there was a quiet interchange of greetings, and then General Grant tilted his head toward the village and asked: "Is General Lee up there?"

22   Sheridan replied that he was, and Grant said: "Very well. Let's go up."

23   The little cavalcade went trotting along the road to the village, and all around them the two armies waited in silence. As the generals neared the end of their ride, a Yankee band in a field near the town struck up "Auld Lang Syne."

QUESTIONS FOR REFLECTION, DISCUSSION, OR WRITING

(1) Point out the various places in this selection where Catton departs from textbook-type history. To what do most of his departures pertain? What desirable effect do they achieve in this narrative?

(2) Try to explain the "strange value beyond values . . . incomprehensively mixed up in it all" (par. 15). Does the "moral equivalent of war" mentioned by Sen. Humphrey and Marquis Childs ("A Plan to Save . . ." and "Peace Corps") refer in any way to this "value"?

(3) Do you think it strange that the "fact of peace" seemed "too big to grasp, right at the moment" (pars. 18-19)? Or have you sometime had a stroke of such good fortune that it failed, at the moment, to really make a full impression? If so, tell about it.

(4) If, after fighting and suffering for four long years because of an enemy, you had him suddenly before you, defeated, would you be apt to find his plight "pitiful, sad, hard and . . . altogether too bad" (par. 20)? If not, what do you suppose caused this feeling in the Union soldiers? If so, what may this tell us about human nature in general?

(5) If self-determinism (the right of peoples to determine their own allegiance and form of government) is a desirable policy today, can you explain why it was not "right" for the Southern Confederacy? Or do you think the South *should* have been permitted this privilege? Is it the same privilege which the United States now supports in various other parts of the world? Either way, explain your stand fully and logically.

John K. Townsend

From A HUNTING PARTY ON THE SNAKE RIVER

JOHN K. TOWNSEND *was a naturalist, a Philadelphian who made the trip to Oregon for scientific purposes, joining a company of 70 traders and missionaries who left Independence, Missouri, in 1834, when he was 35 years old.*

A HUNTING PARTY ON THE SNAKE RIVER, *of which this selection is an excerpt, was one chapter of Townsend's book,* Narrative of a Journey Across the Rocky Mountains to the Columbia River, *published in 1839. Like the rest of the book, it was taken from his original journals and was apparently written when the group was somewhere in the area of present-day Idaho. No changes have been made from the 1839 version, but the writing is remarkably clear and readable even today, almost a century and a third later.*

1   RICHARDSON and Sansbury mention having seen several Blackfoot Indians today, who, on observing them, ran rapidly away,
and, as usual, concealed themselves in the bushes. We are now
certain that our worst enemies are around us, and that they are
only waiting for a favorable time and opportunity to make an
attack. They are not here for nothing, and have probably been
dogging us, and reconnoitering our outposts, so that the greatest
caution and watchfulness will be required to prevent a surprise. We
are but a small company, and there may be at this very moment
hundreds within hearing of our voices.

2   The Blackfoot is a sworn and determined foe to all white men,
and he has often been heard to declare that he would rather hang
the scalp of a "pale face" to his girdle, than kill a buffalo to prevent
his starving.

3   The hostility of this dreaded tribe is, and has for years been,
proverbial. They are, perhaps, the only Indians who do not fear the
power, and who refuse to acknowledge the superiority of the white
man; and though so often beaten in conflicts with them, even by
their own mode of warfare, and generally with numbers vastly
inferior, their indomitable courage and perseverance still urges them
on to renewed attempts; and if a single scalp is taken, it is considered
equal to a great victory, and is hailed as a presage of future and
more extensive triumphs.

4   It must be acknowledged, however, that this determined hostility
does not originate solely in savage malignity, or an abstract thirst for
the blood of white men; it is fomented and kept alive from year
to year by incessant provocatives on the part of white hunters,
trappers, and traders, who are at best but intruders on the rightful
domains of the red man of the wilderness. Many a night have I sat
at the campfire, and listened to the recital of bloody and ferocious
scenes, in which the narrators were the actors, and the poor Indians
the victims, and I have felt my blood tingle with shame, and boil
with indignation, to hear the diabolical acts applauded by those
for whose amusement they were related. Many a precious villain,
and merciless marauder, was made by these midnight tales of
rapine, murder, and robbery; many a stripling, in whose tender
mind the seeds of virtue and honesty had never germinated, burned
for an opportunity of loading his pack-horse with the beaver skins

of some solitary Blackfoot trapper, who was to be murdered and despoiled of the property he had acquired by weeks, and perhaps months, of toil and danger.

5   Acts of this kind are by no means unfrequent, and the subjects of this sort of atrocity are not always the poor and despised Indians: white men themselves often fall by the hands of their companions, when by good fortune and industry they have succeeded in loading their horses with fur. The fortunate trapper is treacherously murdered by one who has eaten from the same dish and drank from the same cup, and the homicide returns triumphantly to his camp with his ill gotten property. If his companion be inquired for, the answer is that some days ago they parted company, and he will probably soon join them.

6   The poor man never returns — no one goes to search for him — he is soon forgotten, or is only remembered by one more steadfast than the rest, who seizes with avidity the first opportunity which is afforded, of murdering an unoffending Indian in revenge for the death of his friend.

QUESTIONS FOR REFLECTION, DISCUSSION, OR WRITING

(1) Do you think Townsend felt very strongly about the white man's treatment of the Indians, or is this part of his journal intended merely as a factual account? What details influence your opinion?

(2) Which do you consider more despicable, the Indians who killed through hatred and frustration, or the white men who killed for furs? Attempt to explain clearly the moral difference (if any, as you see it) and show, if you can, parallels in our modern society.

(3) What do you think of the moral right of white men (throughout all of America's early history) to be "intruders on the rightful domains of the red man of the wilderness"? If you had been living then, would you have felt morally justified in such intrusion? Explain.

Peter Lyon

WYATT EARP AND BAT MASTERSON

PETER LYON *is a New York free-lance writer who has contributed articles to many national magazines, including* Holiday *and* Saturday Evening Post, *as well as* American Heritage. *For many years he was also a writer for a number of radio programs.*

WYATT EARP AND BAT MASTERSON *is one section of an extensive feature article entitled "The Wild, Wild West," published in* American Heritage *(see p. 114) for August 1960. In this selection Lyon exposes the actual men behind two of our legendary western heroes.*

To do this he makes frequent use of another literary device, **irony,** *sometimes classified as a figure of speech. In this literary device (which should not be confused with "irony of fate" or of situation, another matter) the actual intent is exactly the opposite from what the words say. If you call your girlfriend, who has just made a stupid remark, a "real intellectual" — that is irony. When Lyon mentions the "featherweight task of pacifying Tombstone" (par. 3), he means just the opposite — and that is irony. Although in its lighter forms irony is apt to be mere humor, when severe enough it is a form of sarcasm, intended to "cut." Usually not hard to detect in speech, where the voice helps to express the purpose, the real meaning, irony in print is often missed by the dull or inexperienced reader.*

1   HERE ARE two of the regnant superheroes of the televised Wild West. Once upon a time they faced the same foes in the same filmed fables, but times have changed; they have gone their separate ways. This is a pity, for in real life the two were as thick as thieves.

2   Each week we are shown — in bland, bright little slices of televised entertainment — just how they scrubbed the Wild West clean, including the back of its neck and behind its ears. Clean-cut and clean-shaven, Wyatt romances Nellie Cashman, the "miners' angel," or he avenges the murder of some Indian friends, or he traps some mining executives who would thieve silver bullion. Elegant and clean-shaven, Bat foils a horse-race swindler, or he gallantly assists some ladies in their struggle for woman's rights, or by examining the brushwork he perceives that some oil paintings

are spurious. All this is only so much ingenious fretwork on the Earp-Masterson legend, contrived by worthy successors to the staff writers of the *National Police Gazette*. But the legend is itself such an imposing structure as to require no further embellishment.

3   The legend tells us that Marshall Earp cleaned up two Kansas cowtowns, Ellsworth and Wichita, singlehanded. He then joined forces with Bat Masterson to clean up Dodge City, "the wickedest little city in America." So much accomplished, Marshal Earp turned his attention to the featherweight task of pacifying Tombstone, Arizona, a hotbed of outlaws unparalleled in history, whilst Sheriff Masterson proceeded to stamp out sin in the mining camps of Colorado. Thereafter both men retired, breathing easily, having made the Wild West safe for the effete tenderfeet of the East.

4   Both men, the legend adds, were courteous to women, modest, handsome, and blue-eyed. We are also told that Earp was the Wild West's speediest and deadliest gunfighter. For his part, Masterson disdained to pull a gun, preferring to clout an adversary senseless with his cane, whence his nickname. But he was quite willing to testify to his pal's prowess and so contribute to the legend. Earp, so Masterson has assured us, could kill a coyote with his Colt .45 at four hundred yards.*

5   Masterson himself, who was in truth a poor shot, killed at most four men throughout his career (not counting Indians). Indeed, these two differ sharply from other Wild West heroes in that they rarely fired their six-guns in anger. They were both sly, cunning, cautious men, who early learned that shooting might reap a bloody harvest. In consequence, they walked warily, carrying a big bluff. In their time, the Wild West killer and outlaw was dying out, to be replaced by the confidence man. Confidence men rarely kill; they are too artful. Both Earp and Masterson were, among other things, eager students of the technique of early confidence games.

---

* Such skill calls for some respectful analysis. At four hundred yards a coyote cannot be seen against his natural background, so we shall assume the animal is silhouetted against the sky. Even so, an expert using a rifle with a globe sight would congratulate himself if he hit such a target with any regularity, much more if he killed it. A pistol, of course, will not carry so far directly; the marksman must use Kentucky windage — i.e., he must aim appreciably above his target so that his bullet will carry. Masterson admitted that "luck figures largely in such shooting." If, instead of "largely," he had said "completely," he would have come closer to that coyote.

6   They first met in 1872, when both were hunting buffalo on the Salt Fork of the Arkansas, in direct violation of the Indian treaty. Earp was twenty-four; Masterson was nineteen. They seem to have recognized that they were kindred souls, but they parted, not to come together again until the summer of 1876, in Dodge City. During those four years Bat was, so to say, preparing himself to be a peace officer. He stole forty ponies from some Indians and sold them for $1,200, he killed other Indians both as a free-lance buffalo hunter and as an army scout, and he got into a brawl with an army sergeant at Sweetwater, Texas, over a dancehall girl. The girl was killed while trying to shield Masterson; Bat was wounded, but he killed the soldier.

7   Meantime Earp, by his own account, had engaged in even more impressive heroics. First there was his mettlesome exploit at Ellsworth in 1873. To hear him tell it, Earp stepped out of a crowd, unknown and unheralded, and stalked alone across that familiar sun-baked plaza to disarm an able and truculent gunfighter, the Texas gambler Ben Thompson. Not only that, but Thompson was backed up at the time by a hundred pugnacious cowboy friends. How could Earp ever have dared to do it? He would seem to have been cloaked in invisibility, for others who were present never saw him — not the reporter for the Ellsworth newspaper; not Thompson himself; not Deputy Sheriff Hogue, to whom Thompson voluntarily turned over his gun; and not Mayor James Miller, to whom Thompson gave bond for his appearance when he might be wanted later.

8   Is it possible Earp was not there at all?

9   In May, 1874, Earp arrived in Wichita, another rowdy cowtown, where, he said later, Mayor Jim Hope promptly made him the marshal. Let Earp speak: "In two years at Wichita my deputies and I arrested more than eight hundred men. In all that time I had to shoot but one man — and that only to disarm him. All he got was a flesh wound."

10   And now a look at the minutes of the Wichita city commission. They show that Earp was elected on April 21, 1875, as one of two policemen to serve under the marshal and assistant marshal. They show further that on April 19, 1876, the commission voted against rehiring him. A month later it was recommended that the vagrancy act be enforced against Earp and his brother Jim.

11   Judging from the Wichita newspapers, Earp seems not to have
won much of a reputation during his one year as a policeman. They
keep referring to him as "Policeman Erp," which makes him sound
like a walking advertisement for Dr. Brown's Celery Tonic. Now
and then he arrested a suspected horse thief; but the longest
newspaper story about him describes how he was arrested, fined,
and fired from the police force for violating the peace on April 5,
1876. All this resulted from an election-eve fracas in which Earp
slugged an opposition candidate for city marshal. And so he turned
up in Dodge City, another cowtown.

12   Dodge was run by a small clique of saloon-keepers who, as the
years went on, took turns at being mayor. Most saloons were rou-
tinely outfitted with gambling layouts. In 1878 the town council
enacted an ordinance against gambling. Had its members gone out
of their minds? No: they were moved by sound common sense. For,
with a law on the books prohibiting gambling, any chump who
complained that he had been cheated could be forthwith walked
Spanish to the hoosegow on the grounds that he had been breaking
the law.

13   A town run along these lines clearly required something special
in the way of a peace officer: a man who would know how and
when to enforce the freakish laws, who would know how to wink
at the artful ways in which cowpokes from Texas were mulcted. We
are told that the saloon-keeper who was mayor in 1876 sent for
Wyatt Earp.

14   Earp told his skillful biographer, Stuart Lake, that he appointed
Bat Masterson as one of his deputies. Earp also asserted that he
was paid $250 a month, plus a fee of $2.50 for each arrest; he and
his deputies, he said, arrested some three hundred persons a month,
or enough to bring in about $750 a month. (One month in 1877,
he recalled, the fees reached almost $1,000 from nearly four hundred
arrests; that was the peak.) Earp's share would have brought his
income to more than $400 a month, nice money for the time and
place.

15   And now to the town records. Earp was never marshal of Dodge.
He served two terms as assistant marshal: from May, 1876, to
September, 1876, and from May, 1878, to September, 1879. (Dur-
ing that month of 1877 when, by his own account, he and his

deputies arrested nearly four hundred rowdy cowboys, Earp was not a peace officer at all. In fact, he was himself arrested that month for brawling with a dance-hall girl.) His salary as assistant marshal was $75 a month. The fee paid for an arrest (and conviction) was only $2. The docket of the police court shows that during 1878 there were only sixty-four arrests; during 1879 there were only twenty-nine arrests.

16   One interpretation of this remarkable decline in arrests — from three hundred or four hundred a month in 1876-77 to just four a month in 1878-79 — is that lion-hearted Wyatt Earp had tamed the town. There is another interpretation.

17   At all events, it is clear that Earp's income in 1878 could not have been much more than $80 a month — not much money for the time and place. Bat Masterson's income was about the same. Both had to add to it. Both did: as professional gamblers.

18   It has been argued that professional gambling in the Wild West was honest. This is to impose on credulity. Obviously it was no more honest than professional gambling whenever and wherever — which is to say, no more honest than it had to be.

19   Earp was a professional gambler long before he got to Dodge; his reputation around Hays City, according to Dr. Floyd Streeter, a Kansas historian, was that of a card player who was "up to some dishonest trick every time he played."

20   Masterson, who left Dodge in July, 1876, to follow the gold rush to Deadwood, got no further than Cheyenne, Wyoming, where he did so well as a faro banker that he stuck. But he was back in Dodge for the cattle season of 1877. On June 6 he was arrested, jugged, and fined $25 and costs for an act of hooliganism. Then he returned to his faro bank.

21   However, he badly wanted a star. Every professional gambler needed a star; the badge of office permitted its wearer to carry a gun, which in turn provided just the psychological advantage necessary in a game of chance played for high stakes. (Only peace officers were permitted to carry guns in Dodge City; all others were obliged to check their weapons in racks provided for the purpose.) And so Bat decided to run for sheriff of Ford County.

22   His electioneering technique was simplicity itself: he bought an interest in the Lone Star Dance Hall. Only thus could a candidate

convince the bizarre electorate of Dodge City that he was a sound citizen and a responsible taxpayer. In November, 1877, Bat was elected by a three-vote margin. He took office in January, and what is more, he started off in high gear by catching some would-be train robbers. But as the months wore on, like Earp, and like Hickock before them both, he whiled away his evening hours as a professional gambler along with cronies like Doc Holliday, an alcoholic ex-dentist, and Luke Short, a dandiprat. Earp banked faro at the Long Branch Saloon for a percentage of the house's gross. He and Bat and the others spent so many nights in Dodge's brothels that they were nicknamed "the Fighting Pimps."

23   There was justification for the slur. Earp lived with a girl called Mattie Blaylock; since no record of any marriage has ever been found, she is presumed to have been his common-law wife. And Nyle Miller, director of the Kansas State Historical Society, and an authority on the dossiers of Earp and Masterson, has established that, according to the census of 1880, Bat Masterson was living with Annie Ladue, nineteen, described as his "concubine," whilst his younger brother, Jim Masterson, by then Dodge's marshal in his turn, was living with Minnie Roberts, sixteen, also a concubine. As Mr. Miller has commented acidly, "Maybe that was the way some of the officers in those days kept watch over juvenile delinquents. They just lived with them."

24   By that time Bat was no longer sheriff, having been walloped in his bid for re-election by George Hinkle, a bartender. Earp had also turned in his star. Dodge was not appreciably tamer, but the silver strike in the Arizona hills meant that there might be more money lying around loose in Tombstone; he followed his brother Virgil there in December, 1879. With him came Mattie; with him too were other Earps, his brothers Jim and Morgan and their wives; and presently, tagging along after him, came Doc Holliday with his common-law wife, Big Nose Kate Fisher, a Dodge prostitute.

25   Tombstone, they soon found, was strangely unlike Dodge City. Four churches were going up. (Groton's future headmaster, Endicott Peabody, was the young Episcopalian clergyman.) There were carpets in the saloons, forsooth, and French phrases on the menus in restaurants. No doubt about it, the Wild West was running out of steam.

26   Dogged traditionalists, Wyatt Earp got a job as a shotgun messenger for Wells Fargo and his brother Jim caught on as a faro banker.

27   Wyatt was not, as the legend has it, a United States marshal at this time. His brother Virgil was appointed a deputy marshal for southern Arizona in November, 1879, and was appointed an assistant town marshal of Tombstone in October, 1880; but Wyatt, after a brief term as civil deputy sheriff of Pima County, went back to gambling at the Oriental Saloon.

28   A word about Doc Holliday. He was, from every account but Wyatt's, a mean and vicious man. He was Georgia-born, tubercular, and fond of killing. After killing two Negroes in Georgia, he fled; after killing a man in Dallas, he fled; after killing a soldier near Fort Richardson, he fled; after wounding a man in Denver, he fled. It was the pattern of his life. Then he met Earp. "Doc idolized him," Masterson said later. And Earp, for his part, found much to admire in Holliday.

29   "With all of Doc's shortcomings and his undeniably poor disposition," Earp told Stuart Lake, "I found him a loyal friend and good company. . . ."

30   Earp's trouble began on the night of March 15, 1881, when a stagecoach left Tombstone carrying eight passengers, and, we are told, $80,000 worth of bullion.* Bandits attempted to halt this miracle of transportation. They failed, but in the process they killed the driver and one passenger. The killer was, according to a statement by his wife, Doc Holliday; and the talk around town was that the brain behind the bungled holdup was Wyatt Earp's. Moving fast, the Earps persuaded Big Nose Kate to retract her statement and bundled her out of town lest she contradict the retraction. There remained the task of silencing forever Holliday's accomplices.

31   Wyatt went to one of their friends, Ike Clanton, and offered a deal. If Clanton would arrange to have those accomplices hold up another stage so that Earp and Holliday could ambush them, he, Earp, would guarantee that Clanton would be paid the reward for

---

* It is always instructive to examine Wild Western estimates. At $1 per fine ounce, $80,000 worth of bullion would weigh two and a half tons, a load sure to snap the axles of any coach.

their capture. Clanton seems to have considered this offer seriously, but at length he refused. The rebuff was serious, for Ike was a blabbermouth who could not be trusted to keep the offer quiet.

32   Nor did he. Scared stiff that he would be shot for a stool pigeon, Clanton denied everything, so loudly and publicly that Doc Holliday overheard him and reported to Wyatt. That was in mid-October. Something would have to be done.

33   On October 26, Ike Clanton was back in Tombstone with his younger brother, Billy. With them were Frank and Tom McLowry and another youngster, Billy Claiborne. All these men were cattle rustlers or, at the very least, hard cases. That morning Virgil Earp, as town marshal, deputized his brothers Wyatt and Morgan, and thereafter the three prowled the streets, seeking to pick a quarrel with the Clantons or the McLowrys. Virgil Earp clubbed Ike Clanton with the barrel of his revolver. Wyatt Earp deliberately jostled Tom McLowry and then struck him. But despite the provocations, there was no fight.

34   That afternoon the Clanton brothers, the McLowry brothers, and Claiborne went to the O.K. Corral to pick up their horses and ride out of town. Wyatt, Virgil, and Morgan Earp, together with Doc Holliday, went after them. Sheriff John Behan tried to interfere, but he was brushed aside.

35   The Earps and Holliday marched into the corral. Somebody spoke; somebody started shooting. After a couple of minutes, Billy Clanton was dead, Frank and Tom McLowry were dead, and Ike Clanton and Billy Claiborne, having run for their lives, were safe. Morgan Earp was hit in the left shoulder; Virgil in the leg; Holliday in the left hip.

36   The Earp apologists have described these slayings as a triumph of law and order. In Tombstone the reaction was somewhat different. A sign over the caskets of the dead proclaimed: MURDERED IN THE STREETS OF TOMBSTONE. A mining engineer named Lewis, who had witnessed what he called cold-blooded murder, was one of three men appointed by the Citizens' Safety Committee to tell the Earps that there should be no more killing inside the town's limits, and that, if there were, the committee would act without regard to law; finally, Virgil Earp was fired as town marshal on October 29.

37   In any case, friends of those slain took matters into their own hands. Virgil Earp was ambushed and wounded on December 29. In March, 1882, Morgan Earp was picked off in the middle of a billiard game, by a sharpshooter who fired through a window from an alley in back. By this time Wyatt Earp had apparently at long last managed to be deputized by a federal marshal. (No records exist in either the Department of Justice or the National Archives to show that he ever held a regular commission as U.S. marshal or deputy.) He in turn deputized such gunmen as Doc Holliday, Turkey Creek Jack Johnson, and Texas Jack Vermillion, and took off in pursuit of his brother's killers.

38   He rode and he rode, but he never came back. He rode north and east to Colorado where, he hoped, he would be safe. Behind him he left Mattie, his common-law wife, who had taken in sewing at a penny a yard when money was scarce. Behind him, too, he left a town so far from being tamed that President Chester Arthur was obliged, a few months later, to threaten martial law. It was left to a short-spoken, sawed-off, former Texas Ranger named John H. Slaughter to restore order to Cochise County.

39   And meanwhile, what of Bat Masterson? He had hustled back to Dodge City from Tombstone in April, 1881, in response to a hurry-up plea for help from his younger brother Jim. This worthy, still Dodge's marshal and also co-owner of a dance hall, had got into a scrape with his partner, A. J. Peacock, and the man they employed as bartender, Al Updegraff, but Jim Masterson was apparently too timid to do his own fighting. His big brother stepped off the train at noon on April 16. Peacock and Updegraff were there waiting, and once again the tiresome shooting commenced. It was laughable. They all fired their guns empty, without effect. Some unknown hero, using a rifle, wounded Updegraff from behind. Masterson was fined $8 for shooting his pistol on the street. The Ford County *Globe* commented, "The citizens are thoroughly aroused and will not stand any more foolishness," while the Jetmore *Republican* referred caustically to "the old gang." Bat and his brother were ordered out of town.

40   Like a cat, Bat landed on his feet in Trinidad, Colorado, where in addition to running a gambling concession he appears to have been appointed a peace officer. Certainly he had some political

influence. For, when an Arizona sheriff came to Denver with a request for the extradition of Wyatt Earp and Doc Holliday, Masterson helped protect them. He got out a warrant for Holliday's arrest on the charge of running a confidence game. This superseded the request for extradition, after which the charges against Holliday were of course dropped. "I know him well," Bat told a reporter for the Denver *Republican,* speaking of Holliday. "He was with me in Dodge, where he was known as an enemy of the lawless element."

41   But the trail led down from glory. In the 1890's Masterson ran a faro layout at the Arcade in Denver, then notoriously the crookedest town in the country. (Earp was dealing nearby, at the Central.) But around the turn of the century Bat was ordered to leave Denver — it was like being told he was too low for the sewer. In 1902 he went to New York where he was at once arrested. On the train from Chicago he had, it seems, fleeced a Mormon elder of $16,000 by using marked cards in a faro game. No matter: New York was then also corrupt; Bat was bailed by John Considine, a partner of Big Tim Sullivan, who bossed the town. The elder was persuaded to mumble that he must have been mistaken when he identified Masterson. When Bat was again arrested, this time for illegally carrying a gun, his friends pulled on strings that led all the way to the White House; and such was the magic of the Wild West legend that President Theodore Roosevelt appointed Masterson a deputy U.S. marshal for the southern district of New York. The term of appointment was brief. Then Bat was put out to pasture as a sports writer for the *Morning Telegraph.* He died at his desk in 1921.

42   Meantime Earp had married a San Francisco woman named Josephine Marcus. As late as 1911 he was accused of complicity in a confidence game, but in the main he had retired to live off his investments. He died in Los Angeles in 1930. The ugliest bit of his past has been dug up, with some disgust, by Frank Waters. It concerns Mattie, the girl Earp deserted in Tombstone. Alone and friendless, Mattie drifted first to Globe and then to a mining camp near Willcox, Arizona. She was reduced to prostitution for a living. In July, 1888, she died of an overdose of laudanum, a suicide. The coroner who sent her few belongings back to her

family in Iowa tucked into the package a letter in which he wrote that Mattie had been deserted by "a gambler, blackleg, and coward." Among her effects was a Bible that had been presented to Earp when he was in Dodge. The inscription read: "To Wyatt S. Earp as a slight recognition of his many Christian virtues and steady following in the footsteps of the meek and lowly Jesus."

43   Amen.

QUESTIONS FOR REFLECTION, DISCUSSION, OR WRITING

(1) Find examples of *irony* in the following paragraphs: 3, 6, 7, 23, and 39. Is the naïve reader apt to be misled by any of these? How effective are they, once recognized for what they are?

(2) Lyon also makes liberal use of metaphors and similes, especially in his first three paragraphs (and, a good one, in par. 5). Find all of these you can, identify by type, and comment on their originality and effectiveness.

(3) Lyon says that there are "Earp apologists" (par. 36) who interpret this "hero's" actions differently. Can you find any indications (granting your limited acquaintance with any but the TV Earp) that the author may be judging Earp and Masterson unfairly?

(4) Are there other legendary "heroes" of the past that you suspect — or know — to be less heroic than the legends would have us believe? Discuss.

(5) Do you think there is more to be gained than lost in finding out the whole truth about past heroes? Does the statement from "How to Detect Propaganda" that "it may be fun to be fooled . . . but it is more fun and infinitely more to our own interest to know . . ." apply as well to the past as to the present? Or do we, and especially younger people, need all the models of courage and fortitude we can get, whether entirely genuine or not?

(6) Undoubtedly you have sometime been disillusioned when you learned the truth about some living "legendary hero" you had known personally or admired from afar. This disillusionment can provide the topic for a good composition.

Joseph Stocker

THE IMMORTAL MODEL T

JOSEPH STOCKER, *who is now public relations director for the Arizona Education Association, started his career with several years in newspaper work in Oklahoma, Colorado, and Arizona. Since then, however, he has devoted most of the past thirteen years to free-lance writing. He has had one book published,* Arizona: A Guide to Easier Living, *and his articles have appeared in more than 90 different magazines.*

THE IMMORTAL MODEL T *was first published in the December 1959 issue of* Coronet *(which ceased publication, after 25 years, in October 1961). It is an example of the light, informal article which blends narration, description, and exposition.*

1   IN THIS ERA of gaudy, expensive, annually obsolescent automobiles, it is hard to realize that a man once grew rich by manufacturing for 19 years the same car in the same model and the same color.

2   The man was Henry Ford and the car was his remarkable Model T.

3   It was an odd-looking contraption, seven feet tall from top to pavement, as ungraceful as a village pump, as eccentric as the village hermit. It went its way making a noise like the end of the world. But it wrought prodigious changes in our nation's living; it was a revolution on wheels.

4   The Model T Ford — more familiarly referred to as the "flivver," "Tin Lizzie," "Leaping Lena" and "The Spirit of St. Vitus" — made its debut in 1908. By 1927, when he finally discontinued it, Henry Ford had produced 15,458,781 Model T's. This was as many cars as were turned out by all other automobile companies put together.

5   Where Ford's competitors issued new models every year, the Model T remained unchanged, except for minor improvements. It kept its same strange, three-pedal floor board (clutch pedal on the left; reverse pedal in the center; brake on the right). And it was an unvarying black. ("Any customer can have a car painted any color he wants," said Ford, "so long as it is black.")

6   The Model T had other quaint characteristics. There was no

left-front door — only the outline of one stamped into the metal. There was no water pump. When the engine over-heated, you lifted the sides of the hood and folded them under. This, as one eye-witness described it, gave the car the "appearance of a hen with her wings akimbo." There was no gas gauge, either. To find out how much fuel you had, you got out of the car, removed the front seat, unscrewed the gas cap beneath it and thrust in a stick or a ruler.

7   The lights of the Model T operated, not on a battery, but on a magneto (introduced after 1914), and glowed or faded according to the speed of the engine. If you became lost at night and stopped to get your bearings, you had to race your engine for enough light to read a sign or peer up the road ahead.

8   Starting a flivver was a massive test of patience, timing and strength. You turned the ignition switch, jerked the spark down, shoved the accelerator up (in early models both were levers under the steering wheel), set the emergency brake and walked resolutely to the front of the car. Pulling the choke wire which extended through the radiator, you grabbed the crank and gave it a hearty spin. If the engine caught, you raced back and jerked the accelerator down again before your snorting, quivering mount shook itself to pieces.

9   Yet with all its eccentricities, the Model T had three hugely endearing attributes. It was cheap (as low as $265 at one time). It was easy to drive. And it was durable. "She may not be pretty," flivver owners conceded, "but she gets you there and she brings you back."

10   A farmer wrote to the Ford factory that he had bought a second-hand Model T roadster two years old. He used it for 13 years as a farm truck, never had to overhaul it, put it in a repair shop only twice and spent just $40 on mechanical upkeep. "I do not know how many hundreds of thousands of miles it has run," the farmer wrote, "as the speedometer was worn out when I bought the car and I never bothered to put another one on."

11   Henry Ford was in the automobile business five years before he started producing the Model T. He had begun, logically, with the Model A, a two-cylinder car generating eight horsepower. He

Reprinted from *Coronet*, December 1959. Copyright 1959 by Esquire, Inc.

went from that to the four-cylinder Model B and on through the alphabet, although some of the models got no further than the drawing board.

12   Model K, when it came along, almost broke the infant Ford Motor Co. To placate stockholders who thought cars were only for the rich, he priced the Model K at $2,750 — and had to sell every one at a loss.

13   This experience stiffened Ford's determination to produce a cheap car. In due course, there emerged from his factory in the Highland Park suburb of Detroit, a Ford known as the Model T. As one student of the era has since observed, "That car had integrity. Perhaps nothing in it was beautiful — but nothing in it was false."

14   Standardized parts, mass-produced, were a prime reason for the cheapness of the Model T. You could buy a muffler for $2, a front fender for $6, a carburetor for $6. Model T parts were available almost everywhere — including five-and-ten-cent stores — and in some of the world's most out-of-the-way places.

15   One astonished motorist told of having broken the drive-shaft pinion in his Model T's differential gear as he jounced across the wastes of Palestine soon after World War I. While he waited for a horse to tow him out, he sought something to eat in a nearby Arab mud hut village. A villager produced some parched beans and a crude scale, contrived of string and two pans. Into one pan he poured the beans. In the other he placed a weight. It was a Ford drive-shaft pinion. The Arab had picked it up at a British Army repair depot during the war.

16   But the marvel of the Model T was its planetary transmission. There was no gearshift to be jiggled until, with grinding and snarling, you slipped into gear. All you did was push the clutch pedal nearly to the floor, which put you in low gear, and give her the gas. When you were hurtling along at 20 miles per hour, you released the clutch to go into high. For reverse, you depressed the center pedal. A child could do it.

17   Attracted by their simplicity as well as their economy, people bought flivvers in droves. For a long time Ford couldn't make enough of them to supply the demand. From 1918 to 1923, although local Ford dealers advertised, Ford disdained to do so. He didn't have to. One of his top executives was heard to remark, with some

satisfaction and pardonable pride, that the Model T wasn't sold —
it was simply "handed over the counter."

18   And so the flivver proliferated. One wisecrack of the period
was: "Two flies can manufacture 48,876,552,154 new flies in six
months, but they haven't anything on two Ford factories." Model
T's rattled through the towns and cities and along the country
roads. Farmers installed tractor wheels and did their plowing with
Model T's. They jacked up the rear end, removed a tire, attached
a belt and ran buzz saws, pumped water, churned butter, ground
feed and generated electricity. Railroads put flanged wheels on
Model T's and used them as inspection cars. Movie companies
made Model T's collapsible and used them in Keystone Cop
comedies.

19   In the wake of its popularity there sprang up a whole school of
Model T humor:

20   "Why is a Ford like a bathtub?"

21   "You hate to be seen in one."

22   "Didja know that Ford's going to paint his cars yellow so they
can be hung outside of grocery stores and sold in bunches like
bananas?"

23   The Devil (to a new arrival): "Help yourself to any of these
cars and take a spin around Hades."

24   Motorist: "But these are all Fords."

25   Devil: "Sure, that's the Hell of it."

26   "Heard the one about the farmer? He stripped the tin roof
off his barn, sent it to Ford and got back a letter saying, "While
your car was an exceptionally bad wreck, we will be able to complete repairs and return it by the end of the week."

27   These Model T jokes grew so plentiful that ultimately they
were anthologized into books and hawked on railroad trains as,
"Uncanny Stories About a Canny Car."

28   One of the few people who thought Ford jokes unfunny was
James Couzens, who variously served as treasurer and vice president
of the company and later was a U.S. Senator. A Detroit newspaper
reporter wrote a story about the epidemic of Model T jokes and
included several samples. Couzens forthwith sent a tart note
forbidding the paper ever to mention the name of the Ford Motor
Co. again. This, of course, was a fairly meaningless injunction. More

meaningful was the fact that Couzens also cancelled all of Ford's advertising in the paper.

29   The reporter went to see Ford.

30   "Jim has no sense of humor," chuckled Ford. "I'll cancel the cancellation." Then he told the reporter some new Ford stories he'd just heard himself.

31   Plainly, the Model T magnate recognized that Ford jokes — complimentary or otherwise — were fine free publicity. One of his own favorite stories concerned the time he was traveling in a Ford car, inspecting some Michigan lumber properties with several aides. They came onto a farmer who was having trouble with his automobile — a beaten-up Ford. Ford and his men stopped, went to work on the car and, after replacing some spark plugs, got it running again.

32   "How much do I owe you fellers?" asked the farmer.

33   "Nothing," said Ford, rolling down his sleeves.

34   The farmer looked at him dubiously. "Can't make you out," he puzzled. "You talk as if money didn't mean anything to you, but if you've got so much money, why are you running around in a Ford?"

35   Henry Ford did indeed make a lot of money out of the Model T. He became, in fact, one of the two or three wealthiest men in the world. Moreover, the Model T brought fantastic returns to his original stockholders before he bought them all out. A young Detroit lawyer, John W. Anderson, invested $5,000 and got back $12,500,000. Jim Couzens' sister, who skeptically put up $100 (but refused to go as high as $200) collected $95,000 in dividends and was finally paid $260,000 for her $100 interest. In all, $28,000 was invested in the Ford Motor Co. by 12 people, and in ten years they made back a quarter-billion dollars.

36   Henry Ford castigated competitors who brought out new models every year. "It does not please us to have a buyer's car wear out or become obsolete," he said. "We want the man who buys one of our products never to have to buy another."

37   But in the mid-1920s, the flivver began to encounter sales resistance. Other makes, with their gearshifts, accessories, lively colors and annual model changes, were catching the fancy of the public. Ford blamed the Model T's loss of popularity on almost

everything except the Model T. He said that the dealers' "mental attitude" was bad. He said that the American people had "fallen under the spell of salesmanship." But at last, reluctantly, Ford agreed that the Model T had to give way to mechanical progress.

38   The whole nation waited in tingling suspense for news of the new Ford. When the new Model A appeared with stylish lines and in different colors, it made the front page of practically every newspaper in the U.S. And with it came one final Ford joke: "Henry's made a lady out of Lizzie."

39   Not everybody greeted the change-over with great joy. When an elderly woman in New Jersey heard that the Model T's were being discontinued, she bought seven of them and stored them away so she would have Model T's the rest of her life and never have to change.

40   On May 26, 1927, the 15,000,000th Model T rolled off the assembly line. Shortly afterward production of the phenomenal flivvers stopped entirely. An era had ended.

QUESTIONS FOR REFLECTION, DISCUSSION, OR WRITING

(1) What do you think was the author's primary purpose in writing this article? His secondary purpose? How successfully was each achieved? Were they worth achieving?

(2) Find two paragraphs each of straight narration, description, and exposition. Be prepared to tell why you classify them as you do. Is there any argumentation in the article?

(3) Can you explain the current fad of restoring Model T's and other old cars? Does this seem to you worthwhile as a hobby? Why, or why not?

(4) What do you think of Americans' apparent love of "gaudy, expensive, annually obsolescent automobiles" (par. 1) — a love which supports one of our largest industries? Can it be explained merely by the phrase "keeping up with the Joneses"? To what extent has the car become a "status symbol"?

(5) Does the fact that most of the compact foreign cars retain the same model year after year, as did the Model T, have much to do with their increasing popularity in America? What else is responsible for this popularity? In what way, if any, are the foreign compacts also status symbols?

(6) Do you believe the American people have "fallen under the spell of salesmanship," as Ford thought several decades ago (par. 37)? Explain how

this "spell" affects American buying of other products than the automobile? Is there anything we as individuals could or should do about it? Does this kind of "salesmanship" involve any of the "seven devices of propaganda"? Explain.

$*$
$*$

A CASUAL LOOK AROUND

$*$
$*$
$*$
$*$
$*$
$*$
$*$
$*$
$*$
$*$
$*$
$*$
$*$
$*$
$*$
$*$
$*$

George Nelson

**OUT OF THE TRACKLESS BUSH,
A NATIONAL CAPITAL**

GEORGE NELSON *is an architect, president of an industrial design firm in New York City. He has taught at Yale and Columbia universities and Pratt Institute. Also a successful author in the field of architecture, Mr. Nelson has been a member of the staff of* Time, Inc., *a contributing editor of* Interiors Magazine, *editor of several books, and author of others. His articles have been published in such widely varying magazines as* Holiday, Industrial Design, *and* McCall's.

SATURDAY REVIEW, *in which this article first appeared March 12, 1960, is published weekly in New York and circulated in all parts of the world. Founded in 1924 under the name* Saturday Review of Literature, *it soon earned a solid reputation for literary criticism. Since the name was changed to Saturday Review in 1952, the magazine no longer confines its interest to literary matters but now covers a wide range of general information and opinion.*

OUT OF THE TRACKLESS BUSH, A NATIONAL CAPITAL *makes no pretense of telling us everything about Brasília. The author has not even mentioned, for instance, such matters as its cost or the sometimes violent opposition to its construction. But these things are omitted because they are irrelevant to Nelson's* **central theme,** *his* **thesis.**

It is often helpful in understanding an exposition (this exposition, by the way, makes liberal use of description to aid in the explanation) to phrase for ourselves what is apparently the author's theme — in one sentence or so to summarize what he is telling us. If it is a good composition, everything he writes will pertain to this one theme, directly or indirectly, like tributaries flowing into the main river.

In this essay the author comes closer than most to saying, over and over again, "Here is my theme" — e.g. in paragraph 4: "[Brasília] will be the first complete, concrete image of the twentieth century that a layman can understand by simply looking at it." Or, in paragraph 14: "the impact lies in the force with which an image of modern life has been presented . . ."

1   AT SANTOS DUMONT Airport in Rio you get into a plane and fly north and west. You are on the last lap in a series of jet-powered leaps that have taken you from New York to the new capital, Brasília, created out of the Brazilian bush. Coming south now on Varig Airlines Caravelles, the flight plan sounds like a cruise. New York to Nassau in three hours, then Nassau to Trinidad in three and a half. Another three to Belém, three more to Rio. Twice a week Varig brings its new jets into the new capital. On this last lap you fly for a scant two hours, almost all of it over land as empty as Monument Valley. Then, after some 600 miles, there is a stir of excitement in the plane; people lean over to the windows, press forward to the flight deck. Presently there appear up ahead great gashes in the red earth and, at closer range, huge clusters of ultra-modern buildings scattered over a spread of miles. Seen in the vast emptiness of the central plateau, the sight is as shocking as a camel in the Antarctic.

2   In the little wooden terminal, a crowd jostles, drinks coffee, greets new arrivals, gets on planes. People are lean, brown, relaxed,

dressed in jeans or chinos. Inevitably, images of our own West come to mind. Outside, Jeeps and VWs, the two cars which have taken over Brasília, wheel in rust-colored dust and disappear. In the distance one sees the fantastic bunches of towers. It could be a movie set on a scale that would have pauperized even a De-Mille, but it isn't. Even so, the fact of so much gleaming modernity in the middle of 250,000 square miles of nothing is too much to grasp. So you leave the airport for the capital-to-be. Through miles of scrub and scraggly trees goes a road laid out on the scale of a major superhighway.

3   Almost everything about Brasília verges on the fantastic: the boldness of the concept, the scope of the planning, the truly incredible speed with which the city is going up. But there is nothing fantastic about the reasons for it. Here is a country as big as the U.S. with an extra Texas thrown in. Its central regions are bursting with natural wealth while its population clusters in the old cities on or near the seacoast. Since the interior is empty there are no roads. Without roads the resources are inaccessible. The country craves rapid industrial development. What to do? Brasília is one of the answers, and a very daring one. Far from the coast, in the heart of the region awaiting exploitation, a magnet is being constructed. A magnet for people, for roads, for money. To make sure the magnet works, it is designated the national capital. Brasília is going up in extreme haste because in Brazilian politics it is almost a point of honor for a new administration to abandon the projects of its predecessors. President Kubitschek, who dreamed the dream and could not, by law, be reelected, had only three years in which to make the dream come true. When Kubitschek steps down from office, his successor will have to continue, for by then the functions of federal government will have been moved out of Rio.

4   What makes Brasília so utterly remarkable is that the breathtaking sweep of Kubitschek's vision has been matched by the architects. This is no mere collection of large buildings, but a very powerful expression. It happens that Brazil is fortunate in her architects: for thirty years they have maintained a position of international leadership. Brasília, planned by Lucio Costa, its major

buildings designed by Oscar Niemeyer, will be the first complete, concrete image of the twentieth century that a layman can understand by simply looking at it.

5   The architects talk about the city in a relaxed, almost detached way. "It isn't really a city yet, just a framework," says Costa. "It will take ten years to become a city."

6   "Everything we have done here is really quite simple," says Niemeyer. "I have tried to make the buildings beautiful. Beauty lasts."

7   "They didn't give us any time," explains Costa. "We started less than three years ago. So the plan had to be simple and straightforward. There is a major axis, with the most important government buildings on it. There is a minor axis, through the main housing blocks. Where the two cross, we are building a concrete platform on which we have located the entertainment center. Nothing remarkable. It's just a town."

8   "There are many mistakes," says Niemeyer, "but what could one do? They are in a big hurry. That hotel you are staying in had to be designed in one week."

9   Niemeyer, who gave up his Rio office to work full time on Brasília (as a government employee at $250 per month), has a drafting table in a construction shack, a telephone, and apparently no secretary. There are perhaps two dozen draftsmen in an adjoining room. One of his chores is the making of hundreds of on-the-spot decisions in the course of a day.

10   "They are always asking Oscar what to do," said one of his assistants.

11   "Don't you have people who could help?" I asked. Outside there were some 45,000 workmen who were doing, in effect, what Niemeyer had told them to do.

12   "Oscar isn't an organization type," he replied. Suddenly he laughed. "You know, if we had been organized we never could have done it."

13   There is no way of getting at the essence of Brasília by describing its components. Like other cities, it will have fire stations, drugstores, and a golf course. Its most spectacular features, as one might expect, are at the heart of the town, where the top functions of government are exercised. Here again, Brasília differs from other

capitals only in the form and placing of the required structures. One comes closer to an understanding of the special character of the city as one begins to realize that problems taken for granted in older cities simply do not exist here. Traffic, for instance. It is unlikely that there ever will be a traffic or parking problem. The town's design accepts the motor vehicle. Other city problems, such as adequate light and air for all dwellings, do not exist. These amenities have been built in. Safe play areas for children, good school buildings, decentralized shopping — these things also exist. It is a strange experience to be in a town where the typical urban problems have been eliminated.

14   All this suggests that Brasília is a functional design for a community, and while this is true — at least by comparison — it still does not quite take one to the heart of the matter, for the excitement of this place could not be created by a functional solution alone. Niemeyer comes closer when he talks about beauty, but I could imagine someone finding Brasília's architecture far from beautiful, and still sensing the excitement it generates. My best guess is that the impact lies in the force with which an image of modern life has been presented, not at one level, but at many. For example, a town designed to let motor vehicles move around cannot have close-packed buildings on narrow streets: the workable answer puts high buildings in parks, leaving plenty of room for cars. In this sense, Brasília naturally looks "modern" because it is. But the expression goes much deeper. One of the products of modern life is the bureaucrat, the "organization man." In Brasília the government ministries are housed in two rows of absolutely identical office buildings. They give the impression of glass-sided beehives. At 5:00 P.M. the bees (stingless) swarm home to the "quadras" — superblocks filled with eight-story apartment houses on stilts. In the morning they swarm back again. The architectural statement — identical offices, identical apartments — is truthful, disturbing, but also humane. People can live and work decently here. For the individualists who will reject life in Brasília's crystal palaces, there is no strait jacket: there are other kinds of work, and there is plenty of land where a man can put up his own house. The power of the architectural image lies in its multi-layered truth. Brasília, in other words, can be enjoyed and evaluated like any other work

of art; and its creators, like other artists. The significance of the image lies in its depth: the city reflects — accepts — the positive *and* negative aspects of contemporary society. There is no pretense that the little nonentity in Cubicle 99 on Floor 18 is another Simón Bolívar, or, for that matter, even much of an individual. On the other hand, Brasília is no image of 1984. It is going to be a very human, very livable city.

15   Such apparent contradictions as these ("beehive" vs. "human" and so on) are another indication of the maturity and vitality of the artists. Let me cite another example. Niemeyer obviously believes in standardization. Virtually every building of any importance is a vertical slab of the U.N. type: this applies to offices, hospitals, banks, housing. The other important category, including the Supreme Court, Presidential Palace, etc., is a long, low box: the slab, again, now laid on its side. But having accepted the slab, Niemeyer also deviates, as in the Senate (a dome), the Chamber of Deputies (a bowl), the Cathedral (a curved inverted funnel), the Museum (a marble boxcar on a marble stand), and various churches around town. Against the standardized patterns, these departures register on the beholder with terrific force. Curiously enough, the frank acceptance of standardization does not result in monotony at all, and here, I suspect is one of the major lessons for architects.

16   Brasília's plan and architecture have, quite understandably, been the targets of criticism from many quarters. No doubt some of it is justified. In one sense the town is all exterior, from the viewpoint of interest; for Brazil, with far more than its share of brilliant architects, planners, and landscape architects, has not yet produced an interior designer of stature. As a result many of the most important buildings, inside, look as if nobody quite knew what to do with what the architect left behind him. Yet this is minor, for the omissions can be made good in time. I have no particular interest in producing new critical observations at the moment, for it seems to me that the important thing is to acknowledge the unique force, quality, and integrity of the statement.

17   Brasília is a place to be seen and experienced. It is hard to believe that anyone could visit it and come away without some modifications of attitude, whether with respect to modern architecture,

to city planning, or to the emerging shapes of contemporary life. If I were a tourist and had my choice of visiting Brasília or, say, the Taj Mahal, I would pick the former. At this point in time it has much more to say, and it says it with great power and beauty.

QUESTIONS FOR REFLECTION, DISCUSSION, OR WRITING

(1) If you had not already known that the author is an architect, would you have guessed that he might be? Why?

(2) Where else in the essay, besides the paragraphs quoted in the headnotes, does Nelson tell us his *theme*, his central *thesis*, in still other ways? Explain this theme in your own way.

(3) Do any parts of the essay seem irrelevant? Are there any that do not, even indirectly, flow into the "main river" of the author's theme?

(4) Twice (in pars. 14 and 16) the author mentions a "statement," obviously using the word in a way unfamiliar to most of us. Try to explain just how he is using it. Where, especially, do you find the meaning partially clarified in the essay itself?

(5) The author says this architectural statement — *e.g.*, identical offices, identical apartments — is "truthful, disturbing, but also humane." Explain what *he* means by each of the three adjectives.

(6) Consider again the part of paragraph 14 in which the author compares the government employees with bees — and also, at the end of the paragraph, where he says, "There is no pretense that the little nonentity . . . is even much of an individual." Do you find this philosophy depressing? Explain why or why not.

(7) For the average *Saturday Review* reader, who will never even see Brasília, what is to be gained by reading such an article as this? Does it, for example, hold any significance for *you?* If so, explain.

(8) Would you like to live and work in Brasília? If so, would you prefer to live in a "quadra," or would you be one of the "individualists" the author mentions in paragraph 14? Give a full and clear explanation of your reasons.

Time Magazine

BRAZIL'S WILD WEST

TIME *Magazine, the oldest of the weekly "newsmagazines," was started in 1923 and now has a circulation of more than 2½ million. It is printed in four special editions: Atlantic, Pacific, Canadian, and Latin-American editions. Consistent in their distinctive, sprightly style, the articles of* Time *cover all phases of worldwide current affairs. They are usually written by members of the magazine's staff and printed without by-lines.*

BRAZIL'S WILD WEST, *which seems a logical sequel to our preceding essay, was published in* Time's *June 20, 1960, issue. Ordinarily news stories or news features such as this give a reasonably forthright statement of central theme early in the story.*

1   AMERICANS have always dreamed of the great frontier, where the wind blows free — and land is cheap. Last week many a land-hungry U.S. citizen thought that he had found a frontier where land is so cheap that a few cents buys an acre. The new frontier is in Brazil, where a giant land development push is rivaling the rough days of the American West. Along with Brazilians, Japanese and Germans, hundreds of U.S. investors have bought cattle and coffee ranches, speculated heavily in still-uncleared jungle lands along the route of projected highways and railroads.

2   Spurred by Brazil's great push to develop its interior, 15 U.S. companies are peddling land in Brazil. Every month the U.S. embassy gets 100 letters of inquiry about land deals. A Georgia square-dance caller who wanted a plot of land wrote directly to U.S. Ambassador John M. Cabot, promised, "If you help me out, kind sir, we'll build a barn and have a square dance that'll make all sit up and take notice. Free lessons for you and Mrs. Ambassador if you're willing."

3   Like any great speculation, the Brazilian boom has attracted its share of swindlers and shady companies. Convicted Texas Swindler BenJack Cage once promoted a land development company that is now in more reputable hands, has sold nearly 200,000 acres to Americans for more than $1,000,000.

4   *"Texas Ranches."* The Rockefeller brothers own 40% of a

1,000,000-acre cattle ranch in the rich Mato Grosso, which they operate jointly with Brazil's Ambassador to Washington Walther Moreira Salles.

5   Only 50 miles from Brazil's new $500 million inland capital, Brasília (*Time*, April 25), Singer Mary Martin and her husband Richard Halliday have a 1,200-acre ranch where they raise coffee, sugar and chickens. Says Broadway Producer Halliday: "The climate is the amazing thing. It has a steady temperature (about 72°) twelve months of the year." Cowboy Roy Rogers recently bought 2,000 acres near Brasília. Says Rogers optimistically: "Land is dirt cheap there now, just like in the Old West. But in ten or 15 years it will be worth a fortune."

6   Many U.S. buyers have already done well on their Brazilian land speculations. Pan American Airways Vice President Humphrey Toomey bought 105 acres just outside Brasília for $1,800 six months ago. Now he is selling it in quarter-acre lots, expects to get $156,000. Land Developer Mike Borman bought 36,000 acres northeast of Brasília for $15,000 two years ago, is selling it off in 25-acre "Texas Ranches" for $10 down and $10 per month.

7   The impetus for the boom is the recent opening of Brasília and the continued growth of railways and highways in the interior under the sponsorship of Brazil's hurry-up President Juscelino Kubitschek. (His slogan: "Fifty years of progress in five.") Paved highways have increased from 6,000 miles to 10,000 miles in the past four years. Last week Kubitschek embarked on a new project: he ordered a 480-mile highway from Manaus to Pôrto Velho, in the wild Amazonas state, to be built by 1961.

8   *Dry-Gulched.* There are also birds of prey at work. One woebegotten speculator complained to the U.S. embassy in Rio that he had bought, from a group describing themselves as California missionaries, 2,000 eroded acres that proved to be a dirt road instead of a highway, and had a dry gulch in the middle instead of a gushing stream. The embassy warns all comers that titles held even by legitimate land development companies may be clouded, and that in the great growth areas of Mato Grosso or Goiás frequently a purchaser "must take possession and actively defend the

Reprinted by permission from *Time*, the Weekly Newsmagazine; copyright Time, Inc., 1960.

title if he expects to retain effective control of his property." Mary Martin's husband adds: "It's best to go down and see what you're getting and be sure your agent is reliable."

9 For those willing to take the risk, rewards can be sizable, since Brazil has low capital-gains and inheritance taxes. With a good superintendent on a salary or shares, a coffee, cacao, carnauba-wax plantation or cattle ranch can be made to pay for itself within six years.

Some of the boom areas:

10 ¶ Northwest Paraná state, where Brazilian-born, Harvard-educated ('24), Alberto Byington bulldozed 1,000 miles of dirt roads on the 1,000,000-acre site that he received from the Brazilian government for building a railroad. Last year Byington sold $1,000,000 worth of 60-acre sites for coffee farms at $35 per acre.

11 ¶ Northern Goiás state, opened up last year by the new highway between Brasília and Belém, is good for cattle raising, offers land for as low as 50¢ per acre.

12 ¶ Southern Goiás, where land sells for $10 to $20 per acre, is good for cattle and many crops. It has many U.S. land-owners, a new railroad abuilding.

13 ¶ Mato Grosso's southern Pantanal, flood-basin plains, is a first-class cattle country with miserable roads but improving rail service. Land there costs $1.50 to $2 per acre. In the northern Mato Grosso lands of Gleba Arinos (named for the adjoining river), a German-Brazilian family, incorporated as Coromali, is developing 750,000 acres, selling guaranteed titles for $2 per acre. Coromali will also contract to clear, plant and administer ranches.

14 How solid is the boom? As solid as Brazil's future, say top government officials. In the past five years U.S. private investments in Brazil have doubled to more than $1.4 billion. Brazil's real gross national product is increasing 10% a year, and the nation's 65 million population is expected to swell to 100 million by 1975. Although there is wild inflation, land values have risen faster than the cruzeiro has depreciated.

QUESTIONS FOR REFLECTION, DISCUSSION, OR WRITING

(1) In which paragraph does the author give us a neat, one-sentence statement of his theme? What is it? How well does everything else in the story pertain to it?

(2) In what ways might we expect the "development push" of Brazil to differ considerably from the "rough days of the American West"? What might be the similarities?

(3) What is the difference between buying land for "speculation" and buying it for other purposes?

(4) What is meant by the word "titles," which may be "clouded" and may need actively defending in Brazil (par. 8)?

(5) Were you surprised at the cost of Brasília? Does $500 million seem cheap or expensive for a whole new city? Would it have been more or less than that if built in this country? Why?

(6) *Time* says the rewards can be sizable "for those willing to take the risk" (par. 9). How many risks can you think of that would be involved in such a venture? Since this article was written, there have been political troubles and nearly violent administration changes — does this fact suggest any risks to you? Explain.

(7) If someone else would take the financial risk, would you be willing to go to Brazil to live and seek your fortune? Organize a full explanation of your answer into a well developed composition.

Patrick O'Donovan

ANCHORAGE

PATRICK O'DONOVAN *is an English writer, a correspondent for the London Observer. He is a contributor to the British Broadcasting Company, and his articles have frequently appeared in American magazines.*

ANCHORAGE *is one of a series entitled "Portraits of Our Cities," which Mr. O'Donovan wrote for* The New Republic *(see p. 72); it was published in that magazine Aug. 18, 1959. This essay is one of almost pure description — a difficult assignment for any but the most skilled writer, if it is to maintain readers' interest for as many as 1500 words, the approximate length of this one.*

1   IT LOOKS like the northern rim of the world, when the last of
the land, uninhabitable and useless, heaps up in one last rampart
against the sea and the things beyond the mist. The plane heaves
itself over a landscape crowded with mountains from horizon to
horizon. Coal black and streaked with snow, their tips are arrow
sharp and their edges like misused knife blades.

2   The valleys are narrow and choked with ice. Occasionally there
is a trapped lake rimmed with trees and dotted with ice. Sometimes,
pouring motionless between mountains, there is a frozen cataract
of ice, a glacier wrinkled with age and pressure, coming from
nowhere and going nowhere. And nearer to the sea, there are long
gray fjords picking their way between the mountains that start up
direct from the water. It is as harsh as any desert, a ferocious lunar
landscape, black and white, heaved up, tumultuous, motionless
and dead.

3   And then quite suddenly, without foothills, the mountains cease
and there is a city among trees standing on a ledge, seventy-five
miles square, that is thrust out into the water. The ledge looks almost artificial, a reclamation scheme. It is a freak of the debris of
the mountains. The city has a perfunctory Middle Western air, a
hint of skyscrapers at the center, a suggestion of churches, and a
rigid pattern of squared blocks that peter out into suburbs and unused land.

4   This is Anchorage, the largest city in Alaska, with a population
of about 100,000. It began in 1914 as a railway construction camp.
It survived because the railway that runs from the lonely port of
Seward, up through the mountains and onto the tundra for Fair-
banks, set up its repair shops here. It grew with the building of an
airport that has become a crossroads in the planning of international
flights. It was laid out by agents of the federal government. It sits
on the brink of a future that depends, not so much on brave young
pioneers with their bare hands and their picks and ploughs and
axes, as on great corporations who will blast out new communica-
tions, exploit inconveniently placed but limitless minerals, build
a deep-water port and harness rivers for power.

5   The citizens of Anchorage, like other Alaskans in their rare

fanciful moments, like to describe their land as the Last Frontier. It is a pleasant idea but a purely romantic one. It is not the last frontier; it is the new sort of frontier and there are several of them in the world. Siberia, for example, the interior of Australia, Central Africa. They are not waiting for the courage of men with a future to make out of nothing but their manhood. That indeed has been tried and has made only a small impression on these places. What is needed is the financial initiative, the splendid and reliable checks of large corporations and governments, the skill of the graduates of mining schools and men who can build roads.

6   Their work must be half complete before this country can fill the gaps with a large population. In the meantime there are high wages for workmen, especially if they are skilled and can endure monastic discomforts in the wilderness; there are steady jobs for company servants and representatives; there are the usual service jobs and a deal of small private enterprises. But only for the very few and the very fortunate are there the rewards of a frontier — a cattle barony, a mining kingdom.

7   There is unemployment. There are signs of poverty. You can still obtain a holding of 160 acres for next to nothing, and providing you set a dwelling on it, it is yours. But it may take you three generations of peasant labor to clean and create a prosperous farm out of your section of the North and you would be wise to start your holding with a capital of, say, $25,000.

8   These factors are visible in the city of Anchorage. It is not a rip-roaring boom town. Its pace is curiously leisurely, that of an English market town on any day except market day and Sunday. The traffic is sedate and sparse and drivers complain only mildly if their steady progress is checked by a bunch of three ahead or a laden station wagon turning in their path.

9   It is clearly a town caught in a moment of transition. There is no frenzy of building activity, though that clearly will soon start. For miles it is a system of lots in which a small wooden house sits, surrounded by shabby trees, by wasteland, or (in the spring at least) by an explosion of tender flowers. On the outskirts the houses are often little better than shacks, garishly and carelessly painted, with a do-it-yourself air and no sort of care or elegance or pride. Closer in and right into the city, the houses still stand alone,

each with its garden, each with its cylinders of cooking gas under
the eaves, not bothering to be Cape Cod or Colonial, but merely
small, wooden, minimum-expense houses, crammed with nicknacks,
dominated by television sets and china cabinets and bright pictures
of sunlit landscapes — fierce and eloquent assertions of coziness,
warm as toast and classless as all get out.

10   Only at the center does the city coalesce into seven or eight
"city blocks" where the shops stand shoulder to shoulder and each
building is at least two stories high. This is the pleasant center,
designed not so much for the quiet townsfolk as for the workers
who come in from the mountains and the tundra, at the most, once
in six weeks.

11   It is true that there is one place with swinging doors where you
can buy beer by the jug. But the frontier atmosphere is contrived,
and it has a backroom full of teenagers who worship a juke box
there. The bars tend to be of the sort that were designed for the
rich and the spoiled in Europe. They are richly dark. The *banquettes*
are of rich velvet. The chandeliers are crystal. There is an atmosphere of wealth and calculated luxury.

12   They are not clip joints; they fulfill some obvious need in high
salaried, unmarried workers who desire a violent and brief change.
The men drinking are men who will probably not buy homes or
marry here. The company tends to be male. Men in clothes which
shout that they are their best clothes. Youths in jeans and heavy
working boots who yet wear black silk shirts with silver *lamé* in-
serts. Men with cheeks which have been scabbed by the wind and
the cold making a fuss about the lemon peel in their martini. Men
growing tipsy, sometimes, but without the second-hand Irish melancholy of New York. Perhaps, too, an almost continual consciousness
and elation in being in Alaska, in taking part in some monumental
lark.

13   The center is a small, exaggerated city. There are no buildings
with architectural pretensions, not a pillar, not a cornice in the
place. Not a single lapidary cliché carved into marble or its substi-
tutes.

14   There are shops, but of a different sort. There are trinket shops
where you can buy debased Eskimo handicrafts, dreadful little
things carved out of Walrus ivory. There are fragments of dull jade

and soapstone and ashtrays that depict igloos and seal hunts.

15   There are sports shops with windows heaped up with rods, guns, tents, and sensible clothing. There are rather more than any city's share of army surplus stores. There is a charming little shop, run by a kindly white-haired gentleman, which sells, mostly, pistols. He also sells knives of every sort from delicate penknives to great Bowie knives that ought to have names of their own like American swords. He also lends money on watches. He also sells slender stilettos, and, for the life of me, I can only think of one practical use for them.

16   For the real point of Anchorage is not the place itself or its physical appearance, but its surrounding splendors. There is the rim of mountains at the back, there in front is the arm of the inlet which Captain Cook first discovered. The scale is enormous. At one end of the chief street — 4th Avenue — your view is shut by mountains and at the other end it bends in the gray sea. The beaches are gray too, and leave your hand dirty. They are littered with splintered silver driftwood. The water is empty of ships, and when the tide sinks some thirty feet it exposes shining wet mud banks for the sea birds.

17   But above all it is the suggestion of size — the comfortable, unpretentious city under the mountains and beyond the mountains the tundra, and beyond that more mountains and beyond that the arctic slopes, and all on a continental scale.

18   There is juvenile delinquency; there is drunkenness; there is loneliness and destructive disappointment. But above it all is an excitement that does not come from greed. The mountains rising from the ground are a little gentler. The valleys are green just now and loud with streams. The wilderness, which is by tradition the source of the American virtue, is less than an hour's drive away. There are animals to watch or to kill that are as exciting as major works of art. People here do not really expect to grow rich overnight; they do expect a full life in the process of staying alive. Anchorage is a curiously satisfying place.

QUESTIONS FOR REFLECTION, DISCUSSION, OR WRITING

(1) Was O'Donovan successful in creating an interesting, vivid description? Try to analyze the descriptive passages you liked best. What contributed to

their success: the author's selection of details to be shared, his choices of words, uses of figures of speech, or other techniques?

(2) In what ways, if any, might a series of "portraits" of American cities written by a foreigner be more interesting or valuable than one written by an American?

(3) Although in Anchorage there was, at the time of this writing, no frenzy of building activity as in many other American cities, the author says one "clearly will soon start" (par. 9). What will cause this? Will Alaska's statehood be at all responsible? If so, in what way?

(4) Alaska, so far, has made few advancements in any of the arts (including literature, music, architecture). How can you account for this fact?

(5) Explain the author's meaning when he calls the wilderness "by tradition the source of the American virtue" (par. 18)?

(6) Try to explain in other ways the "almost continuous consciousness and elation in being in Alaska, in taking part in some monumental lark" (par. 12), and the "excitement that does not come from greed" (par. 18). Have you ever, under other circumstances, experienced such excitement, elation? Try to describe it.

(7) Discuss the aptness and significance of the metaphor in "a backroom full of teenagers who worship a juke box there" (par. 11). Had this figurative comparison ever occurred to you before?

(8) If someone were to give you the $25,000 development capital (par. 7), would you be interested in trying to "clean and create a prosperous farm" in Alaska? Why, or why not?

(9) Young Americans today are sometimes accused of being too "security-conscious" — less interested in the adventure of challenge than in immediate security. Is this charge true? Do you feel any urge to participate in the development of one of the world's "new frontiers" (par. 5) — if not on a farm, then perhaps in some urban occupation? Explain your feelings in this respect.

(10) If you had a choice, would you rather live in a Brasilian-type "quadra" (see p. 159) or in one of the Anchorage houses that are "merely small . . . [and] classless as all get out" (par. 9)? Explain your reasons.

(11) A good writing assignment might also be your description of some city or town with which you are familiar.

The New Yorker

CANDY

THE NEW YORKER, *contrary to the implication of its name, is a magazine of national circulation — a weekly circulation of approximately half a million in all. Started in 1925, The New Yorker has retained much the same format, style, and sophisticated brand of humor throughout the years. It publishes articles, reviews and commentaries, short stories, verse, and cartoons. The magazine is devoted largely but not exclusively to the many phases of life in the New York area, and always to matters of metropolitan interest. It has always provided an airing-place for worthwhile experimental writing, and many of the country's leading authors have started (and sometimes ended) in* The New Yorker.

CANDY, *taken from the June 3, 1961, issue, was a part of the regular weekly feature, "Talk of the Town," which is staff-written and contains no by-lines. Subject matter may vary in one issue from spring flowers to brief "overheard" remarks, from the Central Intelligence Agency to Kenneth the hair stylist and a "Television Nightmare." (It did so vary, as a matter of fact, in a May issue of 1961.) "Candy," which can hardly be called "typical" of such mixed fare, is at least representative of it.*

1   LONG AGO, when salesmanship was local and unscientific, consumership was an adventurous activity, involving a more or less frivolous exercise of power. One of the last pockets of frivolity was wiped out some months ago with the foundation of the Candy, Chocolate, and Confectionery Institute, a union of forces designed to educate the public in "the many positive appeals of confectionery products," for the defection of candymen to the industrial promotional ranks can only crush what remains of the consumer's spirit of *carpe diem.* According to John A. Mavrakos, president of the C.C.C.I., the candymen had been brooding about their status for some time. "Our industry long has felt the need for a program to communicate the taste appeal, nutritive values, and wholesomeness of our products," he recently told us. And according to a set lecture prepared by the institute, "Industry leaders wondered [several years ago] if the taste appeal was the sole factor. They felt a thorough knowledge of the public's most basic feelings about candy might

provide direction as to the ways promotional campaigns should be set up." We learned from Miss Elinor Ehrman, vice-president of Theodore R. Sills & Co., which is the firm in charge of public relations for the C.C.C.I., that the institute plans to invest a quarter of a million dollars a year in promotional campaigns.

2   The psychological data amassed by the institute's researchers indicate that the public's most basic feelings about candy include associating it with thoughts of home and parents — a happy association, that is. "They either think of some happy occasion, of a happy time with their parents, of an incident at school, or a reward of some kind." As for physiological benefits, research has come up with testimony by *MD* (a medical journal) as to candy's quick "energy-yield"; its usefulness in preventing seasickness, inhibiting alcoholism, and preparing for surgery (it increases blood sugar without adding bulk or fat); and its resistance to mold. (Miss Ehrman confessed that there had been some difficulty about locating congenial dentists.) Furthermore, the National Safety Council has recommended eating candy to prevent drowsiness ("Keep Some in the Glove Compartment"); diet experts are reported to have suggested eating anything from a sourball (thirteen calories) to a chocolate (forty-seven calories) to palliate the craving for richer desserts; and military experts consulted by the candy industry have pointed to a reduced accident rate among candy-eating fliers in the Second World War. Would the Boer War have ended as it did if Queen Victoria had neglected to send her troops five hundred thousand pounds of candy for Christmas in 1899?

3   As a matter of fact, the early history of candy is decidedly military. It seems that sugar was introduced to the West in 325 B.C. by one of Alexander the Great's soldiers, who was impressed by the taste of a plant he found on the banks of the Indus. The Aztecs, presumably before they were quite subdued by Cortés, introduced him to a cold, bitter drink called *cacahuatl*, and he sent a sample to King Charles I of Spain, who civilized it somewhat by adding sugar. (Columbus had supposedly tried to interest Spain in the cacao bean several years earlier, without success.) Spain immediately began setting up cocoa plantations in the colonies, and managed to maintain a monopoly on the method of preparing the drink for a hundred years or so before the secret leaked out (allegedly

through some Spanish monks), first in France and then in England. By 1750, chocolate was being drunk in most of the civilized world. The first chocolate factory in this country was established in New England in 1765. Twenty years later, Thomas Jefferson wrote to John Adams that "the superiority of chocolate, both for health and nourishment, will soon give it the same preference over tea and coffee in America which it has in Spain." But in 1876 a Swiss discovered a way to make solid milk chocolate, and since then people have eaten more chocolate than they have drunk. As for licorice, which had long been considered effective against old age, ugliness, and coughs by the Chinese (Brahma endorsed it), the Egyptians (Tutankhamen was buried with a supply), the Phoenicians, the Cretans, and the Greeks, it was also popular with Alexander's soldiers (They would hold pieces of licorice root in their mouths to relieve thirst on long marches), and, later, with the legions of Rome.

4   Between the days when candy was primarily a medical or military commodity and the foundation of the C.C.C.I., the creation and consumption of candy were at the mercy of human whims and foibles. Peanut brittle evolved from a projected batch of taffy when someone mistakenly added baking soda instead of cream of tartar, and fudge was the result of caramels gone astray. Fudge is still an elusive product, and is known in the business as "a stretch of trouble." The era of modern candy began at Prince Albert's Great Exhibition of 1851, at which chocolate creams, caramels, and hard candy (then called boiled sweets) were introduced to the world. Last year, the dollar volume of the American candy industry was over a billion dollars (about $1,185,000,000), and more than three billion pounds of candy was eaten in this country. Each one of us, in the guise of the average man, ate about seventeen pounds (ten pounds less than the average Englishman). According to the Department of Commerce, forty-three per cent of the total was candy bars; thirty per cent was higher-priced packaged items, including boxed chocolates; fifteeen per cent was bulk candy; and twelve per cent was nickel-and-dime packaged goods. Among the raw materials that went into last year's candy were 418,000,000 pounds of chocolate (largely supplied by Ghana and Nigeria); 1,264,000,-000 pounds of sugar; 622,000,000 pounds of corn syrup; lesser amounts of more than seventy other agricultural products, including

molasses, nuts, fruit, fruit syrup, spices, and items for which we are indebted to the American Indians (maple sugar, wintergreen, peppermint, spearmint, ginger, and sassafras); and 1,065,000,000 pounds of dairy products.

5   A combination of these astronomical statistics, the seasonal nature of candy sales (highest at Christmas, lowest in summer), and the potential customer's penchant for suddenly deciding to go on a diet was what persuaded the candymen to introduce order into the business. On the basis of its research results, the C.C.C.I. has initiated a number of publicity campaigns. In one, it is advocating scheduled candy-eating on the job: "Secretaries, production workers, and the boss work better and are generally in a better mood because of the 'candy break.' The mid-afternoon snack usually does away with that four o'clock slump. . . . Some of the larger factories and offices have instituted a new approach to the candy break and have one of their employees going through the plant 'à la cigarette girl,' so that all employees might enjoy this delicious 'pep-up' food." The industry's brightest hope at the moment, though, is the popularity of candy sales as a means of raising funds for charity. This has become such an important factor in the candy business that there is now at least one firm that manufactures and sells candy solely for fund raising. Among those who have found it profitable for charity to appeal to the American candy weakness are the Hobart, Indiana, Band Mothers; a group of California Camp Fire Girls; the Rocky Mount, North Carolina, Junior Garden Club; the Tulsa, Oklahoma, Will Rogers High School International Understanding Club; and the Oneida, New York, Squadron of the Civil Air Patrol.

6   We think we ought to warn the C.C.C.I. that if its public relations are successful, the next time its researchers set out to discover popular associations with candy they'll find that none of us are thinking any longer of those happy childhod days, since we'll all have learned to associate candy with the hard work it has given us the energy to do and the inordinate sums it has lured us into contributing to local charities.

QUESTIONS FOR REFLECTION, DISCUSSION, OR WRITING

(1) As which of the four basic kinds of writing — exposition, argument (and persuasion), narration, description — would you classify this essay? Why? Are there any elements of one or more of the others?

(2) What are your own "most basic feelings" (par. 2) about candy? With what thoughts do you associate it? Can you explain why?

(3) Why do you suppose the public relations people have had trouble locating "congenial dentists" (par. 2)?

(4) Statistics are often dull to read. What does this essay gain or lose by the inclusion of the numerous statistics in the latter part of paragraph 4?

(5) Compare the problem of the candy promoters with that of the promoters who "made the cigar respectable" (see p. 15). Compare the proposed solution of the candy problem to the solution used by the cigar manufacturers. Do you consider either of these campaigns unethical or unfair to the consumers? Explain why or why not.

(6) How seriously do you think the author's warning (par. 6) is meant to be taken?

Eugene Burdick

From THE UNITED STATES NAVY

EUGENE BURDICK, *himself a* World War II *veteran of the U.S. Navy, is now a professor of political science at the University of California, Berkeley. He is also a successful novelist and magazine writer in other fields than political science. His novels are* The Ninth Wave *and* The Blue of Capricon, *and he co-authored (with William J. Lederer) the famous best-seller* The Ugly American, *published in 1958.*

HOLIDAY, *started in 1946 by the Curtis Publishing Company of Philadelphia (also publishers of* The Saturday Evening Post, Ladies' Home Journal, *and* Jack and Jill), *is one of the few new post-war magazines to survive. It now has a monthly circulation of almost a million. The aim of Holiday, to considerably shorten the editors' own statement, is to "cover all the places, accessible and inaccessible, in the world. . . . [to show] how the world's people live and work and play. . . . in effect, everything and anything that has to do with man's wanderlust, with his healthy urge to go to new places, see new things and know more of the wide, wonderful world he lives in."*

THE UNITED STATES NAVY, *of which the following selection is an excerpt, was*
published in the October 1958 issue of Holiday. *It demonstrates as well as*
the author's novels his crisp, direct, but colorful style of writing — a style
that depends on few, if any, of the usual literary "devices." Take time to
enjoy and appreciate this style.

1   NO AMOUNT of time spent on a yacht or merchant ship or a
luxury liner prepares one for life aboard a Navy ship. A warship is
designed to carry powerful armament over great reaches of sea at
the highest speed possible. Everything is built around the armament. Comfort, recreation, food, stability are all secondary. As a
result, Navy life is intricate, crowded, lacking in privacy, nerve-
racking and most of all it is unnatural. What is puzzling is that it
is also attractive and, in the end, holds a kind of fascination.

2   A day at sea on a warship, any warship at any time, is a thing of
intricacy and pressure. The sailor awakens to the sound of a
bosun's call piping "reveille." This is followed by a prowling
master-at-arms who warns men out of their "racks" with a phrase
that is ancient, unchanging, harsh and too vulgar to be repeated
here. The ship is always in motion and it is always noisy. Even on
a flat burning-hot sea it will heave. Always there is the sound of
generators, the whir of radar gear, the aching ping of sound gear,
the shuffle of men changing watch, the clank of anchor chain,
the endless hammers chipping paint.

3   Breakfast can be anything, but it always includes black bitter
coffee rendered "sweet and blond" by canned milk and sugar, and
ends with cigarettes. The consumption of coffee on any Navy ship
is enormous. It is available at all hours and toward the end of a
watch it gets thick, takes on a deep reddish-brown color and has
enough stimulant power to keep an ordinary person's nerves jangling
for hours.

4   After breakfast the chopped-up, orderly routine of the sailor
begins. In normal cruising condition he is on watch four hours out
of every twelve. He may tend a machine, serve a gun, stare at a
radarscope, stand "lookout" or do any one of a hundred jobs. Between watches he works. The "snipes" of the black gang have

machinery to break down and repair; the gunners clean guns; the deck gang chips paint . . . always, eternally, loudly and with ridiculously small hammers that prolong the chore.

5   Then there are "evolutions" — which are nothing more than drills. There are evolutions for fire fighting, collision, atomic bombings, condition green, condition red and every other conceivable situation. In each of these every man has a precise assignment.

6   In the brief time left over the sailor sleeps, drinks coffee and gripes — or, in Navy parlance, he bitches. He bitches about two things: the Navy and "those people."

7   It is hardly a vision to inspire warmth or admiration. But the words squeeze something out of it, the words, somehow, do not capture the sailor's sense of domination over a difficult world. Sharers in a secret are seldom articulate about their mystery, which is probably part of its allure.

8   But take an example. One black night off Guadalcanal we found ourselves in the midst of a Japanese torpedo-plane attack. It was a confusing and bewildering action and it was done in total blackness — at least in the beginning. But the "evolutions" worked. We went through four separate evolutions and the fourth one found me in the water leading a rescue detail to pick up the survivors from a torpedoed and burning transport. Our detail moved through the debris and burning oil toward the derelict, the sailors from the sinking transport (doing the reverse evolution) moved toward us. All of us were deep in fear, but we rescued everyone that could be rescued. Then we went into a new evolution designed to save as many of the dying as we could.

9   The grimness of the scene, the intensity of the fear have never faded from my mind. But they are overlaid by a kind of quiet awe that our ship could be so competently handled, our purposes so skillfully meshed that we could make order out of the chaos.

10   This is not much in the way of explanation, but it explains both something about the allure of the Navy life and the reason why the sailor mistrusts all others. He has an art, but not the words to describe it.

11   Since its very beginning the United States Navy has had the feeling that it must do its job despite the ignorance of civilians and the opposition of politicians. Indeed, the Navy was originated

in a barefaced piece of political nepotism. In 1775 the Continental
Congress suddenly realized that it was about to fight the world's
most powerful maritime power, but had not a single ship. The
members of the Marine Committee responded with a classic
political move: they appointed relatives to build a navy. Ezek
Hopkins, the brother of one committee member, was made Chief
of Admiralty. The brother-in-law of another was made second-in-
command and the United Colonies Navy was created.

12   Hopkins was a big, outspoken sea captain and had he been able
to escape politics and rum he might have been successful. His only
picture shows him at the end of a monumental carouse in a
Surinam tavern. One of the chief tasks of captains was to keep prize
crews from engulfing the liquor found on captured ships.

13   After endless bickerings Hopkins got a warship ready for sea.
The ship was the converted merchantman, *Alfred*. The unexpected
weight of guns made her top-heavy, she rolled in the slightest sea
and was sluggish in responding to her rudder. In company with
other American ships she chanced upon H.M. Corvette *Glasgow*
off Newport, Rhode Island. But, alas, the crew of *Alfred* was still
half-drunk from rum taken off a prize. In one broadside she lost
twenty men, and the *Glasgow* slipped away.

14   Things did not improve rapidly. Crews suffered from miserable
diet, lack of munitions and mean pay. Naval officers wrote long
letters to the newspapers criticizing the battle tactics of their colleagues and defending themselves against like charges. The climax
came when an American captain came upon a British frigate
aground. It seemed a cheap victory, as the enemy was helpless. But
the captain had an alfresco picnic on a sandbank while he studied
the best way to capture the prize. The British, however, lightened
ship and kedged themselves off the shoal. The American captain
found himself marooned on a sandbank with his victim in pursuit
of his own ship.

15   At last a small gorilla-shaped man with popping eyes appeared
on the scene. He claimed to be the illegitimate son of the Earl of
Selkirk, but no one could be sure. He had a bad temper, and it was
a fact he had once killed a man and fled trial. His name was John
Paul Jones. Jones could and did politick with the best of them. But
he could also talk sweetly to a recruit on the beach, beat down a

mutiny, sail a ship, train a crew and give them pride. He also yearned to fight and that made a difference.

16   The result was that one afternoon Jones brought his ship, the *Bonhomme Richard*, alongside the British ship *Serapis* and after a polite hail let go a broadside. In the subsequent fight, the *Richard* was outmaneuvered by the *Serapis*, and her guns, one by one, were knocked out. Two hundred prisoners who had been locked up below broke free. The *Richard* had seven feet of water in her hold and there were plenty of Americans willing to surrender if only they could be heard above the din of battle.

17   A lesser man might have suffered some dismay, but Jones handled it with quick fury. He turned to a gunner shouting "Quarter" and broke his skull with a pistol, wheeled to the *Serapis* and shouted, "I have not yet begun to fight." He then walked to the hatchway up which the prisoners were surging and reminded them that they would soon drown if they did not man the pumps. In a wild scramble they did precisely that. In a few more moments Jones' topmen had squirmed across the rigging until they were over the *Serapis* and begun dropping hand grenades on the exposed powder. An explosion started, leaped from one British gun to another and resulted in a slaughter that was appalling. The captain of the *Serapis*, stunned by Jones' insane ferocity, struck his colors. Jones transferred his crew to the *Serapis* and took command, leaving the *Richard* to sink. Each ship had lost more than half its crew.

18   It was a magnificent victory, but not enough to save Jones from the plague of politics and envy. He was promised a ship by a Congress temporarily grateful, but the ship became a gift to the king of France. Jones never again served on an American ship and died in Paris, lonely and miserable. But the tradition had been started.

19   There was still too much dueling. When Midshipman Bainbridge challenged the British secretary to the governor of Malta to a duel for an insulting remark about American courage, most of America was thrilled that the Englishman took a bullet between the eyes. But "those people" in Washington were gravely disapproving. Names began to appear that were woven into history. Someone named Decatur took volunteers from two ships named *Constitution* and *Enterprise* and boldly sailed into Tripoli Harbor and burned a

captured ship. A hatchet-faced man named Preble insisted upon hard training and bold action — and got it. Most importantly there was an almost incredible skill at handling ships, when the chips were down, that prevailed over everything else.

20   Between wars the Navy tended to fall into scandals and mistakes of a Gilbert and Sullivan nature. Naval guns sometimes blew up when being tested in front of Cabinet officers. With all of the enthusiasm of a nation of mechanics we loaded gadgets on ships in such abundance that they were ingenious monstrosities. Yet, miraculously, incredibly, the Navy did produce good officers. Men such as Mahan gave the stiffening tradition a theory and a faith. Gradually the ships became better. Annapolis became a first-rate academy and finally the best in the world.

21   But if the officer crops improved it was still a mystery why Americans would sail as enlisted men in the Navy. In the early Navy they suffered a life that was severe beyond description. The food consisted of beef that had hardened into rocklike slabs, biscuits that crawled with weevils, water that was shot through with delicate green slime. The pay consisted of next to nothing.

22   To this day the Navy is reviled by sailors, suspected by politicians and criticized by its own retired officers . . . with the odd result that boys from Iowa and Kansas and city tenements and smart suburbs and all the rest of America come in a steady stream to Navy recruiting stations. They flow to the seaports and boot camps and finally onto ships, like lemmings answering some irresistible primal call. They come over the opposition of their mothers, sweethearts, neighborhood sentiment and common sense . . . but they come. And I was no exception.

23   I went into the Navy effortlessly. No other choice was possible. I was not sure what the secret of the Navy was, but I knew I was attracted. Once in I discovered that the sailor's language is one of the first guards against revealing the secret. It is easily the most bewildering language in the world. Navy talk is an odd and unbelievable combination of arcane language and roaring obscenity. The nonobscene part comes right out of the days of the sailing Navy and is used casually by all good sailors.

24   "Now hear this, I want a clean sweep down fore and aft with no holidays and every part bearing an even strain," a bosun will

tell a group of recruits. "Clew up when you're abaft the gig, but fake down all lines, square away all gear and have nothing adrift. Nothing! Now go on. Be happy in the service."

25   Good sailors use this antique language, which developed on sailing vessels over the centuries, with no sense of unreality. Oddly, there is nothing aboard a huge complex aircraft carrier which cannot be adequately described in this ancient language. Steam catapults, radar, jct planes and helicopters can all be described with words that are centuries old.

26   Beneath the private arcane language of the Navy is a layer of obscenity that must be heard to be believed. The obscenity is a kind of emphasis, a means by which the technical language is transmuted and made flexible. And, of course, it quickly loses its obscene character, for it has high utility, A petty officer who cannot swear well, cannot use the nuances of obscenity, is incapable of giving an order adequately. Regulations have always banned "excessive obscenity," but they are ignored by enlisted men.

27   Officers, however, use very little profanity and to their men they use none. It is also a curious fact that when sailors step off a ship their language changes. I have never yet heard a sailor use offensive language in mixed company ashore. Anxious mothers may suspect, and rightly, that their tender sons are learning a harsh crisp language on board ship, but they could not verify this by what they hear when their boys come home on leave. And for this we can all be grateful.

28   The second big obstacle to learning the secret of the Navy is the surface contempt which all sailors feel for anything to do with the Navy. The fighting man's contempt for the civilian is classic and one anticipates it. But one expects to hear kind things about the Corps from a Marine, about the Army from a dogface, and the zoomie can often find words of praise for the Air Force. This is not so in the Navy. The official view of every sailor is that he hates the Navy — its officers, its paper work, its food, pay, working conditions, guns, lack of liberty. He is contemptuous of a taut ship and also of a slack ship. He loathes the Navy, he could make more money "outside." (I once calculated from listening to the talk of the bridge crew of a destroyer that they averaged $500 a week on the "outside.") He hates the Navy; he will not say a kind

word about it. He says it often and he says it loud. The contempt is as strong the day after a "twenty-year man" ships over for another four years as it was when he was a boot. Quite literally I have *never* heard a sailor say a kind thing about the Navy. It took me four years to discover that this language of contempt is actually an elaborate language of respect and, in many cases, of downright love.

29   One explanation for this is that the atmosphere of Navy boot training is different from what Army or Marine recruits endure. The now-famous drill instructor of the Marine Corps tells recruits that they are being admitted to a sacred fraternity; he will even say flattering things about the Corps. A chief at a Navy boot camp would die before he would utter such words. The Navy does not haze or otherwise humiliate its recruits. It does not harangue them with speeches on the uniqueness of the Navy or tell them the Navy is the first defense of the nation. It merely treats the boots with contempt — a deep-seated belief that they can never become good sailors; and if they do, it is not worth it anyway. By some curious psychological mechanism, the raw boot yearns to know enough so that he, in turn, can become contemptuous. And by the time he does he is a sailor and there is something else which lies just under his contempt: pride at having become a sharer in the secret. The contempt is a mark of the initiated.

30   The difference between a civilian sailor and a "real" sailor rests on his knowledge of just two things: the ship and the sea. It sounds simple but turns out to be fairly complicated.

31   A ship, any ship, is a thing of amazing intricacy. A warship, whether an ancient sailing frigate or a modern carrier, is more intricate and complex than ordinary vessels. The guns alone, the extra crew to service them, the need for quick communication, the storage of ammunition — all these mean that a warship is intensely organized. A warship takes just enough men to service her awesome needs — no more and no less. The result is strange: there are no sad sacks, goof-offs or section eights on a ship. Let a sailor foul up and, with a quiet sign, a kind of collective judgment, he finds himself on the beach. It is a hard judgment and there are few who do not struggle to avoid it.

32   A boot no sooner gets aboard a ship than he makes a great discovery. All warships, even battleships, are fragile. It seems unbe-

lievable that these massive hulks, covered with tons of armor and huge rifles could be vulnerable. The fact is that even in times of peace a warship is in constant danger. A ship can burn, explode, run aground, burst boilers, generate poisonous gases, drag anchor, or roll over in a high sea.

33   Someone said that when naval vessels fight it is like a battle between "egg shells armed with sledge hammers" and that is so. Whenever battle lines have fought one another in earnest the ocean is soon littered with ships, their backs broken by the enormous power of enemy rifles. But every moment of its life, whether safely at anchor or at sea, a ship is in danger. There are literally hundreds of men on board a ship who, by making any one of a thousand mistakes, could destroy it.

34   This explains the arcane language, the contempt for awkwardness, the suspicion of the "outsider" which the Navy man feels. He lives in a delicately balanced world in which every man must do his job perfectly. Everyone is, literally, dependent on everyone else. The net result is that the Navy trains its men to be craftsmen first. If each man does his job perfectly the ship will perform superbly in a fight.

35   Navy men never compliment each other on fighting spirit or team spirit. They would be embarrassed; but they are acutely sensitive to skill. A boot becomes a sailor the day his chief looks at his work and says nothing. The mere lack of criticism is the mark of initiation into a society of craftsmen whose specialty is warships.

36   But a sailor is more than a talented craftsman. After all, one could be a craftsman in a land-bound factory. What makes the difference is the sea. There is no way to put this subtly so I put it baldly. The sea is a seductive mystery. Its vastness, its rhythm, its depth, its strength, its colors, its capacity for change, make the sea the compelling factor. I agree with those who believe that, because we came from the slime of the sea long ago, we carry some dim residual memory of that time. You may not agree, I will not argue with you. Such things cannot be proved. But if you do not sense it you will never be a happy sailor.

37   Whether they come from cities or farms, plains or mountains, the real "thirty-year men" are students of the sea. One is tempted to say they love it, but one does not know. They merely watch it.

Dead flat sea, hot sea, rough sea, windy sea — it makes no difference. They always watch it.

38   Usually there is something to watch. The sea roils, moves in
vast tides and currents, is cut by the lean hard bodies of sharks and
the skittering of flying fish, suddenly turns lead-colored and flat
under a blazing sun. Sailors like a phosphorescent sea. On a dark
night a fast ship moving through phosphorescent water seems to
be cutting the ocean in two. The bow waves are pure silver which
break into billions of gleaming specks that somehow arrange themselves in two long glowing lines astern and reach unbroken to the
horizon.

39   I saw a "green sea" only once, but old salts assure you they have
seen them in all colors. It was off Fiji and the lookouts reported a
discoloration. It was a huge green twisting smear in the water. It
looked as solid as a coral reef although the charts reported the
water "clear." We cut through it slowly and it was the deepest
green I ever saw. It was so green that it seemed like a sign of some
subterranean sickness. No one ever knew what it was. No one
knows yet. But the decks were lined with silent men in skivvy shorts,
watching quietly. When we came to clear water they silently disappeared.

40   The first time I felt the naked power of the sea was off Okinawa,
when we misjudged the position of a typhoon. In a half hour the
face of the water changed; huge, blue-white waves heaved up in
the distance and came rolling down on us with a rush of wind
clocked at seventy-five miles an hour and, later, at 100. The destroyer — 2250 tons of her — rolled slowly sideways. The in-
clinometer showed 60° of roll. Then, as we watched unbelievingly,
it showed 67° — and held there for a deadly several seconds. There
was a crash of crockery, chairs and gear. There was also that awesome groan which a ship makes when it is in distress. No one mistakes this sound for the normal squeaks and grinds of a ship under
way. When the sea let us go and we swung back, I knew something of absolute power. A few hundred miles away a group of
destroyers were capsized with enormous loss of life.

41   For each sailor the sea is a different experience, but all know
it is there, separated from them by the thin metal skin of a destroyer or the thick armor of a battleship. It is waiting to absorb the

losers, and no sailor forgets it. Naval vessels carry no lifeboats and there are, surprisingly, thousands of sailors who cannot swim.

42   Once the ship and the sea are understood, the rest of the Navy makes rough sense — not complete sense, but close to it. This strange world of the warship moves over the seas and this, somehow, makes it different and, however paradoxical it may be, more seductive.

QUESTIONS FOR REFLECTION, DISCUSSION, OR WRITING

(1) What do you consider the author's central theme? Does it involve, in some way, the "secret" which he mentions frequently?

(2) Are all parts of the essay pertinent to its theme? What, for instance, about the 11 paragraphs (11 to 21) of Navy history? Explain how this is or is not a "tributary" flowing into the main theme.

(3) Can you think of any circumstances in civilian life when people are "sharers in a secret" which they find hard to explain to outsiders (or even to themselves) but which still gives them a feeling of pride? If you have been such a "sharer," try to explain the "secret."

(4) If you had a young son in the Navy, how seriously would you be disturbed by his "learning a harsh crisp language on board ship" (pars. 26-27)? Explain. Do you think that, in this respect, he would be better off in the Army, Air Force, or Marines? In the Coast Guard? In a Youth Conservation Corps, such as suggested by Sen. Humphrey in "A Plan to Save . . ."? A Peace Corps?

(5) Does the sea hold any particular fascination for you? How seriously do you take Burdick's theory (and Miss Carson's, in "Mother Sea . . .") that "because we came from the slime of the sea long ago, we carry some dim residual memory of that time" (par. 36)?

(6) What effect, if any, do you think women in the Navy have had on the traditionally male attitudes toward Navy life — the "secret," so to speak? Do you approve of women's being in the Navy? In the other services? Organize an explanation of your opinions in good composition form.

(7) If you have been in the Navy, do you think Burdick wrote the truth? If you have not, would you now be more, or less, apt to join?

Alan Devoe

EVERYONE A NATURALIST

ALAN DEVOE (1909-1955) *was a well known author-naturalist who contributed articles to a wide variety of magazines. He also wrote several books, including* Down to Earth, Live Now! *and* Speaking of Animals.

EVERYONE A NATURALIST *was first published in the January 1949 issue of* American Mercury (*a famous journal of opinion and commentary which was founded in 1924 and continued publication for 30 years*).

In this essay Devoe presents his case for the hobby of studying nature. As in arguing any case, he is obligated to present only his own choice of facts, in a way that will promote his cause. In doing this, the arguer is likely to resort to at least a mild form of some of the "seven devices of propaganda" (see p. 9). Although with this particular topic no damage is likely to come of being "fooled" by such a strategy, it is good to develop the habit of reading all arguments critically.

1   THERE is a great deal of good counsel offered these days in books and magazines to the effect that all of us should cultivate some interest outside our regular business or occupation: some interest in which we can become absorbed in our spare hours and which can take us, so to speak, outside ourselves. Going to an occasional sports event, listening to the radio or watching a television screen, reading a little now and then . . . things like this, after all, are thin and inadequate ways of trying to fill up and round out our lives and give them a sustaining quality and a continuousness of interest. We need to cultivate some special interest in which we can satisfyingly use our minds, and to which we can devote ourselves with a real and continuing enthusiasm, and to which we can turn for complete vacation from the routine of business or housework or whatever in which we are all too easily imprisoned.

2   The good counsellors who make this recommendation are of course quite right. A married man and woman, who take no greater excursions outside themselves than an occasional turning-on of the radio or an occasional watching together of a movie, are both likely to feel frustrated and confined, and to express these obscurely enter-

tained feelings by an everlasting wrangle. It is notorious that the business or professional man, who has confined his whole interest to his business or profession, is likely not to survive his retirement for very long. Ennui, expressing itself *via* heart or kidneys or arteries, drops him in his tracks. The physical organism has no reason to go on continuing. It is equally notable that men devoted to hobbies and similar interests have a way of continuing into great old age, still lively and alert and inquisitive as chipmunks.

3   All very well, then; we should have an outside interest that can absorb us and keep us refreshed. But what?

4   A great many interests, from collecting Japanese prints to cultivating exotic flower-gardens, have the drawback of being expensive. A great many other interests have the drawback that they require their devotee to be in certain special kinds of places or to keep available certain special times or seasons. There are interests that can be indulged only when the strength of the legs is good or money is plentiful, or eyesight is keen, or under the terms of some similarly strict requirement. The man who devotes himself to any of these interests may find himself, by an act of circumstance, suddenly as deprived and forlorn as the dedicated businessman who has been obliged to retire.

5   There ought to be an interest free of these hazards. Happily, there is. It lies open to everyone to be a naturalist.

6   A drudging housewife who is seldom able to leave the kitchen can be a naturalist. A paralyzed man who cannot stir from his bedroom or his wheelchair can be a naturalist. A man of ninety can be one; a boy can be one; there are no conditions that can interfere more than trivially with the lives of naturalists.

II

7   To be a naturalist means simply to give awakened and alert attention to the world around us. It means simply that, instead of seeing birds casually and apathetically, we stare at them attentively and awarely, finding out what their names are, what their songs are, where and how they nest, and what all the intimacies of their lives are like. Being a naturalist means finding out which wildflowers are which, instead of thinking only in the vague general term, "vegetation." It means cocking a sharp eye at the stars, or listening with an

acute ear to the sounds of the night, or smelling with a new keen-
ness of discernment, and a new understanding, the earth-smells that
drift in at the open window. Being a naturalist means simply
being alive to nature, instead of being, as we mostly are, half-
alive or largely dead.

8   It is not necessary to have scientific training in order to be a
naturalist. There are, of course, naturalists who are highly trained
technical scientists; and it is of course the case that every naturalist,
even the most amateur or most late-coming to the field, must
acquire a certain science-mindedness. But advanced training in the
technicalities of science is not necessary for being a naturalist, and
a good one.

9   What famous naturalists offhand come most readily to mind?
Well, there was John Burroughs. When that fine old naturalist
died, he took to the grave with him a nature-lore truly prodigious;
but he was a self-taught man, with no scientific degree to his name.
Ernest Thompson Seton was an animal-observer of extraordinary
attainments, who discovered innumerable nature facts not known
before his time; but of scientific training he had none. Henry
Thoreau and John Muir were not scientists. They were naturalists.
They were good ones. It was likewise so with Mabel Osgood
Wright, that admirable bird-observer, and with John James Audu-
bon, the observer and painter, and with the woodcraft-master, Dan
Beard.

10   If we think of the English naturalists, the same kinds of people
come to mind: Richard Jeffries, sound and accurate and delightful,
but no scientist . . . the incomparable W. H. Hudson, beloved by
many scientists but not originally schooled to belong to their
company . . . the contemporary Henry Williamson who, untrained
as a formal scientist, nevertheless wrote in *Salar the Salmon* what
is perhaps the most informative and profoundly insighted book
about fish-life that has been published.

11   It lies open to everyone to be a naturalist. It lies open to everyone not only to have the experience of richer aliveness, which
inevitably goes with awakening to discovery of the common miracles
of earth, but even to have the experience of discovering brand-new
facts under the sun . . . facts previously unknown even to the most
expert scientists. The other day I had a letter from a woman in

Maine. A farm housewife, she must spend a great deal of her time in the farmhouse kitchen, with nothing to look at but the small dooryard view that can be seen from the kitchen window. Ten or fifteen years ago, she became interested in the robins that nested every year in an apple tree. She began to watch them with a new attentiveness, and she has been watching them with that attentiveness ever since. She has observed every peculiarity of their nest-building each year, and has figured out a theory of the reasons for the variations; she has listened keenly to all the robins' songs and cries and call-notes, and has detected certain patterns in their "language"; she has observed the birds' every behavior, and has written up her notes in her spare time. She is a fine naturalist. Not only has her life been enormously more interesting and expanded, because of her interest, but the manuscript of her accumulated notes — which I forwarded at her request to scientific colleagues — has been pronounced by the ornithological scientists to abound in new discoveries of the liveliest significance.

12   That sort of thing is not at all uncommon. Naturalists, even the most amateur, make discoveries every day in the week. Not huge and dramatic discoveries, it may be, but the finding of all sorts of odd little facts that fill out the chinks and gaps in formal scientific information. The hundred-odd acres of former farm-land that are my own living laboratory have produced dozens of such, over the years of my watching and listening. It is highly unlikely that I shall ever discover a new species of bird, or, squinting up at the country sky on one of these glittering January nights, see a star that none of my astronomer friends has ever noticed. But after fifteen years of watching phoebes, I did see one pull up a worm, robin-fashion, which phoebes are not supposed to do, and the observation has made its way into the scientific phoebe-records. The phenomenon of a robin building nine nests side by side, in nine successive days, and laying three eggs in the first one, two eggs in the second, and one in each of the remaining seven, is not sufficiently arresting to make the front page of the newspapers; but it has been exciting enough to agitate appropriate scientific circles, and it was an exciting thing for me to see. Those of us who are home-acre naturalists, train-window naturalists, housewife or garden-variety naturalists, may find no new stars or discover no new species

of animals. But all of us can make discoveries. All of us can be
pioneers. As Fabre rightly remarked, by no means everything about
even the commonest ant is known to human knowledge. Any small
patch of the planet to which we give attention with alert eyes and
ears and nostrils may at any moment disclose to us unsuspected
secrets.

III

13   It has become a tired platitude to say that the best things in life
are free. But in its platitudinous way the thing is surely everlastingly
true. The world of nature *is* free for our enjoyment, from the glory
of a sunrise to the quaintness of a cricket. It is all here, around us,
for the taking. There is no charge. Not only free, nature has the
priceless advantage of being everywhere. A man may be sick in bed;
nature comes in at his window, in bird songs, in flower scents, in
insect voices, in a thousand kinds of presentation. A deaf man may
be a naturalist. One of our best ones cannot hear a sound. A blind
man may be a naturalist. Clarence Hawkes, writer of a dozen
nature-books, drew his nature-knowledge from what he could hear
and smell and touch. He could not see the earth he loved.

14   We can all of us, in this way or that, be naturalists. We can all
take excursions outside ourselves, vacations from our cramping little
worlds of four walls and every-dayness. We can make the horizon
grow, and our aliveness quicken; we can discover significances in a
snow-crystal and astonishing events occurring under a common leaf.
To be a naturalist is not to "escape" from the world. It is to re-find
it. It is not to run away in fantasy to a far country. It is to come
home. It is to return, that is, to the estate of fresh astonishment
over the wonder of the nature of things, and of kindled curiosity
about it, and of delight to be alive in it and not dead.

15   Everyone can be a naturalist. It carries its incalculable rewards.

QUESTIONS FOR REFLECTION, DISCUSSION, OR WRITING

(1) How convincing do you find Devoe's arguments in favor of being a
naturalist? Do you think he used any degree of "card stacking" in his attempt
to win support? If so, in what ways? Does this annoy you as much as the
same technique if used, for instance, in a political campaign? Why, or why
not?

(2) Analyze Devoe's introduction, which includes the first six paragraphs, trying to see what he is doing, step by step. Is this an effective beginning for his essay?

(3) What, if anything, is gained by the author's inclusion of two whole paragraphs (9-10) of names of famous naturalists, most of whom we are not likely to be familiar with? Does their use effectively support his argument?

(4) Do you think "everyone" could be a naturalist? What about the invalid living in a tenement flat in city slums? Or the busy housewife in a 17th-floor mid-city apartment?

(5) What criteria does he set up (see p. 54) by which to measure the value of a hobby? Is this a necessary step before we could argue about such a topic? Why, or why not?

(6) Can you think of other hobbies that fit even Devoe's requirements (*e.g.*, inexpensiveness)? If so, how well do they compare?

(7) The author says that going to an occasional sports event, listening to the radio or watching TV is "thin and inadequate" as a hobby (par. 1). Is this necessarily true? In what ways, if any, do you think it would be more rewarding to accumulate information on wildflowers than information on the Los Angeles Dodgers — to watch a phoebe pulling up a worm, rather than your neighbor polishing his hot-rod?

(8) Think of the "wrangling" married couples you have known. Do you think the basis of their trouble might be the one suggested by Devoe in paragraph 2? Also consider men you have known who did not "survive retirement" for long. Do you think their trouble may have been "ennui, expressing itself *via* heart or kidneys or arteries" (par. 2)? How about retired acquaintances who had not confined their whole interest to their business or profession?

(9) Whether or not you think this was an entirely convincing essay, do you see any value in having read it? Explain.

(10) Discuss the "tired platitude" (par. 13) that the best things in life are free. Do you believe this? What are some of these "best things," other than those mentioned by Devoe? If really best, then why do so many people pass them by in their pursuit of money, which cannot buy the "best things" at all? This discussion, effectively organized, could make a good composition. Another might be the arguments in favor of your own hobby or one you hope sometime to cultivate. Another: Your own experience or experiences as a naturalist.

Charles G. Finney
WESTERN GLADIATOR

CHARLES G. FINNEY, *a Tucson newspaperman* (Arizona Daily Star), *has written numerous short stories for* The New Yorker, Harper's, Science Fiction, *and other magazines. He is also the author of four novels, one of which,* The Circus of Dr. Lao, *won the National Booksellers award of 1931 for being "the most original novel of the year." His latest,* Old China Hands, *was published in 1961.*

WESTERN GLADIATOR *was first published in the October 1958 issue of* Harper's Magazine *(see p. 15). An expository essay, it represents a much more artistic endeavor than do most expositions: to provide the desired explanation entirely by the processes of narration and description. You can judge how artistic — and satisfying — is the result. In doing this, make yourself aware also of the author's uses of words and sentences; after all, these are to the creative writer what paints are to the artist or musical notes to the musician!*

1   HE WAS BORN on a summer morning in the shady mouth of a cave. Three others were born with him, another male and two females. Each was about five inches long and slimmer than a lead pencil.

2   Their mother left them a few hours after they were born. A day after that his brother and sisters left him also. He was all alone. Nobody cared whether he lived or died. His tiny brain was very dull. He had no arms or legs. His skin was delicate. Nearly everything that walked on the ground or burrowed in it, that flew in the air or swam in the water or climbed trees was his enemy. But he didn't know that. He knew nothing at all. He was aware of his own existence, and that was the sum of his knowledge.

3   The direct rays of the sun could, in a short time, kill him. If the temperature dropped too low he would freeze. Without food he would starve. Without moisture he would die of dehydration. If a man or a horse stepped on him he would be crushed. If anything chased him he could run neither very far nor very fast.

4   Thus it was at the hour of his birth. Thus it would be, with modifications, all his life.

5   But against these drawbacks he had certain qualifications that fitted him to be a competitive creature of this world and equipped him for its warfare. He could exist a long time without food or water. His very smallness at birth protected him when he most needed protection. Instinct provided him with what he lacked in experience. In order to eat he first had to kill; and he was eminently adapted for killing. In sacs in his jaws he secreted a virulent poison. To inject that poison he had two fangs, hollow and pointed. Without that poison and those fangs he would have been among the most helpless creatures on earth. With them he was among the deadliest.

6   He was, of course, a baby rattlesnake, a desert diamondback, named *Crotalus atrox* by the herpetologists Baird and Girard and so listed in the *Catalogue of North American Reptiles* in its issue of 1853. He was grayish brown in color with a series of large dark diamond-shaped blotches on his back. His tail was white with five black cross-bands. It had a button on the end of it.

7   Little Crotalus lay in the dust in the mouth of his cave. Some of his kinfolk lay there too. It was their home. That particular tribe of rattlers had lived there for scores of years.

8   The cave had never been seen by a white man.

9   Sometimes as many as two hundred rattlers occupied the den. Sometimes the numbers shrank to as few as forty or fifty.

10   The tribe members did nothing at all for each other except breed. They hunted singly; they never shared their food. They derived some automatic degree of safety from their numbers, but their actions were never concerted toward using their numbers to any end. If an enemy attacked one of them, the others did nothing about it.

11   Young Crotalus's brother was the first of the litter to go out into the world and the first to die. He achieved a distance of fifty feet from the den when a Sonoran racer, four feet long and hungry, came upon him. The little rattler, despite his poison fangs, was a tidbit. The racer, long skilled in such arts, snatched him up by the head and swallowed him down. Powerful digestive juices in

the racer's stomach did the rest. Then the racer, appetite whetted, prowled around until it found one of Crotalus's little sisters. She went the way of the brother.

12   Nemesis of the second sister was a chaparral cock. This cuckoo, or road runner as it is called, found the baby amid some rocks, uttered a cry of delight, scissored it by the neck, shook it until it was almost lifeless, banged and pounded it upon a rock until life had indeed left it, and then gulped it down.

13   Crotalus, somnolent in a cranny of the cave's mouth, neither knew nor cared. Even if he had, there was nothing he could have done about it.

14   On the fourth day of his life he decided to go out into the world himself. He rippled forth uncertainly, the transverse plates on his belly serving him as legs.

15   He could see things well enough within his limited range, but a five-inch-long snake can command no great field of vision. He had an excellent sense of smell. But, having no ears, he was stone deaf. On the other hand, he had a pit, a deep pock mark between eye and nostril. Unique, this organ was sensitive to animal heat. In pitch blackness, Crotalus, by means of the heat messages recorded in his pit, could tell whether another animal was near and could also judge its size. That was better than an ear.

16   The single button on his tail could not, of course, yet rattle. Crotalus wouldn't be able to rattle until that button had grown into three segments. Then he would be able to buzz.

17   He had a wonderful tongue. It looked like an exposed nerve and was probably exactly that. It was forked, and Crotalus thrust it in and out as he traveled. It told him things that neither his eyes nor his nose nor his pit told him.

18   Snake fashion, Crotalus went forth, not knowing where he was going, for he had never been anywhere before. Hunger was probably his prime mover. In order to satisfy that hunger he had to find something smaller than himself and kill it.

19   He came upon a baby lizard sitting in the sand. Eyes, nose, pit, and tongue told Crotalus it was there. Instinct told him what it was and what to do. Crotalus gave a tiny one-inch strike and bit the lizard. His poison killed it. He took it by the head and swallowed it. Thus was his first meal.

20   During his first two years Crotalus grew rapidly. He attained a
length of two feet; his tail had five rattles on it and its button. He
rarely bothered with lizards any more, preferring baby rabbits,
chipmunks, and round-tailed ground squirrels. Because of his slow
locomotion he could not run down these agile little things. He had
to contrive instead to be where they were when they would pass.
Then he struck swiftly, injected his poison, and ate them after they
died.

21   At two he was formidable. He had grown past the stage where a
racer or road runner could safely tackle him. He had grown to the
size where other desert dwellers — coyotes, foxes, coatis, wildcats
— knew it was better to leave him alone.

22   And, at two, Crotalus became a father, his life being regulated
by cycles. His cycles were plant-like. The peach tree does not
"know" when it is time to flower, but flower it does because its
cycle orders it to do so.

23   In the same way, Crotalus did not "know" when it was time for
young desert diamondback rattlers to pair off and breed. But his
cycle knew.

24   He found "her" on a rainy morning. Crotalus's courtship at first
was sinuous and subtle, slow and stealthy. Then suddenly it became
dynamic. A period of exhaustion followed. Two metabolic machines
had united to produce new metabolic machines.

25   Of that physical union six new rattlesnakes were born. Thus
Crotalus, at two, had carried out his major primary function: he
had reproduced his kind. In two years he had experienced everything that was reasonably possible for desert diamondback rattlesnakes to experience except death.

26   He had not experienced death for the simple reason that there
had never been an opportunity for anything bigger and stronger
than himself to kill him. Now, at two, because he was so formidable, that opportunity became more and more unlikely.

27   He grew more slowly in the years following his initial spurt. At
the age of twelve he was five feet long. Few of the other rattlers
in his den were older or larger than he.

28   He had a castanet of fourteen segments. It had been broken off
occasionally in the past, but with each new molting a new segment
appeared.

29   His first skin-shedding back in his babyhood had been a bewildering experience. He did not know what was happening. His eyes clouded over until he could not see. His skin thickened and dried until it cracked in places. His pit and his nostrils ceased to function. There was only one thing to do and that was to get out of that skin.

30   Crotalus managed it by nosing against the bark of a shrub until he forced the old skin down over his head, bunching it like the rolled top of a stocking around his neck. Then he pushed around among rocks and sticks and branches, literally crawling out of his skin by slow degrees. Wriggling free at last, he looked like a brand new snake. His skin was bright and satiny, his eyes and nostrils were clear, his pit sang with sensation.

31   For the rest of his life he was to molt three or four times a year. Each time he did it he felt as if he had been born again.

32   At twelve he was a magnificent reptile. Not a single scar defaced his rippling symmetry. He was diabolically beautiful and deadly poison.

33   His venom was his only weapon, for he had no power of constriction. Yellowish in color, his poison was odorless and tasteless. It was a highly complex mixture of proteids, each in itself direly toxic. His venom worked on the blood. The more poison he injected with a bite, the more dangerous the wound. The pain rendered by his bite was instantaneous, and the shock accompanying it was profound. Swelling began immediately, to be followed by a ghastly oozing. Injected directly into a large vein, his poison brought death quickly, for the victim died when it reached his heart.

34   At the age of twenty Crotalus was the oldest and largest rattler in his den. He was six feet long and weighed thirteen pounds. His whole world was only about a mile in radius. He had fixed places where he avoided the sun when it was hot and he was away from his cave. He knew his hunting grounds thoroughly, every game trail, every animal burrow.

35   He was a fine old machine, perfectly adapted to his surroundings, accustomed to a life of leisure and comfort. He dominated his little world.

36   The mighty seasonal rhythms of the desert were as vast pulsations, and the lives of the rattlesnakes were attuned to them.

Spring sun beat down, spring rains fell, and, as the plants of the desert ended their winter hibernations, so did the vipers in their lair. The plants opened forth and budded; the den "opened" too, and the snakes crawled forth. The plants fertilized each other, and new plants were born. The snakes bred, and new snakes were produced. The desert was repopulated.

37   In the autumn the plants began to close; in the same fashion the snake den began to close, the reptiles returned to it, lay like lingering blossoms about its entrance for a while, then disappeared within it when winter came. There they slept until summoned forth by a new spring.

38   Crotalus was twenty years old. He was in the golden age of his viperhood.

39   But men were approaching. Spilling out of their cities, men were settling in that part of the desert where Crotalus lived. They built roads and houses, set up fences, dug for water, planted crops.

40   They homesteaded the land. They brought new animals with them — cows, horses, dogs, cats, barnyard fowl.

41   The roads they built were death traps for the desert dwellers. Every morning new dead bodies lay on the road, the bodies of the things the men had run over and crushed in their vehicles.

42   That summer Crotalus met his first dog. It was a German shepherd which had been reared on a farm in the Midwest and there had gained the reputation of being a snake-killer. Black snakes, garter snakes, pilots, water snakes; it delighted in killing them all. It would seize them by the middle, heedless of their tiny teeth, and shake them violently until they died.

43   This dog met Crotalus face to face in the desert at dusk. Crotalus had seen coyotes aplenty and feared them not. Neither did the dog fear Crotalus, although Crotalus then was six feet long, as thick in the middle as a motorcycle tire, and had a head the size of a man's clenched fist. Also this snake buzzed and buzzed and buzzed.

44   The dog was brave, and a snake was a snake. The German shepherd snarled and attacked. Crotalus struck him in the underjaw; his fangs sank in almost half an inch and squirted big blobs of hematoxic poison into the tissues of the dog's flesh.

45   The Shepherd bellowed with pain, backed off, groveled with his jaws in the desert sand, and attacked again. He seized Crotalus

somewhere by the middle of his body and tried to flip him in the air and shake him as, in the past, he had shaken slender black snakes to their death. In return, he received another poison-blurting stab in his flank and a third in the belly and a fourth in the eye as the terrible, writhing snake bit wherever it could sink its fangs.

46   The German shepherd had enough. He dropped the big snake and in sick, agonizing bewilderment crawled somehow back to his master's homestead and died.

47   The homesteader looked at his dead dog and became alarmed. If there was a snake around big enough to kill a dog that size, it could also kill a child and probably a man. It was something that had to be eliminated.

48   The homesteader told his fellow farmers, and they agreed to initiate a war of extermination against the snakes.

49   The campaign during the summer was sporadic. The snakes were scattered over the desert, and it was only by chance that the men came upon them. Even so, at summer's end, twenty-six of the vipers had been killed.

50   When autumn came the men decided to look for the rattlers' den and execute mass slaughter. The homesteaders had become desert-wise and knew what to look for.

51   They found Crotalus's lair without too much trouble — a rock outcropping on a slope that faced the south. Cast-off skins were in evidence in the bushes. Bees flew idly in and out of the den's mouth. Convenient benches and shelves of rock were at hand where the snakes might lie for a final sunning in the autumn air.

52   They killed the three rattlers they found at the den when they first discovered it. They made plans to return in a few more days when more of the snakes had congregated. They decided to bring along dynamite with them and blow up the mouth of the den so that the snakes within would be sealed there forever and the snakes without would have no place to find refuge.

53   On the day the men chose to return, nearly fifty desert diamond-backs were gathered at the portals of the cave. The men shot them, clubbed them, smashed them with rocks. Some of the rattlers escaped the attack and crawled into the den.

54   Crotalus had not yet arrived for the autumn rendezvous. He came that night. The den's mouth was a shattered mass of rock, for

the men had done their dynamiting well. Dead members of his tribe lay everywhere. Crotalus nosed among them, tongue flicking as he slid slowly along.

55   There was no access to the cave anymore. He spent the night outside among the dead. The morning sun warmed him and awakened him. He lay there at full length. He had no place to go.

56   The sun grew hotter upon him and instinctively he began to slide toward some dark shade. Then his senses warned him of some animal presence near by; he stopped, half coiled, raised his head and began to rattle. He saw two upright figures. He did not know what they were because he had never seen men before.

57   "That's the granddaddy of them all," said one of the homesteaders. "It's a good thing we came back." He raised his shotgun.

QUESTIONS FOR REFLECTION, DISCUSSION, OR WRITING

(1) Would this explanation of the life and habits of *Crotalus atrox* have been better if presented as straight exposition? Does your answer depend on the reader-audience and the purpose for which the essay was written? Explain why or why not. For the *Harper's* audience, would straight exposition have been as good? As interesting? As memorable?

(2) Discuss the *artistic* qualities of this essay. Has the author used good creative imagination in casting a deadly viper in the role of "hero," or is this combination too incongruous?

(3) How about the writing itself? It is certainly terse, economical in word use, even in description (the author is a journalist, and journalists are trained to be word frugal) — but has he sacrificed beauty or effectiveness for the sake of this economy? If so, give examples from the writing; if not, point out passages that you find terse yet somehow satisfying artistically.

(4) None of Finney's sentences are very long or complicated. Do you suppose this simplicity was deliberate? What might the reason have been? Why do you think his sentences in paragraphs 2 and 3 are even shorter than the rest? The eighth sentence of paragraph 2 is entirely different, however — what does this difference achieve? (Thoughtful answers to all of these questions will help explain still more about the artistic quality of the essay.)

(5) Do you suppose Finney is a "naturalist" of the Devoe variety ("Everyone a Naturalist") — or a natural scientist? Why?

(6) Finney's Crotalus seems to move through life in a sort of semi-conscious state, regulated almost entirely by instinct and his cycles. Do you have any

reason to doubt this theory? What about other cold-blooded creatures, such as turtles, alligators, fish? The warm-blooded mammals and birds — how much of their activity is governed by any kind of real "thought"?

(7) Most snakes are no more dangerous or unclean than other reptiles or many warm-blooded animals — yet man traditionally, maybe instinctively, despises them. (A most derogatory metaphor, you know, is to call a fellow a "snake.") Can you account for this distaste? Why are *you* horrified or revolted, for instance, by the thought of a snake crawling across your wrist? Or *are* you?

(8) Various topics for writing should suggest themselves here as needed — e.g., the balance of nature, the value of snakes to the farmer, the conservation of wildlife, a snake experience of your own, the life cycle of other animals.

David Cort

SURVIVAL IN THE ZOO

DAVID CORT, *who was for several years foreign editor of* Life Magazine, *is the author of numerous books, including* Is There an American in the House? *This book is a collection of essays, most of which had appeared previously in* The Nation, *the magazine for which Mr. Cort now works as a staff contributor. His novel* The Minstrel Boy *was published in 1961.*

THE NATION *is the country's oldest weekly "journal of opinion"; it was founded in 1865. Avowedly "liberal" in political viewpoint and always disdainful of majority opinion, The Nation has had a colorful but stormy career. At various times and in varying degrees it has been accused, for instance (by the public and, sometimes, by its own staff members), of being too far "left" (in support of socialism) and sometimes too far "right," too pacifistic and, again, too militaristic. The following essay was published March 11, 1961.*

SURVIVAL IN THE ZOO *will be, in parts, much more difficult for the inexperienced reader to manage than was the preceding essay. Read it through first for the over-all impression, marking but not stopping to worry about any troublesome passages. Then return to these for further study of meanings — and of the author's manner of expressing those meanings.*

1   ONE NAME officially given the present period, if we go back perhaps 70,000,000 years, is the Age of Mammals. This Age is still going on. However, a single species or genus of mammals has quite

recently appropriated the whole planet and while bemoaning its own imminent extinction (at its own hands) is bringing to a rapid close the Age of (all the other) Mammals and some birds. At the very worst that can happen, Man is going to do better than the passenger pigeon, Labrador duck, Indian two-horned rhinoceros and quagga. These are already extinct, kaput, finished; and several vanished with a strange, black-out celerity, as the bald eagle and osprey may be about to do. These last try to breed, but suddenly find they cannot. One can imagine a sort of genetic disdain of living in this world of Man's.

2   In the last forty years, conservation in the United States has saved many species. The primary credit for ending the massacre of other species is generally given to the New York Zoological Society and its director, the late William Hornaday. Whether his policies, now enacted into United States law, will be accepted by the politicians of Africa, South America, Asia and the South Pacific in time is of course purely speculative. And so is the practical feasibility of ceding to the other animals large enough areas even of North America, which are coveted by the dominant animal, Man.

3   The official intermediary in this situation is the zoo, here defined as maintaining an international collection of live animals. In the United States, there are thirty-eight first-class zoos, of which the leading three are the New York Zoological Society's Bronx Zoo, Chicago's Brookfield Zoo and the San Diego Zoo. The Bronx Zoo, for example, maintains 3,006 animals divided into 1,099 species. It has 193 species of mammals, 640 of birds, and 266 of reptiles and amphibians. (Fish, of course, are in its Aquarium in Coney Island.)

4   The other zoos cover most enterprising American cities, with oddly blank areas in New England outside Boston, the Southern states down to South Carolina, and the plateau states excluding Colorado. It might be deduced that where people feel superior, they are less interested in the lower orders. There are also innumerable small or specialized exhibits of live animals. Some, as at Bear Mountain in New York and outside Tucson, Arizona, are excellent. But most show unkempt animals, often not identified, and sometimes inspiring more pity and revulsion than interest. The greatest concentration of these amateur collections is in Florida, followed by Southern California and Canada.

5   The end of the Age of Mammals might be put into perspective by the response: "Who needs them?" It is true that nobody wants a wolf in the neighborhood, and U.S. wolves are down to around 1,000 survivors. But the ancestor stock of all our cattle, the aurochs, is extinct, and if we should want to breed from the original strain again, we simply could not do so. All we can do is debate whether the purer aurochs strain is the Spanish fighting bull or an English park breed. Before we say of any species, "Who needs it?" we might do better to give it several centuries of thought.

6   Some fairly radical new answers have been developed by the Bronx Zoo, particularly by its young director, William G. Conway.

7   One is to use theatrical devices to present the animal in a likeness of his natural environment. Another is to research and proceed with the breeding in captivity of species that are endangered in the wild state.

8   The second is not as futile as it may sound. In fact, two mammals that are extinct in the entirely wild state have prospered for some time only in zoos and parks. These are the Père David's deer of China, extinct in China, and the wisent, or European, bison. The Bronx Zoo has eight breeding Père David's deer, and imported a pair of wisent from Holland. (Incidentally, a few Père David's deer have at last been sent back to China.) Other species of mammals undoubtedly have a majority of their surviving populations in zoos; but the element of hope in this depends on their propagation in captivity.

9   "Survival Center" is the name of a projected new division of the Bronx Zoo, for which it is now campaigning for $12,000,000. The name sounds melodramatic, but it is justified for species for which the outside world is an extinction center. Some of the species that will be studied and bred here are bald eagle, nene goose (Hawaii), barnacle goose, sacred crane (northeast Asia), imperial parrot, imperial ivory-billed woodpecker (Mexico), prairie chicken, Asiatic rhinoceros, giant sable antelope, okapi, black-footed ferret, Komodo dragon, tuatera (New Zealand lizard, with which the Bronx Zoo has already set a longevity record — in captivity — of five years). The zoo has succeeded in breeding the pigmy hippopotamus, black-necked swan, Barrows golden-eye and eider (from eggs imported

from Iceland). A Bronx Zoo man was the first to rear whooping cranes in captivity, in 1957.

10   Most mammals — cheetahs are an odd exception — will breed in captivity; but birds, particularly waterfowl, tend to turn celibate. Mr. Conway and his men want to know why; and, more important, how to change the picture. The female swan, for example, will sometimes breed if she has been captured very early, preferably before hatching. Other waterfowl are sometimes persuaded to breed simply by raising the water-level in the enclosure, but why this works is not understood. Much more must be known, and in a hurry, about the breeding patterns of endangered species. In the rearing of whooping cranes, Mr. Conway discovered a great deal about their procedures (*Animal Kingdom*, August, 1957), such as that early feeding is solely of proteins and minerals, grain is first offered the young after a week or so, much food is carefully washed by the parents, the mother was the more conscientious brooder, the father the better feeder, chicks did not respond to parents' calls but waited to be found, the father stays awake all night guarding the nest, and so on.

11   The first reform mentioned, that of presenting every creature *as if* in its wild home, is in large part pure theatricality, and was invented by Carl Hagenbeck in Hamburg over fifty years ago. Neither the animal nor the visitor will be entirely deceived by the new artifices contemplated; but both will enjoy the encounter more than when they stared at each other through bars or wire mesh. And perhaps some of the wild creatures *will* be deceived.

12   In the new aquatic bird house, the shore birds will be seen on a beach retreating before incoming artificial waves; the cliff birds will cling to the face of a sheer cliff with a simulated surf booming below; and the visitors will find themselves looking at eye-level into treetops (the tree trunks descending into a pit beneath) where herons are roosting.

13   The most extraordinary display will be that of those creatures that sleep by day and live by night, and hence are always seen sound asleep by zoo visitors. By keeping the lights up all night, the zoo will persuade them to sleep at night. When the visitors arrive by day, the lights will be dimmed sepulchrally, so that owls, bats,

flying foxes, night monkeys and rattlesnakes will all spring into action. A minor difficulty in this program is getting an import permit for a flying fox, a big bat that feeds on fruit and terrifies the U.S. fruit lobby, no trifling lobby.

14   A Kodiak bear, which stands twelve feet tall and is the world's largest predator, will really get his message across to the visitor when he is met at arm's length through a pane of special glass, in a giant den.

15   The giraffes will at least appear to be feeding naturally on tree-tops, for their food will be placed there, instead of on the ground in a bucket.

16   Emperor penguins will be seen in an Antarctic scene, and air conditioning will throw a reasonably cold blast on the visitor.

17   The present system of putting all the kangaroos together, all the big cats in one house, etc., will eventually be replaced by geographical groupings such as Africa, and this will be subdivided into habitats, such as the forest, veld and bush. In each, the associated animals will be seen together, though separated by hidden moats. Thus, in the American plains scene, the bison, wolf and prairie dog will seem to be associated on the terrain they actually occupy in common. All these rearrangements, of course, will cost a lot of money, while the results give people a vastly truer and more dramatic sense of how the rest of the animal kingdom lives.

18   This zoo of the future will also multiply its own headaches in an already complicated operation. A zoo commissary makes a United Nations dietary look simple, with over 1,000 species plus cranky individuals to feed. Supervising the rearing of young can require twenty-four-hour-a-day surveillance by scientists, who are paid by the New York Zoological Society. (Keepers, food, fuel and half of building costs are provided by New York City.) The new arrangements will certainly present unpredictable difficulties. An example is that if you drain the penguins' pool and then scare them they are likely to dive in on the concrete bottom and brain themselves. The mortality in even well-run zoos is distressing, and usually inexplicable; the aim of the Bronx Zoo is to reduce the inexplicability. New animals are paid for by the New York Zoological Society, not the city.

19   The Bronx Zoo now attracts 2,500,000 visitors every year. These

represent its opportunity to tell the story of the animal kingdom, sympathetically, inspirationally, unforgettably — or dully. Its present management acutely feels the double responsibility — to teach the people, and to save the other species: two interlocked objectives.

20   The renaissance of the zoo, not a moment too soon, is not confined to the New York Zoological Society. In both Washington, D.C., and Los Angeles, citizens' committees are agitating for better zoos. Los Angeles' Mayor Poulson said, "We are still working toward a world-famous zoo. We haven't lowered our sights." In the same area an amateur, Maurice Machris, is trying to set up a conservation research ranch of about 400 acres to breed rare animals. He has already bought fifty species, mostly still in quarantine, and hopes for the incredible total of 900 species. He too has discovered that some important species are down to one or two hundred individuals. He is especially interested in the little-known kouprey of Cambodia, which may possibly be a true wild ox.

21   The spirit of such enterprises is admirable. One measure of the decency of a society must be whether its members care, or even affect to care, about the welfare of other species of no immediate benefit to them. It is not really an insult to mankind to admire a hummingbird, an albatross or a lion.

22   It may be noted that the zoos of Communist Russia are grim, old-fashioned jails. That of Communist East Berlin, however, is excellent, comparable to the fine zoos of Basle and Frankfurt. Such data are surely useful in cultural studies of these countries.

23   In America, the reporting on zoos by the press is invariably more or less "cute," and does not seem to me truthful. The theory may be that the press is addressed only to mammals that can read, and cannot resist giving its readers the assurance that, compared to themselves, okapi and whooping cranes are idiots. The press reaches for the winning side, the procreatively successful animal that can read and has the price of the paper.

QUESTIONS FOR REFLECTION, DISCUSSION, OR WRITING

(I) Do you think Cort's primary purpose is one of exposition or argumentation? Try to state his purpose. How well does he achieve it? Was it worth trying to achieve?

(2) Put in other words the meaning of his sentence, "One can imagine a sort of genetic disdain of living in this world of Man's" (par. 1).

(3) Explain and comment on the author's theory, based on geography, that "where people feel superior, they are less interested in the lower orders" (par. 4). Have you found that people living in one part of the country (or who came from there) are more apt to feel "superior" than those in another part? If so, do the areas coincide with those of his theory?

(4) Do you think we "reading mammals" with the price of a paper need "assurance that, compared to (ourselves), okapi and whooping cranes are idiots" (par. 23)? Do you suppose newspapermen really think we do? Can you think of other reasons instead, why we like to read "cute" stories about animals in the zoo?

(5) Can you picture a situation in which we would need to start all over again in developing cows from aurochs? Is there any other really *practical* reason for preserving such animals?

(6) Discuss Cort's statement that "one measure of the decency of a society must be whether its members care, or even affect to care, about the welfare of other species of no immediate benefit to them" (par. 21). Does this seem to you a valid test for "decency"?

(7) Do you consider it worth the expense and trouble to keep dangerous animals from becoming extinct? Should we be concerned, for instance, about preserving *Crotalus* the rattlesnake and his kind? Why, or why not?

Jack Kerouac
ALONE ON A MOUNTAINTOP

JACK KEROUAC, *who lives in Northport, N.Y., was the first and is probably the most important of the modern "beat" authors. Although he has written occasional short stories and essays, his chief medium of expression is the novel. Some of his titles:* On the Road, The Dharma Bums, The Subterraneans, Doctor Sax, *and* Maggie Cassidy. *Some literary critics think he has great talent; others agree with Eugene Burdick (who wrote "The United States Navy") that "Kerouac is a bad writer and often a silly one. . . . He is like a sensitive eyeball that sweeps and perceives but is not connected to a brain"* (The Reporter, *April 3, 1958).*

ALONE ON A MOUNTAINTOP, *which appeared in* Holiday (*see p. 175*) *for October 1958, and in Kerouac's book* Lonesome Traveler, *seems at first to be a simple account of a young man's summer as a fire lookout. It is an artistic achievement in its blending of earthiness and almost poetic descriptions. But it is not a simple narrative, nor an easy one to understand if we set out to grasp everything the author tries to tell us. (If you think this one is "far out," by the way, you must try some of Kerouac's others!) Perhaps a thing of this kind is best appreciated by reading primarily for the feeling the author can share, without requiring him to be always logical as well.*

*One possible difficulty in this essay is the frequent use of obscure **allusions** (a term applied to casual, indirect references to things outside the subject matter itself — historical or literary figures or events, legends, and such). Allusions can help to enrich writing — but unless used with some consideration for the reader, they can damage it. Some of Kerouac's, for example, would require at least a small-scale research project for us ordinary readers to learn their meaning. You can judge for yourself whether they enrich or damage his art.*

1   ANYBODY who's been to Seattle and missed Alaskan Way, the old water front, has missed the point. Here the totem-pole stores, the waters of Puget Sound washing under old piers, the dark gloomy look of ancient warehouses and pier sheds, and the most antique locomotives in America switching boxcars up and down the water front, give a hint, under the pure cloud-mopped, sparkling skies of the Northwest, of great country to come. Driving north from Seattle on Highway 99 is an exciting experience because suddenly you see the Cascade Mountains rising on the northeast horizon, truly *Komo Kulshan* under their uncountable snows. The great peaks covered with trackless white, worlds of huge rock twisted and heaped and sometimes almost spiraled into fantastic unbelievable shapes.

2   All this is seen far above the dreaming fields of the Stilaquamish and Skagit valleys, agricultural flats of peaceful green, the soil so rich and dark it is proudly referred to by inhabitants as second only to the Nile in fertility. At Milltown, Washington, your car rolls over the bridge across the Skagit River. To the left — seaward, westward — the Skagit flows into Skagit Bay and the Pacific Ocean. At Burlington you turn right and head for the heart of the mountains along a rural valley road through sleepy little towns and one bustling agricultural market center known as Sedro-Woolley with hundreds of cars parked aslant on a typical country-town Main Street of hardware

stores, grain-and-feed stores and five-and-tens. On deeper into the deepening valley, cliffs rich with timber appearing by the side of the road, the narrowing river rushing more swiftly now, a pure translucent green like the green of the ocean on a cloudy day but a saltless rush of melted snow from the High Cascades . . . almost good enough to drink north of Marblemount. The road curves more and more till you reach Concrete, the last town in Skagit Valley with a bank and a five-and-ten; after that the mountains rising secretly behind foothills are so close that now you don't see them but begin to feel them more and more.

3   At Marblemount the river is a swift torrent, the work of the quiet mountains. Fallen logs beside the water provide good seats to enjoy a river wonderland. Leaves jiggling in the good clean northwest wind seem to rejoice. The topmost trees on nearby timbered peaks, swept and dimmed by low-flying clouds, seem contented. The clouds assume the faces of hermits or of nuns, or sometimes look like sad dog acts hurrying off into the wings over the horizon. Snags struggle and gurgle in the heaving bulk of the river. Logs rush by at twenty miles an hour. The air smells of pine and sawdust and bark and mud and twigs; birds flash over the water looking for secretive fish.

4   As you drive north across the bridge at Marblemount and on to Newhalem the road narrows and twists until finally the Skagit is seen pouring over rocks, frothing, and small creeks come tumbling from steep hillsides and pile right in. The mountains rise on all sides, only their shoulders and ribs visible, their heads out of sight and now snowcapped.

5   At Newhalem extensive road construction raises a cloud of dust over shacks and cats and rigs; the dam there is the first in a series that create the Skagit watershed which provides all the power for Seattle.

6   The road ends at Diablo, a peaceful company settlement of neat cottages and green lawns surrounded by close-packed peaks named Pyramid and Colonial and Davis. Here a huge lift takes you one thousand feet up to the level of Diablo Lake and Diablo Dam. Over the dam pours a jet roar of water through which a stray log sometimes goes shooting out like a toothpick in a one-thousand-foot arc. Here for the first time you're high enough really to begin to see the Cascades. Dazzles of light to the north show where Ross Lake

sweeps back all the way to Canada, opening a view of the Mt. Baker National Forest as spectacular as any vista in the Colorado Rockies.

7   The Seattle City Light and Power boat leaves on regular schedule from a little pier near Diablo Dam and heads north between steep timbered rocky cliffs toward Ross Dam, about half an hour's ride. The passengers are power employees, hunters and fishermen and forestry workers. Below Ross Dam the footwork begins; you must climb a rocky trail one thousand feet to the level of the dam. Here the vast lake opens out, disclosing small resort floats offering rooms and boats for vacationists, and just beyond, the floats of the U. S. Forestry Service. From this point on, if you're lucky enough to be a rich man or a forest-fire lookout, you can get packed into the North Cascade Primitive Area by horse and mule and spend a summer of complete solitude.

8   I was a fire lookout and after two nights of trying to sleep in the boom and slap of the Forest Service floats, they came for me one rainy morning — a powerful tugboat lashed to a large corral float bearing four mules and three horses, my own groceries, feed, batteries and equipment. The muleskinner's name was Andy and he wore the same old floppy cowboy hat he'd worn in Wyoming twenty years ago. "Well, boy, now we're gonna put you away where we can't reach ya; you better get ready."

9   "It's just what I want, Andy, be alone for three solid months, nobody to bother me."

10   "It's what you're sayin' now, but you'll change your tune after a week."

11   I didn't believe him. I was looking forward to an experience men seldom earn in this modern world: complete and comfortable solitude in the wilderness, day and night, sixty-three days and nights to be exact. We had no idea how much snow had fallen on my mountain during the winter, and Andy said: "If there's not enough it means you gotta hike two miles down that hard trail every day or every other day with two buckets, boy. I ain't envyin' you. I been back there. And one day it's gonna be hot and you're about ready to broil, and bugs you can't even count 'em; and next day a li'l' ole summer blizzard come hit you around the corner of Hozomeen — which sits right there near Canada in your back yard — and you won't be able to stick logs fast enough in that potbelly stove of

yours." But I had a full rucksack loaded with turtleneck sweaters and warm shirts and pants and long wool socks bought on the Seattle water front, and gloves and an earmuff cap, and lots of instant soup and coffee in my grub list.

12   "Shoulda brought yourself a quart of brandy, boy," said Andy, shaking his head as the tug pushed our corral float up Ross Lake, through the log gate and around to the left dead north, underneath the immense rain shroud of Sourdough Mountain and Ruby Mountain.

13   "Where's Desolation Peak?" I asked, meaning my own mountain (A *mountain to be kept forever*, I'd dreamed all that spring).

14   "You ain't gonna see it today till we're practically on top of it," said Andy, "and by that time you'll be so soakin' wet you won't care."

15   Assistant Ranger Marty Gohlke of Marblemount Ranger Station was with us, too, also giving me tips and instructions. Nobody seemed to envy Desolation Peak except me. After two hours pushing through the storming waves of the long rainy lake with dreary misty timber rising steeply on both sides and the mules and horses chomping on their feedbags patient in the downpour, we arrived at the foot of Desolation Trail and the tugman (who'd been providing us with good hot coffee in the pilot cabin) eased her over and settled the float against a steep muddy slope full of bushes and fallen trees. The muleskinner whacked the first mule and she lurched ahead with her double-sided pack of batteries and canned goods, hit the mud with forehoofs, scrambled, slipped, almost fell back in the lake and finally gave one mighty heave and went skittering out of sight in the fog to wait on the trail for the other mules and her master. We all got off, cut the barge loose, waved to the tug man, mounted our horses, and started up, sad and dripping, in the heavy rain.

16   At first the trail, always steeply rising, was so dense with shrubbery we kept getting shower after shower from overhead and from branches hit by our out-jutting knees. The trail was deep with round rocks that kept causing the animals to slip. At one point a great fallen tree made it impossible to go on until Old Andy and Marty went ahead with axes and cleared a short cut around the tree, sweating and cursing and hacking, as I watched the animals. By-and-by they were ready, but the mules were afraid of the rough steepness of

the short cut and had to be prodded through with sticks. Soon the trail reached alpine meadows powdered with blue lupine everywhere in the drenching mists, and with little red poppies, tiny-budded flowers as delicate as designs on a tiny Japanese teacup. Now the trail zigzagged widely back and forth up the high meadow. Soon we saw the vast foggy heap of a rock-cliff face above and Andy yelled, "Soon's we get up high as that we're almost there but that's another two thousand feet, though you'd think you could reach up and touch it!"

17   I unfolded my nylon poncho and draped it over my head, and, drying a little, or, rather, ceasing to drip, I walked alongside the horse to warm my blood and began to feel better. But the other boys just rode along with their heads bowed in the rain. As for altitude all I could tell was from some occasional frightening spots on the trail where we could look down on distant treetops.

18   The alpine meadow reached to timber line, and suddenly a great wind blew shafts of sleet on us. "Gettin' near the top now!" yelled Andy. And now there was snow on the trail, the horses were chumping through a foot of slush and mud, and to the left and right everything was blinding white in the gray fog. "About five and a half thousand feet right now," said Andy, rolling a cigarette as he rode in the rain.

19   We went down, then up another spell, down again, a slow gradual climb, and then Andy yelled, "There she is!" and up ahead in the mountaintop gloom I saw a little shadowy peaked shack standing alone on the top of the world and I gulped with fear:

20   "This my home all summer? And *this* is summer?"

21   The inside of the shack was even more miserable, damp and dirty, leftover groceries and magazines torn to shreds by rats and mice, the floor muddy, the windows impenetrable. But hardy Old Andy, who'd been through this kind of thing all his life, got a roaring fire crackling in the potbellied stove and had me lay out a pot of water with almost half a can of coffee in it, saying, "Coffee ain't no good 'less it's *strong!*" and pretty soon the coffee was boiling a nice brown aromatic foam and we got our cups out and drank deep.

22   Meanwhile I'd gone out on the roof with Marty and removed the bucket from the chimney and put up the weather pole with the anemometer and done a few other chores; and when we came back

in Andy was frying Spam and eggs in a huge pan and it was almost like a party. Outside, the patient animals chomped on their supper bags and were glad to rest by the old corral fence built of logs by some Desolation lookout of the Thirties.

23   Darkness came, incomprehensible.

24   In the gray morning after they'd slept in sleeping bags on the floor and I on the only bunk in my mummy bag, Andy and Marty left, laughing and saying, "Well, what ayou think now, hey? We been here twelve hours already and you still haven't been able to see more than twelve feet!"

25   "By gosh that's right, what am I going to do for watching fires?"

26   "Don't worry, boy, these clouds'll roll away and you'll be able to see a hunnerd miles in every direction."

27   I didn't believe it and I felt miserable and spent the day trying to clean up the shack or pacing twenty careful feet each way in my "yard" (the ends of which appeared to be sheer drops into silent gorges), and I went to bed early. About bedtime I saw my first star, briefly, then giant phantom clouds billowed all around me and the star was gone. But in that instant I thought I'd seen a mile below me gray-black Ross Lake where Andy and Marty were back in the Forest Service boat which had met them at noon.

28   In the middle of the night I woke up suddenly and my hair was standing on end: I saw a huge black shadow in my window. Then I saw that it had a star above it, and realized that this was Mt. Hozomeen (8080 feet) looking in my window from miles away near Canada. I got up from the forlorn bunk with the mice scattering underneath and went outside and gasped to see black mountain shapes gianting all around; and not only that but the billowing curtains of the northern lights shifting behind the clouds. It was a little too much for a city boy. The fear that the Abominable Snowman might be breathing behind me in the dark sent me back to bed where I buried my head inside my sleeping bag.

29   But in the morning — Sunday, July sixth — I was amazed and overjoyed to see a clear blue sunny sky, and down below, like a radiant pure snow sea, the clouds made a marshmallow cover for all the world and all the lake while I abided in warm sunshine among hundreds of miles of snow-white peaks. I brewed coffee and sang and drank a cup on my drowsy warm doorstep.

30   At noon the clouds vanished and the lake appeared below, beautiful beyond belief, a perfect blue pool twenty-five miles long and more, and the creeks like toy creeks and the timber green and fresh everywhere below and even the fishing boats of vacationists on the lake and in the lagoons. A perfect afternoon of sun, and behind the shack I discovered a snowfield big enough to provide me with buckets of cold water till late September.

31   I had taken this job so I could round up a little grubstake and take off for Mexico for a year, but also I wanted to be alone on the top of a mountain and see what it was like, and besides, all the mountain climbers and loggers I'd known on the West Coast had told me not to miss the High Cascades.

32   My job was to watch for fires. One night a terrific lightning storm made a dry run across the Mt. Baker National Forest without any rainfall. When I saw that ominous black cloud flashing wrathfully toward me I shut off the radio and laid the aerial on the ground and waited for the worst. Hiss! hiss! said the wind, bringing dust and lightning nearer. Tick! said the lightning rod, receiving a strand of electricity from a strike on nearby Skagit Peak. Hiss! Tick! and in my bed I felt the earth move. Fifteen miles to the south, just east of Ruby Peak and somewhere near Panther Creek, a large fire raged, a huge orange spot. At ten o'clock lightning hit it again and it flared up dangerously.

33   I was supposed to note the general area of lightning strikes. By midnight I'd been staring so intently out the dark window I got hallucinations of fires everywhere, three of them right in Lightning Creek, phosphorescent orange verticals of ghost fire that seemed to come and go.

34   In the morning, there at 177°16' where I'd seen the big fire, was a strange brown patch in the snowy rock showing where the fire had raged and sputtered out in the all-night rain that followed the lightning. But the result of this storm was disastrous fifteen miles away at McAllister Creek where a great blaze had outlasted the rain and exploded the following afternoon in a cloud that could be seen from Seattle. I felt sorry for the fellows who had to fight these fires, the smoke-jumpers who parachuted down on them out of planes and the trail crews who hiked to them, climbing and scrambling over slippery rocks and scree slopes, arriving sweaty and exhausted only to face the

wall of heat when they got there. As a lookout I had it pretty easy and only had to concentrate on reporting the exact location (by instrument findings) of every blaze I detected.

35   Most days, though, it was the routine that occupied me. Up at seven or so every day, a pot of coffee brought to a boil over a handful of burning twigs, I'd go out in the alpine yard with a cup of coffee hooked in my thumb and leisurely make my wind speed and wind direction and temperature and moisture readings. Then, after chopping wood, I'd use the two-way radio and report to the relay station on Sourdough. At 10 A.M. I usually got hungry for breakfast, and I'd make delicious pancakes, eating them at my little table that was decorated with bouquets of mountain lupine and sprigs of fir.

36   Early in the afternoon was the usual time for my kick of the day, instant chocolate pudding with hot coffee. Around two or three, I'd lie on my back on the meadowside and watch the clouds float by, or pick blueberries and eat them right there. I had tuned the radio loud enough to hear any calls for Desolation.

37   Then at sunset I'd roust up my supper out of cans of yams and Spam and peas, or sometimes just pea soup with corn muffins baked on top of the wood stove in aluminum foil. Then I'd go out to that precipitous snow slope and shovel my two pails of snow for the water tub and gather an armful of fallen firewood from the hillside like the proverbial Old Woman of Japan. For the chipmunks and conies I put pans of leftovers under the shack; in the middle of the night I could hear them clanking around. The rat would scramble down from the attic and eat some too.

38   Sometimes I'd yell questions at the rocks and trees, and across gorges, or yodel "What is the meaning of the void?" The answer was perfect silence, so I knew.

39   Before bedtime I'd read by kerosene lamp whatever books were in the shack. It's amazing how people in solitary hunger after books. After poring over every word of a medical tome, and the synopsized versions of Shakespeare's plays by Charles and Mary Lamb, I climbed up in the little attic and put together torn cowboy pocket books and magazines the mice had ravaged. I also played stud poker with three imaginary players.

40   Around bedtime I'd bring a cup of milk almost to a boil with a

tablespoon of honey in it, and drink that for my lamby nightcap; then I'd curl up in my sleeping bag.

41 No man should go through life without once experiencing healthy, even bored solitude in the wilderness, finding himself depending solely on himself and thereby learning his true and hidden strength. Learning for instance, to eat when he's hungry and sleep when he's sleepy.

42 Also around bedtime was my singing time. I'd pace up and down the well-worn path in the dust of my rock singing all the show tunes I could remember, at the top of my voice, too, with nobody to hear except the deer and the bear.

43 In the red dusk, the mountains were symphonies in pink snow . . . Jack Mountain, Three Fools Peak, Freezeout Peak, Golden Horn, Mt. Terror, Mt. Fury, Mt. Despair, Crooked Thumb Peak, Mt. Challenger and the incomparable Mt. Baker bigger than the world in the distance . . . and my own little Jackass Ridge that completed the Ridge of Desolation. Pink snow and the clouds all distant and frilly like ancient remote cities of Buddhaland splendor, and the wind working incessantly — whish, whish — booming, at times rattling my shack.

44 For supper I made chop suey and baked some biscuits and put the leftovers in a pan for deer that came in the moonlit night and nibbled like big strange cows of peace — long-antlered buck and does and babies too — as I meditated in the alpine grass facing the magic moon-laned lake. And I could see firs reflected in the moonlit lake five thousand feet below, upside down, pointing to infinity.

45 And all the insects ceased in honor of the moon.

46 Sixty-three sunsets I saw revolve on that perpendicular hill . . . mad raging sunsets pouring in sea foams of cloud through unimaginable crags like the crags you grayly drew in pencil as a child, with every rose tint of hope beyond, making you feel just like them, brilliant and bleak beyond words.

47 Cold mornings with clouds billowing out of Lightning Gorge like smoke from a giant fire but the lake cerulean as ever.

48 August comes in with a blast that shakes your house and augurs little Augusticity . . . then that snowy-air and woodsmoke feeling . . . then the snow comes sweeping your way from Canada, and the

wind rises and dark low clouds rush up as out of a forge. Suddenly a green-rose rainbow appears right on your ridge with steamy clouds all around and an orange sun turmoiling . . .

> *What is a rainbow,*
> *Lord? — a hoop*
> *For the lowly*

. . . and you go out and suddenly your shadow is ringed by the rainbow as you walk on the hilltop, a lovely-haloed mystery making you want to pray.

49   A blade of grass jiggling in the winds of infinity, anchored to a rock, and for your own poor gentle flesh no answer.

50   Your oil lamp burning in infinity.

51   One morning I found bear stool and signs of where the monster had taken a can of frozen milk and squeezed it in his paws and bit into it with one sharp tooth, trying to suck out the paste. In the foggy dawn I looked down the mysterious Ridge of Starvation with its fog-lost firs and its hills humping into invisibility, and the wind blowing the fog by like a faint blizzard, and I realized that somewhere in the fog stalked the bear.

52   And it seemed, as I sat there, that this was the Primordial Bear, and that he owned all the Northwest and all the snow and commanded all the mountains. He was King Bear, who could crush my head in his paws and crack my spine like a stick, and this was his house, his yard, his domain. Though I looked all day, he would not show himself in the mystery of those silent foggy slopes. He prowled at night among unknown lakes, and in the early morning the pearl-pure light that shadowed mountainsides of fir made him blink with respect. He had millenniums of prowling here behind him. He had seen the Indians and Redcoats come and go, and would see much more. He continuously heard the reassuring rapturous rush of silence, except when near creeks; he was aware of the light material the world is made of, yet he never discoursed, nor communicated by signs, nor wasted a breath complaining; he just nibbled and pawed, and lumbered along snags paying no attention to things inanimate or animate. His big mouth chew-chewed in the night, I could hear it across the mountain in the starlight. Soon he would come out of the fog, huge, and come and stare in my window with big burning eyes.

He was Avalokitesvara the Bear, and his sign was the gray wind of autumn.

53   I was waiting for him. He never came.

54   Finally the autumn rains, all-night gales of soaking rain as I lie warm as toast in my sleeping bag and the mornings open cold wild fall days with high wind, racing fogs, racing clouds, sudden bright sun, pristine light on hill patches and my fire crackling as I exult and sing at the top of my voice. Outside my window a wind-swept chipmunk sits up straight on a rock, hands clasped as he nibbles an oat between his paws — the little nutty lord of all he surveys.

55   Thinking of the stars night after night I begin to realize "The stars are words" and all the innumerable worlds in the Milky Way are words, and so is this world too. And I realize that no matter where I am, whether in a little room full of thought, or in this endless universe of stars and mountains, it's all in my mind. There's no need for solitude. So love life for what it is, and form no preconceptions whatever in your mind.

56   When I came down in September a cool old golden look had come into the forest, auguring cold snaps and frost and the eventual howling blizzard that would cover my shack completely, unless those winds at the top of the world would keep her bald. As I reached the bend where the shack would disappear and I would plunge down to the lake to meet the boat that would take me out and home, I turned and blessed Desolation Peak and the little pagoda on top and thanked them for the shelter and the lesson I'd been taught.

QUESTIONS FOR REFLECTION, DISCUSSION, OR WRITING

(1) Examine some of Kerouac's *allusions* — *e.g.*, "*Komo Kulshan*" (par. 1), "the proverbial Old Woman of Japan" (37), "Buddhaland splendor" (43), "Avalokitesvara the Bear" (52). For what percentage of *Holiday's* readers do you suppose all of these are meaningful? Which, if any, are meaningful to you? Does an ignorance of the others seriously impair your understanding of the passages where they are used?

(2) Explain his reference to the Abominable Snowman (par. 28).

(3) Kerouac also makes greater use of metaphors, similes, and personifications (see pp. 15 and 104) than any of our previous authors, and these do usually contribute to the success of his descriptions. Find several of these figures of speech and comment on their originality and effectiveness.

(4) Find several descriptive passages, other than figures of speech, that you consider especially apt or satisfying. Can you find the clue to their success?

(5) The author devoted three paragraphs (51-53), one of them the longest in the essay, to his meditations on the bear. How could he have considered it worth so much? Of what significance is this section? Does the bear, for him, really represent (symbolize) something else entirely? Can you explain what? Is he still looking for the "meaning of the void" (par. 38)?

(6) The real message of this essay, the "meaning" he was seeking and eventually found, is slow in developing (look again at paragraphs 38, 41, 44, 48-50, and 55-56) and even at the last is not fully explained. Would it have been better if the author had not been quite so subtle? Or does he imply that his quest was not one that even he had really understood or been able to phrase exactly? Do you "sense" his meaning, even if you cannot explain it? If so, is this enough?

(7) Kerouac calls this an "experience men seldom earn in this modern world: complete and comfortable solitude in the wilderness." Have you ever experienced complete solitude — in the wilderness or elsewhere? Would you like to? Why, or why not?

(8) Comment on Burdick's *simile* (see headnotes) in his criticism of Kerouac's writing. To what extent do you agree (judging unfairly, perhaps, on only one sample of his writing) that he is "like a sensitive eyeball . . . not connected to a brain"? Explain both Burdick's criticism and your own. Then compare, if possible, the writing of the two authors in respect to the eyeball-brain criticism.

Time Magazine

THE ROOTS OF HOME

TIME *Magazine (see p. 162) used this article for a cover story (always the main feature, introduced by the picture on the front cover) in the June 20, 1960, issue. Although printed without a by-line, the "letter from the publisher" on the index page states that the article was written by* JESSE BIRN-BAUM, *an associate editor of the magazine, who is himself a resident of "suburbia" and who had the help of 21* Time *correspondents interviewing and accumulating information in suburbs in all parts of the United States.*

THE ROOTS OF HOME *concerns a matter which most of us know something about — nearly everyone, it seems, lives in the suburbs, or wishes he did, or is glad he does not. As in most* Time *cover stories, this one is thorough, and the au-*

*thor apparently tried to present all sides of his subject, the good and the bad
alike. But it still should be read critically.*

1   THE WREATH that rings every U.S. metropolis is a green garland
of place names and people collectively called Suburbia. It weaves
through the hills beyond the cities, marches across flatlands that
once were farms and pastures, dips into gullies and woodlands, strad-
dles the rocky hillocks and surrounds the lonesome crossroads. Of-
tener than not it has a lilting polyphony that sings of trees (Stream-
wood, Elmwood, Lakewood, Kirkwood), the rolling country (Cedar
Hill, Cockrell Hill, Forest Hills), or the primeval timberlands (Forest Grove, Park Forest, Oak Park, Deer Park). But it has its roots
in such venerable names as Salem, Greenwich, Chester, Berkeley,
Evanston, Sewickley and Rye.

2   In those towns and hills and groves last week the splendor of a
new summer seemed, as always, to give a new lilt to life. The hills
and fields triumphed with fresh green grass. In the old towns, the
giant oaks and elms threw rich new shade across the white colonial
mansions and the square, peaked-roofed clapboard houses. In fresh-
minted subdivisions, sycamore striplings strained at their stakes to
promise token cover for the bare houses of glass, steel, stone and
shingle that have sprouted (19 million since 1940) as from a bottomless nest of Chinese boxes. School buses headed toward the season's
last mile; power mowers and outboard motors pulsed the season's
first promise. Fragrance of honeysuckle and roses overlay the smell
of charcoal and seared beef. The thud of baseball against mitt, the
abrasive grind of roller skate against concrete, the jarring harmony
of the Good Humor bell tolled the day; the clink of ice, the distant
laugh, the surge of hi-fi through the open window came with the
night.

3   *A March for Causes.* For better or for worse, Suburbia in the
1960s is the U.S.'s grass-roots. In Suburbia live one-third of the nation, roughly 60 million people who represent every patch of democracy's hand-stitched quilt, every economic layer, every laboring and
professional pursuit in the country. Suburbia is the nation's broad-
ening young middle class, staking out its claim across the landscape,

prospecting on a trial-and-error basis for the good way of life for itself and for the children that it produces with such rapidity. It is, as Social Scientist Max Lerner (*America as a Civilization*) has put it, "the focus of most of the forces that are remaking American life today."

4   If Suburbia's avid social honeybees buzz from address to address in search of sweet status, Suburbia is at the same time the home of the talented and distinguished Americans who write the nation's books, paint its paintings, run its corporations and set the patterns. If its legions sometimes march into frantic activity with rigorous unison, they march for such causes as better schools, churches and charities, which are the building blocks of a nation's character. If Suburbia's ardent pursuit of life at backyard barbecues, block parties and committee meetings offends pious city-bred sociologists, its self-conscious strivings to find a better way for men, women and children to live together must impress the same observers.

5   Suburbia is a particular kind of American phenomenon, and its roots lie in a particular kind of American heritage. In a casual, ill-planned way it is the meeting ground between the growing, thriving city and the authentic U.S. legend of small-town life. Says Sociologist Alvin Scaff, who lives in Los Angeles' suburban Claremont: "If you live in the city, you may be a good citizen and interest yourself in a school-board election, but it is seldom meaningful in human terms. In a suburb, the chances are you know the man who is running for the school board, and you vote for or against him with more understanding." Says Don C. Peters, president of Pittsburgh's Mellon-Stuart Co. (construction) and chairman of the board of supervisors of suburban Pine Township: "The American suburb is the last outpost of democracy, the only level left on which the individual citizen can make his wishes felt, directly and immediately. I think there's something idealistic about the search for a home in the suburbs. Call it a return to the soil. It's something that calls most people some time in their lives." When France's Charles de Gaulle saw San Francisco's suburban Palo Alto on his trip to the U.S. six weeks ago, he hailed Suburbia as *"magnifique."*

6   *Hell Is a City.* Man has been moving to the suburbs ever since he invented the urbs. *"Rus mihi dulce sub urbe est,"* sang the Roman epigrammatist Martial in the 1st century A.D. "To me, the country on

the outskirts of the city is sweet." And small wonder, for the towns and walled cities of Europe, from ancient times through the Middle Ages and beyond, were airless, fetid places choking with humanity. The big crisis of the cities came with the Industrial Revolution. In England lonely voices cried out against the grime and stench of the cities. "Hell is a city much like London," wrote Shelley, "a populous and smoky city."

7   By the early 20th century, middle-class Suburbia was a reality in England, and Social Historian C. F. G. Masterman was perhaps the first of a legion of urban critics to draw a bead on it. Each little red house, he wrote in 1909, "boasts its pleasant drawing room, its bow window, its little front garden . . . The women, with their single domestic servants, now so difficult to get, and so exacting when found, find time hangs rather heavy on their hands. But there are excursions to shopping centers in the West End and pious sociabilities, occasional theater visits and the interests of home."

8   *Flowering Green.* Long before England's Masterman had his say, Philadelphians and Bostonians were moving to the outskirts of town. Ben Franklin packed up, left Philadelphia's High Street and unpacked again at the corner of Second and Sassafras, grumbling that "the din of the Market increases upon me: and that with frequent interruptions has, I find, made me say some things twice over." And after all, as one proud New Englander says, "When Paul Revere needed help for the city of Boston, where did he go? The suburbs!"

9   At first the countryside communities leafed and budded with the homes of the well-to-do, who could afford to come and go by the seasons. By the turn of the century, U.S. Suburbia was flowering with permanent residents. Freed from the city by the trolley and rapid-transit services, and then by the automobile, hoisted gradually by a strengthening economy, the new middle-income families swept beyond the gates to buy homes of their own, from which they could commute to their jobs. When World War II ended, the sweep to the suburbs turned into a stampede. The veterans came home, the legion of war workers burst out of crowded city quarters, and in battalions they set out to find homes where the land was greener and cheaper. New settlements spread across acre upon acre; small, sleepy old towns were inundated by newcomers, and the suburban way of life became the visible substance of what a hard-working nation was

working so hard for. "Eventually," observes Humorist-Exurbanite
James Thurber (Cornwall, Conn.) of the steady spread of Suburbia,
"this country will be called the United Cities of America. One suburb will pile into another until in New York State there'll only be
Albany and New York City; and they can really fight it out in the
streets. If they start shoveling in San Diego, buildings will tumble
in Bangor."

10   *The Women.* The key figure in all Suburbia, the thread that
weaves between family and community — the keeper of the suburban dream — is the suburban housewife. In the absence of her commuting, city-working husband, she is first of all the manager of home
and brood, and beyond that a sort of aproned activist with a penchant for keeping the neighborhood and community kettle whistling.
With children on her mind and under her foot, she is breakfast
getter ("You can't have ice cream for breakfast because I say you
can't"), laundress, house cleaner, dishwasher, shopper, gardener,
encyclopedia, arbitrator of children's disputes, policeman ("Tommy,
didn't your mother ever tell you that it's not nice to go into people's
houses and open their refrigerators?")

11   If she is not pregnant, she wonders if she is. She takes her peanut
butter sandwich lunch while standing, thinks she looks a fright,
watches her weight (periodically), jabbers over the short-distance
telephone with the next-door neighbor. She runs a worn track to the
front door, buys more Girl Scout cookies and raffle tickets than she
thinks she should, cringes from the suburban locust — the door-to-
door salesman who peddles everything from storm windows to
potato chips, fire-alarm systems to vacuum cleaners, diaper service
to magazine subscriptions. She keeps the checkbook, frets for the
day that her husband's next raise will top the flood of monthly bills
(it never will) — a tide that never seems to rise as high in the city
as it does in the suburbs.

12   She wonders if her husband will send her flowers (on no special
occasion), shoos the children next door to play at the neighbor's
house for a change, paints her face for her husband's return before
she wrestles with dinner. Spotted through her day are blessed moments of relief or dark thoughts of escape.

13   *Auto Nation.* In Suburbia's pedocracy huge emphasis is placed
on activities for the young (Washington's suburban Montgomery

County, Md. — pop. 358,000 — spends about $34 million a year on youth programs). The suburban housewife might well be a can-opener cook, but she must have an appointment book and a driver's license and must be able to steer a menagerie of leggy youngsters through the streets with the coolness of a driver at the Sebring trials; the suburban sprawl and the near absence of public trans-portation generally mean that any destination is just beyond sensible walking distance. Most children gauge walking distance at two blocks. If the theory of evolution is still working, it may well one day transform the suburban housewife's right foot into a flared paddle, grooved for easy traction on the gas pedal and brake.

14   As her children grow less dependent on her, Suburbia's housewife fills her new-found time with a dizzying assortment of extra-curricular projects that thrust her full steam into community life. Beyond the home-centered dinner parties, Kaffee-klatsches and card parties, there is a directory-sized world of organizations devised for husbands as well as for wives (but it is the wife who keeps things organized). In New Jersey's Levittown, a projected 16,000-unit replica of the Long Island original, energetic suburbanites can sign up for at least 35 different organizations from the Volunteer Fire Department to the Great Books Club, and the Lords and Ladies Dance Club, not to mention the proliferating list of adult-education courses that keep the public school lights glowing into the night. "We have a wonderful adult-education program," says Suburbanite (Levittown, L.I.) Muriel Kane (two children), "where women can learn how to fix their own plumbing and everything."

15   *Fighting in the Thickets.* Since Suburbia was conceived for children (and vice versa), the suburban housewife is the chief jungle fighter for school expansion and reform. Beyond that the path leads easily to the thickets of local politics. Only recently, after the Montgomery County manager whacked $11 million from the 1961 school budget, the county council was invaded by an indignant posse of 1,000 P.T.A. members. The council scrambled to retreat, not only restored the cuts, but added a few projects of its own for good measure. The tax rate jumped 5¢ per $100 valuation as a result, but there was scarcely a whimper.

16   To the north, in New York's suburban Scarsdale, the women's sense of responsibility has the same ring. Says Housewife Rhea

Hertel (Woman's Club, Neighborhood Association, P.T.A., League of Women Voters): "If you're receiving benefits and not contributing, what kind of person are you?" Adds Scarsdale's Grace Fitzwater (Hitchcock Presbyterian Church, Woman's Club, P.T.A.): "When we lived in New York City, I roared with laughter at this sort of thing. I never knew anyone in the city who was civic; out here I don't know anybody who isn't." Says Florence Willett, 44, who is the new mayor of Detroit's suburban Birmingham: "Women feel a greater need for taking their share of the work. With husbands away at work and hampered by long commuting, women can share and contribute more. Don't ever say we run the suburbs, though."

17   *Talent.* With a little prodding from his wife, the suburban husband develops a big yen to mix in Government affairs at the local level. How can the head of the house, father of the brood, refuse to campaign for school bonds or stand for the board of education — particularly when his firm urges him to be civic-minded? The result is that Suburbia often shines with a kind of topnotch talent that makes troubled big-city fathers wince with envy. In Kansas City's suburban Prairie Village, for example, the $1-a-year mayor is a lawyer with a growing practice, the president of the city council is a Procter & Gamble Co. division manager and the head of the village planning commission is assistant to the president of a manufacturing firm. In Philadelphia's suburban Swarthmore, the town council includes a Philadelphia banker, a Du Pont engineer, the president of a pipeline company and a retired executive of Swarthmore College.

18   Biggest of the problems that such people face is Suburbia's growing morass of overlapping services and functions, especially in counties that have experienced a big building rush. In the 17 towns that comprise Denver's four-county suburban area, for example, there are 27 school districts, 35 water districts, 59 sanitation districts. The Suburbia of Portland, Ore. embraces three counties, 178 special service districts, 60 school districts, twelve city governments. And the granddaddy of them all is the megalopolis of Los Angeles which is fish-netted with 72 separate governments and an uncounted array of districts, authorities, and floating unincorporated communities.

19   But suburbanites, more than their urban or rural brethren, tend to want to get things fixed. Lakewood, Calif., 22 miles south of downtown Los Angeles, was just another boondock of 5,000 people

ten years ago when the boom thundered. A development group poured $200 million into 17,000 homes ($8,000-$11,000) and a big shopping center. As residents took hold, the sense of frustration that came from long-distance county rule and the absence of locally administered services flashed into a new, self-starting energy. Lakewood, with a present population of 75,000, incorporated itself in 1954, sank its own home-nurtured political roots and fashioned an identity of its own. Then, while running its own affairs, it devised a method of contracting for police, road maintenance and building maintenance to the county government. The "Lakewood Plan" was later copied by many other California communities. So ably has Lakewood fashioned its living pattern to suit itself that many Lakewood families who might have moved on to more expensive, status-setting locales, have decided to stay where they are.

20   *"Anybody Home?"* The suburbanite has been prodded, poked, gouged, sniffed and tweaked by armies of sociologists and swarms of cityside cynics, but in reality he is his own best critic. Organized suburban living is a relatively new invention, and already some of its victims are wondering if it has too much organization and too little living. The pressure of activity and participation in the model suburb of Lakewood, for example, can be harrowing. The town's recreation league boasts 110 boys' baseball teams (2,000 players), 36 men's softball teams, ten housewives' softball teams. In season, the leagues play 75 boys' and 30 men's basketball teams, 77 football teams, all coached by volunteers, while other activities range through drama, dance and charm classes, bowling, dog-training classes, "Slim 'n Trim" groups, roller skating, photography, woodcraft, and lessons in how to ice a cake. Says Joy Hudson, 35, mother of three children: "There is a problem of getting too busy. Some weeks my husband is home only two nights a week. My little boy often says, 'Anybody going to be home tonight?'" Suburbia, echoed Exurbanite Adlai Stevenson (Libertyville, Ill.) recently, is producing "a strange half-life of divided families and Sunday fathers."

21   The parental press to keep the youngsters busy has created an image of an Organization Child, or Boy in the Gray Flannel Sneakers. The thriving Cub Scout movement is a wondrous machine of 1,822,062 beanie-capped boys who visit fire stations, make kites and tie knots, all *en masse*, and the Little League has more than a mil-

lion little sports who are cheered on by an equal number of over-exuberant daddies. "Some kids," says Long Island School Psychologist Justin Koss, "need the Little League. But some need to dig in their own backyards, too. The trouble is that plenty of parents think that if their kid isn't in Little League, there's something abnormal about him." Declares Shirley Vandenberg, 33 (three children), of Portland Ore.'s suburban Oak Grove: "We don't need Blue Birds and Boy Scouts out here. This is not the slums. The kids out here have the great outdoors. I think people are so bored, they organize the children, and then try to hook everyone else on it. And then the poor kids have no time left to just lie on their beds and daydream." Says Jean Chenoweth (two teen-age children), who moved to a Denver house from the suburbs: "Parents do nine-tenths of the work. I had a Blue Bird Group for three years, and we never accomplished a cotton-picking thing — they just came for the refreshments as far as I could see." Making her choice, Mrs. Chenoweth devotes her spare time to fund raising for a school for handicapped children and making recordings for the blind.

22   In those suburbs where families, income, education and interest are homogenized, suburbanites sometimes wonder whether their children are cocooned from the rest of the world. "A child out here sees virtually no sign of wealth and no sign of poverty," says Suburbanite Alan Rosenthal (Washington's Rock Creek Palisades). "It gives him a tendency to think that everyone else lives just the way he does." Suburbanite-Author, Robert Paul ("*Where Did You Go?*" "*Out.*" "*What Did You Do?*" "*Nothing.*") Smith (New York City's Scarsdale), complains that Scarsdale is "just like a Deanna Durbin movie: all clean and unreal. Hell, I went to school in Mount Vernon, N.Y., with the furnace man's son — you don't get that here."

23   *Den of Conformity.* And what of the grownups themselves? For some, the suburban euphoria often translates itself into the suburban caricature. The neighborhood race for bigger and better plastic swimming pools, cars and power mowers is still being run in some suburbs, and in still others, the chief warm-weather occupation is neighbor watching (Does she hang her laundry outside to dry? Does he leave his trash barrels on the curb after they have been emptied?). In Long Island's staid, old Garden City, observes Hofstra Assistant

Sociology Professor William Dobriner, "they don't care whether you believe in God, but you'd better cut your grass." In close-by Levittown, a poll of householders some time ago showed that the No. 1 topic on people's minds was the complaint that too many dogs were running unleashed on the lawns. Topic No. 2 was the threat of world Communism.

24   The all-weather activities often center on frenzied weekend parties in the "den," attended by neighbors, who each in his turn will throw a potato-chip and cheese-dip party on succeeding weekends. Cries a Chicago suburban woman: "I'm so sick and tired of seeing those same faces every Friday and Saturday night, I could scream." In Kansas City's suburban Overland Park, three jaded couples formed an "Anti-Conformity League" to fight group-think, disbanded it soon afterward because, explains ex-Schoolteacher Ginger Powers (two children), "it was getting just too organized to be anti-conformist."

25   Though suburban wife-swapping stories are the delight of the urban cocktail party, immorality in the suburbs is no more or less prevalent than it is in the cities. But an adventuresome male commuter does have one advantage: he can pursue a clandestine affair easily in the city merely by notifying his suburban wife that he is being kept at the office. One sign of the times is that Private Detective Milton Thompson of suburban Kansas City is also a marriage counselor, has handled 300 marital cases in the past three years. The usual story: "The husband plays on the Missouri side of the river before he gets out here. Maybe it's just a few extra dry martinis with the gang from his office. Maybe not. Anyway, Mama has a little more money than average. She has a maid. That gives her a heck of a lot of time to sit around and think. If hubby is late — boy, does she think."

26   Suburbia's clergymen tend to be most keenly aware of Suburbia's disappointments and Suburbia's promise. "Many people," complains Kansas City Rabbi Samuel Mayerberg, "mistake activity for usefulness." Says Dr. Donald S. Ewing, minister of Wayland's Trinitarian Congregational Church near Boston: "Suburbia is gossipy. So many of the people are on approximately the same level economically and socially. They're scrambling for success. They tend to be new in the community and they're unstable and insecure. When they see some-

one else fail, in work or in a family relationship, they themselves feel a rung higher, and this is a great reason for gossip. I think socially we're flying apart — we don't meet heart to heart any more, we meet at cocktail parties in a superficial way. We value smartness rather than depth, shine rather than spirit. But I think people are sick of it; they want to get out of it."

27   In Chicago's suburban Elk Grove Village, busy Lutheran Minister Martin E. Marty, who writes for the *Christian Century*, and who devotes much of his time to patching up corroding marriages, sighs wearily: "We've all learned that Hell is portable. I think we're seeing a documentable rebellion going on against the post-war idea of mere belongingness and sociability. We all agree that Suburbia means America. It's not different, but it's typical. Solve Suburbia's problems and you solve America's problems."

28   *Buddhas & Babies.* The fact surrounding all the criticism and self-searching is that most suburbanites are having too good a time to realize that they ought to be unhappy with their condition.

29   At week's end, as they nursed their power mowers down the lawn, Suburbia's men paused here and there to enjoy a spell of nothing more salacious than wife-watching. Tanned, brief-clad women sprawled in their chaises and chatted about babies, Khrushchev, Japan and the P.T.A. In the patios, the amateur chefs prepared juicy sacrifices on the suburban Buddhas — the charcoal grills. Mint-flavored iced tea or tart martinis chilled thirsty throats, and from across hedgerows and fences came the cries of exultant youngsters and the yells and laughter of men and women engaged in a rough-and-tumble game of croquet or volleyball. (In Springfield Township, near Philadelphia, nine couples recently pounded through a rousing volleyball match: five of the women were pregnant, but no emergency deliveries were made that day.)

30   Thus the suburban counterpoint leaps forward in optimistic measure, creating a new framework for the American theme. True, as in every place, every suburban husband wishes he earned more money, every mother with young children wishes she had more help, small boys wish there were fewer days of school, small girls wish there were fewer small boys, and babies all wish there was no such thing as strained spinach. Nevertheless, there is scarcely a man or

woman living in all those hills and groves beyond the cities who does not sing with Martial: *Rus mihi dulce sub urbe est.*

QUESTIONS FOR REFLECTION, DISCUSSION, OR WRITING

(1) From the first sentence, almost from the first word, "The Roots of Home" is alive with metaphors. (In fact, the title itself is a metaphor.) Examine three or four paragraphs, locating these figures of speech. How effectively do they assist you in visualizing the author's descriptions?

(2) *Time* Magazine is noted (and sometimes criticized) for its frequent coining, or making-up, of words. Example: "pedocracy" (par. 13). Does the fact that you have never heard this word before — or that you cannot find it in your dictionary — seriously impair your understanding of the sentence where it is used? If you find the prefix "pedo," does the meaning of the word become obvious? Do you see any advantage to the use of such coined words?

(3) Explain the meaning of the statement ". . . but it is seldom meaningful in human terms" (par. 5). Do you agree? Why, or why not?

(4) Although you may never have been in London (which is not too different from many large American cities) and almost certainly have never been in Hell, how do you feel about Shelley's opinion that "Hell is a city much like London" (par. 6)? Do you share this impression of "populous and smoky cities"? Explain.

(5) What do you think is apt to be the effect on children when the mother becomes "the manager of home and brood" (par. 10) — when suburbia produces "a strange half-life of divided families and Sunday fathers" (par. 20)? Relate your ideas, one way or another, to Judge Leibowitz's opinion in "Nine Words That Can Stop Juvenile Delinquency" (p. 30).

(6) Is there any serious danger in children's activities' being so highly organized that the "poor kids have no time left to just lie on their beds and daydream" (par. 21)? Is "daydreaming" really that important?

(7) Do you think there is anything abnormal about the boy who is not in Little League? Explain. Is there anything abnormal about the parents who *think* he is abnormal?

(8) How serious do you consider the charges (or do you even agree with them) that "they don't care whether you believe in God, but you'd better cut your grass" and that the topic of unleashed dogs is more on suburbanites' minds than the threat of world Communism (par. 23)?

(9) Various suitable topics for composition have undoubtedly suggested themselves during this reading — *e.g.*, your preference for the city (suburbs, country town, farm); too much "togetherness" in a housing tract; juvenile delinquency in the suburbs; the value of (or trouble with) Little League.

＊
＊

VIEWS OF MAN

＊
＊ AS HE SEES HIMSELF

＊
＊
＊
＊
＊
＊
＊
＊
＊
＊
＊
＊
＊
＊
＊
＊
＊
＊
＊
＊
＊ *Philip Wylie*
＊
＊ **SCIENCE HAS SPOILED MY SUPPER**
＊

PHILIP WYLIE, *a native of Massachusetts but a resident of Florida, at one time or another has been editor and columnist, member of the staff of* The New Yorker, *publicity writer, advertising director, magazine and motion picture writer, author of more than 20 books, and recipient of many literary awards. Although much of his writing has been controversial, he is also the author of the "Crunch and Des" stories of Florida fishing, the basis of a popular TV series.*

THE ATLANTIC MONTHLY, *where "Science Has Spoiled My Supper" first appeared in April 1954, has been published in Boston since 1857. Since that time it has been a "quality" magazine of the highest reputation in the United States and in many foreign countries. The subject matter of* The Atlantic *is*

widely varied, as are its styles and writing forms, which always include the
essay, the short story, and poetry.

SCIENCE HAS SPOILED MY SUPPER *is typical of Wylie's light but caustic*
approach into a matter of much more concern than, say, what happened to
one man's "supper." Reading the essay will not be difficult, but it will give
you more to think about than you may suspect at first.

1   I AM A FAN for Science. My education is scientific and I have, in
one field, contributed a monograph to a scientific journal. Science,
to my mind, is applied honesty, the one reliable means we have to
find out truth. That is why, when error is committed in the name of
Science, I feel the way a man would if his favorite uncle had taken
to drink.

2   Over the years, I have come to feel that way about what science
has done to food. I agree that America can set as good a table as any
nation in the world. I agree that our food is nutritious and that the
diet of most of us is well-balanced. What America eats is hand-
somely packaged; it is usually clean and pure; it is excellently preserved. The only trouble with it is this: year by year it grows less
good to eat. It appeals increasingly to the eye. But who eats with
his eyes? Almost everything used to taste better when I was a kid.
For quite a long time I thought that observation was merely another
index of advancing age. But some years ago I married a girl whose
mother is an expert cook of the kind called "old-fashioned." This
gifted woman's daughter (my wife) was taught her mother's venerable skills. The mother lives in the country and still plants an old-
fashioned garden. She still buys dairy products from the neighbors
and, insofar as possible, she uses the same materials her mother and
grandmother did — to prepare meals that are superior. They are
just as good, in this Year of Grace, as I recall them from my courtship. After eating for a while at the table of my mother-in-law, it is
sad to go back to eating with my friends — even the alleged "good
cooks" among them. And it is a gruesome experience to have meals
at the best big-city restaurants.

3   Take cheese, for instance. Here and there, in big cities, small

stores and delicatessens specialize in cheese. At such places, one can buy at least some of the first-rate cheeses that we used to eat — such as those we had with pie and in macaroni. The latter were sharp but not too sharp. They were a little crumbly. We called them American cheeses, or even rat cheese; actually, they were Cheddars. Long ago, this cheese began to be supplanted by a material called "cheese foods." Some cheese foods and "processed" cheese are fairly edible; but not one comes within miles of the old kinds — for flavor.

4   A grocer used to be very fussy about his cheese. Cheddar was made and sold by hundreds of little factories. Representatives of the factories had particular customers, and cheese was prepared by hand to suit the grocers, who knew precisely what their patrons wanted in rat cheese, pie cheese, American and other cheeses. Some liked them sharper; some liked them yellower; some liked anise seeds in cheese, or caraway.

5   What happened? Science — or what is called science — stepped in. The old-fashioned cheeses didn't ship well enough. They crumbled, became moldy, dried out. "Scientific" tests disclosed that a great majority of the people will buy a less-good-tasting cheese if that's all they can get. "Scientific marketing" then took effect. Its motto is "Give the people the least quality they'll stand for." In food, as in many other things, the "scientific marketers" regard quality as secondary so long as they can sell most persons anyhow; what they are after is "durability" or "shippability."

6   It is not possible to make the very best cheese in vast quantities at a low average cost. "Scientific sampling" got in its statistically nasty work. It was found that the largest number of people will buy something that is bland and rather tasteless. Those who prefer a product of a pronounced and individualistic flavor have a variety of preferences. Nobody is altogether pleased by bland foodstuff, in other words; but nobody is very violently put off. The result is that a "reason" has been found for turning out zillions of packages of something that will "do" for nearly all and isn't even imagined to be superlatively good by a single soul!

7   Economics entered. It is possible to turn out in quantity a bland, impersonal, practically imperishable substance more or less resembling, say, cheese — at lower cost than cheese. Chain groceries shut

out the independent stores and "standardization" became a principal means of cutting costs.

8   Imitations also came into the cheese business. There are American duplications of most of the celebrated European cheeses, mass-produced and cheaper by far than the imports. They would cause European food-lovers to gag or guffaw — but generally the imitations are all that's available in the supermarkets. People buy them and eat them.

9   Perhaps you don't like cheese — so the fact that decent cheese is hardly ever served in America any more, or used in cooking, doesn't matter to you. Well, take bread. There has been (and still is) something of a hullabaloo about bread. In fact, in the last few years, a few big bakeries have taken to making a fairly good imitation of real bread. It costs much more than what is nowadays called bread, but it is edible. Most persons, however, now eat as "bread" a substance so full of chemicals and so barren of cereals that it approaches a synthetic.

10   Most bakers are interested mainly in how a loaf of bread looks. They are concerned with how little stuff they can put in it — to get how much money. They are deeply interested in using chemicals that will keep bread from molding, make it seem "fresh" for the longest possible time, and so render it marketable and shippable. They have been at this monkeyshine for a generation. Today a loaf of "bread" looks deceptively real; but it is made from heaven knows what and it resembles, as food, a solidified bubble bath. Some months ago I bought a loaf of the stuff and, experimentally, began pressing it together, like an accordion. With a little effort, I squeezed the whole loaf to a length of about one inch!

11   Yesterday, at the home of my mother-in-law, I ate with country-churned butter and home-canned wild strawberry jam several slices of actual bread, the same thing we used to have every day at home. People who have eaten actual bread will know what I mean. They will know that the material commonly called bread is not even related to real bread, except in name.

II

12   For years, I couldn't figure out what had happened to vegetables. I knew, of course, that most vegetables, to be enjoyed in their full de-

liciousness, must be picked fresh and cooked at once. I knew that vegetables cannot be overcooked and remain even edible, in the best sense. They cannot stand on the stove. That set of facts makes it impossible, of course, for any American restaurant — or, indeed, any city-dweller separated from supply by more than a few hours — to have decent fresh vegetables. The Parisians managed by getting their vegetables picked at dawn and rushed in farmers' carts to market, where no middleman or marketman delays produce on its way to the pot.

13   Our vegetables, however, come to us through a long chain of command. There are merchants of several sorts — wholesalers before the retailers, commission men, and so on — with the result that what were once edible products become, in transit, mere wilted leaves and withered tubers.

14   Homes and restaurants do what they can with this stuff — which my mother-in-law would discard on the spot. I have long thought that the famed blindfold test for cigarettes should be applied to city vegetables. For I am sure that if you puréed them and ate them blindfolded, you couldn't tell the beans from the peas, the turnips from the squash, the Brussels sprouts from the broccoli.

15   It is only lately that I have found how much science has had to do with this reduction of noble victuals to pottage. Here the science of genetics is involved. Agronomists and the like have taken to breeding all sorts of vegetables and fruits — changing their original nature. This sounds wonderful and often is insane. For the scientists have not as a rule taken any interest whatsoever in the taste of the things they've tampered with!

16   What they've done is to develop "improved" strains of things for every purpose but eating. They work out, say, peas that will ripen all at once. The farmer can then harvest his peas and thresh them and be done with them. It is extremely profitable because it is efficient. What matter if such peas taste like boiled paper wads?

17   Geneticists have gone crazy over such "opportunities." They've developed string beans that are straight instead of curved, and all one length. This makes them easier to pack in cans, even if, when eating them, you can't tell them from tender string. Ripening time and identity of size and shape are, nowadays, more important in carrots than the fact that they taste like carrots. Personally, I don't

care if they hybridize onions till they are big as your head and come up through the snow; but, in doing so, they are producing onions that only vaguely and feebly remind you of onions. We are getting some varieties, in fact, that have less flavor than the water off last week's leeks. Yet, if people don't eat onions because they taste like onions, what in the name of Luther Burbank do they eat them for?

18   The women's magazines are about one third dedicated to clothes, one third to mild comment on sex, and the other third to recipes and pictures of handsome salads, desserts, and main courses. "Institutes" exist to experiment and tell housewives how to cook attractive meals and how to turn leftovers into works of art. The food thus pictured looks like famous paintings of still life. The only trouble is it's tasteless. It leaves appetite unquenched and merely serves to stave off famine.

19   I wonder if this blandness of our diet doesn't explain why so many of us are overweight and even dangerously so. When things had flavor, we knew what we were eating all the while — and it satisfied us. A teaspoonful of my mother-in-law's wild strawberry jam will not just provide a gastronome's ecstasy: it will entirely satisfy your jam desire. But, of the average tinned or glass-packed strawberry jam, you need half a cupful to get the idea of what you're eating. A slice of my mother-in-law's apple pie will satiate you far better than a whole bakery pie.

20   That thought is worthy of investigation — of genuine scientific investigation. It is merely a hypothesis, so far, and my own. But people — and their ancestors — have been eating according to flavor for upwards of a billion years. The need to satisfy the sense of taste may be innate and important. When food is merely a pretty cascade of viands, with the texture of boiled cardboard and the flavor of library paste, it may be the instinct of *genus homo* to go on eating in the unconscious hope of finally satisfying the ageless craving of the frustrated taste buds. In the days when good-tasting food was the rule in the American home, obesity wasn't such a national curse.

21   How can you feel you've eaten if you haven't tasted, and fully enjoyed tasting? Why (since science is ever so ready to answer the beck and call of mankind) don't people who want to reduce merely give up eating and get the nourishment they must have in measured doses shot into their arms at hospitals? One ready answer to that question

suggests that my theory of overeating is sound: people like to taste! In eating, they try to satisfy that like.

22 The scientific war against deliciousness has been stepped up enormously in the last decade. Some infernal genius found a way to make biscuit batter keep. Housewives began to buy this premixed stuff. It saved work, of course. But any normally intelligent person can learn, in a short period, how to prepare superb baking powder biscuits. I can make better biscuits, myself, than can be made from patent batters. Yet soon after this fiasco became an American staple, it was discovered that a half-baked substitute for all sorts of breads, pastries, rolls, and the like could be mass-manufactured, frozen — and sold for polishing off in the home oven. None of these two-stage creations is as good as even a fair sample of the thing it imitates. A man of taste, who had eaten one of my wife's cinnamon buns, might use the premixed sort to throw at starlings — but not to eat! Cake mixes, too, come ready-prepared — like cement and not much better-tasting compared with true cake.

23 It is, however, "deep-freezing" that has really rung down the curtain on American cookery. Nothing is improved by the process. I have yet to taste a deep-frozen victual that measures up, in flavor, to the fresh, unfrosted original. And most foods, cooked or uncooked, are destroyed in the deep freeze for all people of sense and sensibility. Vegetables with crisp and crackling texture emerge as mush, slippery and stringy as hair nets simmered in Vaseline. The essential oils that make peas peas — and cabbage cabbage — must undergo fission and fusion in freezers. Anyhow, they vanish. Some meats turn to leather. Others to wood pulp. Everything, pretty much, tastes like the mosses of tundra, dug up in midwinter. Even the appearance changes, oftentimes. Handsome comestibles you put down in the summer come out looking very much like the corpses of woolly mammoths recovered from the last Ice Age.

24 Of course, all this scientific "food handling" tends to save money. It certainly preserves food longer. It reduces work at home. But these facts, and especially the last, imply that the first purpose of living is to avoid work — at home, anyhow.

25 Without thinking, we are making an important confession about ourselves as a nation. We are abandoning quality — even, to some extent, the quality of people. The "best" is becoming too good for

us. We are suckling ourselves on machine-made mediocrity. It is bad for our souls, our minds, and our digestion. It is the way our wiser and calmer forebears fed, not people, but hogs: as much as possible and as fast as possible, with no standard of quality.

26   The Germans say, *"Mann ist was er isst* — Man is what he eats." If this be true, the people of the U.S.A. are well on their way to becoming a faceless mob of mediocrities, of robots. And if we apply to other attributes the criteria we apply these days to appetite, that is what would happen! We would not want bright children any more; we'd merely want them to look bright — and get through school fast. We wouldn't be interested in beautiful women — just a good paint job. And we'd be opposed to the most precious quality of man: his individuality, his differentness from the mob.

27   There are some people — sociologists and psychologists among them — who say that is exactly what we Americans are doing, are becoming. Mass man, they say, is on the increase. Conformity, standardization, similarity — all on a cheap and vulgar level — are replacing the great American ideas of colorful liberty and dignified individualism. If this is so, the process may well begin, like most human behavior, in the home — in those homes where a good meal has been replaced by something-to-eat-in-a-hurry. By something not very good to eat, prepared by a mother without very much to do, for a family that doesn't feel it amounts to much anyhow.

28   I call, here, for rebellion.

QUESTIONS FOR REFLECTION, DISCUSSION, OR WRITING

(1) What are the characteristics of this selection by which you can classify it as a familiar essay (see p. 26)? Give illustrations from the essay itself.

(2) What does the author gain by his remarks about Science in the first paragraph? How might we have regarded the whole essay differently if he had omitted this paragraph?

(3) To what extent do the humor and vividness of his writing depend on the author's use of figures of speech (see p. 15)? Locate the similes in paragraphs 10, 16, 18, 22, and 23, and comment on their originality and effectiveness.

(4) How valid do you think is Wylie's theory (pars. 19-21) that the blandness of our diet may explain why so many people are overweight? Do you

suppose excess weight is more of a problem in our day than it was in other generations? If so, what else may be responsible?

(5) What products of modern life, other than foods, are being made more for looks than quality — a result of giving people "the least quality they'll stand for" (par. 5)? Your ideas concerning one or more of these products could be organized into an interesting composition.

(6) Why do you suppose this essay was included here in the more or less philosophical "Views of Man" section, rather than in the one for "Simple Enjoyment"? In what paragraph do you begin to realize that the author is not really so much concerned about American foods as he is about Americans themselves? State in your own words the real *theme* (see p. 156) of this essay, then explain how fully you agree with this thesis, and why.

Henry David Thoreau

From ECONOMY

HENRY DAVID THOREAU (1817-1862) *lived all but one year of his life in Concord, Mass., where he was known as a nonconformist, an eccentric. He did some teaching and lecturing but became best known as an amateur naturalist and, of course, as an author, contributing both verse and prose to magazines and newspapers of the day. In 1849 his first book,* A Week on the Concord and Merrimac Rivers, *was published, and it was followed five years later by his most famous work,* Walden. *After his death (of tuberculosis, in Concord) his other published essays were gathered into three books,* The Maine Woods, A Yankee in Canada, *and* Cape Cod.

ECONOMY, *excerpts of which comprise this selection, is one of the now-famous essays which appeared in* Walden. *Usually considered Thoreau's masterpiece,* Walden *is partially an account of his "experiment in living" (alone, in the woods at Walden Pond), but it is also a careful study of nature, a critical view of then-modern society, and a work of much artistic merit.*

1   . . . I HAVE traveled a good deal in Concord; and everywhere, in shops, and offices, and fields, the inhabitants have appeared to me to be doing penance in a thousand remarkable ways. . . .

2   I see young men, my townsmen, whose misfortune it is to have inherited farms, houses, barns, cattle, and farming tools; for these are more easily acquired than got rid of. Better if they had been born in the open pasture and suckled by a wolf, that they might

have seen with clearer eyes what field they were called to labor in. Who made them serfs of the soil? Why should they eat their sixty acres, when man is condemned to eat only his peck of dirt? Why should they begin digging their graves as soon as they are born? They have got to live a man's life, pushing all these things before them, and get on as well as they can. How many a poor immortal soul have I met well nigh crushed and smothered under its load, creeping down the road of life, pushing before it a barn seventy-five feet by forty, its Augean stables never cleansed, and one hundred acres of land, tillage, mowing, pasture, and wood-lot! The portion-less, who struggle with no such unnecessary inherited encumbrances, find it labor enough to subdue and cultivate a few cubic feet of flesh.

3   But men labor under a mistake. The better part of the man is soon ploughed into the soil for compost. By a seeming fate, commonly called necessity, they are employed, as it says in an old book, laying up treasures which moth and rust will corrupt and thieves break through and steal. It is a fool's life, as they will find when they get to the end of it. . . .

4   Most men, even in this comparatively free country, through mere ignorance and mistake, are so occupied with the factitious cares and superfluously coarse labors of life that its finer fruits cannot be plucked by them. Their fingers, from excessive toil, are too clumsy and tremble too much for that. . . .

5   Some of you, we all know, are poor, find it hard to live, are sometimes, as it were, gasping for breath. I have no doubt that some of you who read this book are unable to pay for all the dinners which you have actually eaten, or for the coats and shoes which are fast wearing or are already worn out, and have come to this page to spend borrowed or stolen time, robbing your creditors of an hour. It is very evident what mean and sneaking lives many of you live, for my sight has been whetted by experience; always on the limits, trying to get into business and trying to get out of debt, a very ancient slough, called by the Latins *aes alienum*, another's brass, for some of their coins were made of brass; still living, and dying, and buried by this other's brass; always promising to pay, promising to pay tomorrow, and dying today, insolvent; seeking to curry favor, to get custom, by how many modes, only not state-prison offenses; lying, flattering, voting, contracting yourselves into a nutshell of civility, or dilating

into an atmosphere of thin and vaporous generosity, that you may persuade your neighbor to let you make his shoes, or his hat, or his coat, or his carriage, or import his groceries for him; making yourselves sick, that you may lay up something against a sick day, something to be tucked away in an old chest, or in a stocking behind the plastering, or, more safely, in the brick bank; no matter where, no matter how much or how little.

6   I sometimes wonder that we can be so frivolous, I may almost say, as to attend to the gross but somewhat foreign form of servitude called Negro Slavery, there are so many keen and subtle masters that enslave both North and South. It is hard to have a Southern overseer; it is worse to have a Northern one; but worst of all when you are the slave-driver of yourself. . . .

QUESTIONS FOR REFLECTION, DISCUSSION, OR WRITING

(1) Explain the allusion (see p. 207) to "Augean stables" in paragraph 2.

(2) Can you think of any circumstances today when it would be better to be "born in the open pasture" than to inherit a farm — or other property? Explain.

(3) Do you agree that it is better to be someone else's slave than your own (par. 6)? Can you imagine any exceptions to your theory? Explain.

(4) Consider the metaphor (see p. 15) in paragraph 4. What do you suppose Thoreau considered the "finer fruits of life"? What do you?

(5) How do you account for the great amount of writing Thoreau did, if he was as opposed to "work" as he claimed to be? Could it be that his writing gave him too much satisfaction for him to consider it drudgery? If so, do you believe the farming his neighbors did might have given them equal satisfaction? How about some other kinds of physical and mental labor today? Make some pertinent comparisons with the work of Thoreau and his neighbors.

(6) Would it be a better world, or worse, if we all adopted a Thoreau-philosophy toward work and stopped trying to "persuade [our] neighbor to let [us] make his shoes, or his hat, or his coat, or his carriage, or import his groceries for him" (par. 5)? Justify your answer fully.

Lin Yutang

MAN, THE ONLY WORKING ANIMAL

LIN YUTANG *was born in China and educated at Shanghai University and in American and German universities. Before the Communist take-over of China, he held positions as dean and as professor of English in Chinese universities, and has served as head of the Arts and Letters Division of UNESCO and as editor of various literary magazines. He has written extensively in both English and Chinese. Some of his books:* My Country and My People, The Wisdom of Confucius, A Leaf in the Storm, Vermillion Gate, *and* From Pagan to Christian. *He now lives in Singapore.*

MAN, THE ONLY WORKING ANIMAL *is one essay of Lin Yutang's most famous book,* The Importance of Living (1937), *where he discusses almost everything from American sex appeal to the art of lying in bed, and to the fallacies of belief in Heaven (fallacies in which he, much later, apparently found fallacies, as he is now a Christian). In "Man, the Only Working Animal" he paints much the same sorry picture of modern living as had Thoreau almost a century earlier and half a world away.*

1   THE FEAST of life is . . . before us, and the only question is what appetite we have for it. The appetite is the thing, and not the feast. After all, the most bewildering thing about man is his idea of work and the amount of work he imposes upon himself, or civilization has imposed upon him. All nature loafs, while man alone works for a living. He works because he has to, because with the progress of civilization life gets incredibly more complex, with duties, responsibilities, fears, inhibitions and ambitions, born not of nature, but of human society. While I am sitting here before my desk, a pigeon is flying about a church steeple before my window, not worrying what it is going to have for lunch. I know that my lunch is a more complicated affair than the pigeon's, and that the few articles of food I take involve thousands of people at work and a highly complicated system of cultivation, merchandising, transportation, delivery and preparation. That is why it is harder for man to get food than for animals. Nevertheless, if a jungle beast were let loose in a city and gained some apprehension of what busy human life was all about, he

would feel a good deal of skepticism and bewilderment about this human society.

2   The first thought that the jungle beast would have is that man is the only working animal. With the exception of a few draught horses or buffalos made to work a mill, even domestic pets don't have to work. Police dogs are but rarely called upon to do their duty; a house dog supposed to watch a house plays most of the time, and takes a good nap in the morning whenever there is good, warm sunshine; the aristocratic cat certainly never works for a living, and gifted with a bodily agility which enables it to disregard a neighbor's fence, it is even unconscious of its captivity — it just goes wherever it likes to go. So, then, we have this toiling humanity alone, caged and domesticated, *but not fed*, forced by this civilization and complex society to work and worry about the matter of feeding itself. Humanity has its own advantages, I am quite aware — the delights of knowledge, the pleasures of conversation and the joys of the imagination, as for instance in watching a stage play. But the essential fact remains that human life has got too complicated and the matter of merely feeding ourselves, directly or indirectly, is occupying well over ninety per cent of our human activities. Civilization is largely a matter of seeking food, while progress is that development which makes food more and more difficult to get. If it had not been made so difficult for man to obtain his food, there would be absolutely no reason why humanity should work so hard. The danger is that we get over-civilized and that we come to a point, as indeed we have already done, when the work of getting food is so strenuous that we lose our appetite for food in the process of getting it. This doesn't seem to make very much sense, from the point of view of either the jungle beast or the philosopher.

3   Every time I see a city skyline or look over a stretch of roofs, I get frightened. It is positively amazing. Two or three water towers, the backs of two or three steel frames for billboards, perhaps a spire or two, and a stretch of asphalt roofing material and bricks going up in square, sharp, vertical outlines without any form or order, sprinkled with some dirty, discolored chimneys and a few washlines and crisscross lines of radio aerials. And looking down into a street, I see again a stretch of gray or discolored red brick walls, with tiny, dark, uniform windows in uniform rows, half open and half hidden by

shades, with perhaps a bottle of milk standing on a windowsill and a few pots of tiny, sickly flowers on some others. A child comes up to the roof with her dog and sits on the roof-stairs every morning to get a bit of sunshine. And as I lift my eyes again, I see rows upon rows of roofs, miles of them, stretching in ugly square outlines to the distance. More water towers, more brick houses. And humanity live here. How do they live, each family behind one or two of these dark windows? What do they do for a living? It is staggering. Behind every two or three windows, a couple go to bed every night like pigeons returning to their pigeon-holes; then they wake up and have their morning coffee and the husband emerges into the street, going somewhere to find bread for the family, while the wife tries persistently and desperately to drive out the dust and keep the little place clean. By four or five o'clock they come out on their doorsteps to chat with and look at their neighbors and get a sniff of fresh air. Then night falls, they are dead tired and go to sleep again. And so they live!

4   There are others, more well-to-do people, living in better apartments. More "arty" rooms and lampshades. Still more orderly and more clean! They have a little more space, but only a little more. To rent a seven-room flat, not to speak of owning it, is considered a luxury! But it does not imply more happiness. Less financial worry and fewer debts to think about, it is true. But also more emotional complications, more divorce, more cat-husbands that don't come home at night, or the couple go prowling together at night, seeking some form of dissipation. *Diversion* is the word. Good Lord, they need to be diverted from these monotonous, uniform brick walls and shining wooden floors! Of course they go to look at naked women. Consequently more neurasthenia, more aspirin, more expensive illnesses, more colitis and appendicitis, more dyspepsia, more softened brains and hardened livers, more ulcerated duodenums and lacerated intestines, overworked stomachs and overtaxed kidneys, inflamed bladders and outraged spleens, dilated hearts and shattered nerves, more flat chests and high blood pressure, more diabetes, Bright's disease, beri-beri, rheumatism, insomnia, arterio-sclerosis, piles, fistulas, chronic dysentery, chronic constipation, loss of appetite and weariness of life. To make the picture perfect, more dogs and fewer children. The matter of happiness depends entirely upon the quality and

temper of the men and women living in these elegant apartments. Some indeed have a jolly life, others simply don't. But on the whole, perhaps they are less happy than the hard-working people; they have more *ennui* and more boredom. But they have a car, and perhaps a country home. Ah, the country home, that is their salvation! So then, people work hard in the country so that they can come to the city so that they can earn sufficient money and go back to the country again.

5   And as you take a stroll through the city, you see that back of the main avenue with beauty parlors and flower shops and shipping firms is another street with drug stores, grocery stores, hardware shops, barber shops, laundries, cheap eating places, news-stands. You wander along for an hour, and if it is a big city, you are still there; you see only more streets, more drug stores, grocery stores, hardware shops, barber shops, laundries, cheap eating places and news-stands. How do these people make their living? And why do they come here? Very simple. The laundrymen wash the clothes of the barbers and restaurant waiters, the restaurant waiters wait upon the laundrymen and barbers while they eat, and the barbers cut the hair of the laundrymen and waiters. That is civilization. Isn't it amazing? I bet some of the laundrymen, barbers and waiters never wander beyond ten blocks from their place of work in their entire life. Thank God they have at least the movies, where they can see birds singing on the screen, trees growing and swaying, Turkey, Egypt, the Himalayas, the Andes, storms, shipwrecks, coronation ceremonies, ants, caterpillars, muskrats, a fight between lizards and scorpions, hills, waves, sands, clouds, and even a moon — all on the screen!

6   O wise humanity, terribly wise humanity! Of thee I sing. How inscrutable is the civilization where men toil and work and worry their hair gray to get a living and forget to play!

QUESTIONS FOR REFLECTION, DISCUSSION, OR WRITING

(1) Compare the attitudes of Lin Yutang and Thoreau toward their readers — do they both seem to include themselves among those afflicted by the evils they describe? Or does either seem to be "preaching" only at other people? Try to analyze the difference, if any, in viewpoint. Which technique is the more effective?

(2) What other "advantages" does humanity have that are not mentioned by Lin Yutang (par. 2)? Has he included the one advantage that you consider the most important? Explain.

(3) Do you think city life in our complex society is as "staggering" as the author does? Or that people's day-by-day routine (par. 3) is as dismal a process as he describes it?

(4) Do you feel particularly sorry for those "well-to-do" people whose emotional complications, he says, bring on such a varied assortment of ailments and unhappiness (par. 4)? Why, or why not?

(5) Have you ever known anyone personally who managed to really practice the Yutang-Thoreau philosophy regarding work? Was he happier than other people, or did he have to pay too great a price for his "jungle-beast" type of freedom from worry and work?

(6) Do you agree with Lin Yutang that the necessity of working to get fed is an evil thing? If not, explain your view. If you do agree, is there anything we can do about it, either as a society or as an individual?

Sloan Wilson
HAPPY IDLE HOURS BECOME A RAT RACE

SLOAN WILSON, *best known as a novelist, has also worked as journalist* (Provincetown Journal *and* Time, Inc.), *as professor of English at Buffalo University, and as assistant director of the White House Conference on Education. He served in the Coast Guard during World War II. A thoughtful critic of public education and our social system, Mr. Wilson became famous for his two best-selling novels,* The Man in the Grey Flannel Suit *and* A Summer Place. *His latest novel,* A Sense of Values, *deals with the same problem he discusses in the following essay, that of overabundant leisure.*

HAPPY IDLE HOURS BECOME A RAT RACE, *first published in the Dec. 28, 1959, issue of* Life *(see p. 26), provides an obvious sequel to the Thoreau and Lin Yutang pieces just finished: now we have the leisure they thought so important, but what shall we do with it? (In other words, to trot out Thoreau's metaphor, where are the "finer fruits" his neighbors had no time to pluck?)*

1   ANYBODY who wants to achieve a reputation for wisdom today has to praise leisure. Exhausted physicians totter home from their hospital rounds to write articles advising everyone to take it easy.

Leaders of government, industry, labor and education interrupt their busy schedules to give speeches calling for a more intelligent use of spare time and, wiping the sweat from their brows, extol the virtues of quiet contemplation. Even the most compulsively driven business executives who used to boast about the endless hours they spent in the office have learned to claim defensively that they "play as hard as they work."

2   Americans, long criticized and admired by foreigners for being the hardest-working, fastest-paced people on earth, today seem intent on making the United States into a hammock society, a happy playground for lovers of fishing, golf and hopscotch for adults. Apparently the national slogan will soon be "Please Do Not Disturb."

3   But in this land of leisure, where are all the leisurely people? In the backyards of the countless suburban homes built since the war, it is common to see elaborate lawn furniture or hammocks, but most of them seem to be empty, rocked only by the wind or by the ghosts of men who worked themselves to death. Diseases associated with nervous tension seem to be everywhere around us. Why do doctors have to keep telling us to take things easy if we all have so much leisure? Something odd happens to free time in this country. We have it, yet we do not. It is almost as if someone were playing an enormous shell game with our idle hours. There they are — we can prove statistically that we have them — but where did they go?

4   The idle hours disappear because we waste and misuse them. We do so because most of us have little conception of the vast difference between the true leisure which is a rewarding, nourishing use of free time and a feckless, aimless meandering which eats up the time before we realize what has happened. Conditioned by our upbringing to a way of life which in the old days granted people far fewer free hours, we are utterly unaccustomed to our strange new bounty. But if Americans find they have a hard time adjusting to their newly won idleness they should not despair, for in truth leisure seems to be an unnatural state for man to inhabit for very long. Man is a creature made not for idleness but for activity, and when he is confronted with long periods of inactivity he often rushes impulsively into them so as to make them seem as much like work as possible. In fact,

many men seem as determined to misuse leisure as they are to win it in the first place.

Keeping Busy Around the Clock

5   The outward signs of this paradox are everywhere at hand. Despite the 40-hour week, most Americans still appear to be busy most of the time. Salesmen, executives and entrepreneurs, large and small, are unaffected by laws passed to limit working hours. Many conscientious or ambitious teachers, office workers and others who in theory are on a short work week actually toil as long as their ancestors did before time clocks were invented. Men and women in jobs strictly controlled by trade unions appear to have the greatest number of free hours, but many of them eagerly seek opportunities for overtime pay, and more than four million "moonlighters" manage to hold two jobs, some working as many as 80 hours a week. More hundreds of thousands of men and women contrive to live far enough from their jobs to use up many hours in commuting. For better or for worse, most Americans are filled with a great restlessness which drives them away from a constructive use of their leisure and leads them to distract themselves either in work or in hectic amusements.

6   To a considerable extent, leisure operates on the principle of the vacuum: as soon as it is created, something has to move in. Just as prisoners pace in their cells, and children on rainy days wail for something to do, most people crave activity. Far from seeking quiet contemplation, they will do almost anything to avoid it. Over and over one hears the remark, "I would like to read more, but I simply don't have time."

7   But all the while we are avoiding leisure we keep talking about it, perhaps because of an uneasy feeling that there is a kind of madness in many of the chores and frantic distractions we invent for ourselves. We may also fear that the great restlessness responsible for these distractions will get out of control, burst the heart, corrode the stomach or unhinge the mind. We have to slow down, we tell ourselves, but many of our efforts to slow down somehow end by causing us to drive too fast or to strain a shoulder muscle. There often seems to be more desperation than contentment on the faces of men clutching the wheels of high-powered outboard motorboats,

careening down icy slopes on skis, or trudging up mountain trails with guns. Relaxation is a hard bird to flush, and harder to shoot down. Even those men who are genuinely capable of spending a Sunday afternoon in a hammock often find themselves painfully prodded by their wives and children. According to one study of the use of leisure, husbands frequently complain that they are tired of "honey-do days" — days at home during which their wives keep saying "Honey, do this" and "Honey, do that." A nagging sense of duty, rather than pleasure, leads many weary parents to engage in exhausting games with their children.

Idleness Begets Misery

8   No matter what praises are sung of leisure, those who have the most of it in the United States seem to be the most miserable. It is common knowledge today that vigorous 60-year-olds show a tendency to fade away and die soon after they retire. Physicians have noted that middle-aged women whose children no longer require mothering and whose husbands supply every material want are among their unhappiest patients. As every newspaper reader knows, men and women who have inherited or made enough money to ensure leisure have their share of difficulties with the divorce courts and the bottle. Youngsters unable to become absorbed in schoolwork and forbidden by child-labor laws to take jobs have added to the ranks of juvenile delinquents.

9   In the United States today the tension is great enough to lead to the consumption last year of 216 million gallons of hard liquor, $172 million worth of sleeping pills and $254 million worth of tranquilizers. A recognized phenomenon of modern life is the "week-end alcoholic" — the man who can stay sober only when he is at work.

10   There is nothing new about mankind's abhorrence of too much leisure. Since being expelled from the Garden of Eden, man has taken it for granted that he was condemned to earn his bread by the sweat of his brow. No matter how much we talk about the necessity of leisure in an age when machines are taking over more and more mental as well as physical work, our relatively recent Puritan past screams in protest. Since the first settlers at Jamestown starved, the need for work was firmly stamped upon the minds of the early colonizers. In both North and South, regulations were made "in detesta-

tion of idleness." Work gained an aura of religious respectability. Even midweek church services were curtailed when they started getting in the way of production. Modern Americans, faced with surpluses of food instead of shortages, can hardly justify a "detestation of idleness" on the grounds of necessity, but we still have a profound feeling that work is good, and that the enjoyment of leisure for more than a short time is vaguely immoral.

11   At first glance, at least, philosophers of the past seem to deride the grim industriousness of the Puritans and to be strong advocates of leisure. Henry Thoreau said, "The order of things should be somewhere reversed; the seventh should be man's day of toil, wherein to earn his living by the sweat of his brow; and the other six his Sabbath of the affections and the soul, in which to range this widespread garden, and drink in the soft influences and sublime revelations of nature."

12   Aristotle said, ". . . We should be able, not only to work well, but to use leisure well; for, as I repeat once more, the first principle of all action is leisure. Both are required, but leisure is better than work and is its end. . . ."

Industrious Philosophers

13   Those husbands who complain about "honey-do days" might have attributed Thoreau's capacity for leisure to his genius at remaining a bachelor, and some observers might say that, like modern physicians, both Thoreau and Aristotle may have talked about leisure more than they enjoyed it. Thoreau was an industrious writer even at Walden Pond, and Aristotle could hardly have written so much so well if he had not labored mightily. But the two philosophers were not hypocritical. They were simply careful about their definitions of leisure. True leisure Aristotle defined as requiring intellectual activities done for their own sake, and a key to his view is the fact that the Greek word for leisure is *schole*, from which the English word "school" is derived.

14   "Clearly we ought not to be amusing ourselves," Aristotle wrote, "for then amusement would be the end of life. . . . We should introduce amusements only at suitable times, and they should be our medicines, for the feeling that they create in the soul is a relaxation, and from the pleasure we get rest."

15   Most Americans right now could undoubtedly devote most of their spare time to the kind of intellectual activity which Aristotle thought essential to leisure — if they really wanted to. But they do not. A recent study showed that only 17% of American citizens were currently reading a book. Even those who can be shown by every known test to have a good share of intelligence often avoid books. It is not laziness alone that limits their minds, for many are industrious at their daily jobs. True, many people are interested primarily in accumulating money, but millions of them get rid of their money even more energetically than they earn it. What are these people working for?

16   Anthropologists have noted that primitive peoples worked to achieve honor, prestige, status and dignity. Boys and men have long sought ways to prove and to advertise their virility. Even when starvation was not a threat in early America, some Indian hunters were ashamed to return home from an expedition empty-handed, and stayed on the trail for weeks, if necessary, simply to demonstrate their skill and strength. On the northwest coast of America there was a tribe which held contests to see who could burn the most valuable goods and kill the most of their slaves. Men and women worked much of the year to make canoes and blankets, not to use, but to destroy with the purpose of confounding their rivals. In less rigorous climates where food and shelter could be obtained without much effort before automation was ever dreamt of, men still worked hard to maintain the superiority of one tribe over another, or of one individual over his neighbor. Primitive man was apparently just as anxious as his modern American brother to avoid leisure.

17   Sometimes an overabundance of leisure is a symptom of social maladjustment. An unsentimental look at people who are presumed to be leisure-loving might show that many are either ill or without hope of improving their situation in life. During the years of slavery, for example, American Negroes were thought to be leisure-loving and were said to need nothing more than a banjo and a good meal to achieve happiness. But what choice did they have in an era when they had no opportunity to work for themselves? Negroes today who have better chances to rise in the world give no indication that they are addicted to leisure any more than anyone else.

18   The millions of people who reportedly stay glued to their televi-

sion sets five and six hours a day have often been cited as examples
of man's willingness to give in completely to passive entertainment.
But who are these viewers, and why do they appear so easily content? Some are children who have little else to do. Others are adults
who through personal misfortune have seen the great opportunities
of the world shrink down for them to the size of the tiny screen.
Many lack the money for other forms of entertainment, or the intelligence or peace of mind that is necessary for reading. The torpor
of their discouragement is different from simple laziness, and no
proof of the inertia of the whole mass of humanity. The rest of us
have amusements, including a modicum of television, for relaxation
and "medicine," just as Aristotle recommends. But we work most of
the time.

19   The traditional reason that Americans have always worked so hard
is that from its very beginning this country gave us reason to expect
that the results would be worth it. Many immigrants to America
came from European class systems in which sons were prevented
from rising far above their fathers and for years had seen no reason
to tire themselves. As soon as they arrived in this country, however,
and realized that it was actually possible for an industrious poor man
to become rich and respected, their attitude changed. To the lure of
accomplishment was added the new shame of failure that could not
reasonably be blamed on "the system." A humble laborer in Europe
could relax in the knowledge that he could not possibly have bet-
tered himself, but his American brother often suffers agonies at the
sight of an old schoolmate driving a Cadillac.

Proud Badges of Rank

20   Moreover, life is a competitive game for many people, and the prize
of prestige or status can be won and kept only by extraordinary effort. The effort is often manifested through spending money rather
than through earning it, partly because the size of one's income is so
important that it is supposed to be kept secret, and partly because
Americans sometimes seem just as proud of their ability to waste the
results of human labor as were the blanket-burning Indians of the
Northwest. As has often been pointed out, the frequently turned-in
automobile, with its unneeded ornamentation, bulk and horsepower,
is far more important as an instrument of status than of transporta-

tion. New houses are today becoming an equally important badge of rank. Many contractors have reported that the showier the house is, the easier it is to sell. And while some people find honest enjoyment in "working around the property," the intensity with which many exhausted homeowners labor over improvements indicates their motive is neighborhood rivalry.

21   For many men a job is simply a tournament entered in order to finance another tournament. Such men try to get the highest salary at the office in order to buy the fastest boat on the lake.

22   Many men also have a neurotic need to work hard. Some have an exaggerated fear of poverty, perhaps remembered from their youth, which no amount of money in the bank can ever fully assuage. Others have an unconscious distrust of their ability to deserve love, which drives them to try unceasingly to purchase affection from their families. Still more try desperately to convert themselves into copies of individuals whom they conceive to be the "right people."

The Overworked Man's Dissipation

23   A man who overworks for neurotic reasons is not automatically cured when he tries to divert himself. The overworked man's play is often more taxing than his labor, and close kin to dissipation. Does this not help explain the enormous appetite for violence which causes such demand for books, movies and television dramas emphasizing loveless sex and the most graphic enactments of killing, shooting and slugging?

24   The violence on television at least has the advantage of being confined to a small box, but similar trouble can erupt openly in the widespread perversions of the pleasures to be found in water sports, automobile driving, skiing and other strenuous activities. It is easy to imagine the horror Thoreau would feel if he were taken today on a weekend drive through traffic jams to spend an afternoon on Walden Pond or were given an opportunity to try out a roaring outboard motorboat capable of cutting figure eights at thirty knots. Whether he would want six Sundays of this to one day of work is doubtful.

25   Ironically, many pleasure-seekers sooner or later become disillusioned with the devices they buy for entertainment. The managers of marinas and boatyards find that people often buy expensive craft with the greatest enthusiasm, only to leave them lying unused and

uncared-for most of the time. Foolishness of this kind might seem to be a weakness of only the very rich, but even poorer homes are full of relatively expensive gadgets which seemed much more desirable on the store shelves than they did when they were taken home.

26   To be sure, there are countless Americans who bear no relation whatever to those cited above and who find in their labor a genuine, healthy pleasure that no entertainment can possibly rival. Many fortunate scholars, artists, scientists and craftsmen find their work is an end in itself which happily brings money as a by-product. At least a few businessmen are unquestionably truthful when they say that they enjoy dealing with people so much, and receive so much pleasure from planning money-making projects, that leisure is dull in comparison. And there are also a good many idealistic individuals who like working for the benefit of mankind or their less fortunate neighbors.

27   Not all of man's drive to work springs from neurotic bases. To be satisfied in his hammock a man needs, among other things, the assurance that his neighbor is not sharpening up his knife to kill him, and what is true of an individual is also true of a nation. We do not think the Russians are joking when they say they intend to bury us, figuratively or otherwise.

28   If it is ever possible for everyone to have a sixteen-room house with a swimming pool under a plastic dome in the backyard and two helicopters in the garage, there will surely be people saying it is a national disgrace to have to put up with such cramped quarters, such miserable facilities for recreation and such antiquated transportation. Our slogan, then, is not "Please Do Not Disturb." Excelsior is the motto, as it has always been, and if man is criticized for it he can always point out that, for better or for worse, it has carried him from the caves to the skies. Like Aristotle's star pupil, Alexander the Great, most men will always seek new worlds to conquer, and like him, most will lack the ability to seek new frontiers within themselves.

29   For the descendants of apelike creatures who refused to be satisfied with enough fruit, work — any task on or off the job done zestfully for its own sake — is the greatest continuing joy. And work done for the benefit of others is the source of the greatest pride. Perhaps the time has come to stop the confusing eulogies of leisure

which, without the most careful definition, seem to be calls for sloppy self-indulgence, and to start a search for more opportunities for meaningful work. Men do not want to be retired yet. The fierce restlessness which wells up in most of them when amusements become too prolonged is no cause for shame — it is the great itch which has always driven mankind. Even if we all become philosophers some day, there will always be philosophies to write, the moon to reach, and after that, the stars.

QUESTIONS FOR REFLECTION, DISCUSSION, OR WRITING

(1) The authors of several previously read essays have considered, in one way or another, this matter of leisure: Drucker, Huxley, Devoe, *Time*, and, of course, Thoreau and Lin Yutang. Review the comments of all these and determine to what extent they agree. Are any in real disagreement with each other? Are Sloan Wilson's theories in actual contradiction to any of the others? (Compare his, especially, with Huxley's.) Explain, using quotations wherever possible.

(2) Do you agree that leisure is an "unnatural state for man to inhabit" (par. 4), that it operates "on the principle of the vacuum" (par. 6)? What is this principle? Use yourself as representative of "man" — how do *you* react to leisure?

(3) Do you share the "uneasy feeling that there is a kind of madness in many of the chores and frantic distractions we invent for ourselves" (par. 7)? Explain, using real-life examples.

(4) To what extent do you think people use their homes and cars as "badges of rank" (par. 20), more commonly referred to as *status symbols*? Is this necessarily bad? What other status symbols can you see in your neighborhood?

(5) In your chosen career, do you expect to be one of those who "find in their labor a genuine, healthy pleasure that no entertainment can possibly rival" (par. 26)? If not, is there another choice you might have made which could have given you this satisfaction? Why did you decide against it?

(6) An interesting topic for composition might be the comparison of two acquaintances: one who uses his leisure time well and happily, the other who fits into one of the unhappy categories described by Wilson.

Joseph Wood Krutch
SPORTSMAN OR PREDATOR?

JOSEPH WOOD KRUTCH, *author-philosopher-naturalist, was born in Knoxville, Tennessee, and now makes his home in Tucson, Arizona. He has taught at various colleges and, before his retirement in 1950, was professor of dramatic literature at Columbia University. An essayist for several magazines, Mr. Krutch was for many years a dramatic critic and associate editor of* The Nation. *Among his books, which total more than 20:* The Desert Year, The Best of Two Worlds, The Measure of Man *(for which he received the National Book Award), and* The Voice of the Desert.

SPORTSMAN OR PREDATOR, *an adaptation of one chapter of Krutch's book* The Great Chain of Life, *was published in the following form in the Aug. 17, 1957, issue of* Saturday Review *(see p. 155). Krutch writes primarily for the "thinking" reader (the kind you should now be considering yourself), and this will not be the easiest reading you have attempted. Although "Sportsman or Predator" is almost certain to arouse the ire of many readers (a result which was undoubtedly expected), the author does present a strong and reasonable case, which requires more than a mere emotional "T'ain't so!" in retort.*

1   IT WOULD not be quite true to say that "some of my best friends are hunters." Nevertheless, I do number among my respected acquaintances some who not only kill for the sake of killing but count it among their keenest pleasures.

2   To me it is inconceivable that anyone should think an animal more interesting dead than alive. I can also easily prove to my own satisfaction that killing "for sport" is the perfect type of that pure evil for which metaphysicians have sometimes sought.

3   Most wicked deeds are done because the doer proposes some good to himself. The liar lies to gain some end; the swindler and the thief want things which, if honestly got, might be good in themselves. Even the murderer may be removing an impediment to normal desires or gaining possession of something which his victim keeps from him. None of these usually does evil for evil's sake. They are selfish or unscrupulous, but their deeds are not gratuitously evil.

4   The killer for sport has no such comprehensible motive. He

prefers death to life, darkness to light. He gets nothing except the satisfaction of saying, "Something which wanted to live is dead. There is that much less vitality, consciousness, and, perhaps, joy in the universe. I am the Spirit that Denies." When a man wantonly destroys one of the works of man we call him Vandal. When he wantonly destroys one of the works of God we call him Sportsman.

5   Now, the typical Sportsman will not accept this parallel. He has his rules, his traditions, his protocols. Apparently he feels toward random slaughterers much as I feel towards even those who observe the rituals. The Sportsman is shocked by a man who will shoot a sitting bird; I am shocked by anyone who will, purely for "sport," shoot a bird at all. To no creature, man or beast, who is full of the desire to live is it any great comfort to know that killing him was done according to the rules. There is a rather well-known short-story (I have ungratefully forgotten the author) about a sportsman who came to the conclusion that man-hunting was the most challenging of all sports and used to give unsuspecting visitors to his island hideout a fair run for their money. Was this sport?

6   I am not a vegetarian, and I am well aware that there are those to whom that makes me as shocking as the "true sportsman" is shocking to me and the mere slaughterer shocking to the Sportsman. I can only ask that we recognize not too scornfully the possibility of these differences of feeling. My position is a rather extreme one, though obviously not the most extreme possible, but I do not think it can fairly be called fanatical because, I freely admit, the Sportsman is not necessarily the monster my own logic seems to make him. Yet, though hunting for food and the destruction of certain animals is probably necessary to civilization, to me it still seems that any activity which includes killing as a pleasurable end in itself is damnable. Even the hunter-for-food may be as wicked and misguided as vegetarians say, but at least he does not kill for the sake of killing. To kill for killing's sake is a terrifying phenomenon — like doing evil not in the hope of gain but for evil's own sake — as strong a proof of that "reality of evil" with which present-day theologians are again concerned as we could have.

From *The Great Chain of Life*, copyright 1956 by Houghton Mifflin Co. Reprinted by permission of Houghton Mifflin Co., and *Saturday Review*.

7   Examples of three different but typical ways of refusing to acknowledge that any defense of such killing is called for may be
plucked out of recent popular periodicals.

8   In the spring of 1955 a magazine called *Sports Illustrated* distributed a questionnaire intended to determine the public attitude
toward hunting. An answer received from a woman in Tampa,
Florida, was as follows: "I am not the sloppy, sentimental type
that thinks it's terrible to shoot birds or animals. What else are
they good for?" And *The New Yorker*, which reprinted her reply,
answered the question with an irony likely to be lost on the asker:
"Bulls can be baited by fierce dogs, and horses sometimes pay
money."

9   About a year before, *The New Yorker* had also, though without
comment and merely in the course of report on the personality of
the new British Permanent Delegate to the United Nations, quoted
Sir Pierson Dixon as remarking genially, apropos of some articles on
sport which he had written for English periodicals: "I like this
shooting thing, stalking some relatively large animal or, even more
enjoyable, shooting birds. It's like the pleasure of hitting a ball."

10   A little later *Time* magazine ran an article about how duck
hunters near Utah's Bear River Migratory Bird Refuge (*sic*) "could
hardly shoot fast enough" to bring down the ducks they found there
and it adorned the article with a quotation from Ernest Hemingway's "Fathers and Sons": "When you have shot one bird flying
you have shot all birds flying, they are all different and they fly
different ways but the sensation is the same and the last one is as
good as the first."

11   Of these three attitudes the first may seem the simplest and the
most elementary, but perhaps it is not. The blank assumption that
the universe had no conceivable use or meaning except in relation
to man may be instinctive; nevertheless, the lady from Tampa is
speaking not merely from naïveté. She is also speaking for all those
minds still tinctured by the thought of the medieval philosophers
who consciously undertook to explain a detail the *raison d'être* of
the curious world of nature by asking for what human use God had
created each species of plant or animal. If any given creature seems
good for nothing except "sport" then it must be for sport that it
was created.

12   Hemingway's utterance, on the other hand, is the most sophisticated of the three and the only one that seems to make the pure pleasure of killing a consciously recognized factor. The mental processes of the Permanent Delegate are neither so corrupt as those of Mr. Hemingway nor so intellectually complicated as those of the lady from Tampa. He is not, like the first, looking for madder music and stronger wine, nor, like the second, attempting to answer the philosophical question of what animals and birds "are for." Because of the dreadful, uncomprehending innocence sometimes said to be found most frequently in the English gentleman, it has simply never occurred to him that the creatures whom he pursues are alive at all — as his phrase "like the pleasure of hitting a ball" clearly reveals. Birds are simply livelier, less predictable clay pigeons. And it is in exactly the same light that those of his class have sometimes regarded the lesser breeds without the law, or even the nearly inanimate members of all the social classes below them.

13   For the attitude farthest removed from this, Albert Schweitzer is the best-known contemporary spokesman. But one can hardly have "reverence for life" without some vivid sense that life exists even in "the lower animals," and it is this vivid sense that is lacking in the vast majority of sportsmen and equally in, say, the abandoners of pets and, not infrequently, one kind of biological scientist. Often not one of them is so much as tinged with the sadism which Hemingway's opinions and activities seem to suggest. It is not that they do not care what the abandoned pet or the experimental animal suffers but that they do not really believe he suffers to any considerable degree. In the case of the hunter it is often not so much that he wants to kill as that he has no vivid sense that he is killing. For him, as for Sir Pierson, it is more or less like "hitting a ball."

14   Hemingway would, of course, say that there was more to it than that. He feels more of a man out there with his gun, bringing down the birds. It's healthy out-of-doors, good for muscle tone, and there's the challenge of a contest, etc. These are exactly the common arguments which, until a few years ago, were advanced to defend war as a legitimate activity.

15   None of the real goods is actually dependent upon the killing of another living creature. How anyone can profess to find animal life interesting and yet take delight in reducing the wonder of any ani-

mal to a bloody mass of fur or feathers is beyond my comprehension. You can go into the woods to share them with your fellow creatures just as well as to slaughter them. Photography is more difficult and challenging than gunnery. The air is sweeter without the odor of spilled blood. And in my opinion anyone who does not recognize this must fall into one of two classes, the one composed of the innocently and the other of the guiltily evil.

16   Thoreau once remarked that many a man went fishing all his life without realizing that it was not fish he was after. That is the type of the innocently evil who have simply never dissociated the pleasurable incidentals of hunting from the killing which comes at the end of it. But I rather suspect that these are a minority, and that the majority belong to the other class — the class of those to whom the final savagery is of essence. They are much like those drinkers who talk about either the fine bouquet of a wine or the conviviality of the cocktail but for whom the "kick" of alcohol is the real *sine qua non*. And I don't like blood lust even when tricked out in the philosophy of a Hemingway.

17   When Thoreau allowed himself to be persuaded to send a turtle as a specimen to the zoologists at Harvard he felt that he had "a murderer's experience in a degree" and that however his specimen might serve science he himself and his relation to nature would be the worse for what he had done. "I pray," he wrote, "that I may walk more innocently and serenely through nature. No reasoning whatever reconciles me to this act."

18   In general, however, professional students of living things are only somewhat more likely than the average man to feel strongly any "reverence for life." One of the most distinguished American students of birds told me that he saw no incompatibility whatever between his interest in birds and his love of "sport." Many, perhaps most, professional students find no reason too trivial to "collect" a bird or animal, though their habitual use of this weasel word may suggest a defensive attitude. And I have often wondered that sportsmen who find themselves subject to many restrictions have not protested as unfair the "collector's license" rather freely granted and sometimes permitting the holder to shoot almost anything almost anywhere and at anytime.

19   Obviously the problem raised by all this is not solvable in any

clear-cut way. The degree of "reverence for life" which man or any other animal can exhibit is limited by the facts of a world he never made. When it was said that the lion and the lamb shall lie down together, the hope that they may someday do so carries with it the obvious implication that they cannot do so now. Even Albert Schweitzer's rule that no life shall be destroyed except in the service of some higher life will be differently interpreted almost from individual to individual.

20   Just how great must be the good that will accrue to the higher animal? Interpreted as strictly as possible, his law would permit killing only in the face of the most desperate and immediate necessity. Interpreted loosely enough, it might justify the slaughter of the 20,000 birds of paradise, the 40,000 hummingbirds, and the 30,000 birds of other species said to have been killed to supply the London feather market alone in the single year 1914. After all, even fashionable ladies are presumably "higher" than birds and they presumably took keen delight in the adornments which the birds were sacrificed to provide.

21   Some pragmatic solution of the rights of man versus the rights of other living creatures does nevertheless have to be made. Undoubtedly it changes from time to time, and it is well that the existing solution should be re-examined periodically. Because the 1914 solution was re-examined, comparatively few birds are now killed for their feathers, and it is not demonstrable that the female population is any the worse for the fact.

22   In India members of the Jain sect sometimes live on liquid food sipped through a veil in order to avoid the possibility that they might inadvertently swallow a gnat. There are always "anti-sentimentalists" who protest against any cultivation of scruples on the ground that they can logically lead only to some such preposterous scrupulosity. But there are extremes at both ends. Those who have scruples are no more likely to end as Jains than those who reject all scruples are likely to end as Adolf Hitlers. The only possible absolutes are reverence for all life and contempt for all life and of these the first is certainly no more to be feared than the second. If there is any such thing as a wise compromise it is not likely to be reached by the refusal to think.

23   In the old days, in this country, these lines were not infrequently

drawn by those students who had interested themselves in old-fashioned natural history and were brought thereby into intimate association with animals and plants. Its aims and its methods demanded an awareness of the living thing as a living thing and, at least until the rise of behaviorism, the suffering and the joy of the lesser creatures was a part of the naturalist's subject matter. But the laboratory scientist of our modern supercharged day is not of necessity drawn into any emotional relationship with animals or plants, and the experiments which of necessity he must perform are more likely to make him more rather than less callous than the ordinary man.

24   At best, compassion, reverence for life, and a sense of the community of living things are not an essential part of his business as they are of the more vaguely defined discipline of the naturalist. And for that reason it is a great pity that the most humane and liberal of the natural sciences should play so small a role in the liberal arts curriculum. While still under the influence of an older tradition, field botany and field zoology were quite commonly taught in American colleges, even in the remoter parts of the United States. Today few liberal arts undergraduates know anything of such subjects and often would find no courses open to them if they were to inquire.

25   The most important things taught by these disciplines were not the shapes of leaves, or the calls of birds, but a philosophy, a certain attitude towards life. It is very hard to argue such a fundamental premise. The Sportsman, who kills living animals merely to recreate himself, obviously thinks that the right attitude is for man to use the life of the earth as he sees fit. This is not for me an acceptable premise. I do not believe that man has a divine right to the unlimited despotism of an oriental potentate; that he is justified when he says "*l'univers, c'est moi*" or that, like the Calvinist God, he may legitimately damn all inferior creatures merely for his own glory. I believe instead that all created things have their rights and that the right to live is one of theirs — unless there are compelling reasons why it should not be.

QUESTIONS FOR REFLECTION, DISCUSSION, OR WRITING

(1) Clarify in your own mind, then explain and discuss Krutch's comparison of the "evil" of the sportsman to the evil of the murderer or the thief (pars. 3-4). Is this a valid comparison? Why, or why not?

(2) Show the differences, if any, between the butcher and the sportsman. Between the butcher and the man who hunts primarily to supply food for his table. Do you see any difference in the "morality" involved? Does Krutch?

(3) The quotation from *The New Yorker* (par. 8) was intended as irony (see p. 137). Can you explain the *real* meaning intended?

(4) Relate the attitude of "the lady from Tampa" with David Cort's "measure of the decency of society," in paragraph 21 of "Survival in the Zoo" (p. 200).

(5) Study paragraph 12 until you understand clearly the distinction Krutch makes among the three philosophies of killing for sport — that of the lady from Tampa, that of Hemingway, and that of the British gentleman. Which do you think he considers purer evil, which most innocently evil? If you are acquainted with sportsmen-hunters (or if you are one yourself), in which of the three categories could most of them be classified? Is there a fourth category that would include still others? Explain it.

(6) Do you understand how, like Hemingway, a man can "feel more of a man out there with his gun, bringing down the birds" (par. 14)? Explain your views.

(7) What does Krutch mean by his statement that the disciplines of *field* botany and zoology are "a philosophy, a certain attitude toward life" (pars. 24-25)? Would Alan Devoe ("Everyone a Naturalist") have agreed? Why is the *laboratory* botanist or zoologist not so apt to develop this philosophy?

(8) What did Thoreau mean when he remarked that many a man went fishing all his life without realizing that it was not fish he was after (par. 16)?

(9) If you are a hunter, explain the reasons for some of the rituals, rules, traditions, or protocols of hunting (par. 5).

(10) Can you reconcile the hunter's love for his dog with his callousness toward the bird or animal he hunts? Explain.

(11) Compare the possible satisfactions of hunting with those of wildlife photography.

(12) Will the reading of this essay tend to influence you, one way or another, in your attitude toward hunting? Explain. Do you feel it important to read some thoughtful explanation of the "pro" side before changing or

long maintaining your former attitude? Why, or why not? (The opposite side, too, was presented in the same issue of *Saturday Review,* and it can also be found, of course, in almost any "outdoors" magazine.)

H. L. Mencken

From ON THE MEANING OF LIFE

H. L. MENCKEN (1880-1956) *had a long and successful career as essayist, critic, and author of many books. He was co-founder and editor of* American Mercury *and for many years a contributing editor of* The Nation. *Mencken was always an outspoken agnostic.*

ON THE MEANING OF LIFE, *from which this selection was taken, is a book-collection of philosophical views, edited by Will Durant.*

In this piece Mencken sometimes uses briefly a means of explanation called analogy, *which is still another form of comparison — comparison, however, for a specific purpose: to explain something abstract or difficult to understand, in terms of something concrete or easy to understand. In this respect the analogy differs from a metaphor or other figures of speech, the purpose of which is merely to* describe, *creating a brief, vivid image. Although an analogy may also create a vivid image, its* primary purpose *is one of exposition, not description; hence it is usually longer than the metaphor, containing more points of similarity. If, for instance, an instructor explains the international situation by a detailed comparison with a neighborhood squabble over property lines, he is using analogy. When Mencken uses the idea of a hen laying eggs to explain why he continues to work, and the idea of a cow giving milk to explain why his work is writing and not something else, he is using a form that is shorter than most, but still analogy.*

1   YOU ASK ME, in brief, what satisfaction I get out of life, and why I go on working. I go on working for the same reason that a hen goes on laying eggs. There is in every living creature an obscure but powerful impulse to active functioning. Life demands to be lived. Inaction, save as a measure of recuperation between bursts of activity, is painful and dangerous to the healthy organism — in fact, it is almost impossible. Only the dying can be really idle.

2   The precise form of an individual's activity is determined, of

Reprinted by permission of Julian Messner, Inc. from *On the Meaning of Life* by Will Durant; copyright, September, 1932, by Will Durant.

course, by the equipment with which he came into the world. In other words, it is determined by his heredity. I do not lay eggs, as a hen does, because I was born without any equipment for it. For the same reason I do not get myself elected to Congress, or play the violoncello, or teach metaphysics in a college, or work in a steel mill. What I do is simply what lies easiest to my hand. It happens that I was born with an intense and insatiable interest in ideas, and thus like to play with them. It happens also that I was born with rather more than the average facility for putting them into words. In consequence, I am a writer and editor, which is to say, a dealer in them and concocter of them.

3   There is very little conscious volition in all this. What I do was ordained by the inscrutable fates, not chosen by me. In my boyhood, yielding to a powerful but still subordinate interest in exact facts, I wanted to be a chemist, and at the same time my poor father tried to make me a business man. At other times, like any other relatively poor man, I have longed to make a lot of money by some easy swindle. But I became a writer all the same, and shall remain one until the end of the chapter, just as a cow goes on giving milk all her life, even though what appears to be her self-interest urges her to give gin.

4   I am far luckier than most men, for I have been able since boyhood to make a good living doing precisely what I have wanted to do — what I would have done for nothing, and very gladly, if there had been no reward for it. Not many men, I believe, are so fortunate. Millions of them have to make their livings at tasks which really do not interest them. As for me, I have had an extraordinarily pleasant life, despite the fact that I have had the usual share of woes. For in the midst of those woes I still enjoyed the immense satisfaction which goes with free activity. I have done, in the main, exactly what I wanted to do. Its possible effects upon other people have interested me very little. I have not written and published to please other people, but to satisfy myself, just as a cow gives milk, not to profit the dairyman, but to satisfy herself. I like to think that most of my ideas have been sound ones, but I really don't care. The world may take them or leave them. I have had my fun hatching them.

5   Next to agreeable work as a means of attaining happiness I put

what Huxley called the domestic affections — the day to day inter-
course with family and friends. My home has seen bitter sorrow,
but it has never seen any serious disputes, and it has never seen
poverty. I was completely happy with my mother and sister, and
I am completely happy with my wife. Most of the men I commonly
associate with are friends of very old standing. I have known some
of them for more than thirty years. I seldom see anyone, intimately,
whom I have known for less than ten years. These friends delight
me. I turn to them when work is done with unfailing eagerness.
We have the same general tastes, and see the world much alike.
Most of them are interested in music, as I am. It has given me
more pleasure in this life than any other external thing. I love it
more every year.

6   As for religion, I am quite devoid of it. Never in my adult life
have I experienced anything that could be plausibly called a religious impulse. My father and grandfather were agnostics before
me, and though I was sent to Sunday-school as a boy and exposed
to the Christian theology I was never taught to believe it. My
father thought that I should learn what it was, but it apparently
never occurred to him that I would accept it. He was a good psychologist. What I got in Sunday-school — besides a wide acquaintance with Christian hymnology — was simply a firm conviction that
the Christian faith was full of palpable absurdities, and the Christian
God preposterous. Since that time I have read a great deal in
theology — perhaps much more than the average clergyman — but
I have never discovered any reason to change my mind.

7   The act of worship, as carried on by Christians, seems to me to
be debasing rather than ennobling. It involves grovelling before a
Being who, if He really exists, deserves to be denounced instead of
respected. I see little evidence in this world of the so-called goodness
of God. On the contrary, it seems to me that, on the strength of
His daily acts, He must be set down a most stupid, cruel and
villainous fellow. I can say this with a clear conscience, for He has
treated me very well — in fact, with vast politeness. But I can't
help thinking of his barbaric torture of most of the rest of humanity.
I simply can't imagine revering the God of war and politics, theology
and cancer.

8   I do not believe in immortality, and have no desire for it. The

belief in it issues from the puerile egos of inferior men. In its Christian form it is little more than a device for getting revenge upon those who are having a better time on this earth. What the meaning of human life may be I don't know: I incline to suspect that it has none. All I know about it is that, to me at least, it is very amusing while it lasts. Even its troubles, indeed, can be amusing. Moreover, they tend to foster the human qualities that I admire most — courage and its analogues. The noblest man, I think, is that one who fights God, and triumphs over Him. I have had little of this to do. When I die I shall be content to vanish into nothingness. No show, however good, could conceivably be good forever.

QUESTIONS FOR REFLECTION, DISCUSSION, OR WRITING

(1) Do Mencken's *analogies* accomplish their purpose — to make his points easier to understand? Would this essay have been more or less effective if he had depended on straight exposition?

(2) Mencken, like Thoreau, was apparently one of the fortunate people who work at something they really enjoy. Both were writers. Should one begin to assume, then, that writing is more satisfying than other kinds of work? Compare it with painting, with dance-band playing, with cabinetmaking, with landscape horticulture. Do these lines of work have anything in common? If so, how might you compare them with the work of a bookkeeper, a salesman, an airplane pilot or stewardess? Do you find any basic difference? If so, might this difference be significant to you, in your choice of work?

(3) Do you feel that you would have liked Mencken as a person? Why, or why not? Does what he says about himself in the latter half of paragraph 4 influence your opinion? Explain.

(4) Anthropologists tell us that nearly all tribes of mankind down through the ages have had some sort of religious impulses and usually some formal religious beliefs and practices. What is your reaction, then, when a man claims *never* to have "experienced anything that could be plausibly called a religious impulse" (par. 6)?

(5) What do you suppose Mencken means when he says the belief in immortality "issues from the puerile egos of inferior men" (par. 8)? Do you agree? If so, then do you consider yourself and Mencken as *superior* people? Do you think *he* thought of himself as superior? Are those "who are having a better time on this earth" also superior people, as he implies? Whether you agree or disagree, be prepared to justify your opinion.

(6) Mencken sees "little evidence in this world of the so-called goodness of God" (par. 7). Do you?

(7) Can you imagine "revering the God of war and politics, theology and cancer" (par. 7)? If so, how do you explain what Mencken calls His "barbaric torture of . . . humanity"?

A. Cressy Morrison

SEVEN REASONS WHY A SCIENTIST
BELIEVES IN GOD

A. CRESSY MORRISON (1864-1951) was a noted scientist and professor of astronomy at Harvard University. He held many executive positions, including those as president of the New York Academy of Sciences; member of the executive board, National Research Council; chairman, Chemical Advisory Committee, U.S. Department of Commerce; and chairman, Committee on Astronomy and Planetarium, American Museum of Natural History. (He also discovered a method for separating oxygen and nitrogen in a magnetic field.)

SEVEN REASONS WHY A SCIENTIST BELIEVES IN GOD was adapted for Reader's Digest from Morrison's book Man Does Not Stand Alone (1944).

To cover all sides of the age-old mystery of God and Heaven in relation to ourselves would fill many volumes; indeed, many library shelves have been filled with smaller religious projects. So, in this book, we will settle for only two men's views of God, those of an agnostic and those of a believer. The essay which follows was not chosen because it contains any neat or complete answer to Mencken's, but partly because it avoids theology (which would soon get out of hand, in our limited space) and because it has few, if any, sectarian implications (which would put us under some obligation to present the viewpoints of many others — and, again, soon get out of hand). The opposing views expressed in the two essays, however, may serve to stimulate some thought and further reading.

1   WE ARE still in the dawn of the scientific age and every increase of light reveals more brightly the handiwork of an intelligent Creator. In the ninety years since Darwin we have made stupen-

dous discoveries; with a spirit of scientific humility and of faith grounded in knowledge we are approaching even nearer to an awareness of God.

2   For myself, I count seven reasons for my faith:

3   First: *By unwavering mathematical law we can prove that our universe was designed and executed by a great engineering Intelligence.*

4   Suppose you put ten pennies, marked from one to ten, into your pocket and give them a good shuffle. Now try to take them out in sequence from one to ten, putting back the coin each time and shaking them all again. Mathematically we know that your chance of first drawing number one is one to ten; of drawing one and two in succession, one to one hundred; of drawing one, two and three in succession, one in a thousand, and so on; your chance of drawing them all, from number one to number ten in succession, would reach the unbelievable figure of one chance in ten billion.

5   By the same reasoning, so many exacting conditions are necessary for life on the earth that they could not possibly exist in proper relationship by chance. The earth rotates on its axis one thousand miles an hour; if it turned at one hundred miles an hour, our days and nights would be ten times as long as now, and the hot sun would then burn up our vegetation each long day while in the long night any surviving sprout would freeze.

6   Again, the sun, source of our life, has a surface temperature of 12,000 degrees Fahrenheit, and our earth is just far enough away so that this "eternal fire" warms us *just enough and not too much!* If the sun gave off only one half its present radiation, we would freeze and if it gave half as much more, we would roast.

7   The slant of the earth, tilted at an angle of 23 degrees, gives us our seasons; if it had not been so tilted, vapors from the ocean would move north and south, piling up for us continents of ice. If our moon was, say, only fifty thousand miles away instead of its actual distance, our tides would be so enormous that twice a day all continents would be submerged; even the mountains would soon be eroded away. If the crust of the earth had been only ten feet thicker, there would be no oxygen, without which animal life must die. Had the ocean been a few feet deeper, carbon dioxide and oxygen would have been absorbed and no vegetable life could exist.

Or if our atmosphere had been much thinner, some of the meteors, now burned in space by the millions every day, would be striking all parts of the earth, setting fires everywhere.

8 Because of these and a host of other examples, there is not one chance in millions that life on our planet is an accident.

9 Second: *The resourcefulness of life to accomplish its purpose is a manifestation of all-pervading Intelligence.*

10 What life itself is, no man has fathomed. It has neither weight nor dimensions, but it does have force; a growing root will crack a rock. Life has conquered water, land and air, mastering the elements, compelling them to dissolve and reform their combinations.

11 Life, the sculptor, shapes all living things; an artist, it designs every leaf of every tree, and colors every flower. Life is a musician and has taught each bird to sing its love songs, the insects to call each other in the music of their multitudinous sounds. Life is a sublime chemist, giving taste to fruits and spices, and perfume to the rose, changing water and carbonic acid into sugar and wood, and, in so doing, releasing oxygen that animals may have the breath of life.

12 Behold an almost invisible drop of protoplasm, transparent, jellylike, capable of motion, drawing energy from the sun. This single cell, this transparent mistlike droplet, holds within itself the germ of life, and has the power to distribute this life to every living thing, great and small. The powers of this droplet are greater than our vegetation and animals and people, for all life came from it. Nature did not create life; fire-blistered rocks and a saltless sea could not meet the necessary requirements.

13 Who, then, has put it here?

14 Third: *Animal wisdom speaks irresistibly of a good Creator who infused instinct into otherwise helpless little creatures.*

15 The young salmon spends years at sea, then comes back to his own river, and travels up the very side of the river into which flows the tributary where he was born. What brings him back so precisely? If you transfer him to another tributary he will know at once that he is off his course and he will fight his way down and back to the main stream and then turn up against the current to finish his destiny accurately.

16 Even more difficult to solve is the mystery of eels. These amazing

creatures migrate at maturity from all ponds and rivers everywhere — those from Europe across thousands of miles of ocean — all bound for the same abysmal deeps near Bermuda. There they breed and die. The little ones, with no apparent means of knowing anything except that they are in a wilderness of water, nevertheless start back and find their way not only to the very shore from which their parents came but thence to the rivers, lakes or little ponds — so that each body of water is always populated with eels. No American eel has ever been caught in Europe, no European eel in American waters. Nature has even delayed the maturity of the European eel by a year or more to make up for its longer journey. Where does the directing impulse originate?

17 A wasp will overpower a grasshopper, dig a hole in the earth, sting the grasshopper in exactly the right place so that he does not die but becomes unconscious and lives on as a form of preserved meat. Then the wasp will lay her eggs handily so that her children when they hatch can nibble without killing the insect on which they feed; to them dead meat would be fatal. The mother then flies away and dies; she never sees her young. Surely the wasp must have done all this right the first time and every time, else there would be no wasps. Such mysterious techniques cannot be explained by adaptation; they were bestowed.

18 Fourth: *Man has something more than animal instinct — the power of reason.*

19 No other animal has ever left a record of its ability to count ten, or even to understand the meaning of ten. Where instinct is like a single note of a flute, beautiful but limited, the human brain contains all the notes of all the instruments in the orchestra. No need to belabor this fourth point; thanks to human reason we can contemplate the possibility that we are what we are only because we have received a spark of Universal Intelligence.

20 Fifth: *Provision for all living is revealed in phenomena which we know today but which Darwin did not know — such as the wonders of genes.*

21 So unspeakably tiny are these genes that, if all of them responsible for all living people in the world could be put in one place, there would be less than a thimbleful. Yet these ultramicroscopic genes and their companions, the chromosomes, inhabit every living cell

and are the absolute keys to all human, animal and vegetable characteristics. A thimble is a small place in which to put all the individual characteristics of two billions of human beings. However, the facts are beyond question. Well, then — how do genes lock up all the normal heredity of a multitude of ancestors and preserve the psychology of each in such an infinitely small space?

22   Here evolution really begins — at the cell, the entity which holds and carries the genes. How a few million atoms, locked up as an ultramicroscopic gene, can absolutely rule all life on earth is an example of profound cunning and provision that could emanate only from a Creative Intelligence; no other hypothesis will serve.

23   Sixth: *By the economy of nature, we are forced to realize that only infinite wisdom could have foreseen and prepared with such astute husbandry.*

24   Many years ago a species of cactus was planted in Australia as a protective fence. Having no insect enemies in Australia the cactus soon began a prodigious growth; the alarming abundance persisted until the plants covered an area as long and wide as England, crowding inhabitants out of the towns and villages, and destroying their farms. Seeking a defense, the entomologists scoured the world; finally they turned up an insect which lived exclusively on cactus, and would eat nothing else. It would breed freely, too; and it had no enemies in Australia. So animal soon conquered vegetable and today the cactus pest has retreated, and with it all but a small protective residue of the insects, enough to hold the cactus in check forever.

25   Such checks and balances have been universally provided. Why have not fast-breeding insects dominated the earth? Because they have no lungs such as man possesses, they breathe through tubes. But when insects grow large, their tubes do not grow in ratio to the increasing size of the body. Hence there never has been an insect of great size; this limitation on growth has held them all in check. If this physical check had not been provided, man could not exist. Imagine meeting a hornet as big as a lion!

26   Seventh: *The fact that man can conceive the idea of God is in itself a unique proof.*

27   The conception of God arises from a divine faculty of man, unshared with the rest of our world — the faculty we call imagination.

By its power, man and man alone can find the evidence of things unseen. The vista that power opens up is unbounded; indeed, as man's perfected imagination becomes a spiritual reality, he may discern in all the evidences of design and purpose the great truth that heaven is wherever and whatever; that God is everywhere and in everything but nowhere so close as in our hearts.

28   It is scientifically as well as imaginatively true, as the Psalmist said: *The heavens declare the glory of God and the firmament showeth His handiwork.*

QUESTIONS FOR REFLECTION, DISCUSSION, OR WRITING

(1) It is sometimes believed, in this Age of Science, that because we cannot see God through either microscope or telescope, He must not exist. Comment on this theory. Can you think of anything that we know to exist but that still cannot be seen?

(2) Does Morrison have anything to say about the "goodness" of God, in any way refuting Mencken's charge that He must be a "most stupid, cruel and villainous fellow"? If so, where and how?

(3) Use *analogy* (perhaps of a parent-child relationship) to explain what we mortals may sometimes regard as God's "cruelty" — or, if you prefer, analogy to show some other view of the matter.

(4) Do you think Morrison does a logical job of proving the existence of God? Would it have been less convincing if he had not been an eminent scientist? More convincing if he had been a priest or minister? Why, or why not?

(5) Take any one of Morrison's "seven reasons" for faith and attempt, in composition form, either to show its lack of convincing logic or to restate the thesis and support it with fresh, if less scientific, illustrations from your own experience or "book-knowledge."

Arthur H. Tasker

OCTOBER BLIZZARD

ARTHUR H. TASKER *is, to quote the magazine in which the essay was first published, a "businessman who turned to writing in the autumn of his life." He was born in Granite Falls, Minnesota, but at the time of writing "October*

Blizzard" was making his headquarters in the Idaho mountains. "I have al-
ways loved words," he wrote, "written words, especially those rising out of the
heart's experience and contemplation."

OCTOBER BLIZZARD *was first published in* The Atlantic Monthly *(see p. 231)*
in October 1957. It is a simply told narrative, and, in the first reading, we
should relax and just enjoy it. Only in having read "October Blizzard" in this
way can we later, when we pause to think about it and then go back to ex-
amine the writing, really appreciate the success of this author's refreshing sim-
plicity in creating his effects and saying something worthwhile.

1   I WOKE to the sound of music, deep, rich, and penetrating. It
filled the whole place — vast music, music from the skies. I was
vitally aware of angels; had been, since my younger brother died
in the swirling waters of the lower dam. I trembled now, but in
some ways I was glad. Then I heard the subdued voices of my
two older brothers, who slept in the other bed. They, too, had heard
the great sound. They did not think of angels; but — what was it,
that pouring sound? Jamie, who was four years older than I, was
speaking but stopped short: "Sh-h-h."

2   Benny, who was in between as to age, was not excitable, and
never afraid. "What is it, what do you think it is?" he asked drowsily.
But Jamie's words roused us to reality: "Geese, *geese*, millions of
them."

3   There was no more sleep for any of us that night, as the huge
choir chanted on in its loud chorus. At daybreak we were up and
out in the warm late Indian summer air. It was October 14; we
knew, for Charlie Dodsworth, our friend, the banker's son, would
be sixteen on October 16, this year of 1880, a boy's way of remembering dates.

4   Daylong and nightlong of the fourteenth and fifteenth, the un-
diminished flight went on. How *could* there be such vast wedges of
Canadian geese and ducks, fairly dimming the skies! Then, on the
morning of the sixteenth, there was a stilling of sound. It was almost startling, this sudden quiet. A few scattered wedges of geese
went wearily south, too driven and worn to make a sound. The old
black hen under the cherry bushes scratched for worms, her chicks

just in the change from soft dark down to edging feathers; she had stolen her nest in the late summer, this hen. And now it was indeed late in the season, this balmy October day — later than any of us could have believed.

5   My father unlocked the door of his hardware store on the west side of the Minnesota River, here in Granite Falls, and busied himself for a time turning paint cans to prevent hardening; I swept the floor and dusted with a damp cloth. There had not been a customer as yet; farmers were wary, something was strange. The door burst open and Matteson thrust in head and shoulders. He was breathless, but managed to say, "Close up, Tasker; hurry home; there's an all hell of a storm coming; run, or you'll never make it!"

6   This was a shock. Father knew this weather-wise old Norwegian meant what he said, however inelegantly phrased. We ran: two long slanting blocks to the bridge, over it speeding, clickety-click, now south and down the steep road to the creek in the beauty of autumn trees, over that bridge and up the slope past the bleak schoolhouse, on, up, and along the ridge path. He was fleet of foot and as nearly scared as an English-born man could be. I was even more alarmed, for indeed a change had come over things. A misty warm pressure, a closing light, was in the air; and then, out of the north and west it came, a rising roar. The riverside trees began to rock; then, like the physical blow of a mysterious hand, a great white mass struck, and sent us staggering — wind that was crushing, snow that closed out the light and sucked the very breath from nostrils or open mouth. Here, within a hundred feet of his home, the place he had left snuggled against this very stone-studded ridge, my father stumbled, losing my hand as he fell.

7   When first the storm had struck, setting the timbers of the house quivering, Mother had opened the woodshed door, only to be hurled against the summer-season stove. But she felt no pain or injury — not then. With Jamie's sturdy help she managed to close the door. "Oh, Tom, Tom, where are you?" She was crying, but Jamie comforted her: "Mother, Mother, no! Just think what time it is. They are at the store. Don't cry."

8   Mother, I fancy, had looked at her first-born in something like surprise. "You're brave," she had tried to say, with a new flood of tears. But what they should have guessed was that the mettlesome

father they had in mind was not one to leave his family in fright
and anxiety, not if he could help it.

9   What that family were thinking, halfway saying, was that they
must wait and wait — for hours; if need be, for days. "O God,
merciful God, help us, save us!" It was, then, a shock that made
my mother scream, when the door again burst open and a blinded,
staggering ghost came in, leading a smaller ghost by the hand, mid
rush, roar, and pelting snow. Our faces were plastered white in
snow; so too my father's beard and small mustache; in every line of
clothing, snow.

10   My mother screamed, but then, quick-witted, a woman of action,
she seized a towel and began swiftly to humanize this man she had
loved since she was sixteen, and then myself — these two whom
she and two staring boys had looked upon, moments ago, in awe.

11   The first words Father said, as soon as he had recovered his
breath, were: "God, and no one else, put my fingers on the latch."
Mother began to cry, and I, too, cried, and even Benny. Oh, we
were home again, we who were so nearly lost. How near indeed.

12   In what was called the parlor or, more often, the front room,
there was a sofa, an uncomfortable couch upholstered in figured
Brussels carpeting, our showpiece, much admired. There Mother
made my father lie down, and she covered him with a padded quilt,
though he protested that he was boiling hot, which from our long
run and the warm, humid day was readily true, howling blizzard
and wintry storm to the contrary. To me it had been less of a
strain. I lived outdoors. I, too, was fleet of foot.

13   When Mother came from the bedroom's huge curly maple
bureau, bearing winter underclothing and towels, we three boys
and our younger sister, Prudence, were shooed from the place to
the kitchen-dining room. What was said there in the front room,
what tears shed, what prayers of gratitude, we, the children, were
never to know.

14   Later in the day, on Father's request, Benny came into the
kitchen with the two clotheslines, and my father showed us the
sailor's knot he had learned in the long voyage from England's
lovely shores; that, too, had been flight.

15   And now the lines were knotted together into a single long line
with a draw loop at one end, which would be fastened to the

clothesline hook outside the woodshed door. At early chore time, Father and stouthearted Jamie, on Mother's insistence, tied themselves loosely together, father and son; then, milk pails swinging, their hands on the guideline, they forced themselves out into the blinding, moving density of blizzard snow.

16   It would be hard to imagine what it must have been like out there in the unprotected barn, with its thin, single-boarded roof and walls. Why, even here in the well-built, plastered house, snuggled close to the protecting hill, we were shouting to each other in an effort to be heard, so deafening now had become the thundering impact of the storm. "Long away?" Try to think of all there was to do: the feeding down from the mow of snow-laden hay, forkful after forkful, to the mangers below; the mixing of ground cow feed with salt, and snow for moisture; oats to be measured and fed to the horses; corn shelled for the ravenous clutter of hens and the yellow-legged fryers; corn on the cob to the three fattening hogs, silent for once in the greater sound.

17   When Jamie had finished telling us all these things they had done, he suddenly paused. "And if you'd climbed with me into the hayloft, you'd have been surprised, for there were five beautiful, scared prairie chickens back in the west end of the hay. Must have flown in at that open place. They kept turning their heads and I thought they were going to fly out again. Poor things!"

18   Benny asked excitedly if they were likely to be there in the morning. And why couldn't we catch them, putting up sheets or something, to keep them from flying out? Jamie looked at Benny in a puzzled way. "Would *you* do *that* . . . to things caught in a storm, just flying in?"

19   Prudence, a very sensitive child, turned her large, round, blue eyes on Benny, and slowly they misted over. She loved him. We were silent. A color of red crept into Benny's cheeks. Benny, the gentlest one of us all, was ashamed! And so, too, was I, who had shared his impulse, his thoughts having been my thoughts. I felt a sudden tenderness for all things lost, or — so nearly lost.

QUESTIONS FOR REFLECTION, DISCUSSION, OR WRITING

(1) Do you see any justification for including "October Blizzard" in the section on "Man as He Sees Himself" (which, of course, is devoted to the creeds and philosophies, large and small, that make people what they really are)? Of what lasting significance, if any, do you think this seemingly minor episode may have had on the author's character? Where in the story are we given at least a glimpse of this effect?

(2) The author says (see headnotes) that he is interested in words that "rise out of the heart's experience and contemplation." What is meant by this? Do you suppose adult "contemplation" has caused him to see more in the blizzard episode than impressed him as a boy? Explain.

(3) In this selection, unlike several others you have read, you probably find few words with which you were not already familiar. Do you feel, because of this, that the author has "written down" to readers such as you, to make the reading easy? Or is his word choice consistent with the purpose and tone of the story itself? How well does he succeed in conveying his impressions? Would "fancier" words have helped?

(4) Consider Tasker's use of figures of speech (see p. 15) in paragraphs 1, 3, 6, 8, and 9. How successful are they in creating vivid description?

(5) This author has succeeded in giving us a full-scale, three-dimensional portrait of a whole family — in only 1400 words, not many for such a task. True, he has given us little idea as to physical appearances, leaving these to our imaginations. But he has carefully selected and dramatized enough details to make us feel that we really know the family personally. List the characteristics of these people, individually and as a family group — qualities that we have seen *in action*, a much more effective way than having the author merely *tell* us they existed.

(6) When the wind hurled Mother against the stove, she "felt no pain or injury — not then." Why did the author add "not then"? Was she injured later?

(7) What do you think would have been H. L. Mencken's response to Father's statement in paragraph 11?

(8) Why is an October blizzard more effective for the author's purpose than, for instance, a January blizzard would be?

(9) What a person really *is*, inside himself, the qualities that keep him from being quite the same as anyone else in the world (call it character, or spirit, or what you will) are often formed as much by the many little things he experiences in his youth as by the few big, spectacular events. What experiences in your early life, large or small, may have helped form you into what you

really are today? One of these will provide the subject for a worthwhile narrative.

William D. Blair, Jr.

JOURNEY INTO FEAR

WILLIAM D. BLAIR, JR., *is a press officer for the U.S. Department of State. Formerly a war correspondent for the* Baltimore Sun *newpsapers, he was wounded while covering the battle for Seoul in October of 1950. After recovery he served as roving correspondent in Europe, then joined the staff of* Newsweek *in 1953, as assistant editor for international affairs. He later served as chief of the magazine's Bonn and Paris bureaus before going to the State Department, where he is now deputy director of the Office of Special Projects.*

V.F.W. MAGAZINE, *in which "Journey into Fear" first appeared in July 1951, is published monthly by the Veterans of Foreign Wars, in Kansas City, Missouri. Founded in 1913, the magazine now has a circulation of well over a million.*

JOURNEY INTO FEAR *is an intimate exposition-description (presented in loose narrative form, thus utilizing three of the four major types of writing) of an emotion men seldom care to discuss. If the fear which Blair describes were limited only to the battlefield, however, the value of his essay would also be very limited. But this fear differs only in degree and intensity from that experienced one way or another, sometime, by most human beings. Hence, his essay has universal meaning.*

Such a subject is extremely difficult for any but a skilled writer to handle, however, without slipping into the literary sin of **sentimentality,** *or* **sentimentalism.** *These are terms used to apply to an excess of sentiment or emotion, "gushing," especially when the writer seems to be making a too-conscious effort to stir his reader. Then such writing becomes* **melodramatic,** *and is apt to be regarded as "sloppy" even by unsophisticated readers. Blair's success or failure in avoiding sentimentality can tell us a great deal about his maturity as a writer.*

1 A VERY FEW hours after arrival at the port of Pusan in Korea we were on a train, jerking toward the west and the enemy. There had been word of guerillas firing on our convoys, and on every flatcar of the train men were holding weapons ready to fire. Sometime during this five-hour journey war came to us all. Wonder at

the strangeness of the place brought with it loneliness and a yearning for home — and then came fear.

2   It may have come first to some as they looked at the skyline and thought about what it would be like to be shot at, to have someone aiming a rifle at them, actually trying to kill them. Probably it came to others at a station, when they saw a South Korean infantryman whose only weapon was a single grenade, hanging by a string from his belt. Maybe some felt it first when we passed a hospital train, returning from the unknown with its load of silent, bandaged figures, or when they noticed the two rigid bodies floating slowly down the river which ran close to the tracks.

3   This first feeling was only a dull fear, hardly more than uneasiness. We were uncertain what lay ahead, we were realizing reluctantly that whatever control we had over our destinies was slipping from us.

4   Arrival in the combat area did nothing to reassure us. A group of lightly wounded soldiers was playing cards on the road near our debarkation point, and one of the newly arrived Marines, mustering his self-confidence, jeered:

5   "Is that the way you people fight a war?"

6   "This isn't the movies, Marines." The cardplayers were tired but superior. "You'll be goddam lucky to do as well as the 27th!" That was the unit the newcomers were to relieve.

7   "You the 27th?"

8   "We're what's left of it."

9   There were many things you weren't afraid of, not knowing; you have to see them first. Death isn't very frightening till you've seen some of its horrible methods. The words "disfigurement," "disablement," don't mean much until you've seen a head without features, and have heard it moan: "Can my wife still love me, with a face like I'll have?"

10   There had been hard fighting at Chindong-ni for over a week. A company of the 27th had been cut off from the rest of the regiment a small distance away and was still surrounded, desperately short of ammunition, water, and rations. Several Marine units were dispatched to effect a rescue. As they set out along a dusty track

and under a malicious sun which made every rod a mile, there was no conversation. Dungarees quickly grew dark with sweat under the heavy loads, and you settled into the automatic, slouching pace which for a time makes thinking unnecessary and postpones fatigue. Instead of excitement there was lethargy, almost unconsciousness as you plodded along past the ruins of Chindong-ni, its mud hovels crumbled and smouldering. Past dead cattle, their legs jutting stiffly in air. Past a dry stream bed. Past an ammunition bearer, who had fainted from heat exhaustion. Past bamboo clumps. And into fear, as two hidden machine guns opened fire from the flank.

11   We stared, ignorantly amazed; then squad by squad we understood and leaped for cover, feeling the sudden singe of terror as we saw the bullets splash dust in the road.

12   Pusan had been the title page, the train ride the preface. This was Chapter One of the text. This was a deeper fear than before; it wiped out the past and the future — every frame of reference except the utter and immediate necessity for safety. We were animals till we found it — wild with fear and moving by instinct alone. In ditches and behind rocks we finally saw that this wasn't, after all, unbearable — not while we lay in relatively safe cover and the danger was only a couple of not very expert machine gunners. Fear subsided, though it didn't altogether disappear, and we were prepared to stay in our ditches indefinitely. And then the officers, swearing, exhorting, brandishing their carbines, stood exposed on the road and ordered us up and on.

13   It is one thing to lie in a snug trench while you listen to the bullets ricocheting from the stones over your head or smacking the turf just beyond; you are calmly afraid, almost pleasurably afraid, as you might be for the hero of a romance. It is another thing to stand where you can easily and unromantically receive a small, hard missile in the hollow of your temple — which itches expectantly at the thought; or in your stomach — which is now bottomless and sick; or in other parts of your so susceptible body. The fear is not nice. It's a frenzied pounding in the breast, a feeling of nakedness, a frantic attempt to blot out everything but the sight of the ground directly ahead and the sound of the voice of command; and to go on, and on, and on until it's done. In days, or weeks, a fear like that becomes determination, which is not the

opposite of being afraid. Or it festers into panic, hysteria, and collapse. It makes man of boy, or child of man.

14   It's a wonderful thing to discover that you're not as afraid as you thought you'd be. It gives green youths an immeasurable lift in their first days of fire. After these initiations they look at each other and smile, because they've shown themselves, maybe for the first time, that they aren't cowards. Unfortunately, the discovery loses its potency in repetition. Mind and body are worn thin; the last drop of will power is wrung out, and you need something more. Providentially, it comes — emotion takes over. The result is a truly marvelous exhilaration, born of the endless fear, and it sweeps the endangered along heedless, even fiercely jubilant, to whatever end of the road. For the survivor, the memory of the interval often lingers. It's like a remembered orgy, which exerts a fascination and arouses a craving. The victim feels a need to indulge it again. It becomes horrible, for men still inflamed by the ecstasy will go back from safety to the battle when for them there is no call.

15   I think it must be this driving intoxication which inspires heroes, the men who hug grenades to their chests to save their fellows, or dash singly against impregnable enemy positions. It must be the thing that makes warriors — for there are some who enjoy war. These are contemporary Achilleses, Launcelots, Rolands, of whom one wants to say that they were born after their time. There was a bearded young lieutenant, possibly still living, in command of a platoon at the bank of the Nam River. Communist raiders were slipping by night into the no-man's-land village on the far bank, setting up mortars and machine guns to harass our outposts. They did little damage, but the insolence piqued the lieutenant's pride. He lay in wait for the raider band alone in a maze of rubble. The trick worked. He killed nearly 20 North Koreans before they could turn and run, and came grinning back to his lines. He was as happy at his work as any man I've known.

16   But the danger-lust is more remarkable in non-warrior types, doing their job as best they can and finding no pleasure in it. These, the fever can transform into something wholly foreign to their natures. One company of soldiers stayed five days on a tiny, T-shaped ridge, surrounded by ten times their number. They ran out of food and low on water, and watched supplies aimed at them drop tanta-

lizingly from American planes into the hands of the enemy. In the night the enemy around would slink into their midst, and in the morning bodies of some soldiers would be found crumpled with knife wounds in their hearts. After what must have been an eternity, a friendly force cut its way to the rescue, and the agonized soldiers could fall back. But they seemed to take no joy in their salvation. "They were so doggone mad they didn't care if they *ever* came back!" marveled a member of the relief.

17   The gruesome sights of the battlefield, in their effect on the soldier, are also subject to the law of diminishing returns. You expect to be shocked and sickened — but that must be an artificial feeling because you don't react fastidiously for long. Burning or crushed or dismembered bodies are only dirt, as the preacher likes to point out, and the sight of them, when the novelty is gone, is little more obnoxious. It's true that at first you are nauseated, and terrified by the thought of the ghastly deaths some of these flesh-heaps have obviously suffered. But you learn to waste little sympathy on the irreparable.

18   There is one true horror, and it has no remedy. I watched two surgeons in a mobile field hospital toil for hours over an almost faceless man. The formless flesh tumbled and came away between the probing instruments. After a long time one of the surgeons sighed and murmured, "I'm sorry, fella." The surgeons tried to make something clean and firm out of a ghastly pulp. Then they bandaged what was left of the head, leaving only an opening for the one functioning eye, and sent him away. "He will die," they said. And horror was the vista of that man's future — not death, but the intervening time in the hospitals, with the opening in the bandage like a window in a tenement, from which the wretched can overlook the vile.

19   Green, scared troops approach their first test by fire, and begin to feel how dependent they are on each other. They begin to reappraise each other, and pray fervently that every man will turn out true. One man's laxity or weakness can kill all the rest. Afterward the survivors feel a hot pride in their collective achievement and a glow of gratitude and trust for each other. In very little time a bond is forged in a company which is stronger than most family ties, for the price of its dissolution is often death. Take a

soldier out of a unit like that and he will be acutely unhappy and afraid; he can't be sure in his new place that the men on his right and left will still be there when the assault waves start to arrive. Many soldiers, comfortably convalescing from wounds in rear-area hospitals, have moved heaven and earth to be sent back to their company, from the first day they could rise out of bed. They would rather go back and fight beside their friends than take their full measure of rest and risk being sent to a different unit.

20   The fraternity of such soldiers is infectious, and it spreads over a whole combat area. Every man who does his job under fire becomes the brother of every other who is in the same fix. After a while you love just about every man you see — each one is suffering for you. It is a common remark among soldiers that the further back you go from the fighting, the less sympathetic are the people. The less hardship the man knows, the less he is driven into the arms of his neighbor, and the more he is just what he was in his peaceful home — self-centered, unfeeling. Under stress a man is noble; left to himself, he is mean. I don't know which is truly the man.

21   Aboard a hospital ship, where men are crowded into a cabin with eight or nine others, mutual sympathy and respect create friendships quickly. The young Marine lieutenant had been speaking of his dread of combat, shame for his post-battle tears, and his greatest terror — when he heard above him in the night the ominous sound of a dozen grenades being primed in unison, to be dropped on his platoon.

22   "But nature is wonderful," he went on. "She doesn't let you remember all the sounds we heard, or all the awful feeling we had or the things we saw. It's just a blur. Just that one sound — the time they banged their grenades, all together, right over us — that stays with me. I'll always remember it. But mostly you forget."

23   So it is. The details, the shades of feeling, the little horrors and pains and fright — these are forgotten. But enough remains to evoke the terrible anguish, the stunning terror again, and always again.

24   Sometimes I wonder what goes into being afraid for your life. Perhaps it is all the other fears which you recognize when you have time to think about your emotions, violently mixed in one moment. Fear that family and friends will suffer, that a wife will

be a widow, that children will be fatherless. Fear that all the little pleasures and joys you find in your life will be felt no more. Fear that you will be judged by your errors; that you will never demonstrate your beliefs. Fear that you will never have lived.

25   In the dense fog near Seoul, a young soldier scrambled back and forth over the hill. His platoon had left him. The order to pull back somehow never had reached him, and finally from the uncanny silence came the conviction that he was alone on the barren height. He tried, frantically, to follow his comrades, but the mist was like a blindfold. After every desperate 20-yard rush he stopped, uncertain, staring at the little space he could see around him. And then, as panic mounted, he heard the scratches of feet against stone, the metallic snick of metal on metal and metal on rock. He had been a soldier long enough, and he knew the sounds. It wasn't his platoon. The impulse to scream was almost too strong to control, but he bit it down. Miraculously, right there in front of him, loomed a huge boulder, reaching angularly away from him out of the ground. He leaped around it and crouched in the tiny cave it afforded. Suddenly two pairs of soft-shoed feet stepped onto the flat rock top above his head, and two voices murmured — not in English. His heart was like a pneumatic drill, crashing and blasting its way through his frame; his eyes blurred with stinging tears. Time became meaningless. The human being can stand no more than so much and slowly he relaxed. It didn't matter, now, once you knew; and it was so peaceful. Life had seldom given him a sweeter moment than this acceptance of its limit. Then he got up, careless and yet confident that his step in the dark would sound like any other, and walked down the hill and through the fields and back to the arms of his brothers.

26   That, in the end, is what war is: Fear. Fear for your life, primarily, till one is so afraid that he can be afraid no more.

QUESTIONS FOR REFLECTION, DISCUSSION, OR WRITING

(1) "Journey into Fear" is hardly a pleasant piece of reading. What, then, *is* the value of reading it? Does this essay convey any meaning for you personally — even if you never go to war? Can it help you to understand yourself and others any better? Explain.

(2) Is the author ever guilty of *sentimentality* in his writing? If so, where? If not, find passages where he might have become overemotional but exercised desirable restraint instead.

(3) Now reconsider "October Blizzard," another essay where the author could easily have "gushed" with sentiment. Did he?

(4) On first impression, this essay and "October Blizzard" seem to be nothing at all alike. Yet they do have certain things in common. What are they?

(5) Does the "fraternity" of soldiers (pars. 19-20) have any parallels in everyday life? If so, is the difference merely one of intensity, or is the civilian variety a different thing altogether? Discuss. Is it the same thing as that of Burdick's "sharers of the secret" (in "The United States Navy")?

(6) If you recall, in Jack London's account of the earthquake (p. 120), he said that "everybody was gracious. The most perfect courtesy obtained. Never . . . were her people so kind and courteous as on this night of terror." In "Journey into Fear" there are references to what could provide an explanation. Find and discuss them in this regard.

(7) Sometimes a personal narrative can become overburdened and boorish with the personal pronoun "I." Blair avoids this hazard. How? What other desirable quality is achieved by his method?

(8) Explain the allusions in paragraph 15.

(9) Many people seem to think fear is the same thing as cowardice, or at least a sign of it. Give a clear explanation of the difference.

(10) You will seldom hear a combat veteran discuss such things as Blair has described in detail. Why is this? Can you find a possible answer or answers in reading paragraphs 22 and 23?

(11) What do you think of the author's explanation of heroism (par. 15)? Does this seem to detract from the glory due our many war heroes? Explain.

(12) Have you ever known, even briefly, a fear that was a "stunning terror," intense enough to make your stomach "bottomless and sick"? Most of us, war veterans or not, have known such fear — and the experience and its effects can be an excellent topic for writing.

(13) Other emotions (*e.g.*, love, hate, anger) can be as intense — and just as difficult to describe — as fear. A worthwhile writing project might be such a description, based on your own experience.

(14) Blair says (par. 20) that under stress a man is noble; left to himself, he is mean. Do you agree? If not, tell why. If so, which do you think is "truly the man"? This answer, too, is worth a full-scale composition.

James P. Cornette
LET THEM BUILD TENTS

JAMES P. CORNETTE, *president of* West Texas State College, Canyon, Texas, *since 1948, has had a varied career as high school teacher and athletic coach, college dean, and professor of English. He is also the author of several books and still writes occasional magazine articles. In recent years he has had two successful television series-shows, "Among My Books" and "Poets Are People Too."*

LADIES' HOME JOURNAL, *a well-known "slick" magazine devoted almost entirely to women's interests, has been published in Philadelphia since 1883. It is owned by the Curtis Publishing Company (also publishers of* The Saturday Evening Post, Holiday, *and* Jack and Jill). *Circulation of the* Journal, *in which "Let Them Build Tents" was published in August 1959, is almost six million.*

LET THEM BUILD TENTS *is a good example of analogy (see p. 264). Whereas Mencken used his analogies only briefly, Cornette uses his to explain an entire structure of ideas. Notice as you read the essay that, while in straight comparison we would be equally concerned with both things compared, in this analogy (as in all analogies) we are concerned with the "tents" only as they help to explain the larger idea.*

1 FOR THREE long Kentucky summer days four of us little boys labored mightily building the tent against the garden fence. It was to be the most wonderful tent ever built! And we were going to have the most wonderful time sitting down and playing in it that four little boys ever had doing anything!

2 And truly it *was* a rather wonderful tent four little boys constructed out of sassafras bean poles and old bed ticking. Our labors done, we sat down to play.

3 But in less than an hour life in the tent had become so dull that we left it and went over to the other side of the garden and started digging a hole — a hole that was to be the biggest hole ever dug and in which we were going to have the most wonderful time playing that four little boys ever had doing anything! We did not return

to the tent. Weeks later mother told us we had to tear it down because it was in the way.

4   Many years went by before I understood the truth first glimpsed on that summer day so long ago: that the real fun is in the building of the tent, rather than in the sitting down and playing in it; in the going, rather than in the having arrived; in the living of life and experiencing as fully as possible all its sweetness and bitterness, rather than in escaping any of it through one's own efforts or those of someone else.

5   One of the tragedies in life is for a man to arrive at the place where he has finished his tent and has nothing to do except to sit down and play in it — with no new tent to begin, and with not even a good place to start digging a hole.

6   There is a tragedy even greater than this, though, possibly the greatest tragedy of all: when a young man is handed a ready-made tent, with the loving admonition, "Here, son, is a beautiful tent made just for you. Now sit down and play in it and have a wonderful time all the rest of your life." At least a man who has built his own has the memories of the building.

7   Now after close to a half century of "building tents" and "digging holes" of my own and a quarter century spent helping thousands of college students and my three sons with theirs, I have come to the conclusion that the really dangerous threat to that which we speak of rather loosely as the "American way of life" lies in the mistaken notion that the "good life" is to be found in sitting down and playing in the tent after it is finished instead of in the building of it. This false idea dominates our national thinking. In the intense and continuing struggle between "labor" and "capital," it is the motivating force; it is the inspiration for our snowballing "protectthe-individual" legislation; and it supplies oil for the idealistic lamps burning in most of our American homes, where suddenly within the last half century the basic essentials of human existence can be provided with a relatively small expenditure of effort and time. With a few exceptions the providing of food, clothing and shelter has kept man busy all his life, so that he has died more or less happy still building and dreaming.

8   When I saw that each of my three boys had the experience of catching his first small-mouth bass in swift water by the time he was

six years of age, and of killing his first quail on the wing by the time he was ten, I was approved of by my friends. I was being "a pal to my boys," teaching them to play.

9   But those same friends thought I was either cruel or crazy when I permitted (and I use the word "permitted" advisedly — boys like to work if they get half a chance) those same boys at eleven to face a Texas Panhandle winter before daylight on a paper route; and at twelve to start "hiring out" to drive tractors and combines in the plains wheat harvest; and in their early teens to start borrowing money at the bank over their own signatures and leasing land and raising cattle and hogs as they went through high school. My sons weren't *slaving* when my friends felt sorry for them; they were *living* — living gloriously, building the tent in great ways.

10   A big pole went up in Bill's on the morning he first spoke of the beauty of a sleeping town waking up against a gray sky, as seen from a moving bicycle. I had introduced him to the beauty of mallards wheeling against the sky at sunrise, but his eleven-year-old discovery was better; especially when with it came a developing awareness of importance to the people turning on lights in houses as he passed.

11   Jim was fourteen when he wouldn't go with us on vacation, because, as he said, "We're through combining and the wheat's all in. But we've still got almost three more sections to plow, and Mr. Byrd *just can't get along without me until the plowing's done*." A big strip went up on Jim's tent on the day he felt that much needed.

12   Nor shall I forget Marv's sixteen-year-old face on the day he came in from the Tri-State Fair with his arms full of grand-champion banners and blue ribbons after his swine had won more prizes than those of any other breeder showing in the open competition at the big fair; or forget the excitement in his voice that night when he telephoned, "Dad, guess what! Our load of steers topped the Fort Worth market today at thirty-eight cents."

13   During the quarter century I have been helping students with the building of their tents, I have seen six college generations come and go. Each fall they have been better fed, clothed and groomed; better poised and better mannered; yes, and better educated, too, as their entrance examinations indicate, certain current writings to the contrary notwithstanding. I have felt proud as each fall I have

watched them come down the receiving line, proud not only of
them but of us American parents for having produced them. In
general, we have done a good job. But along with all the good, we
have done the bad thing of indoctrinating them only too successfully with our own false ideal of the good life.

14   In the eyes of a constantly increasing number of those boys and
girls each fall lies a quiet expectation of being well taken care of
by someone else all the rest of their lives. No wonder that out of
boredom with their "kept" status come sporadic eruptions.

15   We Americans of this parent generation need desperately to
shake ourselves awake and discover the falsity of man's long-cher-
ished Utopian dream of finishing one's tent and sitting down to
play in it; if we will not do it for our own sake, we *must* do it for
the sake of our children. The formula is very simple: Let them build
their own tents.

QUESTIONS FOR REFLECTION, DISCUSSION, OR WRITING

(1) Where in the essay does it become obvious that the author is developing
an analogy, rather than telling a mere story of his childhood? How clear is his
analogy? How frequently (and where?) does he refer to it, directly or indirectly? Try to explain how his technique is more (or less) effective and
memorable than simply *discussing* the merits of letting young people make
their own way.

(2) State in one sentence of your own the author's central theme. Has he
included anything in the essay which is irrelevant, which does not pertain to
this thesis?

(3) Locate and explain the allusion (see p. 207) in paragraph 15.

(4) Compare his theory of idleness to those of other writers of this book,
especially Sloan Wilson's.

(5) Do you think a financially well-off father is either "cruel or crazy" (par.
9) to permit his eleven-year-old son to start making his own way, at twelve to
do a man's work in the fields, and in his early teens to borrow money and
lease land? Would most boys *want* to work so hard, as he says his did? How
could they then have time for Little League, etc.? What about the usual advice of "letting boys be boys"?

(6) Explain in your own words the "false idea of the good life" (par. 13),
with which Cornette thinks we have indoctrinated our young people only too

well. What is that so-called good life? Do you agree that the idea is false? Or that young people are too well indoctrinated with it?

(7) What evidence can you find in your own family or community, or in national news, that boredom with people's "kept status" results in "sporadic eruptions" (par. 14)? Does this account, for instance, for any large percentage of juvenile delinquency? Of adult crime? Explain your views.

(8) Find other illustrations in real life of people who have been "given a tent" of one kind or another — all ready to sit down in for playing. Did the "tent" make them happy?

(9) Tell the story of your own first job and what you gained (or lost) by it.

Robert Paul Smith

HOW NOT TO LISTEN
to somebody else talking until you
can give somebody else the chance
not to listen to you

ROBERT PAUL SMITH *is a versatile New York author whose work has included the writing of radio and TV scripts, magazine articles and stories, and best-selling books, such as* Where did you go? Out. What did you do? Nothing. *He was also the co-author (with Max Shulman) of a successful Broadway play,* The Tender Trap.

BETTER HOMES AND GARDENS, *which published the following essay in the November 1959 issue, is a "home and family service" monthly. Published since 1922 in Des Moines, Iowa, by the Meredith Publishing Company (also owner of* Successful Farming), *it has a circulation of almost five million.*

HOW NOT TO LISTEN . . . , *as one might guess from the title, is a breezy, informal essay — which may still, of course, have something "to say." It demonstrates, too, some of Smith's unconventional techniques which give his writing a style of its own (a style, by the way, not always admired by more conventional readers.)*

1   AT THE dinner table, when I was a kid, conversation flowed over us young 'uns like a mighty, incomprehensible torrent.

2   We paid mighty little attention to what was said unless a sentence detached itself from the main stream, directed itself to us

as a command or reprimand, and required action or compliance. The sentences we heard in this way were, "If you insist upon leaning your head in your hand, you will get mashed potatoes in your hair." "Will you please stop playing with your food (silverware, napkin ring) or leave the table immediately." "Stop teasing your brother (sister)." "Sit up straight, your posture is a disgrace." "Don't gulp your food." "You may be excused." (This was sometimes permission, sometimes a command.) These things were said to us and we understood.

3   From time to time we heard (myself dreamily, as I massaged poached egg into my scalp) certain items of news about Mr. Klauber. This was thorough nonsense to me, because I knew that Mr. Klauber was not a person; he was a hand with a pear in it. He had the only bearing pear tree on the block, and if you managed to pass his house slowly at the proper time, he would call you up, twist a pear off a branch, and give it to you (sometimes, though not often, without a wasp attached). To hand you this pear was Mr. Klauber's function. He had been born, raised, and set down on the block to hand us kids pears, and here were my parents suffering under the delusion that he had another existence. I do not remember his voice, his face, his height, the color of his hair, whether he wore a mustache or a beard. Kids pick out the salient detail of a person as a caricaturist seizes on the single to-be-exaggerated feature. So, Mr. Klauber, to repeat, was a hand with a pear in it.

4   There were certain statements cast in the air above the dinner table about, say, Dr. Reilly. Obvious nonsense again, because Dr. Reilly, I knew, did not walk, talk, eat food, or pay taxes. As Mr. Klauber was a hand, Doctor Reilly was a smell. He was a smell that came into the room where I was running a fever, and upon the entrance of the smell (with, I now presume, Dr. Reilly following soon after) I instantly felt cured. I think now it was bay rum, this smell, but then the smell was Dr. Reilly and the elixir of life.

5   The grown-ups talked and talked, good heavens, how they talked, and we sat there and ate our food. (When dinner was over, I would be able to go out on the block, and there I could talk

"How Not To Listen . . . ," by Robert Paul Smith, reprinted from *Better Homes & Gardens*.

with my peers.) Grown-ups talked so much, and they always talked about the dullest things in the world — other grown-ups. Sometimes they were so entirely depraved they talked about relatives. Now what, in the name of heaven, was there to say about Aunt Cora? She hurt all over, and she never brought presents. Uncle Harry? He lit his cigars once, then chewed them, and left the stubs, looking like nothing so much as puppy dog mess, in every ash tray in the house, and he gave me a quarter every time he came, and he had once been an Eskimo Pie salesman. They talked about the neighbors, and all I can recall of that is that if Father liked someone, my mother did not like his wife, except sometimes, when she did not like the husband, too. And vice versa.

6   I had two older sisters, sometimes known as a fate worse than death, and they got to talk once in a while. They peopled the table with Latin teachers, the cutest boy who was a cheer leader, the real keen wonderful sport who headed up the girls' second basketball team, that terrible girl on Forster Avenue who thought she was so much because she had once met May Singhi Breen, the Ukulele Lady. The girls and my mother talked about letting down hems, putting up hair, lipstick (I still remember that Mother said lip pomade was All Right, but Tangee orange lipstick from the five and ten was All Wrong), Cuban heels, and (not at the dinner table) brassieres and teddies instead of union suits.

7   Once in a great while I got to utter some pitiful statement about long division, or my overdue "liberry" books, or the possibility of sending away for a galena crystal and cat's whisker, or wouldn't everybody at the table like a packet of bluing so I could have a magic lantern. With two older sisters, these opportunities were few. Mostly I pushed my food around the plate moodily, shoved my spinach down the table surreptitiously to the younger sister, who would and did eat anything. Her spinach-eating was partially gluttony and partially affection, because in our house you ate everything on your plate (particularly the more disgusting vegetables, such as cauliflower, cabbage, mashed turnips) or got jawed until your life wasn't worth a nickel, and she was on my side.

8   I have two boys now, and they are so fortunate as to have no older sister, and live in a world where children are believed to be capable of conversation. I was hollering at them the other night,

because they flap their jaws without cease, and here I am, many years later, still sitting at the table hoping to get a word in edgewise. I gagged them both, and tied a rope firmly around their mother's neck, and held forth for some time on the rights of Aged Pa to utter a sentence without having it nipped off at the end and given to the dog to play with.

9   They listened, without interest but with a certain strained politesse, and then the 10-year-old freed himself of his gag and announced that things had changed since the olden days, when I was a boy and George Washington was President.

10   Indeed they have. My kids babble about all manner of things, but I must say, if I have to keep quiet at the table, I would rather hear about neat rockets than Mrs. Klauber. I am more interested in rotten old school than Dr. Reilly's finances.

11   What has not changed is the old cry of parents to children, "You're not listening to a word I say." Well, of course they are not. Nor are we listening to them. Nor, in awful fact, does anybody very much listen to anybody else.

12   Most conversations I am privy to are in no way an exchange of information between two or more sentient things. It is my understanding that when one ant pauses on his way in or out of the hill he calls home, and taps another ant with his antenna, he is saying, "There is a drop of honey three inches by northwest, and you better go and get some of it because my feet are killing me," or "I think you might stop by Entrance Three in the lower tier. Cornelius is having an awful time with those new larvae, and you know how easily he loses his temper," or "Long time no see, Harve, how about coming over to my place for a bite of caterpillar and a noggin of rain water?" It is my further understanding that the other ant says, "I'm laying off honey this week, thanks. It goes right to my thorax," or, "Let Cornelius solve his own problems," or "Let's go." And they do.

13   There is none, so far as I can tell, of this argle bargle: "Great weather for aphids," or "I understand Thatcher is in line for the Decayed Banana account," or "They tell me the 1960 Polliwog has more chrome on its fins than the Monarch Chrysalis." It is, as clearly as I can read antennae, a matter of yea and nay and right

and left and up and down information sent out, information attended to, information absorbed, and the business well in foot.

14   But we don't do that. We perform, in conversation, a sort of ritual dance. Number One enters from stage left, gains the center of the stage, and pirouettes steadily in the exact center of the spotlight, while Number Two does not watch. The minute Number One relinquishes the spot, Number Two in turn hogs the spot, while Number One takes his turn at not watching.

15   We simply don't listen. We wait until someone else shuts up, so we can give the someone else the opportunity not to listen to us.

16   Generally, you cannot turn on one of your peers and accuse him of inattention. But with kids you have height, weight, reach, and volume, and as usual, they catch it. Not that you are in error; they are not listening to you. Your statement is correct. It might be useful to attempt to find out why.

17   One reason is, of course, that it is completely obvious to them that you rarely listen to them, and that you do not even listen to other adults. Children generally obey a law which goes, "Don't do as I say, do as I do."

18   So as usual, what irritates us in our children is the fact that they display our own faults in a transparent way. Being dissemblers, like ourselves, they still do not know how to dissemble very well, and truly, it is not that they do not listen; it is, quite simply, that they make it clear that they are not listening.

19   So, once again, as usual, it is not the kids we're bawling out. It is ourselves. It seems, then, that what we are to examine is why we do not listen.

20   I think we do not listen because we do not talk about the things that really concern us. We are frightened of war, of the Biggest Firecracker in the Whole World, of the appalling lack of moral sense, the decline of manners and kindness.

21   We really do not feel any more that we are in control of our destinies. Perhaps we never were, but, it seems to me, we used to act as if we were, and I imagine that's the first step to control.

22   Never in my lifetime has it appeared to me more necessary for everyone to talk to everyone else, and never has it seemed to me that we have done so less.

23   Kids still talk about the things that deeply concern them, and I
propose that if we have nothing better to talk about than oil burners and the marriages of strolling players, we might as well hold our
peace and see what falls out of the mouths of babes.

24   I guess I will never get, man or boy, to hold forth at the dinner
table. But perhaps the kids will one day say, "You got to give the
old man this: When he had nothing to say — and that was a lot
of the time — he kept his mouth shut."

25   I can think of worse things for them to say.

QUESTIONS FOR REFLECTION, DISCUSSION, OR WRITING

(1) Do you think this essay is appropriately placed in the section on "Views
of Man"? Is what Smith has to say about Man important enough to really
matter? Explain.

(2) What are the techniques (or would you call them "gimmicks"?) which
give Smith's writing its individualistic style? Do you like the style, or do the
techniques themselves "get in the way"?

(3) Where in this selection do you find examples of apparent exaggeration?
Do you consider these a serious offense in an informal essay such as this?
Why, or why not?

(4) Do you think most children are as thoroughly disinterested in neighbors
and relatives as Smith claims to have been? Use illustrations, one way or another, from your own childhood or that of children you know.

(5) Smith says his sons "live in a world where children are believed to be
capable of conversation" (par. 8). Do you think the "modern" policy of letting children talk whenever they feel like it is entirely good? Why, or why not?

(6) The author says that no one listens very much to anybody else (par. 11).
Is this statement true, in your experience?

(7) What is a caricaturist (par. 3)? Explain the similarity between a caricaturist and a child. Do even adults tend to be caricaturists, at least of slight
acquaintances? How many different characteristics of most people do you
really bring to mind when you think of them? What kind of characteristics?

(8) Consider the author's theory (par. 18) that children "display our own
faults in a transparent way." How true is this?

(9) Do you agree with Mr. Smith that we should talk more about such
things as our fear of war, the hydrogen bomb, the lack of morals, the decline

of manners and kindness (par. 20)? Or do you think we may be better off discussing neighborhood affairs, oil burners, and news of relatives? Defend your opinion.

Stephen Vincent Benét

FREEDOM'S A HARD-BOUGHT THING

STEPHEN VINCENT BENÉT (1898-1943) *was an American poet, short-story writer, novelist, and, for a time, radio script writer. He won the Pulitzer Prize for Poetry for his long narrative poem* John Brown's Body. *Selected Works of Stephen Vincent Benét is a collection of his short stories and poems, one volume of each.*

FREEDOM'S A HARD-BOUGHT THING, *a short story written in 1940, is the only fiction used in this anthology outside the "Simple Enjoyment" section. It is included here because its theme is "freedom," and it will serve in a special way to introduce the few essays concerning freedom — a "View of Man" we can hardly ignore.*

Either prose fiction or poetry, although its first purpose should be enjoyment (you must realize by now, of course, that there is more than one kind of "enjoyment" for the mature reader), can serve as well as an essay, sometimes better, to communicate a writer's ideas, his observations on life which he may want to share with us. In "Freedom's a Hard-Bought Thing," Benét has something vital to share and, being a poet as well as a story-writer, he shares it in a beautiful, melodious prose that is near to poetry itself.

Also as poetry often does, this story makes use of **symbolism.** *A* **symbol** *is an object (or person or action) which, besides being real in itself, with a place of its own in the context of the story or poem, also suggests still another level of meaning to the observant reader. Some symbols are more or less universal in their suggestiveness (e.g., the flag suggests country and patriotism, the vulture represents death, the cross symbolizes Christianity), but others are symbolic only in the particular place and manner in which used. An example of this kind in "Freedom's a Hard-Bought Thing" is the imprint of Marster Shepley's heel in Cue's hand — a symbol of subservience which even Cue sensed but did not fully understand.*

But whether or not the characters themselves understand the symbolism which involves them, our understanding can do much to enrich our appreciation of good prose or poetry.

1   A LONG TIME AGO, in times gone by, in slavery times, there was a man named Cue. I want you to think about him. I've got a reason.

2   He got born like the cotton in the boll or the rabbit in the pea
patch. There wasn't any fine doings when he got born, but his
mammy was glad to have him. Yes. He didn't get born in the Big
House, or the overseer's house, or any place where the bearing was
easy or the work light. No, Lord. He came out of his mammy in a
field hand's cabin one sharp winter, and about the first thing he remembered was his mammy's face and the taste of a piece of bacon
rind and the light and shine of the pitch-pine fire up the chimney.
Well, now, he got born and there he was.

3   His daddy worked in the fields and his mammy worked in the
fields when she wasn't bearing. They were slaves; they chopped the
cotton and hoed the corn. They heard the horn blow before the light
came and the horn blow that meant the day's work was done. His
daddy was a strong man — strong in his back and his arms. The
white folks called him Cuffee. His mammy was a good woman, yes,
Lord. The white folks called her Sarah, and she was gentle with her
hands and gentle with her voice. She had a voice like the river going
by in the night, and at night when she wasn't too tired she'd sing
songs to little Cue. Some had foreign words in them — African
words. She couldn't remember what some of them meant, but they'd
come to her down out of time.

4   Now, how am I going to describe and explain about that time
when that time's gone? The white folks lived in the Big House and
they had many to tend on them. Old Marster, he lived there like
Pharaoh and Solomon, mighty splendid and fine. He had his flocks
and his herds, his butler and his baker; his fields ran from the river
to the woods and back again. He'd ride around the fields each day
on his big horse, Black Billy, just like thunder and lightning, and
evenings he'd sit at his table and drink his wine. Man, that was a
sight to see, with all the silver knives and the silver forks, the glass
decanters, and the gentlemen and ladies from all over. It was a sight
to see. When Cue was young, it seemed to him that Old Marster
must own the whole world, right up to the edge of the sky. You can't
blame him for thinking that.

5   There were things that changed on the plantation, but it didn't

From *Selected Works of Stephen Vincent Benét*, Holt, Rinehart and Winston,
Inc. Copyright 1940 by Stephen Vincent Benét. Reprinted by permission of
Brandt and Brandt.

change. There were bad times and good times. There was the time young Marse Edward got bit by the snake, and the time Big Rambo ran away and they caught him with the dogs and brought him back. There was a swivel-eyed overseer that beat folks too much, and then there was Mr. Wade, and he wasn't so bad. There was hog-killing time and Christmas and springtime and summertime. Cue didn't wonder about it or why things happened that way; he didn't expect it to be different. A bee in a hive don't ask you how there come to be a hive in the beginning. Cue grew up strong; he grew up smart with his hands. They put him in the blacksmith shop to help Daddy Jake; he didn't like it, at first, because Daddy Jake was mighty cross-tempered. Then he got to like the work; he learned to forge iron and shape it; he learned to shoe a horse and tire a wagon wheel, and everything a blacksmith does. One time they let him shoe Black Billy, and he shod him light and tight and Old Marster praised him in front of Mr. Wade. He was strong; he was black as night; he was proud of his back and his arms.

6   Now, he might have stayed that way — yes, he might. He heard freedom talk, now and then, but he didn't pay much mind to it. Cue wasn't a talker or a preacher; he was Cue and he worked in the blacksmith shop. He didn't want to be a field hand, but he didn't want to be a house servant either. He'd rather be Cue than poor white trash or owned by poor white trash. That's the way he felt; I'm obliged to tell the truth about that way.

7   Then there was a sickness came and his mammy and his daddy died of it. Old Miss got the doctor for them, but they died just the same. After that, Cue felt lonesome.

8   He felt lonesome and troubled in his mind. He'd seen his daddy and his mammy put in the ground and new slaves come to take their cabin. He didn't repine about that, because he knew things had to be that way. But when he went to bed at night, in the loft over the blacksmith shop, he'd keep thinking about his mammy and his daddy — how strong his daddy was and the songs that his mammy sang. They'd worked all their lives and had children, though he was the only one left, but the only place of their own they had was the place in the burying ground. And yet they'd been good and faithful servants, because Old Marster said so, with his hat off, when he buried them. The Big House stayed, and the cotton and the corn,

but Cue's mammy and daddy were gone like last year's crop. It made Cue wonder and trouble.

9   He began to take notice of things he'd never noticed. When the horn blew in the morning for the hands to go to the fields, he'd wonder who started blowing that horn, in the first place. It wasn't like thunder and lightning; somebody had started it. When he heard Old Marster say, when he was talking to a friend, "This damned epidemic! It's cost me eight prime field hands and the best-trained butler in the state. I'd rather have lost the Flyaway colt than Old Isaac," Cue put that down in his mind and pondered it. Old Marster didn't mean it mean, and he'd sat up with Old Isaac all night before he died. But Isaac and Cue and the Flyaway colt, they all belonged to Old Marster and he owned them, hide and hair. He owned them, like money in his pockets. Well, Cue had known that all his life, but because he was troubled now, it gave him a queer feeling.

10   Well, now, he was shoeing a horse for young Marster Shepley one day, and he shod it light and tight. And when he was through, he made a stirrup for young Marster Shepley, and young Marster Shepley mounted and threw him a silver bit with a laughing word. That shouldn't have bothered Cue, because gentlemen sometimes did that. And Old Marster wasn't mean; he didn't object. But all night Cue kept feeling the print of young Marster Shepley's heel in his hands. And yet he liked young Marster Shepley. He couldn't explain it at all.

11   Finally, Cue decided he must be conjured. He didn't know who had done it or why they'd done it. But he knew what he had to do. He had to go see Aunt Rachel.

12   Aunt Rachel was an old, old woman, and she lived in a cabin by herself, with her granddaughter, Sukey. She'd seen Old Marster's father and his father, and the tale went she'd seen George Washington with his hair all white, and General Lafayette in his gold-plated suit of clothes that the King of France gave him to fight in. Some folks said she was a conjure and some folks said she wasn't, but everybody on the plantation treated her mighty respectful, because, if she put her eye on you, she mightn't take it off. Well, his mammy had been friends with Aunt Rachel, so Cue went to see her.

13   She was sitting alone in her cabin by the low light of a fire. There was a pot on the fire, and now and then you could hear it bubble and

chunk, like a bullfrog chunking in the swamp, but that was the only sound. Cue made his obleegances to her and asked her about the misery in her back. Then he gave her a chicken he happened to bring along. It was a black rooster, and she seemed pleased to get it. She took it in her thin black hands and it fluttered and clucked a minute. So she drew a chalk line from its beak along a board, and then it stayed still and frozen. Well, Cue had seen that trick done before. But it was different, seeing it done in Aunt Rachel's cabin, with the big pot chunking on the fire. It made him feel uneasy and he jingled the bit in his pocket for company.

14   After a while, the old woman spoke. "Well, Son Cue," said she, "that's a fine young rooster you've brought me. What else did you bring me, Son Cue?"

15   "I brought you trouble," said Cue, in a husky voice, because that was all he could think of to say.

16   She nodded her head as if she'd expected that. "They mostly bring me trouble," she said. "They mostly brings trouble to Aunt Rachel. What kind of trouble, Son Cue? Man trouble or woman trouble?"

17   "It's my trouble," said Cue, and he told her the best way he could. When he'd finished, the pot on the fire gave a bubble and a croak, and the old woman took a long spoon and stirred it.

18   "Well, Son Cue, son of Cuffee, son of Shango," she said, "you've got a big trouble, for sure."

19   "Is it going to kill me dead?" said Cue.

20   "I can't tell you right about that," said Aunt Rachel. "I could give you lies and prescriptions. Maybe I would, to some folks. But your Granddaddy Shango was a powerful man. It took three men to put the irons on him, and I saw the irons break his heart. I won't lie to you, Son Cue. You've got a sickness."

21   "Is it a bad sickness?" said Cue.

22   "It's a sickness in your blood," said Aunt Rachel. "It's a sickness in your liver and your veins. Your daddy never had it that I knows of — he took after his mammy's side. But his daddy was a Corromantee, and they is bold and free, and you takes after him. It's the freedom sickness, Son Cue."

23   "The freedom sickness?" said Cue.

24   "The freedom sickness," said the old woman, and her little eyes

glittered like sparks. "Some they break and some they tame down," she said, "and some is neither to be tamed or broken. Don't I know the signs and the sorrow — me, that come through the middle passage on the slavery ship and seen my folks scattered like sand? Ain't I seen it coming, Lord — O Lord, ain't I seen it coming?"

25   "What's coming?" said Cue.

26   "A darkness in the sky and a cloud with a sword in it," said the old woman, stirring the pot, "because they hold our people and they hold our people."

27   Cue began to tremble. "I don't want to get whipped," he said. "I never been whipped — not hard."

28   "They whipped your Granddaddy Shango till the blood ran twinkling down his back," said the old woman, "but some you can't break or tame."

29   "I don't want to be chased by dogs," said Cue. "I don't want to hear the dogs belling and the paterollers after me."

30   The old woman stirred the pot.

31   "Old Marster, he's a good marster," said Cue. "I don't want to do him no harm. I don't want no trouble or projecting to get me into trouble."

32   The old woman stirred the pot and stirred the pot.

33   "O God, I want to be free," said Cue. "I just ache and hone to be free. How I going to be free, Aunt Rachel?"

34   "There's a road that runs underground," said the old woman. "I never seen it, but I knows of it. There's a railroad train that runs, sparking and snorting, underground through the earth. At least that's what they tell me. But I wouldn't know for sure," and she looked at Cue.

35   Cue looked back at her bold enough, for he'd heard about the Underground Railroad himself — just mentions and whispers. But he knew there wasn't any use asking the old woman what she wouldn't tell.

36   "How I going to find that road, Aunt Rachel?" he said.

37   "You look at the rabbit in the brier and you see what he do," said the old woman. "You look at the owl in the woods and you see what he do. You look at the star in the sky and you see what she do. Then you come back and talk to me. Now I'm going to eat, because I'm hungry."

38   That was all the words she'd say to him that night; but when Cue went back to his loft, her words kept boiling around in his mind. All night he could hear that train of railroad cars, snorting and sparking underground through the earth. So, next morning, he ran away.

39   He didn't run far or fast. How could he? He'd never been more than twenty miles from the plantation in his life; he didn't know the roads or the ways. He ran off before the horn, and Mr. Wade caught him before sundown. Now, wasn't he a stupid man, that Cue?

40   When they brought him back, Mr. Wade let him off light, because he was a good boy and never run away before. All the same, he got ten, and ten laid over the ten. Yellow Joe, the head driver, laid them on. The first time the whip cut into him, it was just like a fire on Cue's skin, and he didn't see how he could stand it. Then he got to a place where he could.

41   After it was over, Aunt Rachel crope up to his loft and had her granddaughter, Sukey, put salve on his back. Sukey, she was sixteen, and golden-skinned and pretty as a peach on a peach tree. She worked in the Big House and he never expected her to do a thing like that.

42   "I'm mighty obliged," he said, though he kept thinking it was Aunt Rachel got him into trouble and he didn't feel as obliged as he might.

43   "Is that all you've got to say to me, Son Cue?" said Aunt Rachel, looking down at him. "I told you to watch three things. Did you watch them?"

44   "No'm," said Cue. "I run off in the woods just like I was a wild turkey. I won't never do that no more."

45   "You're right, Son Cue," said the old woman. "Freedom's a hard-bought thing. So, now you've been whipped, I reckon you'll give it up."

46   "I been whipped," said Cue, "but there's a road running underground. You told me so. I been whipped, but I ain't beaten."

47   "Now you're learning a thing to remember," said Aunt Rachel, and went away. But Sukey stayed behind for a while and cooked Cue's supper. He never expected her to do a thing like that, but he liked it when she did.

48   When his back got healed, they put him with the field gang for a while. But then there was blacksmith work that needed to be done

and they put him back in the blacksmith shop. And things went on for a long time just the way they had before. But there was a difference in Cue. It was like he'd lived up till now with his ears and his eyes sealed over. And now he began to open his eyes and his ears.

49   He looked at the rabbit in the brier and he saw it could hide. He looked at the owl in the woods and he saw it went soft through the night. He looked at the star in the sky and he saw she pointed north. Then he began to figure.

50   He couldn't figure things fast, so he had to figure things slow. He figure the owl and the rabbit got wisdom the white folks don't know about. But he figure the white folks got wisdom he don't know about. They got reading and writing wisdom, and it seem mighty powerful. He ask Aunt Rachel if that's so, and she say it's so.

51   That's how come he learned to read and write. He ain't supposed to. But Sukey, she learned some of that wisdom, along with the young misses, and she teach him out of a little book she tote from the Big House. The little book, it's all about bats and rats and cats, and Cue figure whoever wrote it must be sort of touched in the head not to write about things folks would want to know instead of all those trifling animals. But he put himself to it and he learn. It almost bust his head, but he learn. It's a proud day for Cue when he write his name, "Cue," in the dust with the end of a stick and Sukey tell him that's right.

52   Now he began to hear the first rumblings of that train running underground — that train that's the Underground Railroad. Oh, children, remember the names of Levi Coffin and John Hansen! Remember the Quaker saints that hid the fugitive! Remember the names of all those that helped set our people free!

53   There's a word dropped here and a word dropped there and a word that's passed around. Nobody know where the word come from or where it goes, but it's there. There's many a word spoken in the quarters that the Big House never hears about. There's a heap said in front of the fire that never flies up the chimney. There's a name you tell to the grapevine that the grapevine don't tell back.

54   There was a white man, one day, came by, selling maps and pictures. The quality folks, they looked at his maps and pictures and he talked with them mighty pleasant and respectful. But while Cue

was tightening a bolt on his wagon, he dropped a word and a word. The word he said made that underground train come nearer.

55   Cue meet that man one night, all alone, in the woods. He's a quiet man with a thin face. He hold his life in his hands every day he walk about, but he don't make nothing of that. Cue's seen bold folks and bodacious folks, but it's the first time he's seen a man bold that way. It makes him proud to be a man. The man ask Cue questions and Cue give him answers. While he's seeing that man, Cue don't just think about himself any more. He think about all his people that's in trouble.

56   The man say something to him; he say, "No man own the earth. It's too big for one man." He say, "No man own another man; that's too big a thing too." Cue think about those words and ponder them. But when he gets back to his loft, the courage drains out of him and he sits on his straw tick, staring at the wall. That's the time the darkness comes to him and the shadow falls on him.

57   He aches and he hones for freedom, but he aches and he hones for Sukey too. And Long Ti's cabin is empty, and it's a good cabin. All he's got to do is to go to Old Marster and take Sukey with him. Old Marster don't approve to mix the field hand with the house servant, but Cue's different; Cue's a blacksmith. He can see the way Sukey would look, coming back to her in the evening. He can see the way she'd be in the morning before the horn. He can see all that. It ain't freedom, but it's what he's used to. And the other way's long and hard and lonesome and strange.

58   "O Lord, why you put this burden on a man like me?" say Cue. Then he listen a long time for the Lord to tell him, and it seem to him, at last, that he get an answer. The answer ain't in any words, but it's a feeling in his heart.

59   So when the time come and the plan ripe and they get to the boat on the river and they see there's one too many for the boat, Cue know the answer. He don't have to hear the quiet white man say, "There's one too many for the boat." He just pitch Sukey into it before he can think too hard. He don't say a word or a groan. He know it's that way and there's bound to be a reason for it. He stand on the bank in the dark and see the boat pull away, like Israel's children. Then he hear the shouts and the shot. He know what he's

bound to do then, and the reason for it. He know it's the paterollers, and he show himself. When he get back to the plantation, he's worn and tired. But the paterollers, they've chased him, instead of the boat.

60   He creep by Aunt Rachel's cabin and he see the fire at her window. So he scratch at the door and go in. And there she is, sitting by the fire, all hunched up and little.

61   "You looks poorly, Son Cue," she say, when he come in, though she don't take her eye off the pot.

62   "I'm poorly, Aunt Rachel," he say. "I'm sick and sorry and distressed."

63   "What's the mud on your jeans, Son Cue?" she say, and the pot, it bubble and croak.

64   "That's the mud of the swamp where I hid from the paterollers," he say.

65   "What's the hole in your leg, Son Cue?" she say, and the pot, it croak and bubble.

66   "That's the hole from the shot they shot at me," say Cue. "The blood most nearly dried, but it make me lame. But Israel's children, they's safe."

67   "They's across the river?" say the old woman.

68   "They's across the river," say Cue. "They ain't room for no more in the boat. But Sukey, she's across."

69   "And what will you do now, Son Cue?" say the old woman. "For that was your chance and your time, and you give it up for another. And tomorrow morning, Mr. Wade, he'll see that hole in your leg and he'll ask questions. It's a heavy burden you've laid on yourself, Son Cue."

70   "It's a heavy burden," say Cue, "and I wish I was shut of it. I never asked to take no such burden. But freedom's a hard-bought thing."

71   The old woman stand up sudden, and for once she look straight and tall. "Now bless the Lord!" she say. "Bless the Lord and praise him! I come with my mammy in the slavery ship — I come through the middle passage. There ain't many that remember that, these days, or care about it. There ain't many that remember the red flag that witched us on board or how we used to be free. Many thousands gone, and the thousands of many thousands that lived and died in

slavery. But I remember. I remember them all. Then they took me into the Big House — me that was a Mandingo and a witch woman — and the way I live in the Big House, that's between me and my Lord. If I done wrong, I done paid for it — I paid for it with weeping and sorrow. That's before Old Miss' time and I help raise up Old Miss. They sell my daughter to the South and my son to the West, but I raise up Old Miss and tend on her. I ain't going to repine of that. I count the hairs on Old Miss' head when she's young, and she turn to me, and helpless. And for that there'll be a kindness between me and the Big House — a kindness that folks will remember. But my children's children shall be free."

72   "You do this to me," say Cue, and he look at her, and he look dangerous. "You do this to me, old woman," he say, and his breath come harsh in his throat, and his hands twitch.

73   "Yes," she say, and look him straight in the eyes. "I do to you what I never even do for my own. I do it for your Granddaddy Shango, that never turn to me in the light of the fire. He turn to that soft Eboe woman, and I have to see it. He roar like a lion in the chains, and I have to see that. So, when you come, I try you and I test you, to see if you fit to follow after him. And because you fit to follow after him, I put freedom in your heart, Son Cue."

74   "I never going to be free," say Cue, and look at his hands. "I done broke all the rules. They bound to sell me now."

75   "You'll be sold and sold again," say the old woman. "You'll know the chains and the whip. I can't help that. You'll suffer for your people and with your people. But while one man's got freedom in his heart, his children bound to know the tale."

76   She put the lid on the pot and it stop bubbling.

77   "Now I come to the end of my road," she say, "but the tale don't stop there. The tale go backward to Africa and it go forward, like clouds and fire. It go, laughing and grieving forever, through the earth and the air and the waters — my people's tale."

78   Then she drop her hands in her lap and Cue creep out of the cabin. He know then he's bound to be a witness, and it make him feel cold and hot. He know then he's bound to be a witness and tell that tale. O Lord, it's hard to be a witness, and Cue know that. But it help him in the days to come.

79   Now, when he get sold, that's when Cue feel the iron in his heart.

Before that, and all his life, he despise bad servants and bad marsters. He live where the marster's good; he don't take much mind of
other places. He's a slave, but he's Cue, the blacksmith, and Old
Marster and Old Miss, they tend to him. Now he know the iron in
his heart and what it's like to be a slave.

80   He know that on the rice fields in the hot sun. He know that,
working all day for a handful of corn. He know the bad marsters
and the cruel overseers. He know the bite of the whip and the gall
of the iron on the ankle. Yes, Lord, he know tribulation. He know
his own tribulation and the tribulation of his people. But all the
time, somehow, he keep freedom in his heart. Freedom mighty hard
to root out when it's in the heart.

81   He don't know the day or the year, and he forget, half the time,
there ever was a gal named Sukey. All he don't forget is the noise of
the train in his ears, the train snorting and sparking underground.
He think about it at nights till he dream it carry him away. Then he
wake up with the horn. He feel ready to die then, but he don't die.
He live through the whip and the chain; he live through the iron
and the fire. And finally he get away.

82   When he get away, he ain't like the Cue he used to be — not even
back at Old Marster's place. He hide in the woods like a rabbit, he
slip through the night like an owl. He go cold and hungry, but the
star keep shining over him and he keep his eyes on the star. They
set the dogs after him and he hear the dogs belling and yipping
through the woods.

83   He scared when he hear the dogs, but he ain't scared like he used
to be. He ain't more scared than any man. He killed the big dog in
the clearing — the big dog with the big voice — and he do it with his
naked hands. He cross water three times after that to kill the scent,
and he go on.

84   He got nothing to help him — no, Lord — but he got a star. The
star shine in the sky and the star shine — the star point north with
its shining. You put that star in the sky, O Lord; you put it for the
prisoned and the humble. You put it there — you ain't never going
to blink it out.

85   He hungry and he eat green corn and cowpeas. He thirsty and he
drink swamp water. One time he lie two days in the swamp, too
puny to get up on his feet, and he know they hunting around him.

He think that's the end of Cue. But after two days he lift his head and his hand. He kill a snake with a stone, and after he's cut out the poison bag, he eat the snake to strengthen him, and go on.

86 He don't know what the day is when he come to the wide, cold river. The river yellow and foaming, and Cue can't swim. But he hide like a crawdad on the bank; he make himself a little raft with two logs. He know this time's the last time, and he's obliged to drown. But he put out on the raft and it drift him to the freedom side. He mighty weak by then.

87 He mighty weak, but he careful. He know tales of Billy Shea, the slave catcher; he remember those tales. He slide into the town by night, like a shadow, like a ghost. He beg broken victuals at a door; the woman give them to him, but she look at him suspicious. He make up a tale to tell her, but he don't think she believe the tale. In the gutter he find a newspaper; he pick it up and look at the notices. There's a notice about a runaway man named Cue. He look at it and it make the heart beat in his breast.

88 He patient; he mighty careful. He leave that town behind. He got the name of another town, Cincinnati, and a man's name in that town. He don't know where it is; he have to ask his way, but he do it mighty careful. One time he ask a yellow man directions; he don't like the look on the yellow man's face. He remember Aunt Rachel; he tell the yellow man he conjure his liver out if the yellow man tell him wrong. Then the yellow man scared and tell him right. He don't hurt the yellow man; he don't blame him for not wanting trouble. But he make the yellow man change pants with him, because his pants mighty ragged.

89 He patient; he very careful. When he get to the place he been told about, he look all about that place. It's a big house; it don't look right. He creep around to the back — he creep and he crawl. He look in a window; he see white folks eating their supper. They just look like any white folks. He expect them to look different. He feel mighty bad. All the same, he rap at the window the way he been told. They don't nobody pay attention and he just about to go away. Then the white man get up from the table and open the back door a crack. Cue breathe in the darkness.

90 "God bless the stranger the Lord sends us," say the white man in a low, clear voice, and Cue run to him and stumble, and the white

man catch him. He look up and it's a white man, but he ain't like thunder and lightning.

91   He take Cue and wash his wounds and bind them up. He feed him and hide him under the floor of the house. He ask him his name and where he's from. Then he send him on. O Lord, remember thy tried servant, Asaph Brown! Remember his name!

92   They send him from there in a wagon, and he's hidden in the straw at the bottom. They send him from the next place in a closed cart with six others, and they can't say a word all night. One time a tollkeeper ask them what's in the wagon, and the driver say, "Southern calico," and the tollkeeper laugh. Cue always recollect that.

93   One time they get to big water — so big it look like the ocean. They cross that water in a boat; they get to the other side. When they get to the other side, they sing and pray, and white folks look on, curious. But Cue don't even feel happy; he just feel he want to sleep.

94   He sleep like he never sleep before — not for days and years. When he wake up, he wonder; he hardly recollect where he is. He lying in the loft of a barn. Ain't nobody around him. He get up and go out in the air. It's a fine sunny day.

95   He get up and go out. He say to himself, *I'm free*, but it don't take hold yet. He say to himself, *This is Canada and I'm free*, but it don't take hold. Then he start to walk down the street.

96   The first white man he meet on the street, he scrunch up in himself and start to run across the street. But the white man don't pay him any mind. Then he know.

97   He say to himself in his mind, *I'm free. My name's Cue — John H. Cue. I got a strong back and strong arms. I got freedom in my heart. I got a first name and a last name and a middle name. I never had them all before.*

98   He say to himself, *My name's Cue — John H. Cue. I got a name and a tale to tell. I got a hammer to swing. I got a tale to tell my people. I got recollection. I call my first son 'John Freedom Cue.' I call my first daughter 'Come-Out-of-the-Lion's-Mouth.'*

99   Then he walk down the street, and he pass a blacksmith shop. The blacksmith, he's an old man and he lift the hammer heavy. Cue look in that shop and smile.

100   He pass on; he go his way. And soon enough he see a girl like a peach tree — a girl named Sukey — walking free down the street.

QUESTIONS FOR REFLECTION, DISCUSSION, OR WRITING

(1) Man has held man in bondage, of one kind or another, almost since the beginning of human history. Explain how this simple story of one man's yearning and struggle for freedom could be used as a sort of analogy for whole countries, whole races of men, in their yearning and struggle. Is there more than one point of comparison in such an analogy?

(2) Name as many countries as you can whose present status is analogous to some phase of Cue's story.

(3) Select some of the best portions of this story and read them aloud, slowly, letting yourself feel and express Benét's melodious flow and rhythm. (Try the first three paragraphs, as a beginning.)

(4) Explain the *symbolism* of the morning horn (mentioned repeatedly throughout the first part of the story) . . . of Marster Shepley's heel print in Cue's hand (par. 10) . . . of the irons on Shango (20 and later) . . . of the "darkness in the sky and a cloud with a sword in it" (26) . . . of the star (84) . . . of the white man and his welcome (90) . . . of the old blacksmith (99).

(5) In paragraph 5 is an analogy — brief, but useful in explaining a reason. Identify it.

(6) Find the allusions — which, as it happens, are also similes — in paragraphs 4 and 59.

(7) How do you like Benét's choices of metaphors and similes? Consider, especially, "a voice like the river going by in the night" (par. 3) and "gone like last year's crop" (8).

(8) Do you find Benét's use of dialect difficult to read (as dialect frequently is)? Does it contribute to the artistic quality of the story — *i.e.*, to help achieve the soft, melodious quality of the prose? Explain and illustrate.

(9) Does Cue ever learn that Aunt Rachel is not using witchcraft in advising him? If so, where? How does he react?

(10) Now, since reading this story, comment further on Thoreau's remark that "it is hard to have a Southern overseer . . . but worst of all when you are the slave-driver of yourself." Do you suppose Cue or Aunt Rachel would have agreed with him?

Patrick Henry
LIBERTY OR DEATH

PATRICK HENRY, *a Virginia lawyer and political and military leader during the Revolutionary period, delivered his most famous oration, printed below, in 1775. He was addressing the Virginia convention of delegates gathered to discuss the advisability of armed resistance to Britain. Much of the strength of the speech was due to Henry's skillful blending of logical argument and passionate persuasion. The technique was apparently highly successful: his resolutions to fight for freedom, resolutions which had previously met with strong opposition, were now passed without a dissenting vote — and Patrick Henry later became the first governor of the state of Virginia.*

1   MR. PRESIDENT: — No man thinks more highly than I do of the patriotism, as well as abilities, of the very worthy gentlemen who have just addressed the House. But different men often see the same subject in different lights; and, therefore, I hope that it will not be thought disrespectful to those gentlemen, if, entertaining as I do, opinions of a character very opposite to theirs, I shall speak forth my sentiments freely and without reserve. This is no time for ceremony. The question before the House is one of awful moment to this country. For my own part I consider it as nothing less than a question of freedom or slavery; and in proportion to the magnitude of the subject ought to be the freedom of the debate. It is only in this way that we can hope to arrive at truth, and fulfill the great responsibility which we hold to God and our country. Should I keep back my opinions at such a time, through fear of giving offense, I should consider myself as guilty of treason toward my country, and of an act of disloyalty toward the majesty of heaven, which I revere above all earthly kings.

2   Mr. President, it is natural to man to indulge in the illusions of hope. We are apt to shut our eyes against a painful truth, and listen to the song of that siren, till she transforms us into beasts. Is this the part of wise men, engaged in a great and arduous struggle for liberty? Are we disposed to be of the number of those who, having eyes, see not, and having ears, hear not, the things which so nearly concern their temporal salvation? For my part, whatever anguish of spirit it

may cost, I am willing to know the whole truth; to know the worst and to provide for it.

3   I have but one lamp by which my feet are guided; and that is the lamp of experience. I know of no way of judging of the future but by the past. And judging by the past, I wish to know what there has been in the conduct of the British ministry for the last ten years to justify those hopes with which gentlemen have been pleased to solace themselves and the House? Is it that insidious smile with which our petition has been lately received? Trust it not, sir; it will prove a snare to your feet. Suffer not yourselves to be betrayed with a kiss. Ask yourselves how this gracious reception of our petition comports with these warlike preparations which cover our waters and darken our land. Are fleets and armies necessary to a work of love and reconciliation? Have we shown ourselves so unwilling to be reconciled, that force must be called in to win back our love? Let us not deceive ourselves, sir. These are the implements of war and subjugation; the last arguments to which kings resort. I ask gentlemen, sir, what means this martial array, if its purpose be not to force us to submission? Can gentlemen assign any other possible motives for it? Has Great Britain any enemy in this quarter of the world, to call for all this accumulation of navies and armies? No, sir, she has none. They are meant for us; they can be meant for no other. They are sent over to bind and rivet upon us those chains which the British ministry have been so long forging. And what have we to oppose them? Shall we try argument? Sir, we have been trying that for the last ten years. Have we anything new to offer on the subject? Nothing. We have held the subject up in every light of which it is capable; but it has been all in vain. Shall we resort to entreaty and humble supplication? What terms shall we find which have not been already exhausted? Let us not, I beseech you, sir, deceive ourselves longer. Sir, we have done everything that could be done to avert the storm which is now coming on. We have petitioned; we have remonstrated; we have supplicated; we have prostrated ourselves before the throne, and have implored its interposition to arrest the tyrannical hands of the ministry parliament. Our petitions have been slighted; our remonstrances have produced additional violence and insult; our supplications have been disregarded; and we have been spurned, with contempt, from the foot of the throne. In vain, after these things,

may we indulge the fond hope of peace and reconciliation. There is no longer any room for hope. If we wish to be free — if we mean to preserve inviolate those inestimable privileges for which we have been so long contending — if we mean not basely to abandon the noble struggle in which we have been so long engaged, and which we have pledged ourselves never to abandon until the glorious object of our contest shall be obtained, we must fight! I repeat it, sir, we must fight! An appeal to arms and to the God of Hosts is all that is left us!

4   They tell us, sir, that we are weak; unable to cope with so formidable an adversary. But when shall we be stronger? Will it be the next week, or the next year? Will it be when we are totally disarmed, and when a British guard shall be stationed in every house? Shall we gather strength by irresolution and inaction? Shall we acquire the means of effectual resistance by lying supinely on our backs, and hugging the delusive phantom of hope, until our enemies shall have bound us hand and foot? Sir, we are not weak, if we make a proper use of the means which the God of nature hath placed in our power. Three millions of people, armed in the holy cause of liberty, and in such a country as that which we possess, are invincible by any force which our enemy can send against us. Besides, sir, we shall not fight our battles alone. There is a just God who presides over the destinies of nations; and who will raise up friends to fight our battles for us. The battle, sir, is not to the strong alone; it is to the vigilant, the active, the brave. Besides, sir, we have no election. If we were base enough to desire it, it is now too late to retire from the contest. There is no retreat but in submission and slavery! Our chains are forged! Their clanking may be heard on the plains of Boston! The war is inevitable — and let it come! I repeat it, sir, let it come!

5   It is in vain, sir, to extenuate the matter. Gentlemen may cry peace, peace — but there is no peace. The war is actually begun! The next gale that sweeps from the North will bring to our ears the clash of resounding arms! Our brethren are already in the field! Why stand we here idle? What is it that gentlemen wish? What would they have? Is life so dear, or peace so sweet, as to be purchased at the price of chains and slavery? Forbid it, Almighty God! I know not what course others may take; but as for me, give me liberty, or give me death!

QUESTIONS FOR REFLECTION, DISCUSSION, OR WRITING

(1) Do you agree that this historical selection belongs in the "Views of Man" section, rather than in "Exploring the Past"? Do you think the problem and the philosophy expressed by Henry *are* things of the past? Explain.

(2) Where in today's world can we find parallels to the problem the Colonial delegation faced? Do we sometimes still find, in effect, the same fervent answer as Henry expressed in the last sentence of his speech? If so, where in recent years?

(3) Find examples of both argument and persuasion in the speech and try to show why such a combination is sometimes more effective than either if used alone.

(4) Contributing to the power of the speech is Henry's use of strong metaphors, such as "warlike preparations which cover our waters and darken our lands," and "by lying supinely on our backs, and hugging the delusive phantom of hope, until our enemies have bound us hand and foot." Three of the most powerful metaphors use the rather obvious symbol of "chains." Find and study these three (remember Shango's chains, in the preceding story), and then discuss the psychological strategy of this echoing symbol-metaphor.

(5) Explain the allusion involved in his plea, "Suffer not yourself to be betrayed with a kiss."

(6) Compare Henry's liberty-philosophy with that of Cue in "Freedom's a Hard-Bought Thing."

(7) Compare the philosophy here with that of Bertrand Russell and his followers in England (and a few in America, too), whose slogan is "Better Red than Dead!" How do you personally feel about the matter? Do you think the threat of nuclear destruction demands a softer attitude than Henry's? Explain your stand.

David Lawrence

THE BIG PRISON

DAVID LAWRENCE, *long-time Washington correspondent, has been president and editor of U.S. News and World Report since its founding. He also writes frequent articles for other magazines and a newspaper column which is syndicated in 280 dailies of the United States. Among his several books: Nine Honest Men and Diary of a Washington Correspondent.*

U.S. NEWS AND WORLD REPORT *is the result of a merger, in 1948, of* United
States News *(in publication since 1933) and its sister publication,* World Report *(since 1946), both of which David Lawrence was founder and president.
Published in Washington and covering both national and international news,
the magazine now has a weekly circulation of well over a million.*

THE BIG PRISON, *which deals with a more modern-day topic of freedom, was
the* U.S. News and World Report *editorial for the issue of August 28, 1961.*

1   MORE THAN 17,000,000 persons were imprisoned a few days ago
in East Germany.

2   They have committed no crime. They have not trespassed upon
any other people's territory. They are nevertheless confined within
borders prescribed by their Communist masters. Armed guards patrol
the barbed-wire and concrete barriers erected to prevent their leaving the big prison.

3   Across a line through the city of Berlin are many relatives and
friends whom they are forbidden to visit.

4   Alone and unbefriended by any other nation, the East German
people suffer in silence — unable to express their will and bound by
the mandate of their oppressors not to dare to depart to other countries or even to other parts of their own German homeland.

5   The world has not often witnessed in our times such a colossal
act of cruelty.

6   In these days when "self-determination" is the rallying cry of millions of persons in Africa, many of them not yet fit for self-govern-
ment, the majority of nations have given more than lip service to the
idea that colonialism should be abolished and independence granted.

7   But where are the champions of the imprisoned millions in East
Germany? Do the Afro-Asian members of the United Nations lift
their voices in protest or demand special meetings of the General Assembly to seek justice for the 17,000,000 prisoners — educated human beings who obviously deserve a chance to govern themselves?
And what do we in America or our friends in Western Europe do
about it?

8   Timidly and with a mistaken belief that it is important not to
offend Nikita Khrushchev, the American Government's broadcasts

Reprinted from U.S. News & World Report (August 28, 1961), published at
Washington.

to East Germany tell the people there to be calm and to do nothing to bring about disturbances of any kind. This is advice based on our own alleged self-interest. But it is really a form of appeasement reminiscent of the days of Munich.

9   Here, for instance, is an extract from an editorial published in the *New York Times* of August 16 and transmitted by the various press services to the newspapers of Europe:

10   "While the Soviets seek to stir up revolution and war against us wherever they can — even to the perfidy of the Hitler-Stalin pact — we must seek to discourage anti-Communist revolts in order to avert bloodshed and war. We must, under our principles, live with evil even if by doing so we help to stabilize tottering Communist regimes, as in East Germany, and perhaps even expose citadels of freedom, like West Berlin, to slow death by strangulation."

11   Does this expression by one of the leading newspapers of the United States represent the thinking of the American people today? Have we forgotten the ideals of yesteryears — the many words of sympathy we have written into the platforms of both of our political parties in decades past as we openly took our stand by the side of oppressed peoples?

12   Do we really mean to remain passive now lest we offend the Communists? Will this not embolden them to take further steps — perhaps the next time to imprison the people of West Berlin, too?

13   For if we are obsessed with fears and afflicted with a defeatism which makes us afraid even to encourage other peoples to seek their freedom, then the Soviet Union need have no concern about trespassing further on human rights.

14   The West Germans are plainly disappointed that their Western allies have indicated their aloofness toward the problem of the East German people. Small wonder that it was deemed necessary by President Kennedy to send Vice President Lyndon Johnson to West Berlin to help bolster the morale of the people there.

15   True enough, nobody wants to see any incitement to war. But wars come from timorousness, and not from resoluteness.

16   The Soviet Union has committed a major crime in imprisoning the people of East Germany. Will the people of the West fail to speak up against this act of inhumanity?

17   Diplomatic notes of protest are not enough. Throughout the

United States and other Western countries days of mourning should be proclaimed as millions of free men go to their churches to pray to God to give the East German people the strength to rise up against their captors and emerge from their enslavement.

18   Demonstrations in all parts of the world should be held immediately so that there can be recorded the protest of a shocked humanity.

19   For Communism, which boasts of its prowess in science and pledges great achievements in economic fields, reveals its true character as it denies human beings their freedom and their individual liberties.

20   The verdict of the world must be registered, and the United States should take the lead in denouncing the unjustified imprisonment of 17,000,000 human beings behind the walls of imperialistic Communism.

QUESTIONS FOR REFLECTION, DISCUSSION, OR WRITING

(1) Do you see any basic differences between the plight of these 17,000,000 "prisoners" and that of the American Colonials of Patrick Henry's time? Between the 17,000,000 and Cue ("Freedom's a Hard-Bought Thing")? Or between them and the Arabs of Algeria? Explain the differences, if any.

(2) What would have been Patrick Henry's response to the American government broadcasts (par. 8) and the *New York Times'* editorial (10)? Do you agree with the *Times'* line of reasoning? Why, or why not?

(3) Discuss Lawrence's assertion that "wars come from timorousness, and not from resoluteness" (par. 15).

(4) Most of the police and civil officials of East Berlin are Germans, and they helped "imprison" the city. What do you think would cause them to so assist the Russians in their tyranny? How many people do you know who would be so helpful if the same thing were happening in your home town? Can you be sure even of yourself? If so, how?

Norman Cousins

TRIUMPH OVER THE BULLY

NORMAN COUSINS, *editor of* Saturday Review (*see p. 155*) *since 1942, is also a noted lecturer, is active on various important boards and committees, and has been the recipient of numerous awards and citations. At one time he was literary editor and managing editor of* Current History Magazine. *The many books which he has written or edited include* Modern Man Is Obsolete, Talks with Nehru, *and* In God We Trust.

TRIUMPH OVER THE BULLY *was a* Saturday Review *editorial for the May 14, 1960 issue. In it the author suggests (partly by analogy) a way in which, eventually, the freedom of man may be assured. It is an optimistic little essay, but even optimism needs to be looked at critically.*

1   THE BUSINESS of coping with bullies comes close to being the oldest business in the world. Most men have neither the desire nor the stomach for altercation or domination. Those who do frequently have been able to prey on the others. Sometimes, as in the case of the American West, the bullies would put themselves above the law, using guns as the source of both authority and immunity.

2   The individual may have been no match for the bully; but several hundred men could come together and make the decisions that would provide for the common safety. They could draw up the rules of the game, designate those who would have the authority to carry arms, and establish qualified men to guard against the abuse of power. In this way, through law, the weak became strong and the domain of bullies was ended.

3   In a curious sense, the advent of total power has pushed the entire human race back to the time when men were at the mercy of bullies; that is, a time when government either did not exist or was incapable of dealing with lawlessness. The dominant condition of mankind today is anarchy. Whatever the forms of law and order in today's world may be, they have only limited validity. For these forms exist only inside the nation. But the over-riding danger to life comes from the absence of authority over the nation itself. In the absence of a higher tribunal, a nation interprets for itself the require-

ments of justice. It inevitably pursues its own self-interest in contact with other nations. And a nation knows no law except self-determination. But the self-determination of one nation is the anarchy of all. And the ultimate consequences of world anarchy on the individual are even more menacing than they would be inside the nation itself. For the end product of world anarchy could mean the end of the age of man, whereas anarchy inside the nation might inflict its harm only on a limited number.

4   The individual in today's world, therefore, can no longer look to the nation as the main source of his security. It is able no longer to protect him against invasion or assault from other nations. It is able no longer to furnish the main conditions of his growth or to safeguard his values or institutions or culture or property. No matter how wide the oceans that surround the nation, no matter how bristling its defenses, its people are totally vulnerable to shattering attack. The nation possesses retaliatory power, true, but even in the exercise of that power it engages in a form of self-assault, for power in today's world is directed against the delicate and precarious conditions that make existence possible, and, indeed, against the mainstream of life itself.

5   It becomes necessary, then, for the nation to develop new means of performing its historic role. If the existence of force can no longer serve as the main source of a nation's security, something else will have to take its place if human society is to be able to endure and function.

6   As in the case of the individual or the group confronted by the bully, the need is for enough peoples to come together to determine how to protect themselves in the light of existing conditions, and how to establish whatever new approaches or agencies may be required for the common safety. The new power that must be brought into being is power in its most natural form. It is the power represented by the human will — the power of consensus. Out of it can come the energy and momentum for building a new flooring for human society. Out of it, too, can come workable checks on heretofore uncontrolled force.

7   This leads to a paradox. The individual wants to create something beyond the nation that can give him the protections once afforded by the nation, yet the nation itself is his only instrumentality for

achieving it. The only place an individual can find firm footing for a stand is inside a nation; how, therefore, can he be effective outside the nation?

8   Just as there is a concept of natural law that transcends the state, so there is a concept of natural will that can transcend the nation. A new force that is emerging in the world is the force of world public opinion. It is as yet without formal channels or organs of expression. No matter; it is a developing new power and it is becoming increasingly audible. Public opinion inside the nation is at its most powerful when it is concerned with questions of justice or over-riding moral issues. Similarly, world public opinion can make its power felt on the big questions that have moral content or that are concerned with the rational means of safeguarding human life.

9   No freedom is more meaningful for the individual of a free society than to use that freedom in a cause that is not confined to the nation. He can use his footing inside the nation to work for a consensus inside the nation, one that can lead to effective commitments by the nation to an ordered society.

10   It is not necessary for the nation to be dissolved in order to create a situation of safety on earth. It is necessary only for national sovereignty to be made meaningful, to eliminate those attributes that add up to world anarchy and to assure and underwrite those that add up to national responsibility.

QUESTIONS FOR REFLECTION, DISCUSSION, OR WRITING

(1) What do you think was the author's purpose in writing "Triumph over the Bully"? How successful was he in achieving that purpose? Was it worthwhile?

(2) In paragraphs 1, 2, and 6, Cousins uses a simple form of analogy to help us understand his theme. What is his theme? How useful is the analogy?

(3) How important is community public opinion in causing individuals to behave?

(4) Cousins says world public opinion is "without formal channels or organs of expressions" (par. 8). What, then, is the United Nations for? Is it ineffective in this respect?

(5) Would you, any time in the foreseeable future, want to trust your protection, your destiny and that of the United States, to the "opinion" of a

world largely composed of avowed enemies and illiterate or jealous "have-not" nations? Can we much longer have any choice in this matter? Explain your opinion.

(6) Why do you suppose "world opinion" failed (either to develop at all or to do any good) in preventing Russia's renewal of bomb testing? The imprisoning of East Berlin? The fall of Hungary? Of Tibet?

(7) Do you suppose the settlers of the West would have been able to control "the bully" with just opinion and no guns or "hanging trees"? Might we need to stretch Cousins' analogy a bit further to make it realistic enough to be meaningful? If not, what alternatives are there? Be prepared to justify your stand.

John F. Kennedy

INAUGURAL ADDRESS, 1961

JOHN F. KENNEDY, *the whole world's attention focused on him, made the following address at his inauguration on January 20, 1961. The reasons for the world's interest were obvious: he had just become, for better or for worse, the leader of the free world; he was a very young, vigorous man succeeding an old and sometimes sick one; it was only the fifth time in the twentieth century that a U.S. President had succeeded one of the opposite political party, and this by an astonishingly close margin of victory; he had already promised drastic changes in American policies; he was the first Roman Catholic ever to serve as U.S. President. This was a speech that was certain to be widely quoted, discussed, examined in every country of the world.*

And, surprisingly, the speech received little but praise. To quote from Time *Magazine (which had not supported Kennedy in the campaign): "Passages from the speech were compared, as examples of inspired and inspiring eloquence, with the resounding 'The only thing we have to fear is fear itself' of Franklin Roosevelt's 1933 inaugural. . . . Reaction to the speech was immediate. From all shades of political outlook, from people who had voted for Kennedy in November and people who had voted against him, came a surge of praise and congratulation. Even so partisan a Republican as Senate Minority Leader Everett Dirksen described it as 'inspiring' and as a 'very compact message of hope.' "*

If approved and acclaimed by most Americans, political friends and foes alike, then this address must have succeeded in expressing the philosophy of the United States itself. And that is why it is included in this section of the book. We have been reading the credos of individual men — this speech seemed to be the credo, the statement of beliefs, of a whole nation of men in 1961.

1   WE OBSERVE today not a victory of party but a celebration of freedom — symbolizing an end as well as a beginning — signifying renewal as well as change. For I have sworn before you and Almighty God the same solemn oath our forebears prescribed nearly a century and three quarters ago.

2   The world is very different now. For man holds in his mortal hands the power to abolish all form of human poverty and to abolish all form of human life. And yet the same revolutionary beliefs for which our forebears fought are still at issue around the globe — the belief that the rights of man come not from the generosity of the state but from the hand of God.

3   We dare not forget today that we are the heirs of that first revolution. Let the word go forth from this time and place, to friend and foe alike, that the torch has been passed to a new generation of Americans — born in this century, tempered by war, disciplined by a cold and bitter peace, proud of our ancient heritage — and unwilling to witness or permit the slow undoing of those human rights to which this nation has always been committed, and to which we are committed today.

4   Let every nation know, whether it wish us well or ill, that we shall pay any price, bear any burden, meet any hardship, support any friend or oppose any foe in order to assure the survival and success of liberty.

5   This much we pledge — and more.

6   To those old allies whose cultural and spiritual origins we share, we pledge the loyalty of faithful friends. United, there is little we cannot do in a host of new cooperative ventures. Divided, there is little we can do — for we dare not meet a powerful challenge at odds and split asunder.

7   To those new states whom we now welcome to the ranks of the free, we pledge our word that one form of colonial control shall not have passed merely to be replaced by a far more iron tyranny. We shall not always expect to find them supporting our every view. But we shall always hope to find them always strongly supporting their own freedom — and to remember that, in the past, those who foolishly sought to find power by riding on the tiger's back inevitably ended up inside.

8   To those peoples in the huts and villages of half the globe strug-

gling to break the bonds of mass misery, we pledge our best efforts to help them help themselves, for whatever period is required — not because the Communists are doing it, not because we seek their votes, but because it is right. If the free society cannot help the many who are poor, it can never save the few who are rich.

9   To our sister republics south of our border, we offer a special pledge — to convert our good words into good deeds — in a new alliance for progress — to assist free men and free governments in casting off the chains of poverty. But this peaceful revolution of hope cannot become the prey of hostile powers. Let all our neighbors know that we shall join with them to oppose aggression or subversion anywhere in the Americas. And let every other power know that this hemisphere intends to remain the master of its own house.

10   To that world assembly of sovereign states, the United Nations, our last best hope in an age where the instruments of war have far out-paced the instruments of peace, we renew our pledge of support — to prevent its becoming merely a forum for invective — to strengthen its shield of the new and the weak — and to enlarge the area to which its writ may run.

11   Finally, to those nations who would make themselves our adversary, we offer not a pledge but a request: that both sides begin anew the quest for peace, before the dark powers of destruction unleashed by science engulf all humanity in planned or accidental self-destruction.

12   We dare not tempt them with weakness. For only when our arms are sufficient beyond doubt can we be certain beyond doubt that they will never be employed.

13   But neither can two great and powerful groups of nations take comfort from their present course — both sides overburdened by the cost of modern weapons, both rightly alarmed by the steady spread of the deadly atom, yet both racing to alter that uncertain balance of terror that stays the hand of mankind's final war.

14   So let us begin anew — remembering on both sides that civility is not a sign of weakness, and sincerity is always subject to proof. Let us never negotiate out of fear. But let us never fear to negotiate.

15   Let both sides explore what problems unite us instead of belaboring the problems that divide us.

16   Let both sides, for the first time, formulate serious and precise

proposals for the inspection and control of arms — and bring the absolute power to destroy other nations under the absolute control of all nations.

17   Let both sides join to invoke the wonders of science instead of its terrors. Together let us explore the stars, conquer the deserts, eradicate disease, tap the ocean depths and encourage the arts and commerce.

18   Let both sides unite to heed in all corners of the earth the command of Isaiah — to "undo the heavy burdens . . . (and) let the oppressed go free."

19   And if a beach-head of cooperation can be made in the jungles of suspicion, let both sides join in the next task: creating, not a new balance of power, but a new world of law, where the strong are just and the weak secure and the peace preserved forever.

20   All this will not be finished in the first one hundred days. Nor will it be finished in the first one thousand days, nor in the life of this administration, nor even, perhaps, in our lifetime on this planet. But let us begin.

21   In your hands, my fellow citizens, more than in mine, will rest the final success or failure of our course. Since this country was founded, each generation has been summoned to give testimony to its national loyalty. The graves of young Americans who answered that call encircle the globe.

22   Now the trumpet summons us again — not as a call to bear arms, though arms we need — not as a call to battle, though embattled we are — but a call to bear the burden of a long twilight struggle, year in and year out, "rejoicing in hope, patient in tribulation" — a struggle against the common enemies of man: tyranny, poverty, disease and war itself.

23   Can we forge against these enemies a grand and global alliance, north and south, east and west, that can assure a more fruitful life for all mankind? Will you join in that historic effort?

24   In the long history of the world, only a few generations have been granted the role of defending freedom in its hour of maximum danger. I do not shrink from this responsibility — I welcome it. I do not believe that any of us would exchange places with any other people or any other generation. The energy, the faith and the devotion which we bring to this endeavor will light our country and all

who serve it — and the glow from that fire can truly light the world.

25   And so, my fellow Americans: Ask not what your country will do for you — ask what you can do for your country.

26   My fellow citizens of the world: Ask not what America will do for you, but what together we can do for the freedom of man.

27   Finally, whether you are citizens of America or of the world, ask of us the same high standards of strength and sacrifice that we shall ask of you. With a good conscience our only sure reward, with history the final judge of our deeds, let us go forth to lead the land we love, asking His blessing and His help, but knowing that here on earth God's work must truly be our own.

QUESTIONS FOR REFLECTION, DISCUSSION, OR WRITING

(1) You probably had to look up few words used in this speech. Knowing that Kennedy is a well-educated, widely read and experienced man, why do you suppose he used such a simple, everyday vocabulary in his inaugural address?

(2) Patrick Henry, also a shrewd, effect-minded speaker, used many more "difficult" words in his brief oration. Can you account for the difference?

(3) The Kennedy speech fairly glows with metaphors. Such figures of speech as "beach-head of cooperation" and "now the trumpet summons us again" were undoubtedly carefully chosen, not only to add color to the speech but also to assist in achieving clarity and emphasis. Find all the metaphors you can and examine each for its appropriateness. Experiment with a few of them, saying the same thing "straight" and trying to imagine which way would be more effective on the millions of listeners and readers.

(4) *Time* Magazine referred to the "lean, lucid phrases" of the address. Certainly good metaphors fit this description, but there are also many others, such as "to abolish all form of human poverty and to abolish all form of human life." (The word "phrase" is not used here in the narrower grammatical sense.) Select several well-put statements or expressions, other than metaphors, and see how the adjectives "lean" and "lucid" apply to them.

(5) Examine the implied analogy "those who foolishly sought to find power by riding on the tiger's back inevitably ended up inside" (par. 7). Explain the meaning of this, and give examples from your own or the world's experience.

(6) Consider again the rallying slogan "Better Red than Dead!" Compare this philosophy with that expressed by President Kennedy in paragraph 4: ". . . we shall pay any price, bear any burden, meet any hardship, support

any friend or oppose any foe in order to assure the survival and success of liberty." This comparison and a defense of either philosophy can provide (and often has provided) a worthwhile topic for composition.

(6) President Kennedy did not believe that "any of us would exchange places with any other people or any other generation." Do you think this is an exaggerated statement? Would you make such an exchange, if possible — say, to a more serene period of history, when one did not have to worry about hydrogen bombs and automobile wrecks? Explain why or why not.

✳
✳

SIMPLE ENJOYMENT

✳
✳
✱
✱
✱
✱
✱
✱
✱
✱
✱
✱
✱
✱
✱
✱
✱
✱
✱
✱
✱
✱
✱
✱
✱
✱

SOME LAST ADVICE

The authors' primary purpose in writing the next four essays and the several short stories and poems which follow was to give enjoyment. Some, as far as you are concerned, may not have succeeded. But we know by now that "enjoyment," at least in reading, is a broad and elastic term. It includes, of course, the common pleasures of laughter and tears and horror (what else but "pleasure" would explain the popularity of "tear-jerkers" and movies of giant crabs coming out of the earth?). Reading enjoyment is often simply a matter of learning something new and interesting, or gaining a new insight into life that we might have been many years in finding for ourselves . . . it may be only the warm glow of recognition in someone else's emotions or impressions, the same as our own which we had never put into words — or those entirely different from ours, and hence a bit shocking. Enjoyment may be to comprehend a character so fully that we, at the time, almost become the character ourselves . . . it may be to escape for awhile into fantasy, a dream world of sorts, and forget our car expenses. And sometimes it is simply appreciation of an artistic creation, as one might lose himself in music or a sunset, with no greater excuse than beauty. These, and more, are the varied "enjoyments" of reading.

So — you are on your own in this section, to have pleasure with no further editorial advice or bothersome questions to study. But all the literary techniques you have studied already — analogy and figures of speech and allusion and symbolism, and all the rest that are used by writers to make your reading more meaningful — will be found here in even greater abundance. But surely by now you will not need to use our old clinical approach, putting each under a microscope, so to speak (in a sort of analogy-metaphor?), in order to study it. The very act of reading should now include their use as intended.

Still helpful, however, will be to remember that if an essay or story or poem lives long enough to find its way into an anthology, even if its primary purpose is fun and frolic, it probably has something "to say" as well — a theme, if you please — a glimpse of life the author felt like sharing — an observation, however slight, on the human condition. You will do well, then, after reading for the apparent "simple enjoyment," to mull the thing over to find any other significance it may contain: still another enjoyment, perhaps.

After all, who in the world ever loses a chance to get "two for the price of one"?

John Mason Brown

BETWEEN THE DARK AND THE DAYLIGHT

IN THEORY it is a charming picture. Every father who has ever read a book, and hopes his children will read one too, has been haunted by it.

The day's work done. Curtains drawn over the darkening windows. Time halted for the happiest of hiatuses. The world shut out. The family close as a unit. The fire roaring. The lamps lighted. The children, fresh from their tubs, their suppers finished, their homework done; the children stretched out on the floor in their dressing gowns, their eyes dancing with wonder. Their mother on the sofa, sewing. Well, if not that, listening

From *Morning Faces*, by John Mason Brown (New York: Whittlesey House, 1949). Copyright 1949 by John Mason Brown. Reprinted by permission of the author and of McGraw-Hill Book Co., Inc.

contentedly. And father (it would be he), hogging the center of the stage — father at his most *pater familias*; father carrying the torch for culture and continuity; father sitting in the big armchair by the fire, his glasses on, a book spread open in his hands, reading out loud to the entire attentive family.

This is the dream. Every father's dream. But the reality? That's quite a different matter. At least it is in my household. For once, I speak as an authority.

"What about it?" I said to my sons in the late afternoon a few weeks back. By some odd coincidence neither of them happened to be out at a birthday party. It seemed, therefore, like a perfect time for the experiment. You see, it was still cold enough for a fire. Moreover, it was Friday. That meant the older boy had no lessons to do.

"What about our reading a book together?" I suggested, flooded with one of those happy inspirations which intermittently inundate parents. "Let's go in the living room and *you* can light a fire." (This "you" was to the younger boy. It was a low, cheap bribe. It was, however, cheating in a good cause.)

As here recorded in the sweet quiet of print, such an invitation may sound placid enough. But to have that many words heard in my sons' rooms in the late afternoon requires more than conversational stamina. I am afraid bellowing is needed.

My two sons have rooms of their own. Which is all right with them, and me. But each of these adjoining rooms has a radio in it, which they find "neat" and I don't.

They have only recently discovered these radios. They used to get their indoor exercise in other ways than spinning the dials. It humiliates me to remember that once upon a time I, seeing these machines untouched, tried in vain to persuade the boys to listen to them. It's difficult for me to believe, but for months these radios were silent. Now their tubes burn like eternal lights. My boys huddle around them, unwilling and unable to leave them. My hope is, of course, that this is only a phase. My wife and I keep saying to ourselves overexposure to the radio is bound to cure them. If it doesn't, nothing will cure us.

As addicts of the airways, my sons are complete individualists. Their taste in programs is seldom the same. All they share in common is their fondness for noise. Although neither of them is deaf, they both seem to think they are.

They are convinced apparently that a radio cannot be heard unless it is turned on full blast. Strangely enough, each boy is deaf only to the caterwauling of the other's machine. They think nothing of playing Sky King against Superman, Jack Armstrong against Captain Midnight, or opposing Tom Mix to Tennessee Jed. And all of this within fifteen feet of one another. The more thunderous the cacophony, the more abundant their delight.

Trying to speak above these discharging machines is like trying to make oneself heard during a demonstration at a national convention. Yet, hard as it is to hear yourself speak, it is harder still to get the boys' attention when spoken to.

Accordingly, in each of their rooms I had to repeat my suggestion, "What about going into the living room and reading a book together?"

"Why?" asked my younger son, welcoming me with a scowl and with one hand on the dial.

"No," said the older one, adding a "thanks" drowned out by gunshot or a falling airplane, I couldn't tell which.

"But we haven't read together for a long while," I bellowed.

"Sh-h-h, Daddy, p-l-e-a-s-e — it's Superman!"

I ought to have known better. The past two months should have taught me that I was an intruder as unwanted as an atheist at High Mass. Every afternoon for weeks the older boy, on his return from school at about five-ten, had made an Olympic dash from the front door to his own room. Every afternoon, with scarcely a word for anyone and without pausing to remove his coat and cap, he had shut himself in, more securely than a condemned man in solitary, to discover what fresh misadventures were overtaking Superman.

Though hoarse, I was persistent. Apologetic, too, much to my surprise, as I pushed my way through a mountain of comics on the floor. "Sorry," I said, "but please come — as a favor."

"Sure, when it's over."

Then I retreated to the younger boy's room.

"Sh-h-h, don't you know you're intawupting Sky King?" he managed to make me hear over an explosion.

"Oh, I didn't really. But don't forget *you* can light the fire."

"O.K., Dad, when it's over."

This gave me some twelve minutes in which to choose a book. Selecting a book that is right for both a boy of six and one of ten; that can survive the ordeal of being read out loud; yes, and that is endurable to the parents no less than to their young is not as easy as it sounds. I turned to my wife for aid. She blanched a little, less at the problem of choosing the book than at the prospect of being read aloud to.

Fairly soon after our marriage I discovered that my wife hates being read to. A book for her is a lonely delight, not a joint pleasure. It isn't that she is eager to do the reading aloud herself. She dislikes that as violently as she objects to hearing another person read. It's simply that she is one of those people — and their name is Kilroy — who feels the printed word should be encountered in print.

Even after dinner, when we are alone and it is an adult book that I am eager to share, her capacity for listening usually stops with the first paragraph. Her gift for pretending to listen comes to a no less abrupt end with the second. Thereafter, if she is not fortunate enough to have been called by a friend to the telephone, a look of despair steals across her face. No victim of claustrophobia could suffer more.

When it comes to reading out aloud to the children, my wife's attitude is different. She wants them to be read to; she reads to them herself; but she is just as happy, if not happier, when I do the reading.

"Thank God," said I, "we don't have to read *Peter Rabbit*."

There does come a time, and very rapidly, when the most loving parent cannot nestle down with any pretense of pleasure to narratives which start, "Once upon a time there was a pussycat called Ribby, who invited a little dog called Duchess to tea." Or, "Once upon a time there was an old cat, called Mrs. Tabitha Twitchit, who was an anxious parent. She used to lose her kittens continually, and whenever they were lost they were always in mischief!"

"Thank God, too," I continued, "we don't have to read that book about a church mouse. I think I'd commit hara-kiri if I had to repeat once again that little gem — you know the one I mean. The one the children used to love to have me read because they knew I hated it so — the one that runs:

Snap, whack, bang,
Goes the snap-rat bang,
Goes the snap bang,
Goes whack bang,
Fuss, fuss, fuss!

"I don't really think I could face *Little Black Sambo* and those one-hundred-and-sixty-nine pancakes. Or the Babar books, much as I used to like them. Even *Uncle Remus* gets me down after the fifth consecutive run-through. No, let's try . . ."

At this moment the older boy came in, trailed by his younger brother. Both of them looked as if they had just taken their places in a tumbrel headed for the guillotine.

"O.K., Dad," they said with resignation.

So we moved into the living room and set the stage. The younger boy started the fire with his older brother's aid. My wife took her place on the sofa. The lamps were lighted; the curtains drawn. The boys stretched out on the floor, and I sat in the big chair.

I knew better than to reach for *Hiawatha* or *Evangeline*. I had tried them in the past, finding myself in each case in complete sympathy with the revolutions which had broken out by page two.

Somehow I found I was not in an *Ivanhoe* mood. I haven't been for more than thirty years. So I excused myself from Gurth and Wamba by deciding that the book which they slowly start was too old both for a six-year-old and for me.

I knew that *Danny Deever* was reliable. It had always proven so in the past. It had brevity to endear it. What is more, a hanging is a dish the young take to without persuasion. I must admit I had been tempted by Lars Porsena of Clusium and his nine gods. But Horatius and his bridge-work required vocal energy, and I had little voice or energy left. I would like to have read *Alice*, *The Hunting of the Snark*, *Stuart Little*, or *The White Deer*. These, however, were old favorites with the boys.

Treasure Island seemed the perfect solution. It had everything — thrills, pirates, a youthful hero, villains, adventure, buried gold, ships, and a siege. It was literature; a classic. If anything could, it would win them away from the comics and the radio and all those supermen flying around in space, wearing long red underwear and transported by magic capes.

After a brief introduction, less eloquent than the prologue to *Henry V* but on the same general idea, I began, "Chapter One. The Old Sea Dog at the 'Admiral Benbow.' "

"What kind of a dog is a sea dog?" This, needless to say, came from the six-year-old. Time out for a quick explanation.

"Who is Admiral Benbow?" Another explanation.

"Come on, now, let's get going. It'll all explain itself. Just listen."

I cleared my throat, as people will when beginning a new chapter. "Squire Trelawney, Dr. Livesey, and the rest of these gentlemen," I commenced, "having asked me to write down the whole particulars about Treasure Island. . . ."

Everything seemed to be going beautifully. They liked the brown old seaman, with his tarry pigtail, his scarred hands, and a saber cut across one cheek. They were delighted — as who would not be? — with his "Fifteen men on the dead man's chest — Yo-ho-ho, and a bottle of rum!" They were excited about his warnings against "a seafaring man with one leg." Their growing suspense made me very happy. The dream had become an actuality.

Just then the telephone rang. It was for my wife. She was gone in a flash.

"What's 'Dry Tortugas'?" asked the older boy.

"Uh, uh — well, uh —" I did not and do not have the foggiest idea. "Oh, it's just one of those things they have on the Spanish Main." That seemed vague enough. Anyway, it worked.

"What's the Spanish Main?" demanded the younger boy.

Again an expository pause, and fortunately one which this time could be filled in.

Then I went on, becoming so interested myself that I did not look up until enraged cries of "Stop it!" "Hey, you!" "He took my cap pistol!" "You bum!" compelled me to do so.

"Stop it, boys!" I thundered in my most piratical tones. "I don't care who did what. Give me that pistol. Now you come over here." The younger boy stretched out beside my chair.

With a pistol in my lap without a cutlass, I returned to *Treasure Island.*

Everything except me was blessedly quiet for some time. From the corner of my eye I could not help noticing that the younger boy had bellied his way behind my chair. So long as he was silent, I did not object. "This is it," I said to myself as I read on. "This is it!"

I was nearer the truth than I realized. Suddenly, a spitball caught me right in the back of the neck. What is more, it stung. It was not meant for me. That I happily, even proudly, admit. Its target, however, was beside the point.

"Go to your room," I ordered the little boy, though the punishment hurt me far more than it did him. "That's very rude of you." He left at once, without protest, with an unknown docility.

"Now let us go on," I said to the older boy. "*You* like it, don't you?"

"Yes, it's neat. But, say, Daddy, can't I go too?"

"You? Why?"

"Well, uh — uh — couldn't I — uh — uh — read it to myself?"

"Couldn't you what?"

"Read it to myself? It takes so long this way, Daddy."

"Certainly," I replied, I am afraid with a considerable show of hurt feelings.

"You see," he added, sensing that I needed consolation, "there's something I've just got to finish in my room before The Lone Ranger comes on. You don't mind, do you?"

"Not at all; not — at — all, if that's your choice."

He was kind enough not to run to his room. And kind enough to turn at the door to say, "Thanks, Dad. Thanks a million."

I looked at the drawn curtains. I looked at the lighted lamps. I looked at the roaring fire. I looked at the empty room. Then I picked up *Treasure Island*. It remains an excellent book to read to oneself.

But I was glad when dinner was announced. I was lonely.

James Thurber

COURTSHIP THROUGH THE AGES

SURELY NOTHING in the astonishing scheme of life can have nonplussed Nature so much as the fact that none of the females of any of the species she created really cared very much for the male, as such. For the past ten million years Nature has been busily inventing ways to make the male attractive to the female, but the whole business of courtship, from the marine annelids up to man, still lumbers heavily along, like a complicated musical comedy. I have been reading the sad and absorbing story in Volume 6 (Cole to Dama) of the *Encyclopaedia Britannica*. In this volume you can learn all about cricket, cotton, costume designing, crocodiles, crown jewels, and Coleridge, but none of these subjects is so interesting as the Courtship of Animals, which recounts the sorrowful lengths to which all males must go to arouse the interest of a lady.

We all know, I think, that Nature gave man whiskers and a mustache with the quaint idea in mind that these would prove attractive to the female. We all know that, far from attracting her, whiskers and mustaches only made her nervous and gloomy, so that man had to go in for somersaults, tilting with lances, and performing feats of parlor magic to win her attention; he also had to bring her candy, flowers, and the furs of animals. It is common knowledge that in spite of all these "love displays" the male is constantly being turned down, insulted, or thrown out of the house. It is rather comforting, then, to discover that the peacock, for all his gorgeous plumage, does not have a particularly easy time in courtship; none of the males in the world do. The first peahen, it turned out, was only faintly stirred by her suitor's beautiful train. She would often go quietly to sleep while he was whisking it around. The Britannica tells us that the peacock actually had to learn a certain little trick to wake her up and revive her interest: he had to learn to vibrate his quills so as to make a rustling sound. In ancient times man himself, observing the ways of the peacock, probably tried vibrating his whiskers to make a rustling sound; if so, it didn't get him anywhere. He had to go in for something else; so, among other things, he went in for gifts. It is not likely that he got this idea from certain flies and birds who were making no headway at all with rustling sounds.

One of the flies of the family Empidae, who had tried everything, finally hit on something pretty special. He contrived to make a glistening transparent balloon which was even larger than himself. Into this he would put sweetmeats and tidbits and he would carry the whole elaborate envelope through the air to the lady of his choice. This amused her for a time, but she finally got bored with it. She demanded silly little colorful presents, something that you couldn't eat but that would look nice around the house. So the male Empis had to go around gathering flower petals and pieces of bright paper to put into his balloon. On a courtship flight a male Empis cuts quite a figure now, but he can hardly be said to be happy. He never knows how soon the female will demand heavier presents, such as Roman coins and gold collar buttons. It seems probable that one day the courtship of the Empidae will fall down, as man's occasionally does, of its own weight.

The bowerbird is another creature that spends so much time courting the female that he never gets any work done. If all the male bowerbirds became nervous wrecks within the next ten or fifteen years, it would not surprise me. The female bowerbird insists that a playground be built for her with a specially constructed bower at the entrance. This bower is much more elaborate than an ordinary nest and is harder to build; it costs a lot more, too. The female will not come to the playground until the male has filled it up with a great many gifts: silvery leaves, red leaves, rose petals, shells, beads, berries, bones, dice, buttons, cigar bands, Christmas seals, and the Lord knows what else. When the female finally condescends to visit the playground, she is in a coy and silly mood and has to be chased in and out of the bower and up and down the playground before she will quit giggling and stand still long enough even to shake hands. The male bird is, of course, pretty well done in before the chase starts, because he has worn himself out hunting for eyeglass lenses and begonia blossoms. I imagine that many a bowerbird, after chasing a female for two or three hours, says the hell with it and goes home to bed. Next day, of course, he telephones someone else and the same trying ritual is gone through with again. A male bowerbird is as exhausted as a night-club habitué before he is out of his twenties.

The male fiddler crab has a somewhat easier time, but it can hardly be said that he is sitting pretty. He has one enormously large and powerful claw, usually brilliantly colored, and you might suppose that all he had to do was reach out and grab some passing cutie. The very earliest fiddler crabs may have tried this, but, if so, they got slapped for their pains. A female fiddler crab will not tolerate any caveman stuff; she never has and she doesn't intend to start now. To attract a female, a fiddler crab has to stand on tiptoe and brandish his claw in the air. If any female in the neighborhood is interested — and you'd be surprised how many are not — she comes over and engages him in light badinage, for which he is not in the mood. As many as a hundred females may pass the time of day with him and go on about their business. By nightfall of an average courting day, a fiddler crab who has been standing on tiptoe for eight or ten hours waving a heavy claw in the air is in pretty sad shape. As in the case of the males of all species, however, he gets out of bed next morning, dashes some water on his face, and tries again.

The next time you encounter a male web-spinning spider, stop and reflect that he is too busy worrying about his love life to have any desire to bite you. Male web-spinning spiders have a tougher life than any other males in the animal kingdom. This is because the female web-spinning spiders have very poor eyesight. If a male lands on a female's web, she kills him before he has time to lay down his cane and gloves, mistaking him for a fly or a bumblebee who has stumbled into her trap. Before the species figured out what to do about this, millions of males were murdered by ladies they called on. It is the nature of spiders to perform a little dance in front of the female, but before a male spinner could get near enough for the female to see who he was and what he was up to, she would lash out at him with a flat-iron or a pair of garden shears. One night, nobody knows when, a very bright male spinner lay awake worrying about calling on a lady who had been killing suitors right and left. It came to him that this business of dancing as a love display wasn't getting anybody anywhere except the grave. He decided to go in for web-twitching, or strand-vibrating. The next day he tried it on one of the nearsighted girls. Instead of dropping in on her suddenly, he stayed outside the web and began monkeying with one of its strands. He twitched it up and down and in and out with such a lilting rhythm that the female was charmed. The serenade worked beautifully; the female let him live. The Britannica's spider-watchers, however, report that this system is not always successful. Once in a while, even now, a female will fire three bullets into a suitor or run him through with a kitchen knife. She keeps threatening him from the moment he strikes the first low notes on the outside strings, but usually by the time he has got up to the high notes played around the center of the web, he is going to town and she spares his life.

Even the butterfly, as handsome a fellow as he is, can't always win a mate merely by fluttering around and showing off. Many butterflies have to have scent scales on their wings. Hepialus carries a powder puff in a perfumed pouch. He throws perfume at the ladies when they pass. The male tree cricket, Oecanthus, goes Hepialus one better by carrying a tiny bottle of wine with him and giving drinks to such doxies as he has designs on. One of the male snails throws darts to entertain the girls. So it goes, through the long list of animals, from the bristle worm and his rudimentary dance steps to man and his gift of diamonds and sapphires. The golden-eye drake raises a jet of water with his feet as he flies over a lake; Hepialus has his powder puff, Oecanthus his wine bottle, man his etchings. It is a bright and melancholy story, the age-old desire of the male for the female, the age-old desire of the female to be amused and entertained. Of all the creatures on earth, the only males who could be figured as putting any irony into their courtship are the grebes and certain other diving birds. Every now and then a courting grebe slips quietly down to the bottom of a lake and then, with a mighty "Whoosh!," pops out suddenly a few feet from his girl friend, splashing water all over her. She seems to be persuaded that this is a purely loving display, but I like to think that the grebe always has a faint hope of drowning her or scaring her to death.

I will close this investigation into the mournful burdens of the male with the *Britannica's* story about a certain Argus pheasant. It appears that the Argus displays himself in front of a female who stands perfectly still without moving a feather. (If you saw "June Moon" some years age and remember the scene in which the Songwriter sang "Montana Moon" to his grim and motionless wife, you have some idea what the female Argus probably thinks of her mate's display.) The male Argus the Britannica tells about was confined in a cage with a female of another species, a female who kept moving around, emptying ashtrays and fussing with lampshades all the time the male was showing off his talents. Finally, in disgust, he stalked away and began displaying in front of his water trough. He reminds me of a certain male (Homo sapiens) of my acquaintance who one night after dinner asked his wife to put down her detective magazine so that he could read her a poem of which he was very fond. She sat quietly enough until he was well into the middle of the thing, intoning with great ardor and intensity. Then suddenly there came a sharp, disconcerting *slap!* It turned out that all during the male's display, the female had been intent on a circling mosquito and had finally trapped it between the palms of her hands. The male in this case did not stalk away and display in front of a water trough; he went over to Tim's and had a flock of drinks and recited the poem to the fellas. I am sure they all told bitter stories of their own about how their displays had been interrupted by females. I am also sure that they all ended up singing "Honey, Honey, Bless Your Heart."

E. B. White

DOG TRAINING

THERE IS a book out called *Dog Training Made Easy* and it was sent to me the other day by the publisher, who rightly guessed that it would catch my eye. I like to read books on dog training. Being the owner of dachshunds, to me a book on dog discipline becomes a volume of inspired humor. Every sentence is a riot. Some day, if I ever get a chance, I shall write a book, or warning, on the character and temperament of the Dachshund and why he can't be trained and shouldn't be. I would rather train a striped zebra to balance an Indian club than induce a dachshund to heed my slightest command. For a number of years past I have been agreeably encumbered by a very large and dissolute dachshund named Fred. Of all the dogs whom I have served I've never known one who understood so much of what I say or held it in such deep contempt. When I address Fred I never have to raise either my voice or my hopes. He even disobeys me when I instruct him in something that he wants to do. And when I answer his peremptory scratch at the door and hold the door open for him to walk through, he stops in the middle and lights a cigarette, just to hold me up.

"Shopping for a puppy presents a number of problems," writes Mr. Wm. Cary Duncan, author of *Dog Training Made Easy*. Well, shopping for a puppy has never presented many problems for me, as most of the puppies and dogs that have entered my life (and there have been scores of them) were not the result of a shopping trip but of an act of God. The first puppy I owned, when I was about nine years old, was not shopped for — it was born to the collie bitch of the postman of my older sister, who sent it to me by express from Washington, D.C., in a little crate containing, in addition to the puppy, a bar of Peters' chocolate and a ripe frankfurter. And the puppy I own now was not shopped for but was won in a raffle. Between these two extremes there have been many puppies, mostly unshopped for. It is not so much that I acquire dogs as it is that dogs acquire me. Maybe they even shop for me, I don't know. If they do I assume they have many problems, because they certainly always arrive with plenty, which they then turn over to me.

The possession of a dog today is a different thing from the possession of a dog at the turn of the century, when one's dog was fed on mashed potato and brown gravy and lived in a doghouse with an arched portal. Today a dog is fed on scraped beef and Vitamin B_1 and lives in bed with you.

An awful lot of nonsense has been written about dogs by persons who don't know them very well, and the attempt to elevate the purebred to a position of national elegance has been, in the main, a success. Dogs used to mate with other dogs rather casually in my day, and the results were discouraging to the American Kennel Club but entirely satisfactory to small boys who liked puppies. In my suburban town, "respectable" people didn't keep she-dogs. One's washerwoman might keep a bitch, or one's lawn-cutter, but not one's next-door neighbor.

The prejudice against females made a deep impression on me, and I grew up thinking that there was something indecent and unclean about she-things in general. The word bitch of course was never used in polite families. One day a little mut followed me home from school, and after much talk I persuaded my parents to let me keep it — at least until the owner turned up or advertised for it. It dwelt among us only one night. Next morning my father took me aside and in a low voice said: "My son, I don't know whether you realize it, but that dog is a female. It'll have to go."

"But why does it have to?" I asked.

"They're a nuisance," he replied, embarrassed. "We'd have all the other dogs in the neighborhood around here all the time."

That sounded like an idyllic arrangement to me, but I could tell from my father's voice that the stray dog was doomed. We turned her out and she went off toward the more liberal section of town. This sort of incident must have been happening to thousands of American youngsters in those days, and we grew up to find that it had been permanently added to the record by Dorothy Parker in her short story "Mr. Durant."

On our block, in the days of my innocence, there were in addition to my collie, a pug dog, a dachshund named Bruno, a fox terrier named Sunny who spent many years studying one croquet ball, a red setter, and a St. Bernard who carried his mistress's handbag, shuffling along in stately fashion with the drool running out both sides of his jaws. I was scared of this St. Bernard because of his size, and never passed his house without dread. The dachshund was old, surly, and disagreeable, and was endlessly burying bones in the flower border of the DeVries's yard. I should very much doubt if any of those animals ever had its temperature taken rectally, ever was fed raw meat or tomato juice, ever was given distemper inoculations, or ever saw the whites of a veterinary's eyes. They were brought up on chicken bones and gravy and left-over cereal, and were all fine dogs. Most of them never saw the inside of their owners' houses — they knew their place.

The "problem" of caring for a dog has been unnecessarily complicated. Take the matter of housebreaking. In the suburbia of those lovely post-Victorian days of which I write, the question of housebreaking a puppy was met with the simple bold courage characteristic of our forefathers. You simply kept the house away from the puppy. This was not only the simplest way, it was the only practical way, just as it is today. Our parents were in possession of a vital secret — a secret which has been all but lost to the world: the knowledge that a puppy will live and thrive without ever crossing the threshold of a dwelling house, at least till he's big enough so he doesn't wet the rug.

Although our fathers and mothers very sensibly never permitted a puppy to come into the house, they made up for this indignity by always calling the puppy "Sir." In those days a dog didn't expect anything very elaborate in the way of food or medical care, but he did expect to be addressed civilly.

Mr. Duncan discussed housebreaking at some length and assumes, as do all writers of dog books, that the owner of a puppy has little else to do except own the puppy. It is Mr. Duncan's theory that puppies have a sense of modesty and don't like to be stared at when they are doing something. When you are walking the dog, he says, you must "appear utterly uninterested" as you approach some favorite spot. This, as any city dweller knows, is a big order. Anybody who has ever tried to synchronize a puppy's bowels with a rigid office schedule knows that one's interest in the small phenomena of early morning sometimes reaches fever pitch. A dog owner may feign disinterest, but his mask will not suffice. Nothing is more comical than the look on the face of a person at the upper end of a dog leash, pretending not to know what is going on at the lower.

A really companionable and indispensable dog is an accident of nature. You can't get it by breeding for it, and you can't buy it with money. It just happens along. Out of the vast sea of assorted dogs that I have had dealings with, by far the noblest, the best, and the most important was the first, the one my sister sent me in a crate. He was an old-style collie, beautifully marked, with a blunt nose and great natural gentleness and intelligence. When I got him he was what I badly needed. I think probably all these other dogs of mine have been just a groping toward that old dream. I've never dared get another collie for fear the comparison would be too uncomfortable. I can still see my first dog in all the moods and situations that memory has filed him away in, but I think of him oftenest as he used to be right after breakfast on the back porch, listlessly eating up a dish of petrified oatmeal rather than hurt my feelings. For six years he met me at the same place after school and convoyed me home — a service he thought up himself. A boy doesn't forget that sort of association. It is a monstrous trick of fate that now, settled in the country and with sheep to take care of, I am obliged to do my shepherding with the grotesque and sometimes under-handed assistance of two dachshunds and a wire-haired fox terrier.

Bill Helmer

MEXICAN HEY RIDE

It's a pity that here in America it is no longer considered "daring" to drive a car. The old hazards of travel have been so tamed by traffic laws, super highways, motels and elaborate service stations that today even a timorous grandmother might cross the continent by auto, a mission which not so many years ago would have been taken on only by the stoutest hearts — men who would not flinch at treacherous mountain roads, desert wastelands, breakdowns in the wilderness, and sleeping nights beside the road. Indeed, those were the days when driving was a challenge and to cross the Rockies was a feat to be admired.

But no more. The thrill is gone from traveling the U.S. But, there does still exist one great and accessible frontier where driving still demands courage, skill and resourcefulness: The Republic of Mexico.

Ah, yes, Mexico. Even Sebring seems impure and commercial to the man whose engine has screamed and tires squealed in fighting for the inside rail of a Mexico City traffic circle; or who has cornered narrow mountain roads at 65 mph, sideways, in second gear, battling to maintain an eight-foot lead over a thundering Mexican bus. This, *this* is the man, to quote Hemingway, who truly lives his life "all the way up!"

Driving in Mexico is indeed an adventure of skill and daring, not something to be jumped into feet-first, lest you be carried out the same way. Before participating you have to train and practice. Start with the simpler forms of straight, open highway driving and finally you will qualify for the Big League — Mexico, D.F., *Paris of the Americas*.

Seeing Mexico from a hunched-over position behind your steering wheel may give you rare insight into one facet of the national temperament. But we hasten to add that the Mexicans' traditional use or abuse of the road paints a one-sided picture of their country. While you follow the considerations outlined here, we recommend and even urge that you step out of your car occasionally (carefully!) and meet the congenial, friendly people who, when not breathing raw *Gasolmex*, make driving interesting.

Let us assume that you have outwitted customs officials and crossed the border into Mexico. Tighten your seat-belt and adjust your helmet.

Buses, trucks, chuck-holes, bicycle riders, Indians and livestock are some of the interesting sidelights of the Mexican highway system which will help you develop the nerve and skill so essential to successful city driving later. It is wise to start first with a relatively good, straight highway which gradually climbs into the mountains and then deteriorates, thus offering progressive training.

The first thing you will notice is a reassuring (?) absence of patrol cars and radar. You will drive for hours seeing miles and miles of nothing but miles and miles, not even a telephone pole. Here, on these long, lonely stretches you will experience an exhilarating freedom from oppressive law enforcement — freedom American pioneers enjoyed as they traveled through Indian country unhindered by the U.S. Cavalry.

You will probably average an easy 80 or 90 mph over the smooth, wide highway until you meet your first burro. Here your training begins. Be calm, don't panic. Remember, he won't run out in front of you like a cow . . . he's already there, rooted like a tree. Now don't jam on your brakes like a fool tourist and disintegrate in the ditch, but accelerate slightly to improve control and turn your wheel one revolution. Hold on. There, *you've got him!* And with no damage to your radiator. Now correct your skid and keep going.

That was easy, and now you're ready for a *moving* target: bicycles. Mexico is a country of bicycle racers who spend their weekends training by long endurance runs in packs of 30 or 40. These packs command a highway like a herd of sheep and you should approach them as such. Bear down on your horn and aim for the middle of the herd. This panics the leader, causing the rest of the pack to part like the Red Sea.

Another interesting if not too relevant highway phenomenon is the Indian bus-waiter. From out of the dense, uninhabitable brush come Mexican Indians to stand (or squat) by (or on) the road waiting for the bus to take them to the local village. You may be driving across barren wasteland between Matehuala and San Luis Potosi and two miles ahead notice a small speck beside the road which slowly grows into a blanket, a large straw sombrero, two beady eyes, and maybe a rifle. Be calm, this is not a bandit. In fact, he is harmless — the only danger being the American tourists who often stop their Cadillacs in the middle of the road while they get out to take pictures of the quaint natives.

Mexicans have an interesting philosophy toward road construction and detours which you should be aware of lest you devote too much attention to animate obstacles only. If you complain to a local official that you wrecked your car because some idiot dug a trench across the road and didn't mark it, he will inform you that it is not customary to drive over such trenches at high speeds. You might wreck your car. Also, a certain *mañana* attitude is reflected in the lack of highway signs and markers. This is good; it helps you develop an intuitive sense for detecting bridge washouts and wrong roads. (Most roads in Mexico seem to be wrong roads.)

Okay, by now you are ready for a bit of mountain training. The discussion up to this point has not included trucks or buses. Only in mountains do these vehicles perform in full character. The neophyte will feel a tingle of apprehension at first as he maneuvers mountain curves on a road barely wide enough for two Volkswagens and bordered on one side by an unrailed 2000-foot drop. Trucks and buses make this even more interesting.

Drive as far over on your side of the road as possible because your ten-foot-wide opponent will also. Once your initial fear has changed to a fatalistic numbness you can begin to appreciate how exciting it all is: You're on the outside of a negative-banked mountain curve and you feel the road begin to vibrate. Notice that small animals are scurrying for shelter. This means a truck is coming.

Watch as it suddenly appears around the curve ahead, ponderously rising and falling like a battleship in a typhoon, spraying clouds of dust and asphalt chunks from beneath its crushing wheels. Like a god of destruction it bears inexorably down on you, rocking and swaying and roaring. Easy now, and *don't show fear* — they can sense it. Just keep a steady hand on the wheel and casually puff your cigarette to show confidence, and with a thunderclap of sound and wind he will flash by, leaving the air filled with flying gravel and dense, black clouds of pungent diesel smoke as proof that it was no nightmare. See? Nothing to it.

Buses are like trucks except faster and more colorful. For example, some passengers, rather than pay fare, elect to hang on the ladder which runs up the back to the luggage rack. Watch these guys; they throw stuff. In the driver's seat is a huge, laughing, hairy fellow in dark glasses and mustache, crouching low. He is wrestling with the large, flat steering wheel like the tillerman on a hook-and-ladder fire truck. He rears up and down violently as his iron bull lurches in and out of chuckholes and bucks wildly beneath him. You get an exceptionally clear view of all this because of the large windshield and flat front. Better not to look.

The same experience at night is better in one way, worse in another. You can't *see* your fate so clearly, but your imagination may create images even worse. The psychological terror is increased when you look down your hood into the glaring headlights of an oncoming truck, and *suddenly they go out!* Darkness rushes in and with it the first glimpse of the darkened hulk careening toward you with only cab lights burning. But relax. Whatever your first panicky judgment might tell you, this is actually a courteous saftey measure (the only safety measure) which permits you to see the hulking demon (otherwise obscured by glaring headlights), and how far it overlaps into your lane.

A similarly interesting custom is headlight signaling at the approach to a single-lane bridge. If you are approaching such a bridge and the driver approaching from the opposite direction flashes his lights (daytime) or blinks them (night), it means that you are about to die unless you let him come first. Usually the first blinker gets to cross first, others waiting for him to clear before they go ahead. But in the case of the simultaneous blink there enters in the "guts" factor understood only by Mexicans and dead Americans. The rule to remember here is that basically you are a coward.

Surviving to this point, you are now ready to enter the *city* and an entirely new experience in adventurous driving. Unlike the open road where most drivers are going places, in the city you will find a good number driving nowhere special just for the sport of it. Don't feel too daring at first, because while your highway training has prepared your nerves, you now have an additional set of skills to develop.

This discussion will be limited to the *gloriettas* which combine every hazard and obstacle possible. Once you master these you may begin to feel indestructible, but don't cancel your insurance. You may be hit by an American tourist.

Gloriettas — the name is somehow appropriate — are large traffic circles into and out of which funnel speeding vehicles from six or seven different directions. The result is a honking, screeching maelstrom of high-speed traffic thundering 'round and 'round a grassy park in the middle of which stands the statue of some notable like Aztec Chief Ixpopocatuzuitlan, who smiles down vengefully upon his former enemies who are now locked in deadly combat with each other.

Since no two streets in Mexico City run parallel, and most meet at *gloriettas*, you have plenty of battlegrounds from which to choose. Start out with the safer ones first, out Avenida Juarez, and work toward the true challenges on Reforma. When your intermediate successes indicate that you are ready for the Big Moment downtown — Reforma at Columbus Statue — you will feel the thrill of a matador making his first entrance before a hundred thousand eyes in the Plaza Mexico.

Okay, find yourself a nice, long "spoke" street aimed right into the teeming center of the great *glorietta*. This is your big moment — maybe your last one — so you must try to relax. Hold the wheel firmly at ten and two o'clock and begin picking up speed. You have to be traveling at least fifty by the time you reach the outer ring of orbiting cars or they'll never let you in. Faster now. Set your course for the statue at the center of the circle. Begin to steal glances left at the oncoming traffic circling toward you. Keep cool! Notice how drivers are warily eyeing you, trying to judge your experience, determination and susceptibility to bluff.

Don't weaken or waver — they'll see it. The slightest hesitation on your part now will be fatal, like plunging into the unyielding edge of a buzz saw. They are watching you, but *don't look at them!* To acknowledge their approach is to grant them right-of-way. Just plunge right in as if you were blind to their very existence and deaf to their blasting horns, then cut a sharp right into the traffic pattern. You will be pleased to discover that a space has opened for you (probably), and you are now accepted as a fellow electron in orbit whose duty henceforth (while in the outer shell) is to prevent the entry of stray particles like yourself a moment ago. Indeed, this is a science.

Your technique should be learned well because the principle applies in most circumstances. The driver who openly acknowledges the approach of another is obliged to avoid the collision by yielding. When neither, or both, have acknowledged the other, the contest favors the driver going too fast to stop. The slower driver always yields by default since the choice lies only in his hands.

We have, however, one major exception to such spontaneous driving. You will be amazed to discover that Mexico City, a metropolis of almost five million, is practically devoid of stop signs. Instead, you will encounter those tributes of Mexican engineering genius called *topas* (from the Spanish meaning "tank-stopper") which are rows of concrete bumps about five inches high built into the pavement at many intersections. The reasoning here is that the value of a stop sign depends entirely upon the willingness of the driver to voluntarily observe it. This is not true of *topas*. You will "run" only one set of *topas* — only one. Then you will have your car's front end repaired and henceforth come to a complete stop before climbing slowly up over them and proceeding.

In general, the same sporting rules apply to pedestrians as to autos. If you acknowledge one's presence by honking, braking or cursing, he knows that you have seen him and he will pay no further notice. The pedestrian-auto relationship actually is one of the most colorful aspects of driving in Mexico and is derived from the country's national sport of bullfighting. As soon as he steps into the street, the pedestrian begins to picture himself the fearless matador, in flashing silk tights, pitted in a life and death struggle against ferocious, brave bulls. As he steps lithely in front of a taxicab he will execute a classic *veronica*, sweeping his coattails cape-like over the driver's half of the windshield. Then two *chicuelinas* and a *rebolera* and he's safely across to the other side of the street, flushed with victory and perhaps clutching a radio aerial as his reward — the ear.

Conversely, your part in this little drama is to play the bull. When stopped for a traffic light, honk your horns, snort your engine, and lower your head for the charge. In return, he will squint at you, grunt, "Huh! Toro!" a few times, and dramatically plant his switchblade in your front tire. (But here, of course, the bull need not *always* lose . . .)

So there you have it — Mexico — the perfect answer to today's dreary, colorless turnpikery, and the last frontier for the automotive adventurer who would like, once again, to drive by the seat of his pants.

Edna St. Vincent Millay

FIRST FIG

My candle burns at both ends;
   It will not last the night;
But ah, my foes, and oh, my friends —
   It gives a lovely light!

William Saroyan

THE SUMMER OF THE BEAUTIFUL WHITE HORSE

ONE DAY back there in the good old days when I was nine and the world was full of every imaginable kind of magnificence, and life was still a delightful and mysterious dream, my cousin Mourad, who was considered crazy by everybody who knew him except me, came to my house at four in the morning and woke me up by tapping on the window of my room.

Aram, he said.

I jumped out of bed and looked out the window.

I couldn't believe what I saw.

It wasn't morning yet, but it was summer and with daybreak not many minutes around the corner of the world it was light enough for me to know I wasn't dreaming.

My cousin Mourad was sitting on a beautiful white horse.

I stuck my head out of the window and rubbed my eyes.

Yes, he said in Armenian. It's a horse. You're not dreaming. Make it quick if you want a ride.

I knew my cousin Mourad enjoyed being alive more than anybody else who had ever fallen into the world by mistake, but this was more than even I could believe.

In the first place, my earliest memories had been memories of horses and my first longings had been longings to ride.

This was the wonderful part.

In the second place, we were poor.

This was the part that wouldn't permit me to believe what I saw.

We were poor. We had no money. Our whole tribe was poverty-stricken. Every branch of the Garoghlanian family was living in the most amazing and comical poverty in the world. Nobody could understand where we ever got money enough to keep us with food in our bellies, not even the old men of the family. Most important of all, though, we were famous for our honesty. We had been famous for our honesty for something like eleven centuries, even when we had been the wealthiest family in what we liked to think was the world. We were proud first, honest next, and after that we believed in right and wrong. None of us would take advantage of anybody in the world, let alone steal.

Consequently, even though I could see the horse, so magnificent; even though I could *smell* it, so lovely; even though I could *hear* it breathing, so exciting; I couldn't *believe* the horse had anything to do with my cousin Mourad or with me or with any of the other members of our family, asleep or awake, because I *knew* my cousin Mourad couldn't have *bought* the horse, and if he couldn't have bought it he must have *stolen* it, and I refused to believe he had stolen it.

No member of the Garoghlanian family could be a thief.

I stared first at my cousin and then at the horse. There was a pious stillness and humor in each of them which on the one hand delighted me and on the other frightened me.

Mourad, I said, where did you steal this horse?

Leap out of the window, he said, if you want a ride.

It was true, then. He *had* stolen the horse. There was no question about it. He had come to invite me to ride or not, as I chose.

Well, it seemed to me stealing a horse for a ride was not the same thing as stealing something else, such as money. For all I knew, maybe it wasn't stealing at all. If you were crazy about horses the way my cousin Mourad and I were, it wasn't stealing. It wouldn't become stealing until we offered to sell the horse, which of course I knew we would never do.

Let me put on some clothes, I said.

All right, he said, but hurry.

I leaped into my clothes.

I jumped down to the yard from the window and leaped up onto the horse behind my cousin Mourad.

That year we lived at the edge of town, on Walnut Avenue. Behind our house was the country: vineyards, orchards, irrigation ditches, and country roads. In less than three minutes we were on Olive Avenue, and then the horse began to trot. The air was new and lovely to breathe. The feel of the horse running was wonderful. My cousin Mourad who was considered one of the craziest members of our family began to sing. I mean, he began to roar.

Every family has a crazy streak in it somewhere, and my cousin Mourad was considered the natural descendant of the crazy streak in our tribe. Before him was our uncle Khosrove, an enormous man with a powerful head of black hair and the largest mustache in the San Joaquin Valley, a man so furious in temper, so irritable, so impatient that he stopped anyone from talking by roaring, *It is no harm; pay no attention to it.*

That was all, no matter what anybody happened to be talking about. Once it was his own son Arak running eight blocks to the barber shop where his father was having his mustache trimmed to tell him their house was on fire. The man Khosrove sat up in the chair and roared, It is no harm; pay no attention to it. The barber said, But the boy says your house is on fire. So Khosrove roared, Enough, it is no harm, I say.

My cousin Mourad was considered the natural descendant of this man, although Mourad's father was Zorab, who was practical and nothing else. That's how it was in our tribe. A man could be the father of his son's flesh, but that did not mean that he was also the father of his spirit. The distribution of the various kinds of spirit of our tribe had been from the beginning capricious and vagrant.

We rode and my cousin Mourad sang. For all anybody knew we were still in the old country where, at least according to our neighbors, we belonged. We let the horse run as long as it felt like running.

At last my cousin Mourad said, Get down. I want to ride alone.

Will you let me ride alone? I said.

That is up to the horse, my cousin said. Get down.

The *horse* will let me ride, I said.

We shall see, he said. Don't forget that I have a way with a horse.

Well, I said, any way you have with a horse, I have also.

For the sake of your safety, he said, let us hope so. Get down.

All right, I said, but remember you've got to let me try to ride alone.

I got down and my cousin Mourad kicked his heels into the horse and shouted, V*azire*, run. The horse stood on its hind legs, snorted, and burst into a fury of speed that was the loveliest thing I had ever seen. My cousin Mourad raced the horse across a field of dry grass to an irrigation ditch, crossed the ditch on the horse, and five minutes later returned, dripping wet.

The sun was coming up.

Now it's my turn to ride, I said.

My cousin Mourad got off the horse.

Ride, he said.

I leaped to the back of the horse and for a moment knew the awfulest fear imaginable. The horse did not move.

Kick into his muscles, my cousin Mourad said. What are you waiting for? We've got to take him back before everybody in the world is up and about.

I kicked into the muscles of the horse. Once again it reared and snorted. Then it began to run. I didn't know what to do. Instead of running across the field to the irrigation ditch the horse ran down the road to the vineyard of Dikran Halabian where it began to leap over vines. The horse leaped over seven vines before I fell. Then it continued running.

My cousin Mourad came running down the road.

I'm not worried about you, he shouted. We've got to get that horse. You go this way and I'll go this way. If you come upon him, be kindly. I'll be near.

I continued down the road and my cousin Mourad went across the field toward the irrigation ditch.

It took him half an hour to find the horse and bring him back.

All right, he said, jump on. The whole world is awake now.

What will we do? I said.

Well, he said, we'll either take him back or hide him until tomorrow morning.

He didn't sound worried and I knew he'd hide him and not take him back. Not for a while, at any rate.

Where will you hide him? I said.

I know a place, he said.

How long ago did you steal this horse? I said.

It suddenly dawned on me that he had been taking these early morning rides for some time and had come for me this morning only because he knew how much I longed to ride.

Who said anything about stealing a horse? he said.

Anyhow, I said, how long ago did you begin riding every morning?

Not until this morning, he said.

Are you telling the truth? I said.

Of course not, he said, but if we are found out, that's what you're to say. I don't want both of us to be liars. All you know is that we started riding this morning.

All right, I said.

He walked the horse quietly to the barn of a deserted vineyard which at one time had been the pride of a farmer named Fetvajian. There were some oats and dry alfalfa in the barn.

We began walking home.

It wasn't easy, he said, to get the horse to behave so nicely. At first it wanted to run wild, but as I've told you, I have a way with a horse. I can get it to want to do anything I want it to do. Horses understand me.

How do you do it? I said.

I have an understanding with a horse, he said.

Yes, but what sort of an understanding? I said.

A simple and honest one, he said.

Well, I said, I wish I knew how to reach an understanding like that with a horse.

You're still a small boy, he said. When you get to be thirteen you'll know how to do it.

I went home and ate a hearty breakfast.

That afternoon my uncle Khosrove came to our house for coffee and cigarettes. He sat in the parlor, sipping and smoking and remembering the old country. Then another visitor arrived, a farmer named John Byro, an Assyrian who, out of loneliness, had learned to speak Armenian. My mother brought the lonely visitor coffee and tobacco and he rolled a cigarette and sipped and smoked, and then at last, sighing sadly, he said, My white horse which was stolen last month is still gone. I cannot understand it.

My uncle Khosrove became very irritated and shouted, It's no harm. What is the loss of a horse? Haven't we all lost the homeland? What is this crying over a horse?

That may be all right for you, a city dweller, to say, John Byro said, but what of my surrey? What good is a surrey without a horse?

Pay no attention to it, my uncle Khosrove roared.

I walked ten miles to get here, John Byro said.

You have legs, my uncle Khosrove shouted.

My left leg pains me, the farmer said.

Pay no attention to it, my uncle Khosrove roared.

That horse cost me sixty dollars, the farmer said.

I spit on money, my uncle Khosrove said.

He got up and stalked out of the house, slamming the screen door.

My mother explained.

He has a gentle heart, she said. It is simply that he is homesick and such a large man.

The farmer went away and I ran over to my cousin Mourad's house.

He was sitting under a peach tree, trying to repair the hurt wing of a young robin which could not fly. He was talking to the bird.

What is it? he said.

The farmer, John Byro, I said. He visited our house. He wants his horse. You've had it a month. I want you to promise not to take it back until I learn to ride.

It will take you a *year* to learn to ride, my cousin Mourad said.

We could keep the horse a year, I said.

My cousin Mourad leaped to his feet.

What? he roared. Are you inviting a member of the Garoghlanian family to steal? The horse must go back to its true owner.

When? I said.

In six months at the latest, he said.

He threw the bird into the air. The bird tried hard, almost fell twice, but at last flew away, high and straight.

Early every morning for two weeks my cousin Mourad and I took the horse out of the barn of the deserted vineyard where we were hiding it and rode it, and every morning the horse, when it was my turn to ride alone, leaped over grape vines and small trees and threw me and ran away.

Nevertheless, I hoped in time to learn to ride the way my cousin Mourad rode.

One morning on the way to Fetvajian's deserted vineyard we ran into the farmer John Byro who was on his way to town.

Let me do the talking, my cousin Mourad said. I have a way with farmers.

Good morning, John Byro, my cousin Mourad said to the farmer.

The farmer studied the horse eagerly.

Good morning, sons of my friends, he said. What is the name of your horse?

My Heart, my cousin Mourad said in Armenian.

A lovely name, John Byro said, for a lovely horse. I could swear it is the horse that was stolen from me many weeks ago. May I look into its mouth?

Of course, Mourad said.

The farmer looked into the mouth of the horse.

Tooth for tooth, he said. I would swear it *is* my horse if I didn't know your parents. The fame of your family for honesty is well known to me. Yet the horse is the twin of my horse. A suspicious man would believe his eyes instead of his heart. Good day, my young friends.

Good day, John Byro, my cousin Mourad said.

Early the following morning we took the horse to John Byro's vineyard and put it in the barn. The dogs followed us around without making a sound.

The dogs, I whispered to my cousin Mourad. I thought they would bark.

They would at somebody else, he said. I have a way with dogs.

My cousin Mourad put his arms around the horse, pressed his nose into the horse's nose, patted it, and then we went away.

That afternoon John Byro came to our house in his surrey and showed my mother the horse that had been stolen and returned.

I do not know what to think, he said. The horse is stronger than ever. Better-tempered, too. I thank God.

My uncle Khosrove, who was in the parlor, became irritated and shouted, Quiet, man, quiet. Your horse has been returned. Pay no attention to it.

Phyllis McGinley
SEASON AT THE SHORE

Oh, not by sun and not by cloud
And not by whippoorwill, crying loud,
And not by the pricking of my thumbs,
Do I know the way that the summer comes.
Yet here on this seagull-haunted strand,
Hers is an omen I understand —
Sand:

Sand on the beaches,
   Sand at the door,
Sand that screeches
   On the new-swept floor;
In the shower, sand for the foot to crunch on;
Sand in the sandwiches spread for luncheon;
Sand adhesive to son and sibling,
From wallet sifting, from pockets dribbling;
Sand by the beaker
   Nightly shed
From odious sneaker;
   Sand in bed;
Sahara always in my seaside shanty
Like the sand in the voice
Of J. Durante.

Winter is mittens, winter is gaiters
Steaming on various radiators.
Autumn is leaves that bog the broom.
Spring is mud in the living room
Or skates in places one scarcely planned.
But what is summer, her seal and hand?
Sand:

Sand in the closets,
   Sand on the stair,
Desert deposits
   In the parlor chair;
Sand in the halls like the halls of ocean;
Sand in the soap and the sun-tan lotion;
Stirred in the porridge, tossed in the greens,
Poured from the bottoms of rolled-up jeans;
   In the elmy street,
      On the lawny acre;
   Glued to the seat
      Of the Studebaker;
Wrapped in the folds of the *Wall Street Journal;*
Damp sand, dry sand,
Sand eternal.

When I shake my garments at the Lord's command,
What will I scatter in the Promised Land?
Sand.

Ambrose Bierce

THE BOARDED WINDOW

In 1830, only a few miles away from what is now the great city of
Cincinnati, lay an immense and almost unbroken forest. The whole region was sparsely settled by people of the frontier — restless souls who no
sooner had hewn fairly habitable homes out of the wilderness and attained
to that degree of prosperity which today we should call indigence than,
impelled by some mysterious impulse of their nature, they abandoned all
and pushed farther westward, to encounter new perils and privations in
the effort to regain the meager comforts which they had voluntarily renounced. Many of them had already forsaken that region for the remoter
settlements, but among those remaining was one who had been of those
first arriving. He lived alone in a house of logs surrounded on all sides by
the great forest, of whose gloom and silence he seemed a part, for no one
had ever known him to smile nor speak a needless word. His simple wants

were supplied by the sale or barter of skins of wild animals in the river town, for not a thing did he grow upon the land which, if needful, he might have claimed by right of undisturbed possession. There were evidences of "improvement" — a few acres of ground immediately about the house had once been cleared of its trees, the decayed stumps of which were half concealed by the new growth that had been suffered to repair the ravage wrought by the ax. Apparently the man's zeal for agriculture had burned with a failing flame, expiring in penitential ashes.

The little log house, with its chimney of sticks, its roof of warping clapboards weighted with traversing poles and its "chinking" of clay, had a single door and, directly opposite, a window. The latter, however, was boarded up — nobody could remember a time when it was not. And none knew why it was so closed; certainly not because of the occupant's dislike of light and air, for on those rare occasions when a hunter had passed that lonely spot the recluse had commonly been seen sunning himself on his doorstep if heaven had provided sunshine for his need. I fancy there are few persons living today who ever knew the secret of that window, but I am one, as you shall see.

The man's name was said to be Murlock. He was apparently seventy years old, actually about fifty. Something besides years had had a hand in his aging. His hair and long, full beard were white, his gray, lusterless eyes sunken, his face singularly seamed with wrinkles which appeared to belong to two intersecting systems. In figure he was tall and spare, with a stoop of the shoulders — a burden bearer. I never saw him; these particulars I learned from my grandfather, from whom also I got the man's story when I was a lad. He had known him when living near by in that early day.

One day Murlock was found in his cabin, dead. It was not a time and place for coroners and newspapers, and I suppose it was agreed that he had died from natural causes or I should have been told, and should remember. I know only that with what was probably a sense of the fitness of things the body has buried near the cabin, alongside the grave of his wife, who had preceded him by so many years that local tradition had retained hardly a hint of her existence. That closes the final chapter of this true story — excepting, indeed, the circumstance that many years afterward, in company with an equally intrepid spirit, I penetrated to the place and ventured near enough to the ruined cabin to throw a stone against it, and ran away to avoid the ghost which every well-informed boy thereabout knew haunted the spot. But there is an earlier chapter — that supplied by my grandfather.

When Murlock built his cabin and began laying sturdily about with his ax to hew out a farm — the rifle, meanwhile, his means of support — he was young, strong and full of hope. In that eastern country whence he came he had married, as was the fashion, a young woman in all ways worthy of his honest devotion, who shared the dangers and privations of his lot with a willing spirit and light heart. There is no known record of her name; of her charms of mind and person tradition is silent and the doubter is at liberty to entertain his doubt; but God forbid that I should share it! Of their affection and happiness there is abundant assurance in every added day of the man's widowed life; for what but the magnetism of a blessed memory could have chained that venturesome spirit to a lot like that?

One day Murlock returned from gunning in a distant part of the forest to find his wife prostrate with fever, and delirious. There was no physician within miles, no neighbor; nor was she in a condition to be left, to summon help. So he set about the task of nursing her back to health, but at the end of the third day she fell into unconsciousness and so passed away, apparently, with never a gleam of returning reason.

From what we know of a nature like his we may venture to sketch in some of the details of the outline picture drawn by my grandfather. When convinced that she was dead, Murlock had sense enough to remember that the dead must be prepared for burial. In performance of this sacred duty he blundered now and again, did certain things incorrectly, and others which he did correctly were done over and over. His occasional failures to accomplish some simple and ordinary act filled him with astonishment, like that of a drunken man who wonders at the suspension of familiar natural laws. He was surprised, too, that he did not weep — surprised and a little ashamed; surely it is unkind not to weep for the dead. "Tomorrow," he said aloud, "I shall have to make the coffin and dig the grave; and then I shall miss her, when she is no longer in sight; but now — she is dead, of course, but it is all right — it *must* be all right, somehow. Things cannot be so bad as they seem."

He stood over the body in the fading light, adjusting the hair and putting the finishing touches to the simple toilet, doing all mechanically, with soulless care. And still through his consciousness ran an undersense of conviction that all was right — that he should have her again as before, and everything explained. He had had no experience in grief; his capacity had not been enlarged by use. His heart could not contain it all, nor his imagination rightly conceive it. He did not know he was so hard struck; *that* knowledge would come later, and never go. Grief is an artist of powers as various as the instruments upon which he plays his dirges for the dead, evoking from some the sharpest, shrillest notes, from others the low, grave chords that throb recurrent like the slow beating of a distant drum. Some natures it startles; some it stupefies. To one it comes like the stroke of an arrow, stinging all the sensibilities to a keener life; to another as the blow of a bludgeon, which in crushing benumbs. We may conceive Murlock to have been that way affected, for (and here we are upon surer ground than that of conjecture) no sooner had he finished his pious work than, sinking into a chair by the side of the table upon which the body lay, and noting how white the profile showed in the deepening gloom, he laid his arms upon the table's edge, and dropped his face into them, tearless yet and unutterably weary. At that moment came in through the open window a long, wailing sound like the cry of a lost child in the far deeps of the darkening wood! But the man did not move. Again, and nearer than before, sounded that unearthly cry upon his failing sense. Perhaps it was a wild beast; perhaps it was a dream. For Murlock was asleep.

Some hours later, as it afterward appeared, this unfaithful watcher awoke and lifting his head from his arms intently listened — he knew not why. There in the black darkness by the side of the dead, recalling all without a shock, he strained his eyes to see — he knew not what. His senses were all alert, his breath was suspended, his blood had stilled its tides as if to assist the silence. Who — what had waked him, and where was it?

Suddenly the table shook beneath his arms, and at the same moment he heard, or fancied that he heard, a light, soft step — another — sounds as of bare feet upon the floor!

He was terrified beyond the power to cry out or move. Perforce he waited — waited there in the darkness through seeming centuries of such dread as one may know, yet live to tell. He tried vainly to speak the dead woman's name, vainly to stretch forth his hand across the table to learn if she were there. His throat was powerless, his arms and hands were like lead. Then occurred something most frightful. Some heavy body seemed hurled against the table with an impetus that pushed it against his breast so sharply as nearly to overthrow him, and at the same instant he heard and felt the fall of something upon the floor with so violent a thump that the whole house was shaken by the impact. A scuffling ensued, and a confusion of sounds impossible to describe. Murlock had risen to his feet. Fear had by excess forfeited control of his faculties. He flung his hands upon the table. Nothing was there!

There is a point at which terror may turn to madness; and madness incites to action. With no definite intent, from no motive but the wayward impulse of a madman, Murlock sprang to the wall, with a little groping seized his loaded rifle, and without aim discharged it. By the flash which lit up the room with a vivid illumination, he saw an enormous panther dragging the dead woman toward the window, its teeth fixed in her throat! Then there were darkness blacker than before, and silence; and when he returned to consciousness the sun was high and the wood vocal with songs of birds.

The body lay near the window, where the beast had left it when frightened away by the flash and report of the rifle. The clothing was deranged, the long hair in disorder, the limbs lay anyhow. From the throat, dreadfully lacerated, had issued a pool of blood not yet entirely coagulated. The ribbon with which he had bound the wrists was broken; the hands were tightly clenched. Between the teeth was a fragment of the animal's ear.

Carl Sandburg

CHICAGO

Hog Butcher for the World,
Tool Maker, Stacker of Wheat,
Player with Railroads and the Nation's Freight Handler;
Stormy, husky, brawling,
City of the Big Shoulders:

They tell me you are wicked and I believe them, for I have seen
your painted women under the gas lamps luring the farm boys.
And they tell me you are crooked and I answer: Yes, it is true I have
seen the gunman kill and go free to kill again.

And they tell me you are brutal and my reply is: On the faces of
women and children I have seen the marks of wanton hunger.

And having answered so I turn once more to those who sneer at this
my city, and I give them back the sneer and say to them:

Come and show me another city with lifted head singing so proud to
be alive and coarse and strong and cunning.

Flinging magnetic curses amid the toil of piling job on job, here is a
tall bold slugger set vivid against the little soft cities;

Fierce as a dog with tongue lapping for action, cunning as a savage
pitted against the wilderness,

Bareheaded,

Shoveling,

Wrecking,

Planning,

Building, breaking, rebuilding.

Under the smoke, dust all over his mouth, laughing with white
teeth,

Under the terrible burden of destiny laughing as a young man
laughs,

Laughing even as an ignorant fighter laughs who has never lost a
battle,

Bragging and laughing that under his wrist is the pulse, and under
his ribs the heart of the people,

Laughing!

Laughing the stormy, husky, brawling laughter of Youth, half-naked,
sweating, proud to be Hog Butcher, Tool Maker, Stacker of
Wheat, Player with Railroads and Freight Handler to the
Nation.

Julian Mitchell

LAMENT FOR THE COWBOY LIFE

Where the trails met, our herds met, too,
And mingled on their lowing way to slaughter.
Spying ahead, the sky a parching blue,
We tortured valleys for their news of water.

And water found, we shared our food,
And settling by one fire watched nights together.
Waking each day to coffee freshly brewed
I never hungered for more gentle weather.

When outlaws ambushed us, we blazed them back,
We flushed them out, like partridges, from cover.
A double grave means someone's grief and lack,
But who they were the desert can discover.

Coming at last down to the railhead
We sorted herds and haggled for fair prices.
The hands reported not one beast was dead,
Their massive flanks shipped off for butchers' slices.

And you had business there, and mine was on,
Three thousand miles across this continent.
And so we parted, partners, business done,
And whiskey pledged our friendship permanent.

From Salem to Salinas grows this land,
And Massachusetts grass grows dollar-green.
And yet I wish I'd stayed a cattle-hand
And never knew a country lies between.

Against my office window bumps the sun.
Now God herds us, as we those cattle then.
But every evening, on the homeward run,
I ride with cowboys, not with subway men.

William E. Barrett
SEÑOR PAYROLL

LARRY and I were Junior Engineers in the gas plant, which means that we were clerks. Anything that could be classified as paper work came to the flat double desk across which we faced each other. The Main Office downtown sent us a bewildering array of orders and rules that were to be put into effect.

Junior Engineers were beneath the notice of everyone except the Mexican laborers at the plant. To them we were the visible form of a distant, unknowable paymaster. We were Señor Payroll.

Those Mexicans were great workmen; the aristocrats among them were the stokers, big men who worked Herculean eight-hour shifts in the fierce heat of the retorts. They scooped coal with huge shovels and hurled it with uncanny aim at tiny doors. The coal streamed out from the shovels like black water from a high-pressure nozzle, and never missed the narrow opening. The stokers worked stripped to the waist, and there was pride and dignity in them. Few men could do such work, and they were the few.

The Company paid its men only twice a month, on the fifth and on the twentieth. To a Mexican, this was absurd. What man with money will make it last fifteen days? If he hoarded money beyond the spending of three days, he was a miser — and when, Señor, did the blood of Spain flow in the veins of misers? Hence, it was the custom for our stokers to appear every third or fourth day to draw the money due to them.

There was a certain elasticity in the Company rules, and Larry and I sent the necessary forms to the Main Office and received an "advance" against a man's pay check. Then, one day, Downtown favored us with a memorandum:

"There have been too many abuses of the advance-against-wages privilege. Hereafter, no advance against wages will be made to any employee except in a case of genuine emergency."

We had no sooner posted the notice when in came stoker Juan Garcia. He asked for an advance. I pointed to the notice. He spelled it through slowly, then said, "What does this mean, this 'genuine emergency'?"

I explained to him patiently that the Company was kind and sympa-thetic, but that it was a great nuisance to have to pay wages every few days. If someone was ill or if money was urgently needed for some other good reason, then the Company would make an exception to the rule.

Juan Garcia turned his hat over and over slowly in his big hands. "I do not get my money?"

"Next payday, Juan. On the twentieth."

He went out silently and I felt a little ashamed of myself. I looked across the desk at Larry. He avoided my eyes.

In the next hour two other stokers came in, looked at the notice, had it explained and walked solemnly out; then no more came. What we did not know was that Juan Garcia, Pete Mendoza, and Francisco Gonzalez had spread the word, and that every Mexican in the plant was explaining the order to every other Mexican. "To get money now, the wife must be sick. There must be medicine for the baby."

The next morning Juan Garcia's wife was practically dying, Pete Men-doza's mother would hardly last the day, there was a veritable epidemic among children, and, just for variety, there was one sick father. We al-ways suspected that the old man was really sick; no Mexican would other-wise have thought of him. At any rate, nobody paid Larry and me to ex-amine private lives; we made out our forms with an added line describing the "genuine emergency." Our people got paid.

That went on for a week. Then came a new order, curt and to the point: "Hereafter, employees will be paid ONLY on the fifth and the twentieth of the month. No exceptions will be made except in the cases of employees leaving the service of the Company."

The notice went up on the board, and we explained its significance gravely. "No, Juan Garcia, we cannot advance your wages. It is too bad about your wife and your cousins and your aunts, but there is a new rule."

Juan Garcia went out and thought it over. He thought out loud with Mendoza and Gonzales and Ayala, then, in the morning, he was back. "I am quitting this company for different job. You pay me now?"

We argued that it was a good company and that it loved its employees like children, but in the end we paid off, because Juan Garcia quit. And so did Gonzalez, Mendoza, Obregon, Ayala and Ortez, the best stokers, men who could not be replaced.

Larry and I looked at each other; we knew what was coming in about three days. One of our duties was to sit on the hiring line early each morning, engaging transient workers for the handy gangs. Any man was accepted who could walk up and ask for a job without falling down. Never before had we been called upon to hire such skilled virtuosos as stokers for handy-gang work, but we were called upon to hire them now.

The day foreman was wringing his hands and asking the Almighty if he was personally supposed to shovel this condemned coal, while there in a stolid, patient line were skilled men — Garcia, Mendoza, and others — waiting to be hired. We hired them, of course. There was nothing else to do.

Every day we had a line of resigning stokers, and another line of stokers seeking work. Our paper work became very complicated. At the Main Office they were jumping up and down. The procession of forms showing Juan Garcia's resigning and being hired over and over again was too much for them. Sometimes Downtown had Garcia on the payroll twice at the same time when someone down there was slow in entering a resignation. Our phone rang early and often.

Tolerantly and patiently we explained: "There's nothing we can do if a man wants to quit, and if there are stokers available when the plant needs stokers, we hire them."

Out of chaos, Downtown issued another order. I read it and whistled. Larry looked at it and said, "It is going to be very quiet around here."

The order read: "Hereafter, no employee who resigns may be rehired within a period of 30 days."

Juan Garcia was due for another resignation, and when he came in we showed him the order and explained that standing in line the next day would do him no good if he resigned today. "Thirty days is a long time, Juan."

It was a grave matter and he took time to reflect on it. So did Gonzalez, Mendoza, Ayala and Ortez. Ultimately, however, they were all back — and all resigned.

We did our best to dissuade them and we were sad about the parting. This time it was for keeps and they shook hands with us solemnly. It was very nice knowing us. Larry and I looked at each other when they were gone and we both knew that neither of us had been pulling for Downtown to win this duel. It was a blue day.

In the morning, however, they were all back in line. With the utmost gravity, Juan Garcia informed me that he was a stoker looking for a job.

"No dice, Juan," I said. "Come back in thirty days. I warned you."

His eyes looked straight into mine without a flicker. "There is some mistake, Señor," he said. "I am Manuel Hernandez. I work as the stoker in Pueblo, in Santa Fe, in many places."

I stared back at him, remembering the sick wife and the babies without medicine, the mother-in-law in the hospital, the many resignations and the rehirings. I knew that there was a gas plant in Pueblo, and that there wasn't any in Santa Fe; but who was I to argue with a man about his own name? A stoker is a stoker.

So I hired him. I hired Gonzalez, too, who swore that his name was Carrera, and Ayala, who had shamelessly become Smith.

Three days later the resigning started.

Within a week our payroll read like a history of Latin America. Everyone was on it: Lopez and Obregon, Villa, Diaz, Batista, Gomez, and even San Martín and Bolívar. Finally Larry and I, growing weary of staring at familiar faces and writing unfamiliar names, went to the Superintendent and told him the whole story. He tried not to grin, and said, "Damned nonsense!"

The next day the orders were taken down. We called our most prominent stokers into the office and pointed to the board. No rules any more.

"The next time we hire you hombres," Larry said grimly, "come in under the names you like best, because that's the way you are going to stay on the books."

They looked at us and they looked at the board; then for the first time in the long duel, their teeth flashed white. "Si, Señores," they said.

And so it was.

Stephen Crane

"I EXPLAIN THE SILVERED PASSING . . ."

(FROM *War Is Kind*)

I explain the silvered passing of a ship at night,
The sweep of each sad lost wave,
The dwindling boom of the steel thing's striving,
The little cry of a man to a man,

From *The Collected Poems of Stephen Crane*, by permission of Alfred A. Knopf, Inc.

A shadow falling across the greyer night,
And the sinking of the small star;
Then the waste, the far waste of waters,
And the soft lashing of black waves
For long and in loneliness.

Remember, thou, O ship of love,
Thou leavest a far waste of waters,
And the soft lashing of black waves
For long and in loneliness.

Oscar Hammerstein, II

HELLO, YOUNG LOVERS

(FROM *The King and I*)

When I think of Tom
I think about a night
When the earth smelled of summer,
And the sky was streaked with white,
And the soft mist of England was sleeping on a hill;
I remember this
And I always will.
There are new lovers now on the same silent hill,
Looking on the same blue sea.
And I know Tom and I are a part of them all,
And they're all a part of Tom and me.

Hello, young lovers,
Whoever you are,
I hope your troubles are few.
All my good wishes go with you tonight,
I've been in love like you.
Be brave, young lovers, and follow your star,

Be brave and faithful and true.
Cling very close to each other tonight,
I've been in love like you.
I know how it feels to have wings on your heels,
And to fly down a street in a trance.
You fly down a street on a chance that you'll meet,
And you meet not really by chance.
Don't cry, young lovers,
Whatever you do,
Don't cry because I'm alone.
All of my mem'ries are happy tonight —
I've had a love of my own,
I've had a love of my own like yours,
I've had a love of my own.

Robert Fontaine

MY MOTHER'S HANDS

UNTIL a short while ago I wondered how elderly people who had
been married for decades could still find in each other sources of surprise
and wonder, even elements of excitement and provocation. I would visit
my father and mother every day in their small apartment, for an hour or
so, and chat about baseball and hockey and prize fights on TV, with
maybe a few words about the latest scandal in our small city, or who had
died and married and been born.

Now and then, sitting there, drinking the tea my mother inevitably
brewed for me and helping my father out with the *New York Times* Sunday puzzle, searching for the highest peak in the Philippines or the name
of an obscure Swiss commune, I would wonder with part of my mind how
it was with them in their hearts; how they picked up and juggled the days
and made them sparkle, or if they did.

They were in their late seventies and their lives were as quiet outside as
one could imagine — as quiet as the snow or the rain or the rustle of trees
in midsummer.

I would go home to where my wife and children were bustling and bickering, growing up and growing older, partying and dining and hoping for Paris or Broadway or Cape Cod, dreaming of yachts and sleek motors and brave deeds, impulsively finding life filled with twists and turns and fascinating reflections of unseen lights beckoning toward some adventure or other.

I loved them and encouraged them. Life is to be lived, savored, salted and consumed. But what do you dream about when you are almost eighty and have been in love for fifty years? Is not every avenue long ago explored, every lake sailed, every wave broken across a finite and decided shore, every star discovered?

Now and then my wife and I would take my father and mother on short trips. These trips excited but did not overwhelm my parents. They were pleased but not moved. "It's good to get home," my mother always said with a sigh, at last. My father said, "I don't sleep right in a bed that's not my own." "I sleep all right," my mother said, "but I eat too much."

"It's nice," I would observe, "to get away for a while. I mean, for the change."

"It's nice to get back," my father would say.

My father gets up at seven-thirty and takes a brief case and goes for a long walk, all dressed up as if he were an attorney about to stage his most thrilling case. He goes to a downtown hotel and sits in the lobby and smokes a cigar. He likes it there in the lobby early in the day.

After that he walks for miles through stores and shops and the public library. He knows many people, small people, or, I should say, working people; clerks, butchers, newsboys. He talks with them about the weather and the latest sports events. Then he buys a half-dozen doughnuts, puts them in his brief case, goes home, and takes a nap.

My mother markets and plays canasta with her three girl friends once a week. Otherwise they watch television or listen to the radio. They never go to the movies. Years and years ago my father played in movie theaters for silent pictures and afterwards for pictures and vaudeville. He is just as happy if he never sees a motion picture again. I don't believe he has seen one in ten years, with a single exception we shall come to presently.

So the life of my father and mother has flowed on, with me always wondering, "What do they think about? Do they notice each other? Do they have strong emotions about each other? But how could they?" The blood has slowed down. The arms are inelastic. The eyes are dim. The fingers of my father which once rippled along a violin can barely make unpleasant squeaks on that instrument any more. My mother walks carefully, for her glasses do not focus properly where her feet meet the stairs and sidewalks.

Yet one morning I came on my usual call, bringing a New York paper, as is my custom, and some Cape scallops, which are a delicacy both my father and mother appreciate but cannot afford.

When I got in the apartment they were fighting. Now this in itself was most extraordinary. They were bickering and shouting about some obscure matter. As I recall, it had something to do with an event some twenty-five years previously and they had different ideas as to how the event had turned out or where it had occurred, and the discussion got hotter and hotter. At first I was amused and then I was alarmed. My father said, "That's the way you are, always so sure of yourself."

"I ought to know. I was there."

"I was there, too."

"Well, you don't remember then."

"My memory is perfect," my father shouted.

My mother said, "Don't shout at me."

"I'll shout at who I please."

"Not at me, you won't shout."

It went on like this with me standing there holding the scallops in my hand and wondering. They kept at it like newly-weds for about fifteen minutes. Finally my father got real angry and took his hat off the bed he sat beside and rushed out of the apartment slamming the door.

"Let him go," my mother said.

"I guess I'll have to. What were you fighting about?"

My mother shrugged. "I don't remember. He's just so stubborn. I keep hoping he'll outgrow it."

"If he hasn't now he never will."

"Well he better. I won't put up with it much longer."

I sat around for a while and then I put the scallops in the icebox. I was beginning to smell like Gloucester, Mass. I told my mother not to worry. She said, "Humph!" I left.

Around dinnertime I began to wonder again, so I called up. I was all alone. My wife had taken the children to visit her mother. My mother answered the phone and said my father had not come home yet or called on the phone. I did not expect him to call on the phone. I don't believe he has used a telephone for fifteen years. He just does not seem to trust them.

I hopped on a bus and went down to see my mother. She was not as crisp as she had been. She had wilted a little and looked gloomy. "I hope he doesn't do anything foolish," she said. "He's not a young man, you know."

"I know. I'll go roam around downtown. Maybe I can find him."

Now about ten years ago my father had been disconnected from the last real job he held. He had been head of a music school and the school had disbanded. For the first time in his life he had decided to soothe himself with alcohol and he had chosen half-pint bottles of the worst sherry ever made in California. These he drank regularly, after which he became very talkative and a little belligerent, especially for a man five feet six, weighing 130 pounds neat.

After a while he had got over it and never touched the stuff again, not even at birthday parties or Christmas. Yet I had a notion he had probably gone off again, just like a young, rebuffed lover. It was rather amazing to think of him, at his age, being sulky and irritated with my mother and she, for that matter, being wistful and lonesome like a girl at her first quarrel. In a way it was rather refreshing. I did not think they had it in them.

At any rate it had begun to pour rain, so I began walking around the city, starting with the cheery hotel bars and working my way to the North End and the more disreputable places. In each one I expected to find him, full of poor sherry, relating his woes or his boyhood adventures driving a butter wagon or taking violin lessons, to a group of patient souses.

Once or twice I thought I had a glimpse of him, but when I got in out of the rain, into the smell of hops and brews, it was not he but some other sad old character reeling about with a sad, silly grin on his face.

I began to worry. He is an old man, I thought. I must remember that. If he got full and roamed around in the rain it might be dangerous. Of course I was getting soaked myself, and drinking a little too much due to the excessive number of bars I felt I had to patronize.

At about eleven-thirty I gave up. I had enough to drink that I was alternately frightened and full of unexpected laughter. Imagine, my father, almost eighty, having a fight with my mother and running away from home! With hardly a dime in his pocket, too, probably. Running away! I thought. I went down to the NY, NH and H station. He was not there either. At last I went home — or, rather, to my mother's place.

She was weeping gently now. "I believe he has really run away." She would stop weeping, square her shoulders, and say suddenly, "I'll fix him." Then she would slump and weep some more.

I sat there with her, drinking tea, for a long time. We talked of all the old days. She spoke as if they were all over and my father had deserted her for another woman.

At last the door opened and my father walked calmly in. He had a small package in his hands. He smiled quietly and said, "Hello."

"Where've you been?" I asked. My mother was forced to smile. She was so glad to see him.

"I went to a movie."

My mother was stunned. "A movie?"

"The Arcade. All in bright color. It hurt my eyes."

"What was it about?" I asked, to make conversation.

My father shrugged. "A lot of young, foolish girls and their mushy love affairs."

"Oh," I said.

"You want some tea?" my mother asked.

"The movie was out at eleven," I said.

My father shrugged. "I went to Walgreen's to make a purchase."

"I'll make some nice warm tea," my mother said. "You must be tired after all that color and those mushy girls."

"Sentimental stuff," my father said. "Movies don't change. They're just bigger and louder. Here!"

He handed her the package. It was a bottle of hand lotion, the sort that is guaranteed to make your hands as soft as silk. My father handed it to my mother and hung his head a little and blushed. It was quite touching.

My mother beamed. Her eyes gleamed behind her thick spectacles. "What a lovely bottle."

"They say it keeps your hands like velvet," my father said.

My mother's hands have worked for me and others for many, many years; washing, baking, scrubbing, digging in a garden . . . they are gnarled and the veins are prominent and they are rough from years of work. To my father, though, they must have been the hands of a young woman, of a woman he loved, a woman who had stayed for a long time in his heart as precisely the same woman . . . and her hands were as velvet to him and he wanted to keep them that way.

My mother was weeping again but this time with pleasure and love.

I said, "Well, I've got to get along and you better go to bed."

So I went and left them to make up and to smile and to be alone. It was a moment, I am sure, when they preferred no company.

Frederick Eckman
LOVE LIES A-BLEEDING

That they should quarrel
over garbage! Yet he *did*
fail to set it out, & now
it must fill the back porch
   with its putridness
for another three days.

There are no words
to reconcile this: a promise
forgotten, the passionate
   imbecility of love
slashed open. *Her* loss
as well — who, grieving,
slams the cupboard doors
while he sulks on the couch
   his heart drowning
in that mortal stench.

Guy de Maupassant
THE JEWELS OF M. LANTIN

M. LANTIN, having met this young lady at a party given by his immediate superior, was literally enmeshed by love.

She was the daughter of a provincial tax collector who had died a few years previously. With her mother, she had come to Paris. Her mother became friendly with several middle-class families of the neighborhood in hopes of marrying off the young lady. Mother and daughter were poor, honorable, quiet, and gentle. The girl seemed to be the typical dream woman into whose hands any young man would yearn to entrust his entire life. Her modest beauty had an angelic quality, and the imperceptible smile which constantly graced her lips, seemed a reflection of her heart.

Everyone sang her praises; everyone who knew her repeated incessantly: "It will be a lucky fellow who wins her. You couldn't find a better catch!"

M. Lantin, now chief clerk of the Minister of the Interior, at a salary of 3500 francs, asked and received her hand in marriage.

He was unbelievably happy. She managed the house with such skill that their life was one of luxury. There was no delicacy, no whim of her husband's which she did not secure and satisfy; and her personal charm was such that, six years after their first meeting, he loved her even more than he had initially.

He begrudged her only two traits — her love of the theater and her passion for artificial jewels.

Her friends (she knew the wives of several minor functionaries) were always getting her seats for the fashionable plays, sometimes even for first nights; and she dragged her poor husband, willy-nilly, to these entertainments which completely wore him out, tired as he was after a hard day's work. He begged her to agree to go to the theater with some lady friend of hers who would accompany her home. She took a long time to decide, claiming this a most inconvenient arrangement. At last, however, she agreed, and he was profoundly grateful to her.

Now, this taste for the theater naturally stirred in her the need to primp. Her toilette remained simple, to be sure — always modest but in good taste; and her gentle grace, her irresistible, humble, smiling grace seemed to acquire a new savor from the simplicity of her dress, but she became accustomed to wearing two huge rhinestone earrings, which looked like diamonds; and she had strings of artificial pearls around her neck, and wore bracelets of similar gems.

Her husband, who somewhat scorned this love of garish display, said, "Dearest, when you haven't the means to wear real jewelry, you should show yourself adorned only with your own grace and beauty; these are the true pearls."

But she, smiling quietly, would insist, "Can I help it? I love it so. This is my vice. I know, my dear, how absolutely right you are; but I can't really remake myself, can I? I think I would just idolize real jewelry."

And she would roll the pearls in her fingers. "See how perfect," she'd say. "You'd swear they were real."

Sometimes, during the evening, while they sat before the fire, she would bring out her jewel chest, put it on the tea table, and commence to examine the contents with passionate attention, as though there were some subtle and profound secret delight in this pursuit. She persisted in draping strings of pearls around her husband's neck; then she would laugh merrily, crying, "How silly you look, my darling!" And she would throw herself into his arms and kiss him wildly.

One wintry evening, when she had been at the opera, she came home shivering with cold. The next day she was coughing wretchedly. A week later she died.

Lantin nearly followed her into the tomb. His despair was such that, in a month's time, his hair turned completely white. He wept incessantly, his very soul seared by unbearable suffering, haunted by the memory, the smile, the voice — by the overwhelming beauty of his deceased wife.

Even the passage of time failed to stem his grief. Frequently, at his office, while his colleagues were chatting idly, his cheeks would tremble and his eyes would fill with tears; he would grimace horribly and commence to sob.

He kept his wife's room intact, and sealed himself in every day to meditate. All her furniture and even her dresses remained just where they had been on the fatal day.

Living became difficult for him. His income which, under his wife's management, amply supplied the needs of both, now became insufficient for him alone. Dazed, he wondered how she had been able to purchase the superb wines and delicacies which he could no longer afford.

He fell into debt and began to scurry around for money as does anyone suddenly plunged into poverty. One fine morning, finding himself penniless a full week before payday, he thought about selling something. Suddenly the idea swept over him of taking a look at his wife's treasure trove, because, if the truth be told, he had always harbored some resentment towards this store of brilliants. The mere sight of them slightly tarnished the memory of his beloved.

It was a difficult business, searching through the case of jewels, because, even up to the very last days of her life, his wife had shopped stubbornly, bringing home some new bauble practically every night. He finally chose the magnificent necklace she seemed to have preferred, which, he figured, was worth six or seven francs, because, for artificial gems, it was really a masterpiece of craftsmanship.

With the jewels in his pocket he walked towards the Ministry, looking for a reliable jeweler.

Spotting a store, he entered — somewhat chagrined to be making this public display of his poverty and ashamed at attempting to sell so worthless an object.

He approached the merchant. "Excuse me. I wonder what value you would place on this piece."

The man took the necklace, examined it, turned it over, weighed it, called to his partner, talked to him in low tones, placed the necklace on the counter and scrutinized it carefully from a distance as though judging the effect.

M. Lantin, overwhelmed by this process, opened his mouth to protest: "Oh! I know that piece isn't worth anything," but just at that moment the storekeeper said:

"Monsieur, this piece is worth between twelve and fifteen thousand francs, but I cannot buy it until I learn exactly how you came into possession of it."

Lantin stared, wide-eyed, silent — uncomprehending. He finally stammered, "What? You are absolutely sure?"

The gentleman seemed offended by his attitude, and said wryly, "You may go elsewhere if you think you can do better. To me that is worth fifteen thousand at the very most. If you find no better offer, you may come back here."

M. Lantin, stupefied, took the necklace and left, feeling a curious urge to be alone and undisturbed.

But, before he had gone far, he was seized with an impulse to laugh, and he thought, "Imbecile! What a fool! What if I had taken him at his word! What a jeweler — not to know the difference between real gems and fakes!"

And he entered another jewelry store on the Rue de la Paix. As soon as he saw the jewel, the dealer cried, "Of course! I know this necklace well; I sold it!"

Deeply disturbed, M. Lantin asked, "How much is it worth?"

"Sir — I sold it for twenty-five thousand francs. I'm ready to take it back for eighteen thousand, if you will tell me — the law, you know — how you happened to receive it."

This time Lantin sat paralyzed with astonishment. He stuttered, "But — but — examine it very closely, sir. I have always thought it was — artificial."

The jeweler asked, "Would you please tell me your name, sir?"

"Of course. I'm Lantin. I work at the Ministry of the Interior, and I live at 16 Rue des Martyrs."

The merchant opened his ledger, looked through it, and said, "This necklace was sent to Mme. Lantin, 16 Rue des Martyrs, on the twentieth of July, 1876."

And the two men stared at each other, the clerk dumbfounded; the jeweler scenting a robber.

The merchant said, "Would you mind letting me have this for a day? Naturally, I'll give you a receipt."

M. Lantin blurted out, "Of course!" And he left, folding the paper into his pocket.

Then he crossed the street, went back, saw that he had gone out of his way, returned past the Tuileries, saw again he had made a mistake, crossed the Seine, went back to the Champs-Elysées without a single clear notion in his head. He forced himself to think. His wife could not possibly have purchased such valuable jewelry. Absolutely not! Well then? A present? A present? From whom? For what?

He was brought up short, and he stood stock still — there in the middle of the street. A horrible thought flashed across his mind. She? But all those other jewels were also gifts! He felt the earth shiver; a tree just before him seemed to crush him. He threw out his arms and fell, senseless, to the ground.

He regained consciousness in a nearby pharmacy to which passers-by had carried him. He asked that he be taken home, and he locked himself in.

He wept bitterly until nightfall — stuffing a handkerchief into his mouth to stifle his cries. Then he staggered to bed, wrung out with fatigue and chagrin, and he slept heavily.

A ray of sunshine woke him, and he got up slowly to go to his office. After such a blow, it would be hard to carry on with his work. He felt that he could be excused, and he wrote his superior a note. Then he thought that he ought to go back to the jeweler; and he crimsoned with shame. He could not possibly leave the necklace with that man. He dressed hurriedly and went out.

As he walked along, Lantin said to himself, "How easy it is to be happy when you're rich! With money you can even shake off your sorrows; you can go or stay as you please! You can travel and amuse yourself. If only I were really rich!"

Then he became aware of the fact that he was hungry, not having eaten since the previous evening. But his pockets were empty, and he reminded himself of the necklace. Eighteen thousand francs! Eighteen thousand francs! What a fortune!

He reached the Rue de la Paix, and he began pacing up and down opposite the shop. Eighteen thousand francs! More than twenty times he started to enter; but shame always halted him.

He was still hungry — famished — and without a sou. He finally made up his mind, raced across the street so as not to give himself time to think, and burst into the store.

As soon as he saw him, the merchant greeted him royally, offered him a chair with smiling courtesy. The partners then came in and sat down near Lantin, happiness beaming from their eyes and their lips.

The jeweler declared, "I am satisfied, Monsieur, and if you feel as you did yesterday, I am ready to pay you the sum agreed upon."

"Certainly," stammered Lantin.

The merchant took eighteen large notes from a drawer, counted them, gave them to Lantin, who signed a receipt and, with trembling hand, stuffed the money into his pocket.

Then, just as he was going out, he turned back towards the grinning shopkeeper, and, lowering his eyes, murmured, "I — I have some other gems — which came to me in the same way. Would you be willing to buy those from me?"

The jeweler nodded, "Of course, Monsieur."

One of the partners barely stifled a laugh, while the other was forced to leave the room to hide his mirth.

Lantin, impassive and stern, said, "I'll bring them to you."

When he returned to the store, an hour later, he had still not eaten. They set about examining the jewels piece by piece, assessing each one. Then they all went back to Lantin's house.

Now Lantin entered into the spirit of the business, arguing, insisting that they show him the bills of sale, and getting more and more excited as the values rose.

The magnificent earrings were worth twenty thousand francs; the bracelets, thirty-five thousand. The brooches, pins and medallions, sixteen thousand. The whole collection was valued at one hundred ninety-six thousand francs.

The merchant boomed out in a jolly voice, "That's what happens when you put your money into jewelry."

Lantin said solemnly, "That's one way to invest your money!" Then he left, after having agreed with the purchaser to have a second expert appraisal the following day.

When he was out in the street, he looked up at the Vendôme Column. He felt like leaping up to the top. He felt light enough to play leapfrog with the statue of the Emperor perched up there in the clouds.

He went into an elegant restaurant to eat, and he drank wine at twenty francs a bottle.

Then he took a cab and rode around the Bois de Boulogne. He looked at the gleaming carriages, suppressing a desire to cry out, "I'm rich, too! I have two hundred thousand francs!"

He thought of his office. He drove up, entered his Chief's office solemnly, and announced, "Sir — I'm tendering my resignation! I've just inherited three hundred thousand francs!" He went around shaking hands with his colleagues, and telling them all about his plans for the future. Then he went out to dinner at the Café Anglais.

Finding himself seated alongside a distinguished-looking gentleman, he couldn't resist whispering to him, a little archly, that he had just inherited four hundred thousand francs.

For the first time in his life he enjoyed the theater and he spent the night carousing.

Six months later he remarried. His second wife was a most worthy woman, but rather difficult. She made his life unbearable.

William Shakespeare

O MISTRESS MINE

(From *Twelfth Night*)

O mistress mine, where are you roaming?
O, stay and hear, your true love's coming,
    That can sing both high and low:
Trip no further, pretty sweeting,
Journeys end in lovers meeting,
    Every wise man's son doth know.

What is love? 'Tis not hereafter;
Present mirth hath present laughter;
    What's to come is still unsure:
In delay there lies no plenty;
Then come kiss me, sweet and twenty,
    Youth's a stuff will not endure.

Emily Dickinson

"HOPE" IS THE THING WITH FEATHERS

"Hope" is the thing with feathers —
That perches in the soul —
And sings the tune without the words —
And never stops — at all —

And sweetest — in the Gale — is heard —
And sore must be the storm —
That could abash the little Bird
That kept so many warm —

I've heard it in the chillest land —
And on the strangest Sea —
Yet, never, in Extremity,
It asked a crumb — of Me.

Walt Whitman

BEAT! BEAT! DRUMS!

Beat! beat! drums! — blow! bugles! blow!
Through the windows — through doors — burst like a ruthless force,
Into the solemn church, and scatter the congregation,
Into the school where the scholar is studying;
Leave not the bridegroom quiet — no happiness must he have now
    with his bride,
Nor the peaceful farmer any peace, ploughing his field or gathering
    his grain,
So fierce you whirr and pound you drums — so shrill you bugles
    blow.

Beat! beat! drums! — blow! bugles! blow!
Over the traffic of cities — over the rumble of wheels in the streets;
Are beds prepared for sleepers at night in the houses? No sleepers
    must sleep in those beds,
No bargainers' bargains by day — no brokers or speculators — would
    they continue?
Would the lawyers be talking? would the singer attempt to sing?
Would the lawyer rise in the court to state his case before the judge?
Then rattle quicker, heavier drums — you bugles wilder blow.

Beat! beat! drums! — blow! bugles! blow!
Make no parley — stop for no expostulation,
Mind not the timid — mind not the weeper or prayer,
Mind not the old man beseeching the young man,
Let not the child's voice be heard, nor the mother's entreaties,
Make even the trestles to shake the dead where they lie awaiting the
    hearses,
So strong you thump O terrible drums — so loud you bugles blow.

William Ernest Henley

INVICTUS

Out of the night that covers me,
  Black as the Pit from pole to pole,
I thank whatever gods may be
  For my unconquerable soul.

In the fell clutch of circumstance
  I have not winced nor cried aloud.
Under the bludgeonings of chance
  My head is bloody, but unbowed.

Beyond this place of wrath and tears
  Looms but the Horror of the shade,
And yet the menace of the years
  Finds, and shall find me, unafraid.

It matters not how strait the gate,
  How charged with punishments the scroll,
I am the master of my fate:
  I am the captain of my soul.

Edwin Arlington Robinson

RICHARD CORY

Whenever Richard Cory went down town,
We people on the pavement looked at him;
He was a gentleman from sole to crown,
Clean favored, and imperially slim.

And he was always quietly arrayed,
And he was always human when he talked;
But still he fluttered pulses when he said,
"Good-morning," and he glittered when he walked.

And he was rich — yes, richer than a king —
And admirably schooled in every grace;

In fine, we thought that he was every thing
To make us wish that we were in his place.

So on we worked, and waited for the light,
And went without the meat, and cursed the bread;
And Richard Cory, one calm summer night,
Went home and put a bullet through his head.

A. E. Housman

"IS MY TEAM PLOWING . . . ?"

"Is my team plowing,
    That I was used to drive
And hear the harness jingle
    When I was man alive?"

Aye, the horses trample,
    The harness jingles now;
No change though you lie under
    The land you used to plow.

"Is football playing
    Along the river shore,
With lads to chase the leather,
    Now I stand up no more?"

Aye, the ball is flying,
    The lads play heart and soul;
The goal stands up, the keeper
    Stands up to keep the goal.

"Is my girl happy,
    That I thought hard to leave,
And has she tired of weeping
    As she lies down at eve?"

Aye, she lies down lightly,
    She lies not down to weep;
Your girl is well contented.
    Be still, my lad, and sleep.

"Is my friend hearty,
    Now I am thin and pine,
And has he found to sleep in
    A better bed than mine?"

Yes, lad, I lie easy,
    I lie as lads would choose;
I cheer a dead man's sweetheart —
    Never ask me whose.

Shirley Jackson

CHARLES

THE DAY my son Laurie started kindergarten he renounced corduroy overalls with bibs and began wearing blue jeans with a belt. I watched him go off the first morning with the older girl next door, seeing clearly that an era of my life was ended, my sweet-voiced nursery-school tot replaced by a long-trousered, swaggering character who forgot to stop at the corner and wave good-bye to me.

He came home the same way, the front door slamming open, his hat on the floor, and the voice suddenly become raucous shouting, "Isn't anybody *here?*"

At lunch he spoke insolently to his father, spilled his baby sister's milk, and remarked that his teacher said we were not to take the name of the Lord in vain.

"How *was* school today?" I asked, elaborately casual.

"All right," he said.

"Did you learn anything?" his father asked.

Laurie regarded his father coldly. "I didn't learn nothing," he said.

"Anything," I said. "Didn't learn anything."

"The teacher spanked a boy, though," Laurie said, addressing his bread and butter. "For being fresh," he added, with his mouth full.

"What did he do?" I asked. "Who was it?"

Laurie thought. "It was Charles," he said. "He was fresh. The teacher spanked him and made him stand in a corner. He was awfully fresh."

"What did he do?" I asked again, but Laurie slid off his chair, took a cookie, and left, while his father was still saying, "See here, young man."

The next day Laurie remarked at lunch, as soon as he sat down, "Well, Charles was bad again today." He grinned enormously and said, "Today Charles hit the teacher."

"Good heavens," I said, mindful of the Lord's name. "I suppose he got spanked again?"

"He sure did," Laurie said. "Look up," he said to his father.

"What?" his father said, looking up.

"Look down," Laurie said. "Look at my thumb. Gee, you're dumb." He began to laugh insanely.

"Why did Charles hit the teacher?" I asked quickly.

"Because she tried to make him color with red crayons," Laurie said. "Charles wanted to color with green crayons so he hit the teacher and she spanked him and said nobody play with Charles but everybody did."

The third day — it was Wednesday of the first week — Charles bounced a see-saw on the head of a little girl and made her bleed, and the teacher made him stay inside all during recess. Thursday Charles had to stand in a corner during story-time because he kept pounding his feet on the floor. Friday Charles was deprived of blackboard privileges because he threw chalk.

On Saturday I remarked to my husband, "Do you think kindergarten is too unsettling for Laurie? All this toughness and bad grammar, and this Charles boy sounds like such a bad influence."

"It'll be all right," my husband said reassuringly. "Bound to be people like Charles in the world. Might as well meet them now as later."

On Monday Laurie came home late, full of news. "Charles," he shouted as he came up the hill; I was waiting anxiously on the front steps. "Charles," Laurie yelled all the way up the hill, "Charles was bad again."

"Come right in," I said, as soon as he came close enough. "Lunch is waiting."

"You know what Charles did?" he demanded, following me through the door. "Charles yelled so in school they sent a boy in from first grade to tell the teacher she had to make Charles keep quiet, and so Charles had to stay after school. And so all the children stayed to watch him."

"What did he do?" I asked.

"He just sat there," Laurie said, climbing into his chair at the table. "Hi, Pop, y'old dust mop."

"Charles had to stay after school today," I told my husband. "Everyone stayed with him."

"What does this Charles look like?" my husband asked Laurie. "What's his other name?"

"He's bigger than me," Laurie said. "And he doesn't have any rubbers and he doesn't ever wear a jacket."

Monday night was the first Parent-Teachers meeting, and only the fact that the baby had a cold kept me from going; I wanted passionately to meet Charles's mother. On Tuesday Laurie remarked suddenly, "Our teacher had a friend come to see her in school today."

"Charles's mother?" my husband and I asked simultaneously.

"Naaah," Laurie said scornfully. "It was a man who came and made us do exercises, we had to touch our toes. Look." He climbed down from his chair and squatted down and touched his toes. "Like this," he said. He got solemnly back into his chair and said, picking up his fork, "Charles didn't even *do* exercises."

"That's fine," I said heartily. "Didn't Charles want to do the exercises?"

"Naaah," Laurie said. "Charles was so fresh to the teacher's friend he wasn't *let* do exercises."

"Fresh again," I said.

"He kicked the teacher's friend," Laurie said. "The teacher's friend told Charles to touch his toes like I just did and Charles kicked him."

"What are they going to do about Charles, do you suppose?" Laurie's father asked him.

Laurie shrugged elaborately. "Throw him out of school, I guess," he said.

Wednesday and Thursday were routine; Charles yelled during story hour and hit a boy in the stomach and made him cry. On Friday Charles stayed after school again and so did all the other children.

With the third week of kindergarten Charles was an institution in our family; the baby was being a Charles when he filled his wagon full of mud and pulled it through the kitchen; even my husband, when he caught his elbow in the telephone cord and pulled telephone, ashtray, and a bowl of flowers off the table, said, after the first minute, "Looks like Charles."

During the third and fourth weeks it looked like a reformation in

Charles; Laurie reported grimly at lunch on Thursday of the third week, "Charles was so good today the teacher gave him an apple."

"What?" I said, and my husband added warily, "You mean Charles?"

"Charles," Laurie said. "He gave the crayons around and he picked up the books afterward and the teacher said he was her helper."

"What happened?" I asked incredulously.

"He was her helper, that's all," Laurie said, and shrugged.

"Can this be true, about Charles?" I asked my husband that night. "Can something like this happen?"

"Wait and see," my husband said cynically. "When you've got a Charles to deal with, this may mean he's only plotting."

He seemed to be wrong. For over a week Charles was the teacher's helper; each day he handed things out and he picked things up; no one had to stay after school.

"The PTA meeting's next week again," I told my husband one evening. "I'm going to find Charles's mother there."

"Ask her what happened to Charles," my husband said. "I'd like to know."

"I'd like to know myself," I said.

On Friday of that week things were back to normal. "You know what Charles did today?" Laurie demanded at the lunch table, in a voice slightly awed. "He told a little girl to say a word and she said it and the teacher washed her mouth out with soap and Charles laughed."

"What word?" his father asked unwisely, and Laurie said, "I'll have to whisper it to you, it's so bad." He got down off his chair and went around to his father. His father bent his head down and Laurie whispered joyfully. His father's eyes widened.

"Did Charles tell the little girl to say *that*?" he asked respectfully.

"She said it *twice*," Laurie said. "Charles told her to say it *twice*."

"What happened to Charles?" my husband asked.

"Nothing," Laurie said. "He was passing out the crayons."

Monday morning Charles abandoned the little girl and said the evil word himself three or four times, getting his mouth washed out with soap each time. He also threw chalk.

My husband came to the door with me that evening as I set out for the PTA meeting. "Invite her over for a cup of tea after the meeting," he said. "I want to get a look at her."

"If only she's there," I said prayerfully.

"She'll be there," my husband said. "I don't see how they could hold a PTA meeting without Charles's mother."

At the meeting I sat restlessly, scanning each comfortable matronly face, trying to determine which one hid the secret of Charles. None of them looked to me haggard enough. No one stood up in the meeting and apologized for the way her son had been acting. No one mentioned Charles.

After the meeting I identified and sought out Laurie's kindergarten teacher. She had a plate with a cup of tea and a piece of chocolate cake; I had a plate with a cup of tea and a piece of marshmallow cake. We maneuvered up to one another cautiously, and smiled.

"I've been so anxious to meet you," I said. "I'm Laurie's mother."

"We're all so interested in Laurie," she said.

"Well, he certainly likes kindergarten," I said. "He talks about it all the time."

"We had a little trouble adjusting, the first week or so," she said primly, "but now he's a fine little helper. With occasional lapses, of course."

"Laurie usually adjusts very quickly," I said. "I suppose this time it's Charles's influence."

"Charles?"

"Yes," I said, laughing, "you must have your hands full in that kindergarten, with Charles."

"Charles?" she said. "We don't have any Charles in the kindergarten."

Ogden Nash

TO A SMALL BOY
standing on my shoes
while I am wearing them

Let's straighten this out, my little man,
And reach an agreement if we can.
I entered your door as an honored guest.

Reprinted from *Family Reunion* by Ogden Nash, by permission of Little, Brown and Co. Copyright 1931, by Ogden Nash.

My shoes are shined and my trousers are pressed,
And I won't stretch out and read you the funnies
And I won't pretend that we're Easter bunnies.
If you must get somebody down on the floor,
What do you think your parents are for?
I do not like the things that you say
And I hate the games that you want to play.
No matter how frightfully hard you try,
We've little in common, you and I.
The interest I take in my neighbor's nursery
Would have to grow, to be even cursory,
And I would that performing sons and nephews
Were carted away with the daily refuse,
And I hold that frolicsome daughters and nieces
Are ample excuse for breaking leases.
You may take a sock at your daddy's tummy,
Or climb all over your doting mummy,
But keep your attentions to me in check,
Or, sonny boy, I will wring your neck.
A happier man today I'd be
Had someone wrung it ahead of me.

Edgar Allan Poe

THE CASK OF AMONTILLADO

THE THOUSAND injuries of Fortunato I had borne as I best could; but
when he ventured upon insult, I vowed revenge. You, who so well know
the nature of my soul, will not suppose, however, that I gave utterance to
a threat. *At length* I would be avenged; this was a point definitively settled; but the very definitiveness with which it was resolved precluded the
idea of risk. I must not only punish, but punish with impunity. A wrong
is unredressed when retribution overtakes its redresser. It is equally unredressed when the avenger fails to make himself felt as such to him who
has done the wrong.

It must be understood that neither by word nor deed had I given

Fortunato cause to doubt my good-will. I continued, as was my wont, to smile in his face, and he did not perceive that my smile *now* was at the thought of his immolation.

He had a weak point, this Fortunato, although in other regards he was a man to be respected and even feared. He prided himself on his connoisseurship in wine. Few Italians have the true virtuoso spirit. For the most part their enthusiasm is adopted to suit the time and opportunity, to practice imposture upon the British and Austrian millionaires. In painting and gemmary Fortunato, like his countrymen, was a quack; but in the matter of old wines he was sincere. In this respect I did not differ from him materially: I was skillful in the Italian vintages myself, and bought largely whenever I could.

It was about dusk one evening, during the supreme madness of the carnival season, that I encountered my friend. He accosted me with excessive warmth, for he had been drinking much. The man wore motley. He had on a tight-fitting parti-striped dress, and his head was surmounted by the conical cap and bells. I was so pleased to see him that I thought I should never have done wringing his hand.

I said to him: "My dear Fortunato, you are luckily met. How remarkably well you are looking today! But I have received a pipe of what passes for Amontillado, and I have my doubts."

"How?" said he. "Amontillado? A pipe? Impossible! And in the middle of the carnival!"

"I have my doubts," I replied; "and I was silly enough to pay the full Amontillado price without consulting you in the matter. You were not to be found, and I was fearful of losing a bargain."

"Amontillado!"

"I have my doubts."

"Amontillado!"

"And I must satisfy them."

"Amontillado!"

"As you are engaged, I am on my way to Luchesi. If any one has a critical turn, it is he. He will tell me —"

"Luchesi cannot tell Amontillado from sherry."

"And yet some fools will have it that his taste is a match for your own."

"Come, let us go."

"Whither?"

"To your vaults."

"My friend, no; I will not impose upon your good-nature. I perceive you have an engagement. Luchesi —"

"I have no engagement: come."

"My friend, no. It is not the engagement, but the severe cold with which I perceive you are afflicted. The vaults are insufferably damp. They are incrusted with niter."

"Let us go, nevertheless. The cold is merely nothing. Amontillado! You have been imposed upon. And as for Luchesi, he cannot distinguish sherry from Amontillado."

Thus speaking, Fortunato possessed himself of my arm. Putting on a mask of black silk, and drawing a *roquelaure* closely about my person, I suffered him to hurry me to my palazzo.

There were no attendants at home; they had absconded to make merry in honor of the time. I had told them that I should not return until the morning, and had given them explicit orders not to stir from the house. These orders were sufficient, I well knew, to insure their immediate disappearance, one and all, as soon as my back was turned.

I took from their sconces two flambeaux, and, giving one to Fortunato, bowed him through several suites of rooms to the archway that led into the vaults. I passed down a long and winding staircase, requesting him to be cautious as he followed. We came at length to the foot of the descent, and stood together on the damp ground of the catacombs of the Montresors.

The gait of my friend was unsteady, and the bells upon his cap jingled as he strode.

"The pipe?" said he.

"It is farther on," said I; "but observe the white webwork which gleams from these cavern walls."

He turned towards me, and looked into my eyes with two filmy orbs that distilled the rheum of intoxication.

"Niter?" he asked at length.

"Niter," I replied. "How long have you had that cough?"

"Ugh! ugh! ugh! — ugh! ugh! ugh! — ugh! ugh! ugh! — ugh! ugh! ugh! — ugh! ugh! ugh!"

My poor friend found it impossible to reply for many minutes.

"It is nothing," he said, at last.

"Come," I said, with decision, "we will go back; your health is precious. You are rich, respected, admired, beloved; you are happy, as once I was.

You are a man to be missed. For me it is no matter. We will go back; you will be ill, and I cannot be responsible. Besides, there is Luchesi —"

"Enough," he said; "the cough is a mere nothing; it will not kill me. I shall not die of a cough."

"True — true," I replied; "and, indeed, I had no intention of alarming you unnecessarily; but you should use all proper caution. A draught of this Medoc will defend us from the damps."

Here I knocked off the neck of a bottle which I drew from a long row of its fellows that lay upon the mold.

"Drink," I said, presenting him the wine.

He raised it to his lips with a leer. He paused and nodded to me familiarly, while his bells jingled.

"I drink," he said, "to the buried that repose around us."

"And I to your long life."

He again took my arm and we proceeded.

"These vaults," he said, "are extensive."

"The Montresors," I replied, "were a great and numerous family."

"I forget your arms."

"A huge human foot d'or, in a field azure; the foot crushes a serpent rampant whose fangs are imbedded in the heel."

"And the motto?"

"*Nemo me impune lacessit.*" [1]

"Good!" he said.

The wine sparkled in his eyes and the bells jingled. My own fancy grew warm with the Medoc. We had passed through walls of piled bones, with casks and puncheons intermingling, into the inmost recesses of the catacombs. I paused again, and this time I made bold to seize Fortunato by an arm above the elbow.

"The niter!" I said; "see, it increases. It hangs like moss upon the vaults. We are below the river's bed. The drops of moisture trickle among the bones. Come, we will go back ere it is too late. Your cough —"

"It is nothing," he said; "let us go on. But first, another draught of the Medoc."

I broke and reached him a flagon of De Grâve. He emptied it at a breath. His eyes flashed with a fierce light. He laughed and threw the bottle upward with a gesticulation I did not understand.

---

[1] No one injures me with impunity.

I looked at him in surprise. He repeated the movement — a grotesque one.

"You do not comprehend?" he said.

"Not I," I replied.

"Then you are not of the brotherhood."

"How?"

"You are not of the masons."

"Yes, yes," I said; "yes, yes."

"You? Impossible! A mason?"

"A mason," I replied.

"A sign," he said.

"It is this," I answered, producing a trowel from beneath the folds of my *roquelaure*.

"You jest!" he exclaimed, recoiling a few paces. "But let us proceed to the Amontillado."

"Be it so," I said, replacing the tool beneath the cloak, and again offering him my arm. He leaned upon it heavily. We continued our route in search of the Amontillado. We passed through a range of low arches, descended, passed on, and, descending again, arrived at a deep crypt, in which the foulness of the air caused our flambeaux rather to glow than flame.

At the most remote end of the crypt there appeared another less spacious. Its walls had been lined with human remains, piled to the vault overhead, in the fashion of the great catacombs of Paris. Three sides of this interior crypt were still ornamented in this manner. From the fourth the bones had been thrown down, and lay promiscuously upon the earth, forming at one point a mound of some size. Within the wall thus exposed by the displacing of the bones we perceived a still interior recess, in depth about four feet, in width three, in height six or seven. It seemed to have been constructed for no especial use within itself, but formed merely the interval between two of the colossal supports of the roof of the catacombs, and was backed by one of their circumscribing walls of solid granite.

It was in vain that Fortunato, uplifting his dull torch, endeavored to pry into the depth of the recess. Its termination the feeble light did not enable us to see.

"Proceed," I said; "herein is the Amontillado. As for Luchesi —"

"He is an ignoramus," interrupted my friend, as he stepped unsteadily forward, while I followed immediately at his heels. In an instant he had reached the extremity of the niche, and, finding his progress arrested by the rock, stood stupidly bewildered. A moment more and I had fettered him to the granite. In its surface were two iron staples, distant from each other about two feet, horizontally. From one of these depended a short chain, from the other a padlock. Throwing the links about his waist, it was but the work of a few seconds to secure it. He was too much astounded to resist. Withdrawing the key, I stepped back from the recess.

"Pass your hand," I said, "over the wall; you cannot help feeling the niter. Indeed it is *very* damp. Once more let me *implore* you to return. No? Then I must positively leave you. But I must first render you all the little attentions in my power."

"The Amontillado!" ejaculated my friend, not yet recovered from his astonishment.

"True," I replied: "the Amontillado."

As I said these words I busied myself among the pile of bones of which I have before spoken. Throwing them aside, I soon uncovered a quantity of building stone and mortar. With these materials and with the aid of my trowel, I began vigorously to wall up the entrance of the niche.

I had scarcely laid the first tier of the masonry when I discovered that the intoxication of Fortunato had in a great measure worn off. The earliest indication I had of this was a low, moaning cry from the depth of the recess. It was *not* the cry of a drunken man. There was then a long and obstinate silence. I laid the second tier, and the third, and the fourth; and then I heard the furious vibrations of the chain. The noise lasted for several minutes, during which, that I might harken to it with the more satisfaction, I ceased my labors and sat down upon the bones. When at last the clanking subsided, I resumed the trowel, and finished without interruption the fifth, the sixth, and the seventh tier. The wall was now nearly upon a level with my breast. I again paused, and, holding the flambeaux over the masonwork, threw a few feeble rays upon the figure within.

A succession of loud and shrill screams, bursting suddenly from the throat of the chained form, seemed to thrust me violently back. For a brief moment I hesitated, I trembled. Unsheathing my rapier, I began to grope with it about the recess; but the thought of an instant reassured me. I placed my hand upon the solid fabric of the catacombs and felt satisfied. I reapproached the wall. I replied to the yells of him who clamored. I re-echoed, I aided, I surpassed them in volume and in strength. I did this, and the clamorer grew still.

It was now midnight, and my task was drawing to a close. I had completed the eighth, the ninth, and the tenth tier. I had finished a portion of the last and the eleventh; there remained but a single stone to be fitted and plastered in. I struggled with its weight; I placed it partially in its destined position. But now there came from out the niche a low laugh that erected the hairs upon my head. It was succeeded by a sad voice, which I had difficulty in recognizing as that of the noble Fortunato. The voice said:

"Ha! ha! ha! — he! he! — a very good joke indeed, an excellent jest. We will have many a rich laugh about it at the palazzo — he! he! he! — over our wine — he! he! he!"

"The Amontillado!" I said.

"He! he! he! — he! he! he! — yes, the Amontillado. But is it not getting late? Will not they be awaiting us at the palazzo, — the Lady Fortunato and the rest? Let us be gone."

"Yes," I said, "let us be gone."

"*For the love of God, Montresor!*"

"Yes," I said, "for the love of God!"

But to these words I harkened in vain for a reply. I grew impatient. I called aloud:

"Fortunato!"

No answer. I called again.

"Fortunato!"

No answer still. I thrust a torch through the remaining aperture and let it fall within. There came forth in return only a jingling of the bells. My heart grew sick — on account of the dampness of the catacombs. I hastened to make an end of my labor. I forced the last stone into its position; I plastered it up. Against the new masonry I re-erected the old rampart of bones. For the half of a century no mortal has disturbed them. *In pace requiescat!* [2]

---

[2] May he rest in peace.

Karl Shapiro

AUTO WRECK

Its quick soft silver bell beating, beating,
And down the dark one ruby flare
Pulsing out red light like an artery,
The ambulance at top speed floating down
Past beacons and illuminated clocks
Wings in a heavy curve, dips down,
And brakes speed, entering the crowd.
The doors leap open, emptying light;
Stretchers are laid out, the mangled lifted
And stowed into the little hospital.
Then the bell, breaking the hush, tolls once,
And the ambulance with its terrible cargo
Rocking, slightly rocking, moves away,
As the doors, an afterthought, are closed.

We are deranged, walking among the cops
Who sweep glass and are large and composed.
One is still making notes under the light.
One with a bucket douches ponds of blood
Into the street and gutter.
One hangs lanterns on the wrecks that cling,
Empty husks of locusts, to iron poles.
Our throats were tight as tourniquets,
Our feet were bound with splints, but now
Like convalescents intimate and gauche,
We speak through sickly smiles and warn
With the stubborn saw of common sense,
The grim joke and the banal resolution.
The traffic moves around with care,
But we remain, touching a wound
That opens to our richest horror.

Already old, the question Who shall die?
Becomes unspoken Who is innocent?
For death in war is done by hands;
Suicide has cause and stillbirth, logic.
But this invites the occult mind,
Cancels our physics with a sneer,
And spatters all we knew of denouement
Across the expedient and wicked stones.

Frank O'Connor

MY OEDIPUS COMPLEX

FATHER was in the army all through the war — the first war, I mean — so, up to the age of five, I never saw much of him, and what I saw did not worry me. Sometimes I woke and there was a big figure in khaki peering down at me in the candlelight. Sometimes in the early morning I heard the slamming of the front door and the clatter of nailed boots down the cobbles of the lane. These were Father's entrances and exits. Like Santa Claus, he came and went mysteriously.

In fact, I rather liked his visits, though it was an uncomfortable squeeze between Mother and him when I got into the big bed in the early morning. He smoked, which gave him a pleasant musty smell, and shaved, an operation of astounding interest. Each time he left a trail of souvenirs — model tanks and Gurkha knives with handles made of bullet cases, and German helmets and cap badges and button-sticks, and all sorts of military equipment — carefully stowed away in a long box on top of the wardrobe, in case they ever came in handy. There was a bit of the magpie about Father; he expected everything to come in handy. When his back was turned, Mother let me get a chair and rummage through his treasures. She didn't seem to think so highly of them as he did.

The war was the most peaceful period of my life. The window of my attic faced southeast. My mother had curtained it, but that had small effect. I always woke with the first light and, with all the responsibilities of the previous day melted, feeling myself rather like the sun, ready to illumine and rejoice. Life never seemed so simple and clear and full of possibilities as then. I put my feet out from under the clothes — I called them Mrs. Left and Mrs. Right — and invented dramatic situations for them in which they discussed the problems of the day. At least Mrs. Right did; she was very demonstrative, but I hadn't the same control ot Mrs. Left, so she mostly contented herself with nodding agreement.

They discussed what Mother and I should do during the day, what Santa Claus should give a fellow for Christmas, and what steps should be taken to brighten the home. There was that little matter of the baby, for instance. Mother and I could never agree about that. Ours was the only house in the terrace without a new baby, and Mother said we couldn't afford one till Father came back from the war because they cost seventeen and six. That showed how simple she was. The Geneys up the road had a baby, and everyone knew they couldn't afford seventeen and six. It was probably a cheap baby, and Mother wanted something really good, but I felt she was too exclusive. The Geneys' baby would have done us fine.

Having settled my plans for the day, I got up, put a chair under the attic window, and lifted the frame high enough to stick out my head. The window overlooked the front gardens of the terrace behind ours, and beyond these it looked over a deep valley to the tall, red-brick houses terraced up the opposite hillside, which were all still in shadow, while those at our side of the valley were all lit up, though with long strange shadows that made them seem unfamiliar; rigid and painted.

After that I went into Mother's room and climbed into the big bed. She woke and I began to tell her of my schemes. By this time, though I never seem to have noticed it, I was petrified in my nightshirt, and I thawed as I talked until, the last frost melted, I fell asleep beside her and woke again only when I heard her below in the kitchen, making the breakfast.

After breakfast we went into town; heard Mass at St. Augustine's and said a prayer for Father, and did the shopping. If the afternoon was fine we either went for a walk in the country or a visit to Mother's great friend in the convent, Mother St. Dominic. Mother had them all praying for Father, and every night, going to bed, I asked God to send him back safe from the war to us. Little, indeed, did I know what I was praying for!

One morning, I got into the big bed, and there, sure enough, was Father in his usual Santa Claus manner, but later, instead of uniform, he put on his best blue suit, and Mother was as pleased as anything. I saw nothing to be pleased about, because, out of uniform, Father was altogether less interesting, but she only beamed, and explained that our prayers had been answered, and off we went to Mass to thank God for having brought Father safely home.

The irony of it! That very day when he came in to dinner he took off his boots and put on his slippers, donned the dirty old cap he wore about the house to save him from colds, crossed his legs, and began to talk gravely to Mother, who looked anxious. Naturally, I disliked her looking anxious, because it destroyed her good looks, so I interrupted him.

"Just a moment, Larry!" she said gently.

This was only what she said when we had boring visitors, so I attached no importance to it and went on talking.

"Do be quiet, Larry!" she said impatiently. "Don't you hear me talking to Daddy?"

This was the first time I had heard those ominous words, "talking to Daddy," and I couldn't help feeling that if this was how God answered prayers, he couldn't listen to them very attentively.

"Why are you talking to Daddy?" I asked with as great a show of indifference as I could muster.

"Because Daddy and I have business to discuss. Now, don't interrupt again!"

In the afternoon, at Mother's request, Father took me for a walk. This time we went into town instead of out to the country, and I thought at first, in my usual optimistic way, that it might be an improvement. It was nothing of the sort. Father and I had quite different notions of a walk in town. He had no proper interest in trams, ships, and horses, and the only thing that seemed to divert him was talking to fellows as old as himself. When I wanted to stop he simply went on, dragging me behind him by the hand; when he wanted to stop I had no alternative but to do the same. I noticed that it seemed to be a sign that he wanted to stop for a long time whenever he leaned against a wall. The second time I saw him do it I got wild. He seemed to be settling himself forever. I pulled him by the coat and trousers, but, unlike Mother who, if you were too persistent, got into a wax and said: "Larry, if you don't behave yourself, I'll give you a good slap," Father had an extraordinary capacity for amiable inattention. I sized him up and wondered would I cry, but he seemed to be too remote to be annoyed even by that. Really, it was like going for a walk with a mountain! He either ignored the wrenching and pummeling entirely, or else glanced down with a grin of amusement from his peak. I had never met anyone so absorbed in himself as he seemed.

At teatime, "talking to Daddy" began again, complicated this time by the fact that he had an evening paper, and every few minutes he put it down and told Mother something new out of it. I felt this was foul play. Man for man, I was prepared to compete with him any time for Mother's attention, but when he had it all made up for him by other people it left me no chance. Several times I tried to change the subject without success.

"You must be quiet while Daddy is reading, Larry," Mother said impatiently.

It was clear that she either genuinely liked talking to Father better than talking to me, or else that he had some terrible hold on her which made her afraid to admit the truth.

"Mummy," I said that night when she was tucking me up, "do you think if I prayed hard God would send Daddy back to the war?"

She seemed to think about that for a moment.

"No, dear," she said with a smile. "I don't think he would."

"Why wouldn't he, Mummy?"

"Because there isn't a war any longer, dear."

"But, Mummy, couldn't God make another war, if He liked?"

"He wouldn't like to, dear. It's not God who makes wars, but bad people."

"Oh!" I said.

I was disappointed about that. I began to think that God wasn't quite what he was cracked up to be.

Next morning I woke at my usual hour, feeling like a bottle of champagne. I put out my feet and invented a long conversation in which Mrs. Right talked of the trouble she had with her own father till she put him in the Home. I didn't quite know what the Home was but it sounded the right place for Father. Then I got my chair and stuck my head out of the attic window. Dawn was just breaking, with a guilty air that made me feel I had caught it in the act. My head bursting with stories and schemes, I stumbled in next door, and in the half-darkness scrambled into the big bed. There was no room at Mother's side so I had to get between her and Father. For the time being I had forgotten about him, and for several minutes I sat bolt upright, racking my brains to know what I could do with him. He was taking up more than his fair share of the bed, and I couldn't get comfortable, so I gave him several kicks that made him grunt and stretch. He made room all right, though. Mother waked and felt for me. I settled back comfortably in the warmth of the bed with my thumb in my mouth.

"Mummy!" I hummed, loudly and contentedly.

"Sssh! dear," she whispered. "Don't wake Daddy!"

This was a new development, which threatened to be even more serious than "talking to Daddy." Life without my early-morning conferences was unthinkable.

"Why?" I asked severely.

"Because poor Daddy is tired."

This seemed to me a quite inadequate reason, and I was sickened by the sentimentality of her "poor Daddy." I never liked that sort of gush; it always struck me as insincere.

"Oh!" I said lightly. Then in my most winning tone: "Do you know where I want to go with you today, Mummy?"

"No, dear," she sighed.

"I want to go down the Glen and fish for thornybacks with my new net, and then I want to go out to the Fox and Hounds, and —"

"Don't-wake-Daddy!" she hissed angrily, clapping her hand across my mouth.

But it was too late. He was awake, or nearly so. He grunted and reached for the matches. Then he stared incredulously at his watch.

"Like a cup of tea, dear?" asked Mother in a meek, hushed voice I had never heard her use before. It sounded almost as though she were afraid.

"'Tea?" he exclaimed indignantly. "Do you know what the time is?"

"And after that I want to go up the Rathcooney Road," I said loudly, afraid I'd forget something in all those interruptions.

"Go to sleep at once, Larry!" she said sharply.

I began to snivel. I couldn't concentrate, the way that pair went on, and smothering my early-morning schemes was like burying a family from the cradle.

Father said nothing, but lit his pipe and sucked it, looking out into the shadows without minding Mother or me. I knew he was mad. Every time I made a remark Mother hushed me irritably. I was mortified. I felt it wasn't fair; there was even something sinister in it. Every time I had pointed out to her the waste of making two beds when we could both sleep in one, she had told me it was healthier like that, and now here was this man, this stranger, sleeping with her without the least regard for her health!

He got up early and made tea, but though he brought Mother a cup he brought none for me.

"Mummy," I shouted, "I want a cup of tea, too."

"Yes, dear," she said patiently. "You can drink from Mummy's saucer."

That settled it. Either Father or I would have to leave the house. I didn't want to drink from Mother's saucer; I wanted to be treated as an equal in my own home, so, just to spite her, I drank it all and left none for her. She took that quietly, too.

But that night when she was putting me to bed she said gently:

"Larry, I want you to promise me something."

"What is it?" I asked.

"Not to come in and disturb poor Daddy in the morning. Promise?"

"Poor Daddy" again! I was becoming suspicious of everything involving that quite impossible man.

"Why?" I asked.

"Because poor Daddy is worried and tired and he doesn't sleep well."

"Why doesn't he, Mummy?"

"Well, you know, don't you, that while he was at the war Mummy got the pennies from the Post Office?"

"From Miss MacCarthy?"

"That's right. But now, you see, Miss MacCarthy hasn't any more pennies, so Daddy must go out and find us some. You know what would happen if he couldn't?"

"No," I said, "tell us."

"Well, I think we might have to go out and beg for them like the poor old woman on Fridays. We wouldn't like that, would we?"

"No," I agreed. "We wouldn't."

"So you'll promise not to come in and wake him?"

"Promise."

Mind you, I meant that. I knew pennies were a serious matter, and I was all against having to go out and beg like the old woman on Fridays. Mother laid out all my toys in a complete ring round the bed so that, whatever way I got out, I was bound to fall over one of them.

When I woke I remembered my promise all right. I got up and sat on the floor and played — for hours, it seemed to me. Then I got my chair and looked out the attic window for more hours. I wished it was time for

Father to wake; I wished someone would make me a cup of tea. I didn't feel in the least like the sun; instead, I was bored and so very, very cold! I simply longed for the warmth and depth of the big featherbed.

At last I could stand it no longer. I went into the next room. As there was still no room at Mother's side I climbed over her and she woke with a start.

"Larry," she whispered, gripping my arm very tightly, "what did you promise?"

"But I did, Mummy," I wailed, caught in the very act. "I was quiet for ever so long."

"Oh, dear, and you're perished!" she said sadly, feeling me all over. "Now, if I let you stay will you promise not to talk?"

"But I want to talk, Mummy," I wailed.

"That has nothing to do with it," she said with a firmness that was new to me. "Daddy wants to sleep. Now, do you understand that?"

I understood it only too well. I wanted to talk, he wanted to sleep — whose house was it, anyway?

"Mummy," I said with equal firmness, "I think it would be healthier for Daddy to sleep in his own bed."

That seemed to stagger her, because she said nothing for a while.

"Now, once for all," she went on, "you're to be perfectly quiet or go back to your own bed. Which is it to be?"

The injustice of it got me down. I had convicted her out of her own mouth of inconsistency and unreasonableness, and she hadn't even attempted to reply. Full of spite, I gave Father a kick, which she didn't notice but which made him grunt and open his eyes in alarm.

"What time is it?" he asked in a panic-stricken voice, not looking at Mother but at the door, as if he saw someone there.

"It's early yet," she replied soothingly. "It's only the child. Go to sleep again. . . . Now, Larry," she added, getting out of bed, "you've wakened Daddy and you must go back."

This time, for all her quiet air, I knew she meant it, and knew that my principal rights and privileges were as good as lost unless I asserted them at once. As she lifted me, I gave a screech, enough to wake the dead, not to mind Father. He groaned.

"That damn child! Doesn't he ever sleep?"

"It's only a habit, dear," she said quietly, though I could see she was vexed.

"Well, it's time he got out of it," shouted Father, beginning to heave in the bed. He suddenly gathered all the bedclothes about him, turned to the wall, and then looked back over his shoulder with nothing showing only two small, spiteful, dark eyes. The man looked very wicked.

To open the bedroom door, Mother had to let me down, and I broke free and dashed for the farthest corner, screeching. Father sat bolt upright in bed.

"Shut up, you little puppy!" he said in a choking voice.

I was so astonished that I stopped screeching. Never, never had anyone spoken to me in that tone before. I looked at him incredulously and saw his face convulsed with rage. It was only then that I fully realized how God had codded me, listening to my prayers for the safe return of this monster.

"Shut up, you!" I bawled, beside myself.

"What's that you said?" shouted Father, making a wild leap out of the bed.

"Mick, Mick!" cried Mother. "Don't you see the child isn't used to you?"

"I see he's better fed than taught," snarled Father, waving his arms wildly. "He wants his bottom smacked."

All his previous shouting was as nothing to these obscene words referring to my person. They really made my blood boil.

"Smack your own!" I screamed hysterically. "Smack your own! Shut up! Shut up!"

At this he lost his patience and let fly at me. He did it with the lack of conviction you'd expect of a man under Mother's horrified eyes, and it ended up as a mere tap, but the sheer indignity of being struck at all by a stranger, a total stranger who had cajoled his way back from the war into our big bed as a result of my innocent intercession, made me completely dotty. I shrieked and shrieked, and danced in my bare feet, and Father, looking awkward and hairy in nothing but a short grey army shirt, glared down at me like a mountain out for murder. I think it must have been then that I realized he was jealous too. And there stood Mother in her nightdress, looking as if her heart was broken between us. I hoped she felt as she looked. It seemed to me that she deserved it all.

From that morning out my life was a hell. Father and I were enemies, open and avowed. We conducted a series of skirmishes against one another, he trying to steal my time with Mother and I his. When she was sitting on my bed, telling me a story, he took to looking for some pair of old boots which he alleged he had left behind him at the beginning of the war. While he talked to Mother I played loudly with my toys to show my total lack of concern. He created a terrible scene one evening when he came in from work and found me at his box, playing with his regimental badges, Gurkha knives and button-sticks. Mother got up and took the box from me.

"You mustn't play with Daddy's toys unless he lets you, Larry," she said severely. "Daddy doesn't play with yours."

For some reason Father looked at her as if she had struck him and then turned away with a scowl.

"Those are not toys," he growled, taking down the box again to see had I lifted anything. "Some of those curios are very rare and valuable."

But as time went on I saw more and more how he managed to alienate Mother and me. What made it worse was that I couldn't grasp his method or see what attraction he had for Mother. In every possible way he was less winning than I. He had a common accent and made noises at his tea. I thought for a while that it might be the newspapers she was interested in, so I made up bits of news of my own to read to her. Then I thought it might be the smoking, which I personally thought attractive, and took his pipes and went round the house dribbling into them till he caught me. I even made noises at my tea, but Mother only told me I was disgusting. It all seemed to hinge round that unhealthy habit of sleeping together, so I made a point of dropping into their bedroom and nosing round, talking to myself, so that they wouldn't know I was watching them, but they were never up to anything that I could see. In the end it beat me. It seemed to depend on being grown-up and giving people rings, and I realized I'd have to wait.

But at the same time I wanted him to see that I was only waiting, not giving up the fight. One evening when he was being particularly obnoxious, chattering away well above my head, I let him have it.

"Mummy," I said, "do you know what I'm going to do when I grow up?"

"No, dear," she replied. "What?"

"I'm going to marry you," I said quietly.

Father gave a great guffaw out of him, but he didn't take me in. I knew it must only be pretence. And Mother, in spite of everything, was pleased. I felt she was probably relieved to know that one day Father's hold on her would be broken.

"Won't that be nice?" she said with a smile.

"It'll be very nice," I said confidently. "Because we're going to have lots and lots of babies."

"That's right, dear," she said placidly. "I think we'll have one soon, and then you'll have plenty of company."

I was no end pleased about that because it showed that in spite of the way she gave in to Father she still considered my wishes. Besides, it would put the Geneys in their place.

It didn't turn out like that, though. To begin with, she was very preoccupied — I supposed about where she would get the seventeen and six — and though Father took to staying out late in the evenings it did me no particular good. She stopped taking me for walks, became as touchy as blazes, and smacked me for nothing at all. Sometimes I wished I'd never mentioned the confounded baby — I seemed to have a genius for bringing calamity on myself.

And calamity it was! Sonny arrived in the most appalling hullabaloo — even that much he couldn't do without a fuss — and from the first moment I disliked him. He was a difficult child — so far as I was concerned he was always difficult — and demanded far too much attention. Mother was simply silly about him, and couldn't see when he was only showing off. As company he was worse than useless. He slept all day, and I had to go round the house on tiptoe to avoid waking him. It wasn't any longer a question of not waking Father. The slogan now was "Don't-wake-Sonny!" I couldn't understand why the child wouldn't sleep at the proper time, so whenever Mother's back was turned I woke him. Sometimes to keep him awake I pinched him as well. Mother caught me at it one day and gave me a most unmerciful flaking.

One evening, when Father was coming in from work, I was playing trains in the front garden. I let on not to notice him; instead, I pretended to be talking to myself, and said in a loud voice: "If another bloody baby comes into this house, I'm going out."

Father stopped dead and looked at me over his shoulder.

"What's that you said?" he asked sternly.

"I was only talking to myself," I replied, trying to conceal my panic. "It's private."

He turned and went in without a word. Mind you, I intended it as a solemn warning, but its effect was quite different. Father started being quite nice to me. I could understand that, of course. Mother was quite sickening about Sonny. Even at mealtimes she'd get up and gawk at him in the cradle with an idiotic smile, and tell Father to do the same. He was always polite about it, but he looked so puzzled you could see he didn't know what she was talking about. He complained of the way Sonny cried at night, but she only got cross and said that Sonny never cried except when there was something up with him — which was a flaming lie, because Sonny never had anything up with him, and only cried for attention. It was really painful to see how simple-minded she was. Father wasn't attractive, but he had a fine intelligence. He saw through Sonny, and now he knew that I saw through him as well.

One night I woke with a start. There was someone beside me in the bed. For one wild moment I felt sure it must be Mother, having come to her senses and left Father for good, but then I heard Sonny in convulsions in the next room, and Mother saying: "There! There! There!" and I knew it wasn't she. It was Father. He was lying beside me, wide awake, breathing hard and apparently as mad as hell.

After a while it came to me what he was mad about. It was his turn now. After turning me out of the big bed, he had been turned out himself. Mother had no consideration now for anyone but that poisonous pup, Sonny. I couldn't help feeling sorry for Father. I had been through it all myself, and even at that age I was magnanimous. I began to stroke him down and say: "There! There!" He wasn't exactly responsive.

"Aren't you asleep either?" he snarled.

"Ah, come on and put your arm around us, can't you?" I said, and he did, in a sort of way. Gingerly, I suppose, is how you'd describe it. He was very bony but better than nothing.

At Christmas he went out of his way to buy me a really nice model railway.

Edna St. Vincent Millay

GOD'S WORLD

O world, I cannot hold thee close enough!
  Thy winds, thy wide grey skies!
  Thy mists, that roll and rise!
Thy woods, this autumn day, that ache and sag
And all but cry with colour! That gaunt crag
To crush! To lift the lean of that black bluff!
World, World, I cannot get thee close enough!

Long have I known a glory in it all,
  But never knew I this:
  Here such a passion is
As stretcheth me apart, — Lord, I do fear
Thou'st made the world too beautiful this year;
My soul is all but out of me, — let fall
No burning leaf; prithee, let no bird call.

From *Collected Poems*, Harper & Brothers, 1913-1922-1940-1950,
by Edna St. Vincent Millay. By permission of Norma Millay Ellis.

INDEX

Allusion, 207
"Alone on a Mountaintop," 206
American Heritage, 114
American Mercury, 186
Analogy, 264
"Anchorage," 165
Argument, 37
Atlantic Monthly, The, 231
"Auto Wreck," 398
Barrett, William E., 365
"Basketball Is for the Birds," 47
"Beat! Beat! Drums!" 383
Benchley, Nathaniel, 114
Benét, Stephen Vincent, 297
Better Homes and Gardens, 291
"Between the Dark and the Day-
    light," 330
Bierce, Ambrose, 358
"Big Prison, The," 315
Birnbaum, Jesse, 218
Blair, William D., Jr., 279
"Boarded Window, The," 358
"Brazil's Wild West," 162
Brown, John Mason, 330
Burdick, Eugene, 175
"Candy," 171
Carson, Rachel, 103
"Cask of Amontillado, The," 391

Catton, Bruce, 128
"Charles," 386
"Chicago," 362
Childs, Marquis, 76
Collier's, 120
Conklin, Paul, 72
Cornette, James P., 287
Coronet, 148
Cort, David, 200
"Courtship Through the Ages," 336
Cousins, Norman, 319
Crane, Stephen, 368
de Maupassant, Guy, 375
Devoe, Alan, 186
Dickinson, Emily, 382
"Dog Training," 341
Drucker, Peter F., 79
"Earthquake, The," 120
Eckman, Frederick, 375
"Economy," 239
"Everyone a Naturalist," 186
Exaggeration, 47
Exposition, 8
Familiar Essay, 26
Figure of Speech, 15
Finney, Charles G., 192
"First Fig," 350
Fontaine, Robert, 370

"Force of Youth as a Force for Peace, A," 66

Formal Essay, 26

Fortune, 80

"Freedom's a Hard-Bought Thing," 297

"God's World," 410

Great Chain of Life, The, 256

Hammerstein, Oscar, II, 369

"Happy Idle Hours . . ." 246

Harper's, 15

"Hello, Young Lovers," 369

Helmer, Bill, 344

Henley, William Ernest, 384

Henry, Patrick, 312

Holiday, 175

" 'Hope' Is the Thing with Feathers," 382

Housman, A. E., 385

"How Not to Listen . . ." 291

"How to Be an Employee," 79

"How to Detect Propaganda," 7

Humphrey, Hubert, 37

"Hunting Party on the Snake River, A," 134

Huxley, Aldous, 94

"I Explain the Silvered Passing . . ." 368

"Immortal Model T, The," 148

Importance of Living, The, 242

"Inaugural Address, 1961," 322

Informal Essay, 26

Institute for Propaganda Analysis, The, 7

"Invictus," 384

Irony, 137

"I Say Bastketball's Our Best Game," 54

"Is My Team Plowing . . . ?" 385

Jackson, Shirley, 386

"Jewels of M. Lantin, The," 375

"Journey into Fear," 279

Kennedy, John F., 322

Kerouac, Jack, 206

Krutch, Joseph Wood, 256

Ladies' Home Journal, 287

"Lament for the Cowboy Life," 364

Lawrence, David, 315

Leibowitz, Samuel S., 30

"Let Them Build Tents," 287

"Liberty or Death," 312

Life, 26

Lin Yutang, 242

Loeffler, Ken D., 54

Logical Argument, 47

London, Jack, 120

"Love Lies A-Bleeding," 375

Lyon, Peter, 137

Man Does Not Stand Alone, 268

"Man, the Only Working Animal," 242

McGinley, Phyllis, 357

Mencken, H. L., 264

Metaphor, 15

"Mexican Hey Ride," 344

Millay, Edna St. Vincent, 350, 410

Mitchell, Julian, 364

Monroe, Keith, 15

Morrison, A. Cressy, 268

"Mother Sea: The Gray Beginnings," 103

"My Mother's Hands," 370

"My Oedipus Complex," 399

Narration, 15

Nash, Ogden, 390

Nation, The, 200

Nelson, George, 155

New Republic, The, 72

New Yorker, The, 171

New York Times Magazine, The, 66

"Nine Words That Can Stop Juvenile Delinquency," 30

Objective (writing), 94

O'Connor, Frank, 399

"October Blizzard," 273

O'Donovan, Patrick, 165

"O Mistress Mine," 382

On the Meaning of Life, 264

"Out of the Trackless Bush . . ." 155

Paxton, Harry T., 54

"Peace Corps," 76

Personification, 104

Persuasion, 47

"Plan to Save Trees, Land, and Boys, A," 37

Poe, Edgar Allan, 391

Povich, Shirley, 47

Purpose (in writing), 31

"Richard Cory," 384

Robinson, Edwin Arlington, 384

"Roots of Home, The," 218

Samuels, Gertrude, 66

Sandburg, Carl, 362

Sarcasm, 47

Saroyan, William, 350

Saturday Evening Post, The, 54

Saturday Review, 155

"Science Has Spoiled My Supper," 231

Sea Around Us, The, 103

"Season at the Shore," 357

"Señor Payroll," 365

Sentimentality, 279

"Seven Reasons Why a Scientist Believes in God," 268

Shakespeare, William, 382

"Shape of Things in 1986, The," 94

Shapiro, Karl, 398

Simile, 15

Skinner, Cornelia Otis, 25

Smith, Robert Paul, 291

Sports Illustrated, 47

"Sportsman or Predator," 256

Stillness at Appomattox, A, 128

Stocker, Joseph, 148

"Summer of the Beautiful White Horse, The," 350

"Survival in the Zoo," 200

Symbolism, 297

Tasker, Arthur H., 273

Theme, 156

"They Made the Cigar Respectable," 15

This Week, 30

Thoreau, Henry David, 239

Thurber, James, 336

Time, 162

"To a Small Boy . . ." 390

Townsend, John K., 134

"Triumph over the Bully," 319

True, 94

"$24 Swindle, The," 114

"United States Navy, The," 175

U. S. News and World Report, 316

V.F.W. Magazine, 279

Walden, 239

"We Don't Want to Be Won," 72

"Western Gladiator," 192

White, E. B., 341

Whitman, Walt, 383

Wilson, Sloan, 246

"Women Are Misguided," 25

"Wyatt Earp and Bat Masterson," 137

Wylie, Philip, 231